Imam Husain's Brothers in Arms

by Ayatollāh Sayyid Alī Khāmeneī

An Interpolative Rendition into English with Annotations
by Blake Archer Williams

Copyright © 2021 by Blake Archer Williams

All rights reserved. No part of this publication may be reproduced, distributed, or transmitted in any form or by any means, including photocopying, recording, or other electronic or mechanical methods, without the prior written permission of the publisher, except in the case of brief quotations embodied in critical reviews and certain other noncommercial uses permitted by copyright law. For permission requests, write to the publisher, addressed "Attention: - Permissions (Imam Husain's Brothers in Arms)," at the email address below.

Lantern Publications
info@lanternpublications.com
www.lanternpublications.com

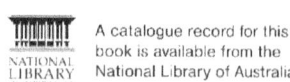

A catalogue record for this book is available from the National Library of Australia

Ordering Information:
Quantity sales. Special discounts are available on quantity purchases by corporations, associations, and others. For details, contact the distributor at the address below.

Shia Books Australia
www.shiabooks.com.au
info@shiabooks.com.au

ISBN-978-1-922583-24-6

First Edition

In the Name of God,
the Most Compassionate, the Most Merciful

Prayers of God's Peace and Blessings

In keeping with the Islamic practice of showing respect for the name of God, and sending prayers of God's peace and blessings whenever the name of His blessed Prophet, Lady Fātima, and the Twelve Imams is mentioned. Additionally, for asking God to hasten the reappearance of the Lord of the Age on this Earthly plane; one or more of the following Arabic symbols have been employed throughout the text. They are repeated for their great rewards.

 Used exclusively after the name of God, meaning "the Sublimely Exalted", or, as a prayer, "[May His name be] Sublimely Exalted".

 Used exclusively after the name of the Prophet, meaning "May the peace and blessings of God be unto him and unto [the purified and inerrant members of] his family"

 Used for any of the Twelve Imams or past prophets of God, meaning "May God's peace be unto him".

 Used for two or more of the Twelve Imams or past prophets of God, meaning "May God's peace be unto them".

 Used for Lady Fātima, meaning "May God's peace be unto her".

 Used for a plurality of the Fourteen Immaculates, meaning "May God's peace be unto them all collectively".

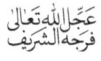 Used for the Lord of the Age (the Twelfth Imam), meaning "May God hasten the advent of his noble person".

Table of Contents

A Note on Transliteration 6

The Names and Dates of the Twelve Imams 14

Translator's Foreword 15

1. Various Approaches to Leadership of the Community 17

2. The True Identity of the Imams 37

3. The Meaning and Purpose of the Imamate 59

4. The 250-Year-Old Warrior 91

5. The Four Phases of the Imamate 113

6. The Initial Period of the Fourth Phase of the Imamate 139

7. The Political Life of Imam Ṣādiq 169

8. The Imams' Politicism and their Militant Actions 209

9. The Revolutionary Sons of the Imams 253

10. Precautionary Dissimulation (*Taqīya*) 279

A Note on Transliteration

The transliteration system used in this book is basically that of the ICAS Press method (which is based on the Library of Congress Romanization Tables), with the following changes: The *shamsi* and *qamari* consonants appear in the definitive article 'al' (in place of the 'l'). This is so that those who are not familiar with the pronunciation of the Arabic words can become familiar with the words as they should be pronounced (as opposed to how they are written), enabling them to pronounce the words properly. Persian words of Arabic origin are transliterated as they are pronounced in the Arabic language, rather than their Persian pronunciations. However, Persian words, proper names, and personal names are transliterated to reflect their proper Persian pronunciation. Thus, 'Bukhārī' is Bokhāri, Kulaynī is Kolayni, Khumaynī is Khomeini, Khāmini'ī is Khāmeneī, etc. In such cases, the sound for the *kasra* is romanized by 'e' rather than by 'i', and the *ḍamma* by 'o' rather than by 'a' or 'u'. Similarly, the ض, ذ, and ظ letters are all Romanized by the letter 'z' (for Persian words only). Thus, the *ezāfe* (*iḍāfa*) is Romanized *-e* after a consonant, and *-ah* or *-ye* after a vowel.

Detailed Table of Contents

A Note on Transliteration 6

The Names and Dates of the Twelve Imams 14

Translator's Foreword 15

1. Various Approaches to Leadership of the Community 17

    1. The discussion concerning the necessity of the Imamate 18

    2. The discussion concerning the succession to the Prophet 19

    3. The discussion concerning the attributes and characteristics of the Imam of the community of Muslims and the conditions under which investiture to the office of the Imamate is appropriate 20

    4. The discussion concerning the role of the Imams ﷺ and their [intellectual and practical] posture concerning insurrection against the forces of illegitimate governance (or the Islamic counter-revolution) 26

    5. The principles of comprehending the way of the Imams ﷺ and the criteria for determining their success 29

    6. The relationship of the leader and the follower: the relationship between one who is deferred to and one who defers 30

    7. The Importance of becoming aware of the benefits of the Imamate and of the Function of the Imams 31

    8. The necessity of understanding the approach of the Imams ﷺ towards their followers (Shīʿayān), the caliphs, and the court-allied religious scholars 33

2. The True Identity of the Imams 37

    1. The dearth of knowledge of the Shīʿa concerning the social and political posture of the Imams 38

    2. Two Benefits of becoming Aware of the Personalities of the Imams 40

    2.1 Learning how one should lead one's life 41

    2.2 Becoming motivated and increasing one's sense of religious self-confidence 44

    3. Two methods of the enemies of nations for eliminating national heroes and heroines 47
        3.1 Forbidding the mentioning of the hero's name to wipe his memory from public discourse 47
        3.2 Distorting and falsifying the image of the hero 49

    4. Our failure to fully appreciate the two benefits of knowing the way of the Imams 51

5. Evidence against the thesis of the Imams ﷺ being reconciled with the caliphs 53

6. A summary of the contents of the rest of the book 56

3. The Meaning and Purpose of the Imamate 59

1. The imperative of attaining to a deep understanding of the character and way of the Imams 61

2. The first step toward understanding the Imam: acknowledging one's ignorance of their way 64

3. The Imperative of attaining to a deep understanding of the character and way of the Imams ﷺ as a "250 Year Old Person" 65

4. The meaning and purpose of the institution of the Imamate 72

5. Two objectives of the Prophet ﷺ: Bringing about a [counter-] revolution in a wayward society, and establishing a new social order 73

6. The struggle of the Prophet Muhammad ﷺ in establishing the Islamic social order 75

7. Islamic ordinances for the creation of an Islamic social order 77

8. The continuity of the Islamic dispensational order after the passing of the Prophet ﷺ 78

9. Two duties of the Imam after the passing of the Prophet ﷺ: The explication of the religion and harmonizing it with the needs of society 79

10. The incumbency on the Imam of taking back the office of leadership 83

11. The transference by the Prophet ﷺ of two prophetic functions to the commander of the faithful and to the rest of the Imams ﷺ after him 84

12. Attributes of the true Shīʿa: Understanding the duties of the Imam and following in his footsteps 86

13. Attributes of the Shīʿa who lived during the Time of the Imams: Living the Life of the Faithful and Engendering Faith 87

4. The 250-Year-Old Warrior 91

1. Two functions of the Imam: The explication of Islam and the political leadership of society 93

2. The duty of the Imam: to struggle to actualize his two functions 94

3. Two duties of the Imam concerning Islam and society 98

4. The way of the Imams: Brothers in arms or appeasers? 99

5. The 250-Year-Old warrior 100

6. The martyrdom of the Imams ﷺ as the general reason for their being warriors 101

7. What is meant by the *Jihād* of the Imams 103

8. Two mistaken definitions and one correct definition of the word Jihād 104

9. A mistaken Definition: *Jihād* defined as any type of struggle whatsoever 105

10. A Second mistaken definition: *Jihād* defined as armed struggle 107

11. The correct definition of *Jihād*: struggling against an Enemy 108

12. Financial *Jihād* 110

13. The poetic *Jihād* of Kumayt 111

14. Armed *Jihād* 112

15. The correct meaning of *Jihād* 112

16. All of the acts of the Imams ﷺ are a form of *Jihād* 112

5. The Four Phases of the Imamate 113

1. The four phases of the life of the 250-Year-Old person 115

2. Imam Ali's ﷺ Two Options after the Usurpation of the Caliphate 116

3. The first phase: 25 Years of expedientiary cooperation 119

4. The second phase: The phase of the establishment of Islamic governance 121

5. The third phase: The phase of the preparation of a covert organization for bringing about insurrection 124

6. The fourth phase: The phase of organized resistance against the ruling authorities, and the expansion of true Islam 131

6. The Initial Period of the Fourth Phase of the Imamate 139

1. The division of the 250-Year duration of the Imamate into four phases 140

2. Two actions of the Imams ﷺ in the fourth phase of the Imamate 142
   2.1 The revivification of the intellectual basis of Islam 142
   2.2 The formation and management of a religio-political party 145

3. Islamic asceticism 148

4. Imam Sajjād's ﷺ efforts at increasing the Shī'a population 149

5. Imam Bāqir's ﷺ taking advantage of umayyad weaknesses and the increasing of the Shī'a ranks 150

6. Imam Bāqir's ﷺ being called to Damascus was due to his being intent on forming a government 154

7. The presence of Imam Bāqir ﷺ in the caliphal capital at Damascus 155

8. The all-out struggle of the Imams ﷺ with the ruling powers from Imam Sajjād ﷺ to Imam Hasan al-Askarī ﷺ (inclusive) 160

9. Hishām orders that Imams Bāqir ﷺ and Sādiq ﷺ be imprisoned in Damascus 161

10. Two teriods within the life of resistance of Imam Sādiq ﷺ 162
   The First Period 162
   The Second Period 165

11. The Āshūrā Movement: the mother of all Shī'a movements 166

7. The Political Life of Imam Sādiq 169

1. The plethora of information on Imam Sādiq ﷺ comingled with misleading information 170

2. The necessity of intellectual activities prior to and during the resistance struggle 171

3. The beginning of the Shī'a intellectual movement with Imam Husain ﷺ 171

4. An analysis of Imam Husain's insurrectionary movement 172

5. Imam Husain's principle objective: the revival of the Prophet's Islamic revolution 174

6. Two responsibilities of Imams Sajjād and Bāqir ﷺ: The explication of authentic Islam and creating a well-equipped following 174

7. Imam Sādiq ﷺ continues his father's methods 175

8. The Reason for the inability of Imam Sādiq ﷺ to form a government after the fall of the Umayyads 176

9. The consolidation of Abbāsid power makes Imam Sādiq's task more difficult 177

10. The Intellectual Efforts of Imam Sādiq ﷺ for the Dissemination of Shī'a Islam and the Training of the Shī'a Cadres 179

11. A Hadith Report about the Negative Effects of Umayyad Propaganda against the Ahl al-Bayt ﷺ 180

12. The Paucity of the Number of True Shī'a during the Time of Imam Sādiq 183

13. The insurrection of Zaid b. Ali from the perspective of the Imams 185

14. Imam Sādiq's position concerning Muhammad b. Abdullāh's insurrection 186

15. Evidence of Imam Sādiq's not intervening to prevent insurrections against the oppressor Caliphs 188

16. Imam Sādiq's position with respect to the caliphs of his time 190

17. Hadith reports which relate clashes between Imam Sādiq ﷺ and the caliphs 192

18. A preamble regarding precautionary dissimulation (*taqīya*) 195

19. Two blows struck by Imam Sādiq ﷺ to Mansūr after his martyrdom 197
   19.1 The recommendation of weeping for him [= for his martyrdom] in Mina 197

19.2 Depriving Manṣūr of any pretext by assigning several heirs and successors in Imam Ṣādiq's last will and testament 199

20. Imam Kāẓim's ؑ way 199

21. Imam Kāẓim's insistence on his right to the caliphate in Hārūn's presence 201

22. The boundaries of the Fadak Lands as described by Imam Kāẓim ؑ to Hārūn 203

23. The Condition of the Shīʻa during the Imamate of Imam Kāẓim 206

24. The Imperative to Seek Forgiveness for [One's] False Appraisals [of the Character] of the Imams 207

25. All of the Imams ؑ are Imam Husain's Brothers in Arms 208

8. The Imams' Politicism and their Militant Actions 209

1. Hadith reports claiming that the Imams ؑ were appeasers are forgeries 210

2. Giving preference to reports of the courage of the Imams ؑ to those which report the opposite 211

3. Veins of active resistance in the lives of the Imams 214

4. The harsh treatment of the Imams ؑ by the caliphs as reason for the militant nature of their activities 217

5. The important subject of the clash of the Imams ؑ with the court-allied Scholars of Religion and poets 219

6. The Scholars of Religion: the intellectual and cultural leaders within the history of Islam 220

7. Muʻāwiya puts the court-allied scholars of religion to use 221

8. Examples of hadith report forgeries 224

9. All of the oppressors utilized the services of the court-allied clergy 228

10. Muhammad Zuhrī: A prominent example of the court-allied clergy 229

11. Abdullāh b. Umar in the service of Muʻāwiya's objectives 232

12. The ascetics welcome al-Manṣūr the Abbāsid 233

13. The Imams' harsh response to the court-allied men of religion 234

14. Imam Bāqir's harsh words to ʻIkrama 234

15. Two hadith reports concerning Zuhrī's allegiance to the caliphal court 236

16. Muhammad b. Shahāb az-Zuhrī takes a lashing from Imam Sajjād's admonishments 238

17. The Imams' utilization of their Shīʻa warrior-poets 244

18. The Imams ؑ reprimand court-allied poets and encourage Shīʻa poets 247

19. The role of weeping and redemptive suffering in the growth of Shīʻa Islam 249

20. The passion of Imam Husain ﷺ as told by Di'bal al-Khuzāī in the presence of Imam Reza ﷺ 250

9. The Revolutionary Sons of the Imams 253

1. The important and misunderstood matter of the revolutionary sons and posterity of the Imams 254

2. Two positions regarding the revolutionary Imāmzādahs 254
   2.1 The position asserting the rightfulness of the insurrections of the Imāmzādahs 255
   2.2 The position asserting the wrongfulness of theinsurrections of the Imāmzādahs 255

3. The wrongfulness of the second position 256

4. The aspersions cast by the oppressor regimes posited as the main reason for the disrepute of the revolutionary Imāmzādahs 256

5. The division of the Imāmzādahs into two groups 261
   5.1 The Imāmzādahs whose values and priorities are centered on the lower world (*dunyā*) 261
   5.2 Imāmzādahs who were righteous and who sought to establish justice 265

6. Zaid b. Ali b. al-Husain 266

7. The objectives of Zaid's uprising and the Imams' opinions of him 268

8. An examination of the hadith reports concerning the disapprobation of Zaid 273

9. The formation of the Zaidīya sect after Zaid's martyrdom 277

10. Precautionary Dissimulation (Taqīya) 279

1. The indubitability of the principle of *taqīya* is Sh'īa Islam 280

2. The lack of an exact equivalent for the word taqīya in the Persian language 281

3. The mistaken common conception of *taqīya* 282

4. An allegory clarifying the difference between the correct and mistaken conceptions of *taqīya* 282

5. *Taqīya* in the Quran and the Hadith report corpus: A correct tool for attaining to one's goals 284

6. The conditions for the correct employment of *Taqīya* 285
   6.1 Maintaining order and being faithful to the principles of the objective 285
   6.2 Concealment 285
   6.3 Getting things done by way of a hierarchic organizational structure 286

7. Examples of covert actions by way of *Taqīya* 287
   7.1 Anonymity in communications by letter 287
   7.2 A well-organized political resistance structure 289
   7.3 Sending secret letters 291

8. Project nomenclature posited as scriptural proofs of *Taqīya* 293
   8.1 The Imams' stipulation that their partisans are to maintain secret communications with each other 294
   8.2 A party organization that is as secretive as a fort is strong 294
   8.3 The office of the *Bāb* (Portal) for the special access of the companions of the Imams 296
   8.4 Secret aides-de-camp of the Imams 298
   8.5 Characterizing *Taqīya* as an endeavor 300
   8.7 The companions of the cave 304

9. The falsity of the definition of *taqīya* as 'not taking any action' 307

10. Taqīya is intertwined with action and endeavor (*Jihād*) 307

The Names and Dates of the Twelve Imams

			Dates of Birth-Death	
No	Konya	Name	Islamic	Christian
1	Ab'al-Hasan	Ali b.AbuTalib	-23 to 40	600–661
2	Abu Md.	Hasan ibn Ali	3–50	624–670
3	Abu Abdillah	Husain b. Ali	4–61	626–680
4	Abu Md.	Ali b. Husain	38–95	658–712
5	Abu Ja'far	Md. ibn Ali	57–114	677–732
6	Abu Abdillah	Ja'far ibn Md.	83–148	702–765
7	Ab'al-Hasan	Musa b. Ja'far	128–183	744–799
8	Ab'al-Hasan	Ali ibn Musa	148–203	765–817
9	Abu Ja'far	Md. ibn Ali	195–220	810–835
10	Ab'al-Hasan	Ali ibn Md.	212–254	827–868
11	Abu Md.	Hasan ibn Ali	232–260	846–874
12	Ab'al-Qasim	Md. B. Hasan	255–Present	868–Present

Translator's Foreword

Imam Husain's Brothers in Arms consists of a series of ten lectures delivered in the Ansār al-Husain Husainieh[1] in Tehran in the month of Muharram of 1393 (September of 1972), approximately seven years prior to the triumph of the Islamic Revolution of Iran, and seven years prior to the dawning of the new (15th) Islamic lunar century. There are other lectures in the archives that have been redacted that predate even this early date, some of which I have translated and hope to publish in 2021 with the help of Lantern's esteemed and learned publisher, Dr. Abidali Mohamedali. What is interesting to note is that these lecture series were occurring at approximately the same time and in parallel with Imam Khomeini's lectures on Islamic Governance which he delivered in the seminary at Najaf during his years of exile around 1968-9, which were published as a book in 1970 under the title *hukūmat-e islāmī* (Islamic Governance), and which became the spark that eventually led to the Islamic Revolution of Iran less than a decade later. What is interesting to note is how Ayatollah Khāmeneī's thoughts and work were occurring at the same time and in parallel with those of Imam Khomeini's.

It should also be noted that Ayatollah Khāmeneī's theory that the Imams were, one and all, engaged in a concerted clandestine effort with an organized or party-like organization for the overthrow of the Umayyad and later Abbāsid orders is highly controversial among senior seminarians in Qom (let alone Najaf). But the Ayatollah certainly brings his reasons to bear in this work and elsewhere, and it is up to the reader to decide the cogency of his arguments.

Blake Archer Williams
January 2021

Acknowledgment: All translations of the verses of the Quran are Muhammad Asad's, with the occasional minor change.

---

[1] A Husainieh is a congregation hall for Shi'a commemoration ceremonies and rites, especially those associated with mourning in the month of Moharram for the martyrdom of Imam Husain, the third Imam of the Shī'a.

1. Various Approaches to Leadership of the Community

[God ﷻ the All-Knowing and All-Wise has stated in His Sacred Writ:]

$$رَبَّنَا لَا تُزِغْ قُلُوبَنَا بَعْدَ إِذْ هَدَيْتَنَا وَهَبْ لَنَا مِن لَّدُنكَ رَحْمَةً ۚ إِنَّكَ أَنتَ الْوَهَّابُ ﴿٨﴾$$

[3:8] "O our Sustainer! Let not our hearts swerve from the truth after Thou hast guided us; and bestow upon us the gift of Thy grace: verily, Thou art the [true] Giver of Gifts.

$$وَلَمَّا بَرَزُوا لِجَالُوتَ وَجُنُودِهِ قَالُوا رَبَّنَا أَفْرِغْ عَلَيْنَا صَبْرًا وَثَبِّتْ أَقْدَامَنَا وَانصُرْنَا عَلَى الْقَوْمِ الْكَافِرِينَ ﴿٢٥٠﴾$$

[2:250] And when they came face to face with Goliath and his forces, they prayed: "O our Sustainer! Shower us with patience in adversity, and make firm our steps, and succor us against the people who deny the truth!"

$$وَجَعَلْنَا مِنْهُمْ أَئِمَّةً يَهْدُونَ بِأَمْرِنَا لَمَّا صَبَرُوا ۖ وَكَانُوا بِآيَاتِنَا يُوقِنُونَ ﴿٢٤﴾$$

[32:24] and [as] We raised among them Imams (leaders) who, so long as they bore themselves with patience and had sure faith in Our messages, guided [their people] in accordance with Our behest [so, too, shall it be with the divine writ revealed unto thee, O Muhammad.]

وَجَعَلْنَاهُمْ أَئِمَّةً يَهْدُونَ بِأَمْرِنَا وَأَوْحَيْنَا إِلَيْهِمْ فِعْلَ الْخَيْرَاتِ وَإِقَامَ الصَّلَاةِ وَإِيتَاءَ الزَّكَاةِ ۖ وَكَانُوا لَنَا عَابِدِينَ ﴿٧٣﴾

[21:73] and made them Imams (leaders) who would guide [others] in accordance with Our behest: for We inspired them [with a will] to do good works, and to be constant in prayer, and to dispense charity: and Us [alone] did they worship.

The subject which I shall be speaking about over the next [ten] days pertains to a portion of the larger subject of [the institution of] the Imamate, [or the Islamic (religio-political) conception and form of the leadership of the community]. Now there are various ways of approaching our subject matter, and it is incumbent upon me to explain the approach which I shall be taking. Thus, it will suffice our purposes for today if we are able to elucidate for you gentlemen the [essence of] the subject matter [and the approach we plan to take towards it] in the next few days.

1. The discussion concerning the necessity of the Imamate

One of the aspects of the general discussion on the Imamate has to do with establishing its necessity. In such a discussion, one must prove that the institution of the imamate is necessary in addition to that of the institution of prophethood; and in such discussions, the basic philosophy of the imamate [and its tenets] must be presented. But this is not the subject of our discussion; it is not because we do not consider such discussions necessary. To the contrary: we do consider such discussions necessary, and have discussed this issue in the past, and continue to do so. But we have another aspect of the subject in mind for the present discussion and for the present gathering which is, generally speaking, more pressing.

1. Various Approaches to Leadership of the Community

2. The discussion concerning the succession to the Prophet

Another aspect of the discussion revolves around the issue of the succession to the Prophet ﷺ and the identity of the [rightful] successor(s) to the Prophet ﷺ. This has been the primary concern of the Shi'a in their discussions concerning the issue of the imamate throughout their history, i.e. the question as to who the rightful successor was, the reasons for this position, and why it was not anyone else [other than Ali b. Abī-Tālib ؏]; why this was not the case. And again, this too is not the subject of my discussion. Any discussion must have its purpose, and the purpose of our discussion is to disabuse the minds of those present of some misunderstandings, or to inform them of something that they are not already aware of; and I do not think that there is anyone in the audience who has any doubts that the rightful successor to the Most Noble Prophet ﷺ was His Holy Eminence Ali b. Abi-Tālib. None of us has the least doubt about this fact, which is why I shall not be treating this issue either [in the present series of talks].

True: if there was an occasion where we were somewhere outside the territories of Shi'a Islam and in the company of a group of people who were not convinced of this fact [= the rightfulness of the right of Imam Ali ؏ to succession to the leadership of the community], then we could establish, when appropriate, using rational and scriptural proofs, that the rightful successor to the Most Noble Prophet ﷺ was His Holy Eminence Ali b. Abi-Tālib. But this discussion is not necessary for those of us gathered in this assembly. And you should also know that such discussions are not necessary in [any] Shi'a *milieu*. What I mean is that exacting discussions that bring all sorts of scholarly minutia and esoterica concerning the subject to bear are unnecessary [as these discussions have already taken place in bygone centuries and the issues have been examined in detail and settled]. Needless to say, I do not mean to imply that such discussions will not or should not take place: they will continue to take place; but they are not germane and necessary for those presently gathered. This is because everyone knows the truth of the matter, and even those [among us Shi'a believers] who have ventured to study the Sunni positions on the issue have not been swayed by them, and there is no one is the whole Shi'a world who harbors the slightest doubt concerning the matter [of the rightfulness of Imam Ali's ﷺ succession]. Therefore, this is not a subject which we need to discuss.

3. The discussion concerning the attributes and characteristics of the Imam of the community of Muslims and the conditions under which investiture to the office of the Imamate is appropriate

Another discussion concerning the issue of the Imamate centers on the question as to what attributes are necessary for the Imam [of the community and his investiture in the office of leadership]. In other words, what attributes and characteristics should the Imam have, and under what conditions [can such a person properly be vested into the office of the Imamate].

For example: what should the level of the Imam's knowledge be? Should his knowledge cover all possible subjects, and if so, why? And conversely, if not, why not. Or, another example: the discussion concerning the issue of the Imam's immaculacy (*ismat*).[2] Or, the discussion concerning the extent of the spiritual [= supernatural] powers of the Imam; this is yet another discussion concerning the subject of the Imamate. But this too is not the subject of our discussion. Such discussions are entirely necessary and appropriate in their own right. Fortunately, the great early scholars of Shi'a Islam have addressed these issues in their detailed and voluminous books, such that if one were to pick up this discussion and write a treatise about it, it would not amount to more than a very small corner of what the great scholars of the first centuries have already addressed. These discussions have all taken place frequently and in exhaustive detail, and certain tenets and beliefs have arisen out of this intellectual discourse and process. And so, in our opinion, we should not enter into these kinds of discussions either, given the audience at hand.

---

[2] Immaculacy (*ismat* = sinlessness as well as inerrancy). The Shī'a believe the Prophet ﷺ, Lady Fātima, and the Twelve Imāms to be immaculate, meaning that they are inerrant as well as sinless. Inerrant means one who does not commit any gross error, be it intentional or unintentional. *Ismat* is a continual state of inerrancy as well as sinlessness in the Shī'a definition of the term (whereas Sunni Islam limits its scope to the person of the Prophet ﷺ and only in his function as bringer of revelation).

1. Various Approaches to Leadership of the Community

Why? Because in the conditions under which you and I are living, being surrounded with a wall of false memes and misconceptions concerning what [true] Islamic culture should be, it would be a gross error of judgement to choose to discuss a topic which has no practical effect on the way in which we are to transact our lives.

Today, there are two types of questions. The first is the question as to whether or not Almighty God ﷻ will indeed hold us to account for our actions, and whether there will be a Reckoning. This is an issue which has a direct impact on your life and my life; for if I believe that there will be a Reckoning, I will live my life in one way, and if I believe that there will not be any such Reckoning, then I will live my life in a different way. Is this not the case? The same principle applies to all of us. Thus, belief in the reality of the Resurrection, in the reality of the fact that God ﷻ will weigh our Book of Deeds in his Scale of Justice plays a determinative role in the way we transact each of our lives:

وَقَالَ الَّذِينَ كَفَرُوا لَا تَأْتِينَا السَّاعَةُ ۖ قُلْ بَلَىٰ وَرَبِّي لَتَأْتِيَنَّكُمْ عَالِمِ الْغَيْبِ ۖ لَا يَعْزُبُ عَنْهُ مِثْقَالُ ذَرَّةٍ فِي السَّمَاوَاتِ وَلَا فِي الْأَرْضِ وَلَا أَصْغَرُ مِن ذَٰلِكَ وَلَا أَكْبَرُ إِلَّا فِي كِتَابٍ مُبِينٍ ﴿٣﴾ لِيَجْزِيَ الَّذِينَ آمَنُوا وَعَمِلُوا الصَّالِحَاتِ ۚ أُولَٰئِكَ لَهُم مَّغْفِرَةٌ وَرِزْقٌ كَرِيمٌ ﴿٤﴾

[34:3] And yet, they who are bent on denying the truth assert, "Never will the Last Hour come upon us!" Say: "Nay, by my Sustainer! By Him who knows all that is beyond the reach of a created being's perception: it will most certainly come upon you!" Not an atom's weight [of whatever there is] in the heavens or on earth escapes His knowledge; and neither is there anything smaller than that, or larger, but is recorded in [His] clear decree, [34:4] to the end that He may reward those who believe and do right-eous deeds: [for] it is they whom forgiveness of sins awaits, and a most excellent sustenance

يَوْمَئِذٍ يَصْدُرُ النَّاسُ أَشْتَاتًا لِّيُرَوْا أَعْمَالَهُمْ ﴿٦﴾ فَمَن يَعْمَلْ مِثْقَالَ ذَرَّةٍ خَيْرًا يَرَهُ ﴿٧﴾ وَمَن يَعْمَلْ مِثْقَالَ ذَرَّةٍ شَرًّا يَرَهُ ﴿٨﴾

[99:6] On that Day will all men come forward, cut off from one another, to be shown their [past] deeds. [99:7] And so, he who shall have done an atom's weight of good, shall behold it; [99:8] and he who shall have done an atom's weight of evil, shall behold it.

Now there are other kinds of beliefs that do not have such a determinative effect. For example, there is the belief, based on *hadīth*[3] reports in the authoritative Shi'a hadith report corpus, that on the first night of our deaths, [once we have entered the realm of the *Barzakh*[4]], we will be visited by the angels Nakīr and Munkar [to question us concerning our deeds in the world which we have just left behind]. The question is whether these two angels will appear in the form of human beings or in

---

[3] *Hadīth*: An authoritative report of a saying or deed of the Prophet ﷺ, and in Shi'a Islam, of one of the Fourteen Immaculates (the Prophet ﷺ, Lady Fātima, and the Twelve Imāms).

[4] *Barzakh* - This word is usually translated, in my view mistakenly, as "isthmus" or "the isthmus", which is why I have put it in quotes. While it is true that *barzakh* literally means isthmus (a narrow neck of land, bordered on both sides by water, connecting two larger bodies of land), and that it is even true that this analogy holds for one of the definitions of the *barzakh* in so far as it is an intermediate stage between this world and the hereafter, it is misleading to translate it as such, because the other more important definition, which is understood in the Arabic and other Islamic languages, is ignored; namely, that the *barzakh* is a class of reality that actually encompasses the reality of the *dunyā* or of this, the lower world, and that some of the attributes of this world are actually parts of the *barzakh*, which is a higher level of reality. These include any phenomena which do not have "extension" or dimension and cannot be measured or sensed by the senses, such as thought, imagination, dreams, intuition, visions and hallucinations. Henry Corbin used to refer to the *barzakh* as the "Imaginal World". But perhaps a better way to think of it is to think of this this world as the womb of the *barzakh*: we are in it while we are "in the womb", but we enter it proper upon our death, when its veil is lifted. The Noble Prophet ﷺ is authoritatively reported to have said about the relationship of this world to the *barzakh*: "This world is but a dream from which we awake upon our deaths."

1. Various Approaches to Leadership of the Community

some other form, whether they will be tall or short, etc. These are also issues [which some people concern themselves with]. And of course, knowing something is better than not knowing anything, but this is not an issue of the first order [of importance]. Furthermore, what possible affect can the knowledge of the height and weight of these angels have on one's lives?! Or take another question, for example: What is the length of time between my death and the advent of the Day of Resurrection? Or: How long will the Day of Resurrection take? And we can go on like this concerning many other beliefs about our creed. What I am getting at is a general rule: there are certain issues which do not have any palpable effect on one's life no matter which side of the issue one takes or how it is resolved. [Therefore, what I commend you to do] about any issue that crosses your mind is to first examine it to see whether it is an issue which has any effect on your lives and on the program you have for your future and how you want to live your life. Does it give direction to your life [or take you away from your intended ideals and objectives]? If so, then you should release it and let it go. This is not an era where we [have the luxury and time to] solve each and every problem which comes up, because we do not even have a good grasp of our primary problems and challenges; we still have not been able to identify the most pressing and urgent problems facing our lives. And I am loath to stand on ceremony on this issue, for the issue of the possibility of distortion and falsification in our scriptural sources of the first rank [excluding the Quran, of course[5]], exists, and numerous truths are veiled from us. This is one of the issues which I will be talking about over the next few days, and you will see, God grant, what havoc the hands of the distorters and falsifiers [of hadith

---

[5] Reference is probably to the "Four Books" or the *kutub al-arba'a*. The "Four Books" are the four best-known Shi'a compilations of hadith reports. The quotes are added so as not to give the impression that the contents of these Four Books are considered to be absolutely sound and reliable (*sahīh*) by Shi'a scholarship. This is not the case. Unlike the case with Sunni dogmatics which holds the contents of all six of their canonical books to be *sahīh* and beyond reproach, Shi'a scholarship holds that the reliability of each hadith report must be evaluated individually on its merits based on the state of knowledge of the day. The soundness and authenticity and integrity of the Quran, of course, has never been in question. See: *The Immunity of the Quran to Distortion & Falsification* by Abdul-Rahim Musawi (Author), Blake Archer Williams (Translator).

scripture] have wrought [on the beliefs and lives of the community of the faithful].

We are suffering from [a deep and entrenched] ignorance and lack of awareness concerning our very first issues of concern. And so, what possible justification can there be for us to pursue questions that can have no impact on the direction of our lives and on the determination and reevaluation of our values and objectives? Therefore, why should we [waste what precious time we have on] engaging in such discussions?

It has been said that Zurāra, who was one of Imam Sādiq's [preeminent] companions who lived in Kūfa (whereas the Imam lived in Madina), was asked upon the Imam's death who he would turn to [for obtaining the responsa to his religio-legal questions]. Now according to the hadith report corpus which has come down to us, which I believe to be correct [on this issue], Zurāra knew [the identity of] the Imam who was to succeed Imam Sādiq. However, for various reasons it was not expedient for him to mention the name of Imam Kāẓim.[6] He therefore practiced precautionary or prudential dissimulation (*taqīya*) and picked up a copy of the Quran and said, "Know that I accept the imamate of he whose person is affirmed by the logic [and teachings] of the Quran."[7] This is a profitable way in which a person or two people who do not agree on a matter of secondary importance which does not have any significant impact on how one is to lead one's life, can resolve their differences, and submit to [the logic and teachings of the Quran] and to what Almighty God ❀ has determined [for them]. It is these kinds of useless discussions of irrelevant minutia have brought the people of this nation to its knees – discussions which will have no significance to the welfare and lives of the people irrespective of whether or not they are discussed now or a hundred

---

[6] Most likely for security reasons, as the possibility existed that the authorities might kill the new Imam before he had had a chance to establish his base.

[7] Citations and references to Persian and Arabic sources: the book whose translation is before you is full of footnotes citing the references for these quotes, but as all the sources are in Persian or Arabic, those who are able to refer to them (and hence, those for whom such citations have any use) have the ability to refer to the original Persian text in order to access the references. Thus, in the interest of not cluttering up the text with unnecessary footnotes, I have decided not to translate them, and refer the scholar and researcher to the original Persian text.

1. Various Approaches to Leadership of the Community

years from now; even if they do happen to unveil the truth at times – they nevertheless remain entirely unnecessary; and they have inflicted great harm to our nation. Nor should you think that it is only in Iran that these kinds of useless discussions concerning irrelevant and meaningless matters takes place. To the contrary! Rather, it is a phenomenon that can be seen throughout the Islamic world; and this is something that we have encountered in books. [The phenomenon] exists in India, in Egypt, and in various other parts [of the Islamic world]. The moment a vein of light appears in the discourse within Islamic nations which manifests a correct understanding of a social matter or of Islam [more generally], they immediately come up with something to divert the discourse away from that vein of correct understanding, and, unfortunately, they have usually been successful.

Therefore, I cannot enter into a discussion here concerning the conditions [necessary] for the Imam [to be vested in the Imamate]. My advice to you is that whatever portion [of this question] becomes clear and convincing to you based on correct proofs, that you should accept it without spending a lot of your time on it; and to relegate whatever portion that is not clear to you to God ﷻ:

ا أَيُّهَا الَّذِينَ آمَنُوا أَطِيعُوا اللَّهَ وَأَطِيعُوا الرَّسُولَ وَأُولِي الْأَمْرِ مِنكُمْ ۖ فَإِن تَنَازَعْتُمْ فِي شَيْءٍ فَرُدُّوهُ إِلَى اللَّهِ وَالرَّسُولِ إِن كُنتُمْ تُؤْمِنُونَ بِاللَّهِ وَالْيَوْمِ الْآخِرِ ۚ ذَٰلِكَ خَيْرٌ وَأَحْسَنُ تَأْوِيلًا ﴿٥٩﴾

> [4:59] O you who have attained to faith! Pay heed unto God ﷻ, and pay heed unto the Apostle and unto those from among you who have been entrusted with authority; and if you are at variance over any matter, *refer it unto God* ﷻ *and the Apostle*, if you [truly] believe in God ﷻ and the Last Day. This is the best [for you], and best in the end.

In other words, take the posture that says, "I accept and submit to that which God ﷻ has ordained." The identity and character of our Twelve Imams ﷺ is abundantly clear; nor is there to be a thirteenth Imam for us to want to search for signs by which we will know such a person. Our Imams ؏ are Imam Ali ؏ and Imam Hasan ؏ and Imam Husain ؏ and nine progenies in the line of Imam Husain ؏, up to the Twelfth Imam, the *Hujjat* and the Qāim ؏.[8]

These Imams ؏ we all accept, as does the entirety of the Shi'a world [as our Imams ؏ or religio-political leaders and spiritual guides]. So what possible reason can there be for us to sit and discuss whether or not such and such an attribute or characteristic is or is not necessary; and for me, say, to prove that yes, such and such an attribute is indeed necessary; and then for you to harbor a doubt in your mind regardless, or not – as the case may be – but in either event, to accept what I have said so as not to break the bounds of social decorum and to while away the time in one fashion or another? Thus, we shall not be discussing this issue either.

4. The discussion concerning the role of the Imams ؏ and their [intellectual and practical] posture concerning insurrection against the forces of illegitimate governance (or the Islamic counter-revolution)

There may be other discussions concerning the lives of the Imams, but that is not the intended purpose of our discussion either; and we shall refrain from entering into those discussions as well. What we intend to discuss is the role of [all of] our Imams ؏ (which we have identified above, and in whose imamates we believe) and the nature of their [intellectual and practical] posture concerning the insurrection against the forces of illegitimate governance (or the Islamic counter-revolution). This is the question that occupies the minds of those who are awake [to the political

---

[8] These are both *kunyas* or patronymics of the Twelfth Imam Q. *Hujjat* or *Hujjatullāh*: the Proof [of God ﷻ] [36:12] ... For of all things do We take account in a manifest Imām (*imāmin mubīn*) [who shall be called to testify and provide evidence on all matters on the Day of Judgment]. This is the meaning of the word *Hujjatullāh* or God's proof for mankind, which is one of the names given to the Imāms by the Quran: The *Hujjat* is the perfect embodiment and "clear evidence" of all truth on Earth and the conclusive argument and evidentiary proof against all falsehood on Judgement Day. *Al-Qāim* Q: the One who will Arise [in insurrection against the forces of tyranny to establish justice on Earth].

1. Various Approaches to Leadership of the Community

realities of their day]. It is entirely possible that this issue is not a concern for one who is not paying close attention [to what is happening around him socially or politically]. But it *will* become a concern of his tomorrow. Tomorrow, this same question will be posed, and a certain number of people who are heedless [of contemporary realities] will be snared up with the response to this question and will be taken away [by the authorities (?)].⁹

[The advent of Islam in Arabia in the early seventh century] brought about an Islamic revolution and [the Prophet ﷺ of Islam] laid the foundations of a new social order by introducing a new vision and sacred creed (*idéologie*).¹⁰ The Prophet ﷺ, who headed this new social order, was given the Quran [by God ﷻ, over a period of twenty-three years]. He in turn presented it to those who accepted Islam, together with the creedal principles and tenets of the Islamic teachings, and together with all of the sacred ordinances and laws which this Divine Writ entailed; after which he left the material plane.

We Shī'a believe that Twelve Imams ؑ [were divinely appointed to] follow in the Prophet's ﷺ wake one after the other [in an uninterrupted series or Golden Chain, not to bring any new laws or to change the Muhammadan dispensation in any way, but in order to interpret the sacred scripture of that dispensation, the Quran and the Prophetic *sunna* or paradigmatic example, and to act as immaculate models and guides for the new way of life which God ﷻ had revealed through His prophet Muhammad]. [Because of the divine nature of their appointment and investiture to the leadership of society (the *imāmate*),] we consider them to be an [integral] part of the religion of Islam. And we consider the words and deeds of these Imams ؑ to be 'at the side of' [i.e. a necessary supplement to] the Quran, and honor them as we honor the

---

⁹ The reference is possibly to the Savak or the Shah's secret intelligence service who was notorious for "disappearing" activists and taking them away to political prisons and torture chambers where any trace of them would be lost.

¹⁰ The Persianized version of the French word *idéologie* has not been translated as "ideology" so as to avoid the synthetic or man-made implications which the word carries in English, but which is not carried over the French word in its Persianized form; i.e. *idéologie* does not necessarily connote a system of ideas which are human in origin, as is the case in its European secular usage.

Most Noble Prophet ﷺ (unto whom and unto whose purified and immaculate progeny be God's everlasting peace).

A questioner might ask what function these Twelve Lights and great personages – as we characterize them – served in Islamic society? Why was their existence necessary? The other question that naturally follows in the wake of the first one, which is whether or not these Twelve Luminous Personalities – whose beings, as we maintain, had an existential significance [to Islam] – did in fact carry out their functions and live out their lives according to their function (which we have yet to elaborate on)? Because some of the historical evidence that is cited concerning their lives and which has currency among the general population, are contradictory. Some of what is said, concerning them contradicts their [alleged] existential role and function, and other such reports of their sacred histories [i.e. things that have come down to us concerning their lives, sayings and deeds] are at loggerheads with the basic teachings and creedal tenets of Islam itself. These contradictions must be resolved. We must investigate and see whether or not that which we posit as the nature and function of the imamate or the Islamic form of the leadership of the community of those who have attained to faith is correct, or whether in fact that which is related here and there about the lives of those great men, some of which are not self-consistent or consistent with each other, is correct. Which is it? At all events, this is the issue that must be deliberated upon.

The net result of what I have said is that there are two discussions, or, better to say, two aspects of a single unitary issue. The first is that we want to discuss the question as to what the role of the Imams ؏ (whose characters and lives we are familiar with, more or less) was with respect to the [interpretation and] explication of Islam. In other words, what role had Islam determined for them? What burden of responsibility did it place upon their shoulders? What benefit was their existence expected to bestow? In other words, what purpose did Almighty God ﷻ have in mind when he chose these Twelve Imams ؏ and appointed them and commissioned them to the institution of the imamate and to the office of the leadership of the community of the faithful? The second concomitant issue, once we know the *purpose and function* to which they were commissioned, is to see to what *extent* they were able to *fulfill* their function. Do we find, upon examination, the usefulness and benefit for which these noble personages were commissioned come to fruition in the lives of these men, or don't we?

5. The principles of comprehending the way of the Imams ﷺ and the criteria for determining their success

There are, of course, numerous benefits to this discussion, which I shall discuss later; but in summary, when one becomes aware of the role and function of the imams and becomes convinced that one's Imams ﷺ did indeed fulfill these functions, then, firstly, one's belief in the Imams ﷺ will become stronger and it will be based on a sturdier and more informed footing. Secondly, [it is only] when one understands the Imams ﷺ [properly] that one can follow [their example properly]. For it is only once one knows what choices one's Imam made in his own life that he or she can use that model to make similar choices in his or her[11] own life. After all, the [literal] meaning of Imam means leader, one who stands in front and leads by example.

Unfortunately, the matter of leadership and following the exemplary models provided to us by the lives of the Imams ﷺ does not enjoy the place of honor that it should among the public within Shi'a culture.[12] As soon as one says, for example, that "Imam Sādiq ﷺ performed in such and such a way in a given situation, and so what would *you* do?" People immediately respond by saying, "But sir! Imam Sādiq ﷺ was an *Imam!!* As soon as you cite the exemplary models of the other Imams, it is the same: they say, "But these were *Imams!!*" Whereas each of their exemplary lives were models and paragons of the glory and mythic grandeur of perfected humanity whose achievement was the reason for the revelation of the Islamic dispensation. [But these people have it all wrong], it is precisely on account of their being Imams ﷺ that their

---

[11] Her Eminence Lady Fātima ﷺ is considered to be immaculate by the Shi'a and is the exemplary model and paradigmatic example for women within Shi'a Islam.
[12] Note that this speech was delivered 47 years ago (as of the time of this translation, or late 2019). The Islamic Republic has tried to change that, of course; with mixed results.

example must be followed! For no one would beseech you to live by their example if they were not Imams! We [Muslims] do not beseech each other to follow the example of, say, Gandhi, who was and is an imam or leader for a different nation of peoples; and so it is not as if you are being asked to emulate and follow the example of one in whose example you have no faith. Rather, you are asked to emulate one's exemplary model on account of his being your Imam. It is *because* he is an Imam that you are duty-bound to pay heed to his words and deeds. What sense does it make to say that I cannot act like he does and follow in his footsteps because he is an Imam?! This is a very gross error [of judgment], and a very clear one at that. When we identify and recognize a person as an Imam and leader, we must inform ourselves of his *way* as well, so that we can follow the way in which he lived his life so that we ourselves can speak and act in the way he or they did.

6. The relationship of the leader and the follower: the relationship between one who is deferred to and one who defers

The Commander of the Faithful [Ali b. Abī-Tālib] ﷺ said: "Verily it is not other than the case that each deferrer has a deferee to which he defers." For if this were not the case, then one would not be a deferrer, and the other would not be his deferee. We can thus conclude that deferring to and following the way of a deferee and leader is a logical necessity of the relationship between the two. [Failing to accept such a basic rule of logic] would be tantamount to one who goes to a congregational or communal prayer, falls in line with the rest of the supplicants who await the cue of the prayer leader to determine when to bow down, when to prostrate themselves, and when to stand back up and repeat the cycle. This individual continues to follow this pattern, but then somewhere in the middle of, say, the second cycle, he starts to bow and prostrate himself off cue and out of sync with the rest of the supplicants, but still maintains, [absurdly,] that he participated in the communal prayer and that he deferred to the prayer leader. Needless to say, such a statement and claim will do nothing but engender laughter and ridicule.

1. Various Approaches to Leadership of the Community

Imam Hasan 🕊 performed a certain act in a specific situation,[13] and it is our contention that his act is still not properly understood by his followers. At the same time, they somehow are also able to maintain that they are followers of Imam Hasan, and pretend to themselves that they have shed a tear or two for the calamities which befell that great Imam; whereas they have not understood the Imam at all. Do we not say that tears shed without understanding [the true reasons for shedding such tears] are useless [in God's eyes, i.e. in terms of worldly and other-worldly rewards]? These are words of wisdom. The same is true for going on a pilgrimage without knowing the true purpose of doing so. And the idioms that are current in the general population concerning these truths are acknowledged by everyone because they are true. For tears shed in ignorance and pilgrimages undertaken in ignorance truly *are* useless activities. And this is even the case, if the Imam [who is the subject of one's ignorant pilgrimage] were alive, and people made pilgrimage to him, visited him, without knowing who he was and what he stood for: that too would be a futile waste of time in which no benefit would accrue to the person paying the visit. Similarly, Imam Husain 🕊 acted in a particular [selfless and self-sacrificing] manner, and there are people who act in a [selfish and self-seeking] manner but who still consider themselves followers of Imam Husain 🕊. Well, truly, this is a great error, a very great error.

7. The Importance of becoming aware of the benefits of the Imamate and of the Function of the Imams

[Therefore, given the importance of becoming aware of the benefits of the imamate and of the function of the Imams], we shall be speaking briefly in the next few days about the basic question of the reason for the necessity [of the institution] of the imamate, and what benefits it bestows from the vantage of [the overall pattern of the teachings] of Islam. [The institution of] prophethood was inaugurated [by God 🕊], and we all know

---

[13] Reference to the peace treaty which the Imam was forced into signing with Mu'āwiya as a consequence of the lack of support that the Imam received during the muster calls to go to war against him.

the reasons for it. But what of [the institution and office of] the imamate? What is that for?

There is a relatively more complex discussion concerning the issue of the function of the Imams, and particularly the eight Imams ﷺ from Imam [Ali b. al-Husain] as-Sajjād ﷺ, [the Fourth Imam] on down to Imam [Hasan b. Ali] al-Askari ﷺ [the Eleventh Imam, inclusive]. The discussion revolves around the particular conditions of their times, the circumstances under which they lived, the role they played in life [and in the lives of their followers], and how they reacted and responded to the [political] events which confronted them. And so, the subject of our discussion over the next few days shall [also include] a summary introduction to the spiritual and intellectual sacred biography (*sīra*) of the Imams ﷺ. [But the general] discussion is a detailed one which has been occupying my mind for some time now, and which I have studied for some time – of course, not for the purposes of this [ten-day] presentation, but generally – and taken some notes on. I have also spoken [on this subject] on occasion, but I have not [had the chance to] organize [the series of talks as I would have liked]; thus, it will not be a thoroughly thought-out and polished presentation. Nor will the subject matter be able to be covered in the handful of session in which I will be at your disposal. I will be summarizing and compressing the [entire] subject matter to the extent that is possible and treating it with summary glosses in the hope that the very presentation of the issue will have an effect which will bring about, God ﷻ willing, a change in our conception and envisioning of these great personalities. This is because they are central both to our worldly concerns, as well as to our concerns about our fates in the afterlife; so it is imperative that we become intimately familiar with them and the way they lived their lives. The discussion will begin simply, and gradually take on greater complexity, God ﷻ grant. I also look forward to and encourage your comments, so that I can benefit from them and so that the benefit of the lectures will be increased.

1. Various Approaches to Leadership of the Community

8. The necessity of understanding the approach of the Imams ﷺ towards their followers (*Shī'ayān*), the caliphs, and the court-allied religious scholars

What is the Way of the Divine Guides [= the Imams], these people whom we accept as our leaders and to whom we defer? How do they approach life and how do they transact it? How did they react to the events of their day and the currents of their times? What was their relationship with their followers or partisans (their "Shī'a", in Arabic)? How did they relate to their enemies, the caliphs of the day; and what was their posture toward the religious scholars who had ties to the court of the caliphs, such as the likes of Abū-Yūsuf[14], Zuhrī[15], and others? Is it not necessary to be aware of these things? And if this *is* a necessity, then, have you attained to this awareness? Now of course it is possible that some scattered facts about this knowledge might cross your mind, but I know that you have not attained to any such awareness [that is complete or even at an acceptable level of completion]. It is not my intention, of course, to insult [your intelligence] by mentioning this; but [to point out and obviate the fact] that an extraordinarily powerful force has been at work in this field for a very long time, which is the work of the distortion and falsification [of the true identity of the Imams, and their essentially politically active (rather than 'quietist') character in particular]. The history of this effort of falsification and distortion goes back to the time of the Imams ﷺ themselves, at which time it was engaged in an attempt to provide a distorted portrayal of the way in which they lived.

Let us assume that there is someone in whom you have confidence and whose word you have complete trust in, but that this person is not in

---

[14] Ya'qūb ibn Ibrahim al-Anṣārī, better known as Abu Yusuf (Arabic: أبو يوسف) (d.798) was a student of jurist Abu Hanifah (d.767) who helped spread the influence of the Hanafi school of Islamic law through his writings and the government positions he held. He served as the chief judge (*qadi al-qudat*) during reign of Harun al-Rashid. His most famous work was *Kitab al-Kharāj*, a treatise on taxation and fiscal problems of the state.

[15] Muhammad ibn Muslim ibn Ubaydullah ibn Shihab al-Zuhri (Arabic: ابن شهاب الزهري; died AH 124/741-2), usually referred to simply as Ibn Shihab or al-Zuhri in hadith literature. He was a central figure among the early collectors of *sīra*—biographies of the Islamic prophet, Muhammad and hadith literature.

your vicinity [such that you have no access to him]. Now let us further suppose that there is another unscrupulous party who is after his own self-interest. It is very natural for such a person – who benefits personally from the distortion of the facts [concerning the person in whom you have implicit trust] – to come and tell you that so and so said such and such a thing or took such a position on an issue – all of which would be fabrications in his favor, the purpose being to make you take a similar position. This is a very natural occurrence. It is very much in the nature of things that Rabī', the servant and confidant of [the Abbāsid caliph] al-Mansūr, should say that Imam Sādiq ﷺ, the leader of the Shī'a, has come to the court of our lord and master al-Mansūr and humbled himself in such and such a manner, and kissed his hand in this way, and praised him and fawned on him in such and such a manner. What else can be expected from a character such as Rabī'? Can one expect him to testify that Imam Sādiq ﷺ spoke up against al-Mansur in a gathering in his own court? After all is said and done, Rabī' is who he is; he is al-Mansūr's servant and can do naught but behave in this manner. And then Rabī''s son relates a report from him, and then his grandson does the same, and then a Shī'a simpleton comes along and relates that report from Rabī''s grandson! The end result is that it will be recorded [in books of history] that "[It is related] from Muhammad b. Sulaymān b. Rabī'" – one of the noble and truly reputable and prominent Shī'a personalities – who is a self-avowed Shī'a – that Rabī''s grandson was a Shī'a"! Then they will say that it was on account of the "fact" that Rabī''s grandson was a Shī'a that he related this report to us, and that he would not have done so if he were a Sunni! "... From his father, [who related the report] from *his* father [before him, that Rabī'] – who was a famous personality – who said that he was in the company of a gathering of [the caliph] al-Mansūr's when Imam Sādiq ﷺ entered. After much praised of the caliph, he said, "O Commander of the Faithful![16] Forgive me! [for] you are magnanimous; [therefore I beseech you to] act in the manner of the Fathers; in the [magnanimous] manner of Jacob, Joseph, and Solomon!"[17] For the love of God ﷻ, pay attention to

---

[16] This is a title of honor which the Shī'a reserve exclusively for Imam Ali ﷺ.
[17] This *hadith* report is related in the great hadith compendium by the 17th century scholar of hadith science (or historian of sacred history) Allāma Muhammad Bāqir

1. Various Approaches to Leadership of the Community

[the enormity of] the distortion and falsification [of history] that has taken place! Imam Sādiq ﷺ, who is the progeny of the Prophet ﷺ of Islam, should address al-Manṣūr, the continuation of the line of Nimrod and Pharaoh – and according to their own accolades, the "Pharaoh of the Community" (*fir'awn hadhaʾ al-umma*) – in such a [self-demeaning] manner? It is entirely possible for one to veil one's intentions in a different manner: if Imam Sādiq ﷺ wanted to avoid death in that gathering, there were a thousand ways to sweet-talk (*bolbol-zabānī*) [himself out of such a tight spot]. There were a thousand other ways to wax eloquent; [so that] there was no need to fabricate a patent lie [which demeans] all that which is sacred in the world, and [the entirety of the line of] the prophets [and the institution of prophethood] and this [uninterrupted] chain of all that is true, good and just (*haqq*) and which is grounded in God's reality (*haqqāniat*). There was no need to fabricate a patent lie [by comparing al-Manṣūr, who is the paragon of the antithesis of these things, with the great prophets of the past]. It is thus clear that this [*hadith* report] is a lie. But [still, (they say)] the narrator *has* related it... [But] *who* is the narrator?? Rabī'!

The hand of distortion and falsification was molded in the very same days that Imam Sādiq ﷺ was alive and moved about within society and lived among the people. There can be no doubt that all of what you have heard about the lives of our Imams ﷺ and their Book of Deeds relative to these [tyrannical] rulers being ones wherein the Imams ﷺ were obsequious and sycophantic, and where they displayed nothing but fawning and servile compliance and a desire to associate with them as a way of self-exoneration, is a lie. The reason is that there are things [which have taken place] in the lives of the Imams ﷺ which undermine and belie this contrary position. It is not possible for a single person, being possessed of a single way of thinking, to act in two different ways under the same [or similar] circumstances. Thus, if there are two reports concerning the same person which are contradictory, then one of them must be false. It is the narrative report which goes against the Imams'

Majlisī (d. 1110/1698), the *Biḥār al-Anwār* (Oceans of Light), which was completed between 1106 AH (1694 AD) and 1110 AH (1698 AD) (Kohlberg).

general approach and intellectual and creedal principles which is untrue. It is certainly valid to make such an analogical comparison (*qiyās*).[18]

We will, God 🌸 willing, go into [the details of] the relations the Imams 🌿 had with their partisans (*Shī'a*), with the caliphs of their respective times, as well as how they related to the court-allied doctors of religion. We will also go into how they related to the "extremist" elements in the Islamic society of their day, by which of course I mean extremist from the perspective of the ruling apparatus, that is, with those among the progeny of the Imams 🌿 who were bent on insurrection. This is a very important chapter, and one in which much distortion and falsification [of history] has occurred; in which [the ruling powers] constantly put out reports about what Imam Ṣādiq 🌿 [allegedly] said about Zaid [b. Ali b. al-Husain], about Muhammad b. Abdullāh [al-Mahdh], or about [Ibrāhim b. Ismāīl b. Ibrāhim] aṭ-Ṭabāṭabāī, and so on. When one sees the truth [of the matter], tears of sorrow well up involuntarily in one's eyes. When one sees what Imam Ṣādiq 🌿 has [actually] said about Zaid, and compares that with the opinion that a large number of Twelver Shī'a have of him, which is that of a loathsome and accursed personality, a deep sorrow of remorse casts its shadow in one's heart about why it should be the case that a given truth should be distorted to the limit of its exact opposite. In any event, these are issues which we shall be discussing.

---

[18] Literally: "[The justified and valid logical grounds for] such analogical reasoning (*qīyās*) exists".

2. The True Identity of the Imams

[God ﷻ the All-Knowing and All-Wise has stated in His Sacred Writ:]

$$رَبَّنَا لَا تُزِغْ قُلُوبَنَا بَعْدَ إِذْ هَدَيْتَنَا وَهَبْ لَنَا مِن لَّدُنكَ رَحْمَةً ۚ إِنَّكَ أَنتَ الْوَهَّابُ ﴿٨﴾$$

[3:8] "O our Sustainer! Let not our hearts swerve from the truth after Thou hast guided us; and bestow upon us the gift of Thy grace: verily, Thou art the [true] Giver of Gifts.

$$وَلَمَّا بَرَزُوا لِجَالُوتَ وَجُنُودِهِ قَالُوا رَبَّنَا أَفْرِغْ عَلَيْنَا صَبْرًا وَثَبِّتْ أَقْدَامَنَا وَانصُرْنَا عَلَى الْقَوْمِ الْكَافِرِينَ ﴿٢٥٠﴾$$

[2:250] And when they came face to face with Goliath and his forces, they prayed: "O our Sustainer! Shower us with patience in adversity, and make firm our steps, and succor us against the people who deny the truth!"

O our Sustainer and Lord of Providence! [I beseech you] by [the right and station of spiritual proximity to You which] Muhammad ﷺ and his [Purified and Immaculate] Progeny ﷺ [have], make our lives, for as long as we are alive, modeled on the lives that they led and when it is our time to die, choose for us the most glorious and noble death from among the way in which Muhammad ﷺ and his [Purified and Immaculate] Progeny ﷺ died.

[God ﷻ the All-Knowing and All-Wise has stated in His Sacred Writ]:

وَجَعَلْنَا مِنْهُمْ أَئِمَّةً يَهْدُونَ بِأَمْرِنَا لَمَّا صَبَرُوا ۖ وَكَانُوا بِآيَاتِنَا يُوقِنُونَ ﴿٢٤﴾

[32:24] and [as] We raised among them Imams (leaders) who, so long as they bore themselves with patience and had sure faith in Our messages, guided [their people] in accordance with Our behest [so, too, shall it be with the divine writ revealed unto thee, O Muhammad.]

وَجَعَلْنَاهُمْ أَئِمَّةً يَهْدُونَ بِأَمْرِنَا وَأَوْحَيْنَا إِلَيْهِمْ فِعْلَ الْخَيْرَاتِ وَإِقَامَ الصَّلَاةِ وَإِيتَاءَ الزَّكَاةِ ۖ وَكَانُوا لَنَا عَابِدِينَ ﴿٧٣﴾

[21:73] and made them Imams ﷺ (leaders) who would guide [others] in accordance with Our behest: for We inspired them [with a will] to do good works, and to be constant in prayer, and to dispense charity: and Us [alone] did they worship.

1. The dearth of knowledge of the Shī'a concerning the social and political posture of the Imams

We stated that the subject of our discussion would be about becoming more familiar with the character of the Imams; because we recognize the fact that they were the ones who rekindled the grandeur and glory of the *tawhīdic*[19] [vision of] Islam and brought it back for everyone. The names

---

[19] *Tawhīd*: the Islamic conception of monotheism: 1. The unicity of the creatorship of the universe; 2. The unicity of the order of creation; 3. The exclusivity of providential lordship (*tawhīd-e rubūbīat*). God's integral order of creation (*tawhīd*). Fidelity (*tawhīd*) and Infidelity (*shirk*) to the Exclusivity of God's

2. The True Identity of the Imams

of these Imams ﷺ are well known to us. From our point of view, the people who competed with the Imams ﷺ throughout the course of history and claimed their rightful station [as political as well as religio-legal leaders of the community] as their own, are to be rejected. We harbor no doubts that it is the Imams ﷺ who are our [rightful] leaders. When I say that "we" harbor no doubts, I am referring to the community of their partisans or their Shī'a; inclusive, even, of the general Shī'a population: we *all* know and recognize them as our leaders. Those who are not aware of the details of their lives, have a summary understanding. If they do not know the exact dates of their births or deaths, they know, for example, that Imam Mūsā al-Kāẓim ﷺ, was the Seventh Imam, that Imam Riḍā ﷺ was the Eight Imam, and so on. Thus, there is no doubt concerning this matter in the Shī'a world.

What is shameful for us is that even though we know the names and identities and [lofty spiritual] stations of these great personages, we are not familiar with how they lived out their lives. Thus, our discussion will be focused on how the prophesied Twelve Immaculate Imams ﷺ transacted their lives, what their objectives were, and what the ideals which determined their objectives were. As I mentioned yesterday: [we

---

Providential Lordship in the Social Order. *Tawḥīd* is the first principle of the Islamic faith and is usually translated as Monotheism or as the unicity of God ﷻ. Here it refers to the unicity of God ﷻ not just in His capacity as Creator (i.e. unicity of Creatorship), but also refers to the seamlessness of the order within creation (including man's social order) as a corollary of that act of creation. Thus, *tawḥīd* here refers to the integrality of creation with the social order that is intended for that creation by God ﷻ the integral (*tawḥīdic*) Islamic society. The Islamic vision of monotheism is an integral vision of the universe where belief in the unicity of creatorship is seamlessly intertwined and combined with the belief that providential lordship over the world and the individual and collective affairs of man are the exclusive domain of God ﷻ. *Tawḥīd* is the primary tenet and creedal principle of Islam that holds that God ﷻ is the sole creator of the world, and that the right of providential lordship over His creation belongs exclusively to Him. The exclusivity (*tawḥīd*) of this providential overlordship (*rubūbīat*) encompasses all domains of creation including man's individual and social affairs. Man's *fiṭric* nature (his primordial and original disposition) is *tawḥīdic*; that is, it is in harmony with the ontic unicity or existential oneness of God ﷻ, it is monotheistic: it is naturally inclined toward and accepts God's sovereignty over him and is innately inclined to serve only He who is his Maker.

shall be discussing, firstly,] what their relations were with the rulers and powers of their day; secondly, their relations with their followers and co-religionists; and thirdly, how they related to the doctors of religion who were allied with the caliphal courts.

I believe that there is a dearth of information concerning this [essential] subject. I am not sure about you, but my own opinion is that there is scant information concerning this subject. I say this because the level of my own understanding about the Imams ﷺ prior to my having started to look into the subject and to research it was also a scant and summary opinion which was mingled with misconceptions and erroneous beliefs. Then, after I looked into the matter, I saw that there were indeed many details which are available [in the sources] which have not seen the light of day. In fact, there is so much untold information that has remained dormant that it should not come as a surprise if it were to be said that the Shī'a have not come to a proper understanding of themselves; one should not take the position that this is an exaggeration, for, indeed, this is something whose veracity has already been established.

2. Two Benefits of becoming Aware of the Personalities of the Imams

In keeping with the traditional approach taken in the Islamic seminaries, where the benefits of studying the subject at hand are discussed by way of a preliminary, what I shall be talking about today concerns the benefits which accrue from the proper understanding of the personalities of the Imams ﷺ.[20] For example, the seminary student who wanted to start studying the science of logic first needed to learn the benefits that accrue from the science and how he will be improved by its study; and he would not be able to start his studies of the subject until he had an understanding of the benefits of the science. Thus, we too, must first determine the

---

[20] The traditional approach in the *hawza* or Islamic seminary is to discuss the eight-fold aspects of a given science, these being: a description of the science, its subject matter, its benefits, who founded it, its issues (or 'problematics'), its position relative to the other sciences, what is intended by its study, and the various methods by which it can be approached.

2. The True Identity of the Imams

benefits of studying our subject. There are two benefits for attaining a proper understanding of the personalities and ways of the Imams:

2.1 Learning how one should lead one's life

One benefit has to do with the matter of how one should lead one's life. Once the words and deeds and way of life of a leader become known to his followers, one of the great and important benefits which accrue is that the followers will then know how to lead their own lives [in such a way as to be in conformance with their leader's words and deeds and values]. Why does such a benefit accrue from becoming aware of the words and deeds and way of life of a leader? Because that is what leading means; or, in other words, this is one of the dimensions of leadership. It is only natural that if one is not aware of the character of someone whom one considers to be one's leader and is not aware of how he would act in a given situation or the position he would take on a given matter, that one will not be able to follow him and thus act as his follower [in practice].

What is the function of the *mukabbir*[21] in the communal prayers? The fact that he indicates that the prayer leader (*imām*) entered into the sitting position or arose into the standing position, or that he is now bowing, or is in the position of prostration. This is something that is necessary, for if one does not know that the prayer leader has come out of the prostration position, he or she might remain in that position. Similarly, if one does not know that the prayer leader has gotten up from the sitting position and is now standing, he or she might remain seated. What kind of prayer leading and following would *that* be? Hence, this is why one of the four[22] sources [for the derivation of sacred law] in the tradition of our sacred jurisprudence (*fiqh*) is *Sunna*^{t} (the paradigmatic

---

[21] *Mukabbir*: Because the ritual devotions of Islam require that the devotees bow down and prostrate themselves in humility to God, they are not able to do so and to follow the movements of the prayer leader at the same time. Because of this, a person is assigned to signal to the participants that the prayer leader has entered the position of prostration, for example, or has come out of that position, so that the followers know that it is now time for them also to come out of the position of prostration and to stand erect; and so on.

[22] The other sources are the Quran, discursive reasoning (*'aql*), and magisterial or juridical consensus (*ijmā'*).

example and the exemplary pattern of behavior) [of the Most Noble Prophet 􀀀 and Twelve Imams 􀀀 and Her Eminence, Lady Fātima 􀀀]. In other words, when a doctor of sacred jurisprudence wants to engage in the act of the derivation of sacred law, he must first be able to carry the burden [of comprehending] the Quran which is referred to as *al-kitāb* (sacred writ); and next to the sacred writ is the *Sunnaᵗ*. What is the *Sunnaᵗ*? It consists of the words and deeds and taciturnity, inaction, and tacit acceptance or approval (*taqrīr*) of the [Fourteen] Immaculates.²³ Their words are what constitute the hadith reports in the hadith report corpus which has reached us by having been recorded and handed down through the generations. It is their words that tell us to do such and such a deed, and to refrain from doing such and such. Their deeds consist in how they lived their lives, so that if we become aware of how the Fourteen Immaculates transacted their lives, then we will have cottoned on to this part of the *Sunnaᵗ* as well. Thus, one of the parts of the *Sunnaᵗ* is the deeds of the Fourteen Immaculates as they relate to one's personal and individual lives. This is one of the calamities and great distortions and falsifications which has befallen Islam.

The focus has always been on, for example, precisely how Imam Sādiq 􀀀 entered into and stayed in the position of prostration; or whether he closed his eyes or kept them open; or the mannerisms of how he would eat his meals; or whether he would glance in different directions when walking, or keep his gaze directly ahead of him; and so on. They would not bother to clarify how Imam Sādiq 􀀀 transacted his *social* life within this caravan of humanity which is moving through history. Nor would they bother to clarify how he acted out his historical role with respect to the illegitimate powers (*tāghūt*)²⁴ of his day, whose roots go all the way

---

²³ "Fourteen Immaculates": the Prophet 􀀀, Lady Fātima, and the Twelve Imams, all of whom are believed by the Shī'a to be sinless and inerrant exemplary models commissioned by Almighty God 􀀀 to act as guides and leaders for mankind.

²⁴ *Tāghūt*: the false or illegitimate authority of anything or anyone other than God; the social orders established and maintained by illegitimate powers; forms of idolatry and heathenism; hegemonic powers and the forces of idolatry; imposter powers who are pretenders to the throne of legitimate sovereignty supposedly sanctioned by God; social orders based on idol worship of any kind: [16:36] *And indeed, within every community have We raised up an apostle*

2. The True Identity of the Imams

back in history to the time of the great prophets and the great divinely-guided personalities of history [and their rebellion against them], i.e. to Pharaoh and Nimrod, and back to before their times as well. They [the traditional scholars of the seminaries of Shī'a Islam] were not interested in seeing how Imam Sādiq ﷺ acted with respect to this inordinate historical front; or, if they were, they have not written anything which we can benefit from today.

When we search for sources which shed light on the way in which the Immaculate Imams ﷺ transacted their social life and on their political posture, we are forced, like the scholars of sacred history of the 3rd and 4th centuries, to forage in the corpus of the original hadith reports among reports whose veracity and reliability is indeterminate. This is because there are no monographs or wider studies available which have worked the subject and given it some form and semblance of order which would preclude us from having to 'invent the wheel' or start 'from scratch'. But such studies are not available, so we have to act like those researchers of the 3rd and 4th centuries of Islam for hadith reports which have been narrated by certain narrators [whose veracity we must determine on our own] in order to cobble together and derive a narrative [concerning the political posture of the Imams ﷺ which can then be presented as such]. Since this [vital] work [of research] has not yet taken place; for if it had occurred, we would not be in this position of indigence which we find ourselves in.

Therefore, one of the benefits of understanding how the Imams ﷺ lived their lives is that we will learn how to live our own [social] lives and what kind of political posture to take concerning social issues. It teaches the Shī'a what kind of political position we should take concerning various social and historical issues if we are to follow our Imams ﷺ aright. It teaches one who is vested in the office of leadership in lieu of the Imam how to carry out the functions and duties of the office of leadership, and

---

[entrusted with this message]: "Worship God, and shun the powers of idolatry and false deities (at-tāghūt)!" Ayatollah Khāmeneī depicts the tāghūt in terms of "those who are the guardians of this false social order, and those who have rebelled against all of the authentic human values, and who have imposed false and empty values on others in order to secure and enhance their own oppressive positions and interests."

how to navigate the ship of state [through the stormy currents of history]. It will also teach those who are the followers of the Imams ﷺ how to interpret their words, on which points to follow them, and on which points he has latitude to make his own determinations. This is the first point.

2.2 Becoming motivated and increasing one's sense of religious self-confidence

The second benefit which accrues from attaining to an understanding of the character of leaders are the emotional and spiritual benefits rather than the practical ones. A society is like a family. Consider the children of a family: the child in a family who does not believe that his father has a noble and honorable character, or one who does not have a father at all, will be a very different child compared to one who believes his father has a noble and honorable character and who is a source of pride for him. One of the things which has become abundantly clear in today's world is that one of the most important elements for fostering a noble character and independent spirit within any given nation in the world is for the people of such a nation to have a luminous and brilliant model and paradigmatic example to emulate. This fosters the spirit of pride in them. Look, for example, at how the French treat Joan of Arc[25], who is one of their heroines. One of the things which we hear frequently is that those who do not have a prominent personality or character or cannot rely on it for whatever reason will substitute the Unknown Soldier as a symbol of that character, before which everyone pays their homage and respect. They

---

[25] Joan of Arc (French: Jeanne d'Arc); c. 1412 – 30 May 1431), nicknamed "The Maid of Orléans", is considered a heroine of France for her role during the Lancastrian phase of the Hundred Years' War, and was canonized as a Roman Catholic saint. She was born to Jacques d'Arc and Isabelle Romée, a peasant family, at Domrémy in northeast France. Joan claimed to have received visions of the archangel Michael, Saint Margaret, and Saint Catherine of Alexandria instructing her to support Charles VII and recover France from English domination late in the Hundred Years' War. The uncrowned King Charles VII sent Joan to the Siege of Orléans as part of a relief army. She gained prominence after the siege was lifted only nine days later. Several additional swift victories led to Charles VII's coronation at Reims. This long-awaited event boosted French morale and paved the way for the final French victory.

2. The True Identity of the Imams

will search in the barrens of history for traces of past civilizations and extract them and polish away the dust and grime of the heedlessness that the passage of time has assigned to them, and place these relics before the hungry and indigently curious eyes of their respective nations, telling them that this is who you were in bygone centuries. "Look at yourself in the Mirror of your Past!" they tell them; this is an actuality that indeed occurs today.

However, it goes beyond this. We see that even between nations which have no racial [or ethnic] ties, but share common interests and objectives and values, that these nations will take the prominent personalities of their allied nations and place them before the eyes of their people and use them as beloved symbols and praiseworthy exemplars worthy of emulation. For example, Mahatma Gandhi might be of a different race than the nation of Egypt, but Egyptians have no qualms about praising his character. It is a general rule that a nation which was in the throes of development and growth, as was Egypt when it was fighting its enemies,[26] has no qualms whatsoever to characterize Gandhi as a great personality and to use him for their cultural purposes, writing books about him, and so on. Why is this? Because while it is true that the two do not have a racial connection, they nevertheless share the same need, which is political independence. We see Vietnam, for example, in a far corner of the world, praising a champion in another far-flung region [such as Cuba's Fidel Castro or Che Guevara] who share the same needs or the same enemy [the United States]. Why? Because whenever a luminous personality becomes a champion and beloved of a nation for whatever reason, be it because he or she is of the same race of the nation, or lives in the same region, or for some other reason (because he or she shared the same needs and objectives with the nation), it serves the purposes of rejuvenating that nation to revivify the personality and memory of that hero and make it known to the people.

And today, one takes pleasure in reading Gandhi's biography, or that of Djamila Bupasha,[27] or that of some other hero who lives in some

---

[26] Reference to the 1967 war with the Zionist entity.
[27] Djamila Boupasha was an Algerian freedom fighter who opposed the French colonial rule of Algeria. She was an important member of the Algerian National

other part of the world; one feels a shared sense of solidarity, and it engenders a sense of pride due to the shared goals which one shares with the hero or heroine. Thus, this is the benefit which derives from attaining to an understanding of a leader from the second, spiritual and emotional, aspect. It so happens that the people and forces which have wanted to weaken nations and strip them of their intellectual independence, unique character and sense of identity throughout history, have focused on this very issue; the issue of the most luminous and brightest personalities among the people. They deprive the people of their leaders and leadership cadre. The question as to how they do this will be discussed later.

When the feeling is engendered in someone that no prominent personality exists in his or her [nation's or community's] past history, this will instill a feeling of inferiority in such a person. When this person feels inferior, then the dominating tyrant will have a lot more latitude. The best way to dominate someone is to first belittle him and make him feel inferior, and to make him feel that he is unimportant, a nobody. In order to do this, one must first convince him or her that there is not a single positive thing in his or her life. When one comes to believe that their life is of no account, that their character is of no value, that they are rootless and inferior, then they will be easily dominated. This is something that [is so obvious] to all of you that it does not stand in need of any argument or proof. You have seen how the proud past histories of nations and peoples condemned [to colonial exploitation] are vacated and wiped out; and what methods and pretexts have been used to wipe them out; and how beautiful and luminous characters are portrayed as unattractive. Thus, when the colonizer is intent on dominating and exploiting a country, and on infiltrating it and to secure its own interests at that nation's expense, this is one of the strategies and deceptions that it uses: to deprive its target nation of its heroes and heroines.

Liberation Front (FLN) who was arrested in 1960 and imprisoned and tortured by the French authorities. She was freed when Algeria gained its independence from France.

2. The True Identity of the Imams

3. Two methods of the enemies of nations for eliminating national heroes and heroines

We can see that this objective can be achieved in one of two ways:

3.1 Forbidding the mentioning of the hero's name to wipe his memory from public discourse

One method is when the forces of exploitation [attempt to] completely wipe the hero or heroine's memory from public discourse, after which a conspiracy of silence is erected concerning them. The person is not talked about, and no mention is made of the wonders and beautiful things of his or her life. Or it can go even further than that, where mentioning someone name becomes a crime punishable by law. This is the method used by Muʿāwiya during his reign, where an edict was issued from [the caliphal capital] Damascus to all the regions within the dominion of Islam to the effect that anyone who utters a sentence about [Imam] Ali or about his House will no longer enjoy the protection of the Islamic state. What this meant was that such a person would no longer be considered a Muslim and would be treated like an "alien combatant" [(to use the contemporary term)]. What this, in turn, meant, was that as far as the state was concerned, people were free to do whatever they wanted with them: anyone could slander or assault such a person, remove his name from the roster of the public treasury, usurp his property, and even kill him, with immunity from the state; the state would have no problem with any of that. In other words, such a person would become someone who has no social standing or rights whatsoever, and nothing that he said or did would be creditable. This was a law that was pursued for some time and pursued vigorously. I am not aware of any ruler or caliph other than Muʿāwiya who brought about such a [barbaric] situation; but I have not researched the issue in detail.

Of course, the situation was somewhat similar during the reigns of Abd al-Mālik and Hām, but the scope was not as broad, and the policies were not pursued as vigilantly was the case during Muʿāwiya's reign. Muʿāwiya had issued an edict forbidding the narration of any report from and/ or concerning Imam Ali ﷺ and forbade everyone from keeping the company of Imam Ali's ﷺ [known] partisans. The situation had gotten to the point that if an enmity arose between two people, one or the other of them would accuse the other of being a partisan (*Shī'a*) of Imam Ali ﷺ, and such a slander required no juridical process or evidence!²⁸ When one was accused of being a partisan of Ali's, what this meant was that the person would be arrested and imprisoned in an Umayyad dungeon somewhere, executed and 'disappeared'. As the historians have said, if a person fell under suspicion of such a charge, he would be arrested, and if he was indicted, he would be executed.

The reign of the Umayyad dynasty came to a close. But I know of a caliph during the Abbāsid dynasty [which followed in its wake] who acted in the same way. This was the Abbāsid caliph al-Mutawakkil, who was intent on wiping out the name of the House and progeny of the Prophet ﷺ. [I do not need to repeat] the tragedy of Karbalā²⁹ and the act of the Umayyad army in closing off access to water for Imam Husain ﷺ and his family and retinue, as those present here have heard it all before, more than is [strictly] necessary (*bīsh az ān miqdāri ke lāzim ast*). This is one way of destroying [the memory of a national hero]. But how effective is such a tactic? The answer is that it is not very effective at all. Shaykh Radī Āl al-Yā-Sīn the great author of the book, *Sulh al-Hasan* (Hasan's Peace) says, "The character of brute force and tyranny – which is a veritable tradition – has been such from the genesis of creation, that every time pressure is brought to bear on an intellectual issue or on an intellectual current, such pressure will cause the issue or current to grow. This is a natural phenomenon." It so happens that our experience validates this position. For this has not been a very successful strategy, and you can

---

²⁸ This is reminiscent of a similar situation which was created by the US presence in Afghanistan, where innocent people were sent to the Guantanamo Bay prison simply because one of their enemies had informed the US authorities that the person was secretly a member of Al-Qā'ida.

²⁹ Recall that this series of ten lectures is taking place during the first ten days of the month of Muharram, which is a ten-day period of mourning culminating in the tenth day which is known as Āshūrā. The event of Āshūrā marks the anniversary of the Battle of Karbalā, when Imam Husain ﷺ, the grandson of the Prophet ﷺ Muhammad, was martyred by the forces of the accursed Umayyad caliph Yazīd in the 61st year of the Islamic calendar or on October 10, 680. The commemoration of this event during the yearly mourning season, with the Day of Āshūrā as the focal date, has served to define Shia communal identity.

2. The True Identity of the Imams

see that during Mu'āwiya's own time, all of the pressures which were brought to bear, and all of the efforts at repression, came to naught. This was to such an extent that an uprising took place in Kūfa once his son [Yazīd] acceded to power. Imam Husain ﷺ began his movement from Madina itself, Abdullāh b. Zubayr [refused to pay allegiance to Yazīd and fought against the Umayyads], and the flames which burned hidden under the ashes came to a flash point and were rekindled and became manifest again. We can therefore conclude that such a method was not successful.

3.2 Distorting and falsifying the image of the hero
Let me just say that it would have been better if all of the Umayyad and Abbāsid caliphs would have made the same mistake that Mu'āwiya made and followed in his footsteps in this regard. But alas, they did not make the same mistake, but came up with a more effective way than Mu'āwiya was able to come up with, which was this: rather than trying to eliminate the image of the hero and to bury it under tons of soil, they thought it best to falsify and distort the hero's image. And this was dangerous, because it worked. It worked so well, and their arrow hit the center of the bullseye in such a way that both the Umayyad dynasties came and went, and centuries passed over [the time when this strategy was implemented], and still the friends of the *Ahl al-Bayt* ﷺ (the [Purified and Immaculate] Members of the Household [of the Prophet ﷺ]) think of them as did their enemies. This great crime was brought off successfully against the lives of the *Ahl al-Bayt* ﷺ. This great crime was brought off successfully against the lives of the *Ahl al-Bayt* ﷺ. The situation is still such that a partisan (*shī'a*) of Imam Sādiq ﷺ, who considers himself to be a proponent and propagator of Imam Sādiq's words [and deeds], describes the Imam in such a way that if one were to be described in such terms, one would take offense at being insulted so grossly. And if a prominent personality were to be described today in such terms, it would be considered a serious breach of etiquette. Imām [Ali b. al-Husain] as-Sajjād ﷺ has been characterized in similar terms: as a weak and spineless invalid and plaything: the "Invalid Imām"! Was it not possible to come up with any other title that would be more insulting than that? Is that why they settled on it?? And for whom?? For what kind of an Imam?! The Fourth Imam who, in our opinion, was the founder of the covert movement of the Shī'a

after the event of Karbalā. The Imam who was responsible for shaking the pillars of the Umayyad dynasty; the person who was the guarantor (*zāmin*) of all of the [political and insurrectionary] movements that have occurred throughout Shī'a history. Imam Sajjād ﷺ was the progenitor of all of these [movements]. Today, the Shī'a think of Imam Sajjād ﷺ as an invalid,[30] whereas what has reached us through the annals of history concerning his illness was limited to those few days during which the Battle of Karbalā was waged [and in which he subsequently was not able to participate]. Well, everyone is subject to illness: you and I and even the burliest of sportsmen fall ill occasionally. But this is no reason for the label of 'invalid' to stay with anyone for the rest of history. What's wrong with the following epithets which engender pride? The Warrior Imam; the Imam of the World; the Aware Imam; the Organizer Imam; the Imam who is the progenitor of insurrectionary movements; the Imam who is the beating heart of the history of Shī'a [resistance against injustice]. But no, it has to be the *Invalid* Imam!!

So you see that this tactic of the enemy has been truly successful, and that we are faced with a millennial falsification of history; with a tissue of lies of incredible density. And what is required, therefore, is for us to rediscover and extract the luminous truth that is hidden behind the dense darkness that has been created by this canopy of lies. And to be sure, it is a difficult task, but one that is doable.

We said that there are two ways of becoming aware of the personalities of the Imams. Firstly, by learning how one should lead one's life, and secondly, by becoming motivated to increasing one's sense of religious self-confidence. Moreover, there is a more comprehensive way of expressing the latter benefit, and that is that it engenders a spirit of pride in the followers of the Imams ﷺ because one becomes more confident that the path that the Imams ﷺ forged and the path that I as a Shī'a or partisan of the Imams ﷺ follow, is the path and Way of God ﷻ; it is a path that one can justly take pride in and which one must thus follow. These are the two benefits of becoming aware of the personalities and path of the Imams ﷺ.

---

[30] I use the term in the sense of the first definition of the word, i.e. a person suffering from disablement or chronic ill health.

4. Our failure to fully appreciate the two benefits of knowing the way of the Imams

Unfortunately, we are the beneficiaries of neither of these two benefits today. We have neither learned how to lead one's life in accordance with the way the Imams ﷺ did (i.e. the practical benefit); nor are we beneficiaries of the spiritual and emotional benefits. When we look at the lives of the Divine Guides, no benefit accrues for us in doing so. If we are to look at the matter on its surface, [the biographies of] their lives provide us with ambivalent [signals]. According to the view of the general public and those who affirm this view, Imam Hasan ﷺ lived his life in one way, and Imam Husain ﷺ lived his in a way that was its diametrical opposite. And both of these ways are different than that of the Fourth Imam's; and all three of these are different still from that of the Eighth Imam's. All four of these life styles are different from that of the Commander of the Faithful's, and all five of these life styles differ from that of the Twelfth Imam's ﷺ. Is this not a contradiction? Did these [Imams ﷺ *actually*] act differently [from each other]? Well, as it happens, the contradiction of this inconsistency is acceptable to certain types *as* a contradiction. To these types of people, when you point out a contradiction, they ask for your evidence. When one provides them with the evidence from the words of Imam Husain ﷺ or the deeds of Imam Hasan, they become recalcitrant and resort to *ad hominem* arguments about one's [understanding] of Imam Hasan. It is as if the actions of Imam Hasan ﷺ and Imam Husain ﷺ are contradictory [in their essence] in their minds, which is why they resort to *ad hominem* arguments and attacks, implying that you do not know what you are talking about.

The way to deal with this kind of mentality is immediately to tell them something to this effect. "Listen, brother. You and I are fake 'brothers': our words and deeds and ways of life are inconsistent with each other. But Imam Hasan ﷺ and Imam Husain ﷺ are true brothers: they are kindred spirits intellectually and in terms of their creed and faith as well as being biological brothers, and so it is impossible for their actions and their way to be inconsistent and contradictory. If one accepts that Imam Husain ﷺ acted in a certain way, you must necessarily also accept that

Imam Hasan 🕊 acted in the same way. If you see it differently, revise your opinion and know that you were mistaken; [67:4] *Yea, turn thy vision [upon it] again and yet again: [and every time] thy vision will fall back upon thee, dazzled and truly defeated....* Take another look at the life of Imam Hasan 🕊 and see how he lived his life."

This kind of inconsistency exists in their minds. They cite [instances] in the lives of the eight Imams 🕊 after Imam Husain: "[But] sir! Why did Imam Sādiq 🕊 act is such and such a way? [And] why did Imam Riḍā act like so?" If we were to continue our discussion in the manner in which we have been doing so far, [we would see] strange contradictions in the lives of each and every Imam which are very clear and in no way reconcilable. On the one hand, our Imams 🕊 were people who were quiet. The majority (*ma'rūf, mashhūr*) and common opinion is that the Imams 🕊 were mute (*sāmit*), tame, and obedient (*muṭī'*), and even confirmatory and corroboratory (*mu'ayyad*) [of the rightfulness and legitimacy of the Umayyad and Abbāsid caliphs' right to rule over the Muslim community]. They were so validatory (*mu'ayyad*), in point of fact, that one of the Imam writes a letter to the mother of the caliph who had just died (and who had succeeded to the position of his brother[31]) in which he expresses the desire that he were the caliph's ransom or sacrifice.[32] This in a letter that is not even addressed to the caliph himself! Well, if someone wants to be fawning and obsequious, he will be so in person; why in a letter?! What possible occasion can there be for the Imam to write a letter to the caliph's mother expressing the desire to be the caliph's ransom or that God 🕊 should sacrifice him for [the sake of] the caliph, and that God 🕊 should make him the recipient of any and all misfortune (*sharr*) which He intends for the caliph to receive? Like I say, on one hand, there is this kind of behavior [evidenced in the hadith report corpus and in the minds of some people]; and on the other hand, we see this same Imam or

---

[31] Probable reference to Abū Mūsā Muhammad ibn Hārūn or-Rashīd, better known by his regnal name of al-Amīn, the sixth Abbāsid caliph (who succeeded his father, Harun or-Rashīd, in 809) and his half-brother, al-Ma'mūn, who killed al-Amīn in 813, during the civil war which al-Ma'mūn had initiated.

[32] A fawning or obsequious utterance.

the son of this Imam reported to have spent many long years living out his life in the dark dungeons [of these caliphs].

5. Evidence against the thesis of the Imams ﷺ being reconciled with the caliphs

All of the Imams ﷺ after Imam Sajjād ﷺ, – that is, Imam Bāqir ﷺ, Imam Sādiq ﷺ, Imam Kāẓim ﷺ, Imam Riḍā, Imam Jawād, Imam Hādī ﷺ, and Imam Askarī ﷺ – have each been imprisoned at least once, and in some cases twice or three times, and have been exiled. Notably, of course, the Eighth Imam was kept a close watch on under different circumstances. Now I put the question to you: that if it were indeed the case that the Seventh Imam really was cozy and of a single mind with the ruling power of his time, (and that this proximity is such that he expresses the desire to "be the caliph's ransom" and to take on the burdens of whatever ills he is fated for), then is it an at all reasonable act for the governing apparatus to imprison and even to murder this person? Such a person is, after all, [according to the logic of this position], a [highly notable] person who is a supporter of the establishment and wants nothing but good for it. Would any rational mind do such a thing? Would you do such a thing if you were in Hārūn's position? Assume that he is someone who likes you and supports you, both privately as well as in public. As far as his public appearances are concerned, he is present at the communal prayers on Fridays and defers to you to be its prayer leader, and is an obedient citizen: whatever day you happen to choose to fast, he too fasts, and whatever day you decide not to fast, he does not fast either, even if it be a day during [the fasting month of] Ramadān. He openly tells you that he is your slave to do with as you like, be it to kill him or to set him free.[33] This is [a hadith report which is] reported concerning the Fourth Imam – one of those gross distortions whose falsity is evident on its surface. [The question is put to you concerning] such a person, who on one hand is so close to you and supportive of you, and on the other hand, has a large following who considers every word which he utters to be revelation revealed from on high, so that if he harbored any enmity toward you, then so would all his

---

[33] This is a reference to a hadith which makes its appearance in the *Bihār al-Anwār* collection of Allāma Majlisī. Ayatollah Khāmeneī will return to this hadīth later in his talks.

followers. And conversely, because he is on friendly terms with you and in unison with you [politically], that this would also be the case with all his followers. Would you ever have such a person killed? Or confined in a dungeon? Would you even want to risk upsetting him? And if you did, would anyone think you to be acting rationally and of being in your right mind? Obviously not. And so how is it that Hārūn or-Rashīd's mind did not have the acumen that yours does? Or al-Mansūr's? Truly: how do you respond to this question?

Well, Imam Kāẓim ﷺ, the Seventh Imam, *had* such a numerous following throughout the territories of Islam... I investigated this; there were whole towns which were famous for their love of the *Ahl al-Bayt* ﷺ (the [Purified and Immaculate] Members of the Household [of the Prophet ﷺ]), such as Kūfa, Qom, and [the province of] Khorāsān. Where is Khorāsān? At the [eastern] limit of the Islamic territories [during the time of the period under discussion], which spread as far [east] as Sind or to the region known as Pakistan today. It was [considered] Khorāsān up to that limit back then. We find that the people of these far-off territories who had a certain latitude and freedom of action [due to their remoteness] had a love for and supported Imam Kāẓim ﷺ, the Seventh Imam. He, in turn, [we are supposed to believe,] liked and supported Hārūn, or followed [policies] which were in line with his interests; or, if he did not support him in his heart, and thought of him as a Sunni, or as an unbeliever and an enemy of the Commander of the Faithful, he was, [we are told,] obedient to his order in practice; he was as tame and meek as a lamb to the slaughter?!? Is it really logical for Hārūn to kill such an obsequious and fawning person who has all these followers? For one thing, he would be losing a good supporter. Secondly, he would be losing the goodwill of a large number of people. Does it make any sense? And if it does not, then it is not something that Hārūn would do, because he is a very rational actor. But it is not just Hārūn who is rational; al-Ma'mūn also acts very much in his rational self-interest; as does al-Mansūr. During that period of the history of Islam, during the reigns of the Umayyad and Abbāsid dynasties, all the persons who were vested in the highest office of Islamic society were rational actors who acted in their own rational self-interests. By this I do not mean reason (*'aql*) as in [the hadith report from Imam

2. The True Identity of the Imams

Ṣādiq ﷺ where he is reported by Shaykh Koleynī in his *Kāfī* compendium to have defined reason as] 'that [faculty of the mind] by means of which [man] devotes him- or herself to God ﷻ" (*mā abad bihī ar-rahmān*). No; rather, what I am referring to is the ordinary sense of the word which [is the faculty which enables] people to get up to all kinds of mischief. Well, these [caliphs] had a mind [for this kind of mischief] which was exceedingly excellent [for such purposes]. They were able to quell all their rivals with their minds and [conquer and] administer [vast] territories. Consider, for example, Khosrow Parvīz,[34] or other conquerors of the past: Xerxes, Darius, Ardeshīr Bābakān, and so on. Were these [leaders] not rational? How could they administer such vast territories if they were not rational? Whereas the territories under the dominion of Hārūn were larger than that of any of these earlier rulers. Was Hārūn not rational? Did he not understand [the bare minimum requirements of statesmanship of having to act in one's rational self-interest if one is to maintain power as an autocrat]?

So there must be some other factor at play here, my brothers; something else must be happening. Either he was not a rational actor and was mad or did not act in his rational self-interest due to some other factor; or, Imam Mūsā b. Ja'far, Imam Kāẓim ﷺ, the Seventh Imam, was not the person whom you envisage. He was not an appeaser. He was a person who was more dangerous to Hārūn alive than dead, even though murdering him was also a highly risky and dangerous proposition for the caliph. Murdering him ran the risk of inflaming the ire of his subjects and agitating them into social discord and even insurrection – which is exactly what happened. This was a proposition which ran the risk of making the people of Baghdad, the caliphal capital at the time, aware of the fact that the person who had been murdered was a grandson of the Prophet ﷺ, unto whom be God's peace; which they ultimately did become cognizant of. But [the reality is that] despite the fact that these dangers did exist [and were very real], it was the existence of the Imam that posed a much

---

[34] Khosrow II, known as Khosrow Parvīz (Persian: "Khosrow the Victorious"), (died AD 628), was a late-Sāsānian king of Persia (reigned 590–628), under whom the empire achieved its greatest expansion. He was defeated in a war with the Byzantines, and was deposed in a palace revolution and executed (Britannica).

greater danger, compared to which these other risks paled in comparison, [which is how the Imam's murder was "justified" in the caliph's heinous calculus].

So, these are issues which we need to get to. What I have said so far in the latest parts of my talks is what I have discerned and have so far not been presented as anything other than a claim on my part. However, I believe that [the veracity of] this [claim] will become clearer as we proceed with the presentation of other issues.

6. A summary of the contents of the rest of the book
To wit, we shall be presenting the following material in the days to come.

We shall first define what [the institution of] the imamate is and why there must be an Imam within the community after the passing of the Prophet ﷺ. We shall also be talking about the functions and benefits of [the institution of] the imamate; what affect it has on society, and its primary reason for its institution [by God ﷻ]. We will then follow this with a discussion of what the general Way of the Imams ﷺ was, and whether or not the functions and objectives of the Imamate were reflected in the lives of the Imams; and if so, how this was the case within their respective historical contexts. We shall offer a scheme whereby the lives of the Imams ﷺ are subdivided and categorized. After this, we shall go on to discuss the relations which the Imams ﷺ had with the powers of their day, such as with al-Manṣūr and Hārūn and others, as well as how they related to their own partisans and followers (*Shīʿa*). We shall address the question as to whether their followers were devotees of a master by the name of Mūsā b. Jaʿfar who did not know each other, or whether they were cognizant of each other and had social interactions, and were organized [as a cadre or a nucleus of trained personnel] around a larger organization. We shall look into this issue by examining some of the hadith reports and bringing these to bear as they relate to our subject.

We will then proceed to examine a group of people who unfortunately have a certain notoriety from the perspective of the historians and historiographers of the sacred history of Shīʿa Islam. People [who are accursed by some but] who are not cursed by those who are very cautious, but who relegate their fate to that which God ﷻ determines is

2. The True Identity of the Imams

best. Who are the people whom I have in mind? I am thinking of a certain number of people who number among the sons and progeny of the Imams ﷺ (*imāmzāda*). What was their crime? Their crime was that they rose up in [righteous] insurrection against the rulers of their day and were mostly killed as a result; although some died natural deaths. These include people such as Zaid b. Alī b. Husain, Muhammad b. Abdullāh b. Hasan b. Hasan b. Alī (a great-grandson of Imam Hasan's), Husain b. Ali (another of Imam Hasan's progeny who rose up in insurrection against the Abbāsid caliph al-Hādī and was martyred in the environs of Fakh), Muhammad b. Ibrāhīm b. Ismā'īl b. Tabātabāī (the eponymous progenitor of the Tabātabāī branch of the descendants of the Prophet ﷺ), and Ibrāhīm b. Abdullāh b. Hasan (another of Imam Hasan's progeny who rose up in insurrection against the Abbāsid caliph al-Mansūr and was martyred in the environs of Kūfa).

There are some people concerning which the history books report the Imams ﷺ weeping at the news of their deaths. But they are nevertheless notorious and accursed rather than being renowned. This is justified by saying that these were people who rose up in rebellion, rather than in insurrection, because their uprising did not have the permission and blessing of the respective Imams ﷺ of their day. And so there will be a discussion concerning this group of people which examines the issue of whether this was indeed the case and whether they were truly accursed by the Imams, or whether things were different. If they were not accursed by the Imams, were they then operating with the blessing and permission and even support of the Imams? We shall examine these questions in more detail than the other topics under discussion, and bring historical evidence to bear, God ﷻ willing.

This brings up the issue of cautionary or prudential dissimulation (*taqīya*) which will need to be addressed. The issue of *taqīya* is a very complex one that is addressed under the auspices of sacred jurisprudence (*fiqh*); and it would require several 10-lecture series such as the one that I am presenting to cover the subject fully. However, our discussion of the subject is tangential and touches on the issue in so far as whenever we present the issue of [the politically active disposition of] the Imams, there are certain people who always jump in with the comment, "But sir! What about *taqīya*? Did the Imams ﷺ not resort to *taqīya*??" And so we shall explain the question as to whether or not [the Shīʿa belief in the permissibility of] *taqīya*, is at odds with our interpretation of the lives of the Imams ﷺ. And we shall also address the corollary issue that if the politically active posture which we claim the Imams ﷺ had is not at odds with the Shīʿa tenet of *taqīya*, then when and under what circumstances does the need for prudential dissimulation arise and how did the Imams ﷺ practice it? We shall refer to the relevant hadith reports concerning *taqīya* during the course of our analysis. Once the meaning of *taqīya* has been clarified, the way in which the Imams ﷺ practiced it will also become clear.

There are some other secondary and ancillary matters which we shall be discussing also throughout the course of our discussions, which I believe will take another five or six days, which is all the time we have. This means that I will have to compress much of the discussion and present it in summary form; and that we will have to avoid tangential discussions as much as possible.

3. The Meaning and Purpose of the Imamate

[God ﷻ the All-Knowing and All-Wise has stated in His Sacred Writ:]

$$\text{رَبَّنَا عَلَيْكَ تَوَكَّلْنَا وَإِلَيْكَ أَنَبْنَا وَإِلَيْكَ الْمَصِيرُ ﴿٤﴾}$$

[60:4] ... "O our Sustainer and Lord of Providence (*parvardegār*; Arabic: *rabb*)! In Thee have we placed our trust, and unto Thee do we turn: for unto Thee is all journeys' end.

$$\text{رَبَّنَا هَبْ لَنَا مِنْ أَزْوَاجِنَا وَذُرِّيَّاتِنَا قُرَّةَ أَعْيُنٍ وَاجْعَلْنَا لِلْمُتَّقِينَ إِمَامًا ﴿٧٣﴾}$$

[25:74] ... "O our Sustainer and Lord of Providence! Grant that our spouses and our offspring be a joy to our eyes, and cause us to be foremost among those who are conscious of Thee!"

$$\text{وَلَمَّا بَرَزُوا لِجَالُوتَ وَجُنُودِهِ قَالُوا رَبَّنَا أَفْرِغْ عَلَيْنَا صَبْرًا وَثَبِّتْ أَقْدَامَنَا وَانصُرْنَا عَلَى الْقَوْمِ الْكَافِرِينَ ﴿٢٥٠﴾}$$

[2:250] And when they came face to face with Goliath and his forces, they prayed: "O our Sustainer! Shower us with patience in adversity, and make firm our steps, and succor us against the people who deny the truth!"

رَبِّ أَوْزِعْنِي أَنْ أَشْكُرَ نِعْمَتَكَ الَّتِي أَنْعَمْتَ عَلَيَّ وَعَلَىٰ وَالِدَيَّ وَأَنْ أَعْمَلَ صَالِحًا تَرْضَاهُ وَأَصْلِحْ لِي فِي ذُرِّيَّتِي ۖ إِنِّي تُبْتُ إِلَيْكَ وَإِنِّي مِنَ الْمُسْلِمِينَ ﴿١٥﴾

[46:15] ... "O my Sustainer and Lord of Providence! Inspire me so that I may forever be grateful for those blessings of Thine with which Thou hast graced me and my parents, and that I may do what is right [in a manner] that will meet with Thy goodly acceptance; and grant me righteousness in my offspring [as well]. Verily, unto Thee have I turned in repentance: for, verily, I am of those who have surrendered themselves unto Thee!"

O our Sustainer and Lord of Providence! [I beseech you] by [the right and station of spiritual proximity to You which] Muhammad ﷺ and his [Purified and Immaculate] Progeny ؑ [have]! Grant us ears that pay heed unto *al-haqq* (that which is real and true and just and everlasting) Grant us a mind that can appreciate and distinguish *al-haqq* [from that which is unreal and false and unjust and ephemeral]. Grant us a heart which is [open to and] accepts *al-haqq*.

O our Sustainer and Lord of Providence! Make it such that what we say and hear and [all of] our efforts [this evening and forevermore] become for us [an act of devotion] in our move toward self-perfection and human self-transformation!

O our Sustainer and Lord of Providence! Save us from [the state of] satisfaction with the summit of the carnal body and contentment with the limits of the senses and superficial trappings! Grant us as part of our daily sustenance [which we receive from You], the flight toward the world of meaning and the movement toward the summit of humanity which [in

3. The Meaning and Purpose of the Imamate

Your all-encompassing wisdom] You have determined [best] prearranged (*moqaddar*) for humanity.

O our Sustainer and Lord of Providence! Do not allow our hearts [or the cores of our being] to be afflicted with blindness and soullessness and stagnation and ossification once we have seen the *āyāt* (signs, revelations) of Your mercy! Do not turn us [or allow us to turn], Lord, from faith to unbelief!

وَجَعَلْنَاهُمْ أَئِمَّةً يَهْدُونَ بِأَمْرِنَا وَأَوْحَيْنَا إِلَيْهِمْ فِعْلَ الْخَيْرَاتِ وَإِقَامَ الصَّلَاةِ وَإِيتَاءَ الزَّكَاةِ ۖ وَكَانُوا لَنَا عَابِدِينَ ﴿٧٣﴾

[21:73] and made them leaders who would guide [others] in accordance with Our behest: for We inspired them [with a will] to do good works, and to be constant in prayer, and to dispense charity: and Us [alone] did they worship.

1. The imperative of attaining to a deep understanding of the character and way of the Imams

We have addressed the fact that to our mind, the ways of the Imams ﷺ were unknown, and that our path should be towards attaining a [better] understanding of the ways of these great men of the history of Islam. We also said that knowing these men simply by their names is not bringing any new [solutions to the problem]: the fact that we know, for example, what year of the Islamic calendar the Third Imam was born, or, say, during which Abbāsid caliph's reign the Sixth Imam was born – we either know these things already, or if we don't, we have no need to know such things. That which is necessary in the field of understanding these great and divinely [inspired and appointed] noblemen is attaining to a deep understanding of their true character: that which is referred to nowadays as a [full intellectual and spiritual] biography. What should such a biography consist of? Should it consist of a given Imam's dates of birth and death, and the number of his children and the names of his wives? Or should it rather consist of the elements which make up his character? What elements contribute to the character of such a person?

If someone talks about or writes a book about a famous personality such as Gandhi, in which there is nothing entered but the dates of his birth and death, the names and attributes of his father and mother, the place of his birth, the time of his birth, his horoscope sign, how many times he married, how many children he had, and so on, would someone who is not a follower of Gandhi be satisfied with such a book (which would be a very short book indeed), and think that they have understood Gandhi? He certainly would not be satisfied! Because that which would provide satisfaction concerning the understanding of a character such as Gandhi would be for one to know what he did in India, who was the enemy he was up against, what were his motivations for going up against this enemy, what program and which instruments he used the implementation of his program, and what were his relations with other prominent personalities and characters in India at the time; all these things are important. Now take a look at some of the famous biographies that are available which have been penned by famous biographers such as Romain Rolland[35] about famous personalities and see how they have been written. Then, once you have made such an examination, turn your gaze back to the other side of your bookshelves and look at what passes as biographies of the Imams ﷺ of the *Ahl al-Bayt* ﷺ (the [Purified and Immaculate] Members of the Household [of the Prophet ﷺ]), which have been written by those who love and support them and are their partisans and followers (*Shī'a*).

At this point you will suffer a severe shock, because you will see that nothing of these sorts of matters exists in this second category of books! When all is said and done, [the end result is that] after fourteen centuries, a Shī'a such as yourself has no idea what the substance of what Imam Sādiq ﷺ had to say in this world is. Did he, for example, want to live out his life as someone who is fond of and loyal to the rulers of the Umayyad Dynasty (at the beginning of his life), and to rulers of the

---

[35] Romain Rolland (29 January 1866 – 30 December 1944) was a French dramatist, novelist, essayist, art historian and mystic who was awarded the Nobel Prize for Literature in 1915 "as a tribute to the lofty idealism of his literary production and to the sympathy and love of truth with which he has described different types of human beings".

3. The Meaning and Purpose of the Imamate

Abbāsid Dynasty (at the end of his life)? Or rather, was it the case that he was against them? And if he was against them, did he hold his dislike in his breast like it is related in the stories that are told in the religious mourning ceremonies (*rowzeh-khānī*),[36] to the point that it resulted in his death? Or did he manifest his antipathy in some way? It is not at all clear! But the question as to who his mother was is something that is usually well known, because we have heard it repeated a hundred times before, because they (the *rowzeh-khūns*) have repeated it a hundred times before. We have heard it repeated on several occasions who his children were, for example. And if we do not know these things, it is due to a failure of memory, because these things have been written [in the books that are available] and have been spoken of [in our religious ceremonies].

Numerous versions of the dates of birth and death of the Imams ﷺ have been recited. This is why today, in an age when Shī'a Islam is on the ascendant, and in an age of the intellectual and cultural progress of the world, especially of the world's revolutionary culture, testify to the authenticity of Shī'a Islam. This is testimony to the veracity of Shī'a Islam's principles and their conformance with the Way of God ﷻ and the fact that it is on the right side of history. In an age where it is appropriate and fitting to get to know the words [and deeds and characters] of the Imams ﷺ, when we take a moment and look back to the early history of Islam, we see that the character of the great men of this sect is unknown.

---

[36] *Rowzeh*: a religious ceremony and mourning ritual where people gather to hear a popular religious authority (a *rowzeh-khūn*) discuss social or moral issues, which usually ends with an elegiac eulogy of one of the Imams ﷺ or members of the household of the Prophet ﷺ who died as martyrs in the cause of Islam. Such ceremonies are usually but not always centered around the martyrdom of Imam Husain ﷺ and his entourage at the Plain of Karbalā; or they are dedicated to one of the Imams ﷺ on the anniversary of his martyrdom; or are dedicated to commemorating Lady Fātima ﷺ the Luminous (*az-zahrā*), the blessed daughter of the Prophet ﷺ of Islam. Ayatollah Khāmeneī is bemoaning the fact that these ritual mourning ceremonies have turned into useless occasions where people turn up and mourn the martyrdom of the Imams ﷺ concerning whom they know little to nothing about, rather than attending classes about them where they can get a deep appreciation of their true character or read a good book that would give them that same understanding. (Of course, he is also bemoaning the dearth of such books...)

If it were not for the efforts of a few of the great men among the early adopters of Shī'a Islam who memorized the words of the Imams ﷺ and wrote them down for posterity, we would know nothing about Shī'a Islam today because we would have no understanding of the characters of the great personalities of the religion.

This is the background of the ailment. And the ailment is obtained through research, and continued efforts and feeling a sense of responsibility on the part of scholars and researchers, and through the continued expression of a desire on the part of the general Shī'a population to attain to a deeper understanding of their Imams ﷺ. Needless to say, the handful of hours which we will be spending over the next few days is but a small step – as I mentioned on the first day also – and it is an unworthy effort of a few steps in this long and winding and arduous road.

2. The first step toward understanding the Imam: acknowledging one's ignorance of their way

[The first step towards attaining to a deep understanding of the way of the Imams ﷺ is] to first acknowledge and accept and believe that we are ignorant in this regard. If this happens, then, in my opinion, a part of the way will [already] have been forded. The great challenge is [recognizing] our ignorance; it is the false belief that we have a good understanding of our Imams ﷺ. And those who have delved their heads more in themselves than in the sources of historical research, and who have been more preoccupied with their own thoughts than with the realities of the time of the Imams, content themselves that when they shed a tear in sympathy [with the tragic plight of the Imams], they are doing so in light of a full knowledge and understanding [of their character and circumstances]. But we do not accept that these tears are tears which are shed with such knowledge and understanding; but we do accept the tenet that tears shed without due knowledge are worthless. What is required are tears which are shed with due knowledge [of the correct reasons they are being shed].

It is necessary for one to have attained to a proper understanding of the character of Imam Bāqir ﷺ in order for ten years of weeping in Minā to have any effect (as had been willed by His Eminence to his son,

3. The Meaning and Purpose of the Imamate

Imam Ja'far as-Sādiq ﷺ); for else, Imam Bāqir's death would have been an ordinary death which, although it was caused by poisoning, no one would have known this [fact]. That people should weep for the Imam for ten years in Minā is not a matter that the Imam himself would have stipulated in his will. An Imam who places no value on the life of this world; an Imam whose forgiveness [at the hands of God ﷻ] is not dependent on the forgiveness of the people; an Imam who did not place any importance on the allure of the ornate trappings of the world, and who lived his life in austerity and was martyred while living a life of austerity: such an Imam does not have so much love for the world to say something like: "Weep for me after my death, people!" This [kind of talk] belongs to those who are 'of this world' [= committed to worldly values over other-worldly ones]. It is only those who are devoted to worldly values who want people to look to them while they are in the worldly plane; and who want people to sing eulogies in praise of them and to weep for them [= their absence]. Why would Imam Bāqir ﷺ stipulate in his last will and testament that people should mourn his death? It can be for no other reason that he wanted to ensure that his character would become [better] known [and not forgotten] in the most public of gathering places for Muslim, i.e. in Minā. [Recall that Minā is a place in the environs of Mecca whose visitation is part of the major Hajj pilgrimage,] where people come from all parts of the Islamic world and come together in a gathering in commemoration of Imam Muhammad b. Ali al-Bāqir ﷺ, and recall that he had willed that people should gather and weep and mourn his loss. Thus, tens of questions are generated in the minds of the people [there gathered], and it is these questions which open the doors for their [better and deeper] understanding [of the character and personality] of the Imam. This is what was intended.

3. The Imperative of attaining to a deep understanding of the character and way of the Imams ﷺ as a "250 Year Old Person"

Some of our friends [here gathered] have suggested that it would be good for me to move on to talk about as many of the Imams ﷺ as possible on account of the limitations of the time that we have. What I told them was that this was not the approach that I have chosen. The method which I have chosen to adopt in discussing the lives of the Imams ۩ – the contents of which I touched on in yesterday's talk – is that I will not talk about each of the Imams ۩ individually. From the tenth year of the Islamic calendar, which ushered in a new chapter in the history of Islam – i.e. the beginning of the Era or Cycle of the Imamate – until the day that this cycle came to an end in its apparent phase and people were no longer in face to face contact with the Imam [of their day], i.e. until the beginning of the Minor Occultation[37], is about 250 years. We view this period as a unitary epoch during which twelve Imams ۩ lived. The first of these was Ali b. Abī-Tālib ۩, the Commander of the Faithful, and the last of them was His Eminence Muhammad b. al-Hasan al-Askarī ۩ (may God ۩ hasten the noble advent of his noble person). Of course, because the Twelfth Imam ۩ was but a small child during the last years of his father's (Imam Hasan al-Askarī's ۩) Imamate (during which time the former had not been

---

[37] The Occultation (*al-ghayba*) is the event whereat the Twelfth Imam Q disappeared from the physical plane (in the year 260 HQ/ 874 CE) at God's behest in order to protect him from being murdered by the Abbāsid authorities. The Shi'a believe that he will return to the physical plane at a time appointed by God ۩ "to fill the earth with equity and justice, where it had hitherto been filled with iniquity and oppression." The Minor Occultation (*al-Ghaybat as-Sughrā*, 874–941) refers to the period when the Twelfth Imam or the Imam al-Mahdi Q still maintained contact with his followers via deputies (*an-nuwwāb al-arba'a*). These four deputies were:
    1. Uthmān b. Sa'īd al-'Amrī (260/ 874 – 875)
    2. Muhammad b. Uthmān al-'Amrī (d. 304/ 916 – 917)
    3. Al-Husain b. Rūh an-Nowbakhtī (d. 326/ 937 – 938)
    4. Ali b. Muhammad as-Sāmarrī (d. 329/ 940 – 941)
During this period of about 67 years (from 260 – 329 H (lunar)/ 874 – 941 CE), the deputies represented him and acted as agents between him and the faithful of the community. In 941 (329 AH), the fourth deputy announced an order by the Imām al-Mahdī Q (the Twelfth Imām), that the deputy would soon die and that the period of the deputyship would end and the period of the Major Occultation would begin. The fourth deputy died six days later. The Major Occultation denotes the second, longer portion of the Occultation, which continues to the present day, in which no specific deputy was designated by the Twelfth Imam Q to represent him, but in which the general class of persons, namely the magisters of sacred jurisprudence (*the fuqahā or ulamā*) are named by him to act in a leadership and guidance capacity while the occultation lasts. The disappeared Imām's Shī'a (partisans or followers) continue to await his reappearance.

3. The Meaning and Purpose of the Imamate

vested in the office of the Imamate), and because the Minor Occultation occurred when the Twelfth Imam ﷺ was so vested in the office, [the details of] his life do not concern us with respect to our present discussion. Thus, we will not be talking about the life of the Twelfth Imam ﷺ. Because we are concerned about talking about the passage of the lives of the Imams ﷺ and the life of the Twelfth Imam ﷺ has no objective reality to which we are privy, we shall be talking about the lives of the first Eleven Imams ﷺ.

We consider these Eleven Imams ﷺ to be a single, unitary human being – a 250 year old person – because the Imams ﷺ themselves have stipulated that they are as such.[38] At times they have also stated that whatever you have heard from us, you can assign to [having been heard from] any of the other Imams ﷺ.[39] This is something that exists in our hadith report corpus; and furthermore, it is something which is acted upon ("*ma'mūl^{on} bih*" *ham hast*) [by the magisters or doctors of Shīʻa sacred jurisprudence]. [And what this means in practice is that] if you had heard a hadith report which had been narrated from Imam Sādiq ﷺ [as its initiating source], but you were not sure if the source of the hadith report was Imam Sādiq ﷺ, there is no [juridical] objection for you to say that the hadith report was narrated from Imam Bāqir ﷺ, because these are not two separate entities, but one person, in reality. The criterion of unicity exists in these [two], and that is the unicity or oneness of their intellectual and spiritual character and *kullahum nūr^{un} wāhid* – these are all a single light; meaning that they [are Divinely-commissioned Guides who] guide mankind in a single direction, because [their unitary] light guides. They are [all] indicators of the guidance of humanity in a single, unitary direction. Thus, they are a single, unitary person [in this central sense].

If for example we see something in the life of the Commander of the Faithful which is contradicted by something else in the life of Imam Sādiq ﷺ, this will appear to us as a contradiction, and [rightly so because] it is [in fact] a contradiction; just as it would be the case if we saw these two contradictory instances in the lives of the Commander of the Faithful himself – a contradiction which would be unacceptable. [And the same is

---

[38] In the *Bihār al-Anwār* compendium (v. 22, p. 6).
[39] *Kāfī* 1:51.

true] if we see two mutually contradictory instances [of speech or behavior] between the life of Imam Ali ﷺ and the life of his son Imam Hasan ﷺ, or in the life of his [other son] Imam Husain ﷺ, or in the life of his [great, great grand-] son Imam Sādiq ﷺ: we will truly and actually consider these to be a contradiction [which stands in need of resolution], because these are not two people: they are the individual members and elements of a guidance group – a group whose members are bonded together with the most fundamental of bonds, i.e. a bond forged by God ﷻ.

Therefore, when we want to study the lives of the Imams, we do not examine each of their lives individually; rather, we think of a single person who was born on the day of the Prophet's ﷺ passing from the material plane, and who died in the year 260 – the year in which the Eleventh Imam passed from the material plane. We think of a 250-year-old person.

This person's life has had its ups and downs. And it is possible for these to appear to us as contradictions because we know firstly that he is a single person; and secondly, that his life had a single direction and was inspired by the same source throughout. In other words, it was inspired from the Sacred Writ of God ﷻ [the Quran] and from the exemplary model and paradigmatic example (*sunna*) of the Most Noble Prophet ﷺ (unto whom and unto whose purified and immaculate progeny be God's everlasting peace). And because we know that the knowledge which the Lord of Providence concerning the affairs of His religion bestowed on him [was unitary and integral] and served a unitary purpose and objective, i.e. for [drawing men's souls closer to] God ﷻ, and for the transcendence of humanity and for the creation of a perfected human society whose members [all] self-surrender and submit their wills to the will of God ﷻ. Because this unity is a reality, we must pay heed to it and resolve any contradictions which crop up. It just so happens that wherever we do pay attention, these seeming contradictions resolve themselves automatically.

If we want to use the analogy of a single person with a unitary objective for these Eleven Imams, we need to compare them to a person who is on a journey and who is headed towards a particular location. Such a person is a wayfarer or passenger from the moment he steps out of his

3. The Meaning and Purpose of the Imamate

house, or from the moment he steps out of his room. He packs his suitcase, picks it up and leaves his house. He might get a taxi, or he might choose to travel by train, or just walk. Let us suppose that he takes a taxi to the train station and boards the train. The train embarks from the station and makes several stops on the way. At times, the train's direction is straight and at other times it moves in a serpentine line, sometimes heading back in a direction which is opposite to that of its general and ultimate destination, and sometimes it stops for a break. When this person whom we have in mind gets off to stretch his legs, we do not immediately conclude that he has changed his mind and will not be completing his journey because he has gotten off the train. True, a [train] passenger does not travel on foot, but sometimes he will feel a need to stretch his legs. Sometimes it is in the nature of a train to move slowly, where it is moving up a steep incline or a sharp curve or perilous bridge. By the same token, the train moves faster on solid ground and stretches of wide expanse. When there is a large obstacle such as an unpassable mountain, the path of the train will have to fold back on itself, but it does so not in order to head back from the original destination but in order to bypass the obstacle it has encountered so as to ensure that it will reach its intended destination. Thus, if we are not to make superficial judgements and if we are to avoid making judgements without thinking things through, and if it is not our first time making a journey by train, when you see the train reversing direction, you will not immediately get up and say to your fellow passengers, "Here we go back to Tehran!" No, we are still moving toward our intended destination. For example, we are headed for Qom; we have not changed direction and are not headed back to Tehran. It is true that the direction of the train is headed back north again, but this change of direction is the necessary prerequisite for continuing to head south to Qom. Making stops along the way is a necessity of the journey: for refueling, for letting passengers get on and off the train, and for other reasons.

Similarly, the person who has decided to go on a journey is the same person from the moment he leaves his bedroom to the time he leaves the house and takes a taxi to the train station and boards the train and travels through the path of the train tracks, both straight and meandering, until he reaches his final destination. If he makes a stop for coffee at a certain station, he cannot say that his journey is therefore completed; only a simpleton would come to such a conclusion. This kind of [gross] simplemindedness is not expected of the simplest of people, even of those simpletons who have never travelled by train in their lives, so that if they happen to say something like, "Well, it seems we have reached the big city" when the train has just made a stop in the middle of nowhere; we would not take such a statement seriously or at face value. [And this is because everyone realizes that] making pit stops and taking breaks are a necessary part of the journey. So, we have a passenger who started on his journey in the tenth year of the Islamic calendar, which had a unitary ultimate destination. I do not want to enter into the discussion, which is usually talked about, which posits that some scroll descended unto each of the Imams ﷺ from on high on which certain things were written and certain commands were made by God ﷻ which commands were imperative and could not be countermanded by the Imams ﷺ. Because first of all, discussing these matters is not effective for our purpose of attaining to a deep understanding of the character of the Imams; and secondly, there are no reliable documents and texts to support such claims. Those who are expert in the science of sacred jurisprudence (*fiqh*) and in creedal matters (*'aqāid*) know that a hadith report which has been reported by no more than one transmitter in any of the levels or generations (*tabaqāt*) of its provenance titles (*asnād*) (i.e. an *al-khabar al-wāhid* or 'single'-transmitter hadith report) cannot be used as a source of definitive logical proof or as an unassailable substantiating authority or justification (*hujjīat*) [in such matters], even if [the chain of transmitters of] the provenance title is sturdy and unassailable.[40] Therefore, those who raise such issues cannot detract us from the line of thought and method

---

[40] This is a matter of dispute between the Scripturalists (*akhbārīs*) and the Principlists (*usūlīs*) in Shī'a Islam. The *akhbārīs* do use these types of hadith reports for both purposes, for, they argue, if these were to be eliminated for such purposes, more than half of the reports in the entirety of the hadith report corpus would have to be set aside. Most *usūlīs*, on the other hand, refer to this category of hadith for practical or juridical (*fiqh*) purposes, but not for establishing creedal beliefs (*'aqāid*).

3. The Meaning and Purpose of the Imamate

which we have chosen to approach the subject of the character and way of life of the Imams, and there is no need to address the issue further.

The point is that the experienced traveler who is intent on reaching his final destination will disembark on his journey and will act as the conditions of the journey dictate, and in any way which is appropriate and conducive to attaining the goal of arriving at the journey's final destination. We do not of course mean to imply that the Imams ﷺ employed a principle of expedience whenever and wherever they felt like it. Not at all; this was not the way of the Imams ﷺ. What I mean to say is that they acted in a way that was in conformance with what was expedient to the interests of Islam and its values and objectives, and not to their own interests.

This fully trained, experienced and tireless mountaineer who had a mastery of his calling, was faced with a summit with a very high altitude which could only be conquered under extreme conditions of pressure, endurance, forbearance and perseverance. At one point in this journey, he reached a pass at which he needed to open his eyes and pay close attention and take the journey step by step in order to be able to cross this close and demanding pass, so as not to fall; and that is precisely what he did. At another part of the journey there were some bandits who surrounded him and wanted to cut him off, kill him and wipe any trace of him away, because it was not in their interest for the mountaineer to climb this mountain and to make it to the end of his journey. Here he took off his shoes and stepped gingerly on his toes so as not to make any noise, lowered his head [so as to mix in with the crowd, if you will forgive the mixed metaphor], and snuck past the bandits before they realized that he had passed them by. And then a little later they saw him on the other side of the deep valley holding his friends' hands and looking back with a smile on his face, as if he were mocking them. And he is still moving toward his goal! This traveler journeyed in this same way for 250 years, not entering doubts about his final destination or veering from it for a single moment or taking a single step in a direction which was counter to that which the path [and the greater interest of Islam] demanded. Whatever steps he took in this long and perilous journey were for the sake of the overarching goal of getting closer and closer to its final destination.

This is a summary of the life of the Imams ﷺ. If you were a skilled painter and wanted to paint such a person, you would need to paint a person who is carrying a backpack, is wearing shoes of steel and carrying a legendary staff of steel, who is forging his way through this path with his eyes fixed on the horizon before him, heedless of all of the perils and obstacles which confront him; and his face would need to be drawn to show such an intensity of determination that if the path were to take 2,500 years rather than 250, he would still undertake the journey.

4. The meaning and purpose of the institution of the Imamate

There is a point which has yet to be mentioned. Of course, the whole discussion is still before us; we have not entered into any of the details, and what we have said so far has been by way of summary and preamble; and we will get into the details in due course, God ﷻ willing. However, the point which we have yet to touch upon concerns the question of what the purpose and objective which this experienced climber is heading towards with his steel shoes and staff, and taking a train of followers in his wake? In other words, what is the purpose of the institution of the imamate? What function does the Imam and the station of the Imamate serve once the Prophet ﷺ has passed [and the Cycle of Prophecy has come to an end]? What are the duties and responsibilities of the Imam? We are not concerned here about the conditions which are necessary for investiture in the office of the imamate; these discussions have already taken place aplenty in the past, and at times to excess. This is what we need to examine.

The way I see it, the continuation of [the Cycle of] Prophethood in the form of [the Cycle of] the Imamate and the generation of a line known as the Imamate from the line known as Prophethood, is for two purposes: the first is the explication and systematization of the creed and religion of Islam; and the other is [ensuring] the continuation of the path of [the institution of] prophethood, and the securement of the values and objectives of the Prophet ﷺ. The questions as to why a prophet is commissioned by God ﷻ for a mission on Earth, and the how's and whereof's of his mission were presented by me in a rather detailed discussion on the same occasion here three years ago. If you remember

3. The Meaning and Purpose of the Imamate

those discussions, you have a strong memory, as I myself do not remember all of the details. But I know that these were the headings of the subject; and I had also taken some notes.

5. Two objectives of the Prophet ﷺ: Bringing about a [counter-] revolution in a wayward society, and establishing a new social order

Prophets are commissioned and appear to human societies at particular times [throughout history] when the coming of a prophet is necessitated, and that is the point when human society is in need of a turning point, and of a [counter-][41] revolution. For centuries, anti-human powers have done their best to falsify and distort the values and ideals of human society, turning society into grotesque and toxic forms; and it is at this juncture that prophets are commissioned. In other words, a prophet comes to destroy the present [distorted] form of society and to extinguish the principles and tenets upon which the decadent and degenerate society is based. Prophets are commissioned in order to change the form of society and to replace the reactionary and false old principles and values with the revolutionary principles and values of Islam, creating a new social order based on the unalloyed dispensation of Islam.

So, if you pay attention, we can see that there are two functions which the prophet must perform: the first consists of presenting a series of revolutionary principles and engendering and fostering a revolution based on these principles; and the second is the establishment and institution of a new social order and dispensation. Of course, when I say

---

[41] The Catholics viewed the Reformation as a revolution and the Counter-Reformation as a counter-revolution. This is because they were the established power and any pivotal change in society was deemed revolutionary and undesirable. But the reverse is true of Shī'a Islam which has remained persecuted and marginalized for the vast majority of its existence, and this is even the case in the larger world of Islam even after the triumph of the Islamic Revolution of Iran. Hence, the Shī'a scholars of religion have always referred to righteous insurrectionary movements whose goal is the establishment of the Quranic dispensation as "revolutionary"; and the use of this word, unlike that of usage in a Catholic context, always has a positive connotation. Thus, I shall be using the word "revolution" from here on in the text, but I will be using it in the Shī'a context, with its concomitant positive connotations.

prophet (*nabī*), what I have in mind are the great prophets or the *ulu'l-azm*[42] apostles who were tasked with bringing about a revolution in the state of affairs of the community to which they were sent. If one such prophet comes to a nation and proclaims such a revolutionary program but fails to establish a new social order based on these principles, his mission is incomplete.

Suppose, for example, that the great prophet Moses is commissioned to the nation of Pharaonic Egypt, appears in its midst and starts his agitation and revolutionary behavior, drawing Pharaoh's attention to his activity. Suppose further that he proclaims some new principles and tenets to the people of that land, and that he is successful in bringing about an insurrection and in killing Pharaoh and unseating him from his throne, and completely destroying the old social order. But suppose further that in doing so, he fails to establish a new social order in accordance with the new dispensation that he has been tasked to bring, and fails to hand over such a new social order to that nation [prior to the end of his life and ministry and mission]; that he fails to seat himself at the head of this social order, and fails to hand over this office to an appropriate successor who is then tasked to maintain the program that he instituted for moving the society forward in the direction dictated by the sacred dispensation. In this event, Moses would not have carried out and fulfilled the duties of his mission. Now we know that all of the divinely-commissioned prophets have established [new] social orders, at least on a small or even on a minimal scale, in accordance with the principles and tenets and values and ideals and objectives which they had in mind. They

---

[42] Those endowed with [a great] resolve. There are "124,000" prophets to which God ﷻ has spoken throughout the ages. Of these, approximately 300 have been apostles, i.e. those prophets who have been tasked with communicating God's will to mankind. In turn, of these 300, there have been five who have been given a Sacred Writ or "Book" and who have brought a new sharī'aᵗ or Sacred Law and Dispensation to various peoples; namely: the prophets Noah, Abraham, Moses, Jesus and Muhammad, may the peace and blessings of God ﷻ be with them all. Muhammad is the last of these five *ulu'l-azm* apostles (literally meaning 'those endowed with a great resolve'), and was given the Quran as his sacred writ upon which to build the new dispensational order.

3. The Meaning and Purpose of the Imamate

established this society or community on a sound footing, and the issue of whether or not that community survived intact is another matter entirely. However, the establishment of a new social order [no matter how small and no matter how sustainable] is part of their function. It is no different in the case of [the Prophet ﷺ of] Islam.

6. The struggle of the Prophet Muhammad ﷺ in establishing the Islamic social order

Islam arrived and its clarion call brought about the preliminary prerequisites of [a social] revolution. This preliminary stage took thirteen years to reach maturity and come to fruition. While the Prophet ﷺ was still domiciled in Mecca, [and had yet to migrate to Madina with his community and establish a new community there,] it was all work and effort; work and effort which from the perspective of the short sighted is futile and for naught. It is nothing but making sacrifices and being tortured [for one's beliefs] and being alienated from one's erstwhile kith and kin, and being subjected to group exile in the Sha'b of Abū-Tālib [where the Prophet ﷺ and his followers were forced into exile in, and where they endured three years of economic siege from the seventh to the tenth year of the Prophet ﷺ's mission, i.e. from the year minus three to the year zero of the Islamic calendar or to the year of the migration from Mecca to Madina]. For those with a weak faith, [those early years prior to the migration were nothing but] suffering the pangs of hunger, indigence and depravation, suffering damage, despondency, despair, doubts and misgivings. These were the necessary preliminaries of revolution; they were the necessities required for reaching that summit which was occupied by the rulers of the society; and [reaching the point of no return, which is] the Prophet's migration to Madina. Here the revolution reaches the point where all of its efforts begin to bear fruit; whereat a new society is born.

I might have mentioned this point in those earlier talks that the Prophet's migration was not an unpredictable event or one which was brought about by happenstance. This is the usual take on the migration; i.e. that a number of the people of Yathrib [which was later to come to be known as Madina, which means the City of the Prophet ﷺ] known as the

Helpers (*ansār*) came and listened to the recitation of verses from the Quran, after which they invited the Prophet ﷺ to their city, in a similar fashion that one might invite a preacher to some ceremony or other in Tehran [from Qom, say]. The Prophet ﷺ was invited to Madina, and went there and began preaching until his death [thirteen years later]! But that is not how the story unfolds. At that time, there were two needs which were juxtaposed before each other. There were two things which stood in dire need of each other. Madina was in desperate need of a new social order to transform it [out of the mess of tribalism and the endless cycle of petty and ritualized revenge that its degenerate social mores had landed it in]. Madina had grown tired and weary of the [internecine tribal] wars; fratricide had taken such a toll on its denizens that they had given up all hope. So there was a Madina which was in dire need, indigent, wretched and humiliated, which had become the plaything of the Jewish tribes of that city. It was a city where the leaders could not get along with each other, let alone with its underlings and lower classes. Madina was in need of a power and a program – I don't mean to imply that it felt the need for a Divine program, for it did not have enough sense and wisdom to feel such a need. But it felt the need for a [new] law, a [new] order; it was in need of someone who had the ability to come and take over the management and administration of the city. This, then, was one need.

The second need was the need of the Prophet ﷺ of Islam. After the Prophet's message was rejected in Mecca, his clan and tribe ostracized him and tortured his Companions. He was also rejected in the town of Tā'if, where they greeted him with a shower of stones, not allowing him even to tarry for a single night (Ibn Hām's *Sīra* 2:266). The other tribes around Mecca all rejected his message in one form or another, and the noblest of the tribes in that region demanded the right to choose the successor to his ministry after his death (Ibn Shahrāshūb, *Manāqib* 1:257). After the Prophet ﷺ put these inevitable and unavoidable defeats behind him – defeats which a movement cannot succeed if it does not overcome them – defeats which were like the early years of maturity, the years that a ten and eleven and twelve year old must go through before it can reach his fourteenth, fifteenth, and sixteenth years – these are in need of a ready and predisposed ground, in need of a Madina and a group of exhausted warring factions. Just like a field that has been cleared after a forest fire has burned the trees and made new fertile soil available for someone to come along and sow healthy and fecund seeds in it.

These two needs are suddenly juxtaposed before each other. The Prophet ﷺ calls them to Islam, and they in turn see what a good thing it would be for them, and accept. Later, the Prophet ﷺ fortifies the foundations of his work by entering a covenant with them, after which he flies by night, telling his followers to follow him to Madina, and that this is an obligation that is religiously incumbent on all of the Meccan community of Muslims. In Madina, the Prophet ﷺ creates and begins to establish a new governmental order, a new society, a new civil and administrative order, and an ideal polity and format for human [social as well as individual] existence. This is the function and purpose of [the institution of] prophethood.

7. Islamic ordinances for the creation of an Islamic social order

A new dispensation was revealed from on high for the administration of this new society; a series of principles and tenets and teachings, and a series of ordinances and commandments and laws. If you steal, then this is the punishment for it; if you assault someone, then this is the punishment for it. And you, o ruler! If you rule with injustice, then this is the punishment for it. And you, O ruler! If you saw someone and failed to act in such and such a way, or if you acted in such and such a way, then this is the punishment for it. This is the punishment for those who impose their will by brute force. Those who want to draw closer to God ﷻ: this is the way to do it. And those who are not inclined to abide by those principles which foster the interests of Islam and the Islamic state must seek the remedy in such and such a manner. A series of necessary provisions had been envisioned [in this divinely revealed dispensation] in order to ensure that the order is perpetuated through eternity [until the Day of Resurrection]. This new creature whose name is "Islam" must remain until perpetuity, and in order for this to occur, there must be a series of commandments which are revealed to the Prophet ﷺ and he in turn orders that they be recorded and collected in the form of a book, which is then placed under the arm of the Islamic society, telling it to refer to it when and as the need arises and to continue its path in accordance with its tenets and teachings. What is this book? Note that it is not only the Quran that is meant by [the analogy of] this "book". Let me repeat that: I am not referring only to the Quran when I talk about this "book". What I mean, rather, is the sum total of the collection of ordinances and ethical precepts and legal regulations and all of the rest of the things that appear in the annals of the teachings and culture of Islam, inclusive of the Sacred Writ (*kitāb*), the paradigmatic example and way (*sunna*) of the Prophet ﷺ, his words and deeds, and so on. They give this "book" to the newly founded society, telling it, "This is in your hands. This medicine is necessary for the continued sustenance of your life. This guidance is vitally important; make sure you hold on to it."

8. The continuity of the Islamic dispensational order after the passing of the Prophet ﷺ

The Prophet ﷺ passes from the material plane.

وَمَا مُحَمَّدٌ إِلَّا رَسُولٌ قَدْ خَلَتْ مِن قَبْلِهِ الرُّسُلُ ۚ أَفَإِن مَّاتَ أَوْ قُتِلَ انقَلَبْتُمْ عَلَىٰ أَعْقَابِكُمْ ۚ وَمَن يَنقَلِبْ عَلَىٰ عَقِبَيْهِ فَلَن يَضُرَّ اللَّهَ شَيْئًا ۗ وَسَيَجْزِي اللَّهُ الشَّاكِرِينَ ﴿١٤٤﴾

> [3:144] And Muhammad ﷺ is only an apostle; all the [other] apostles have passed away before him: if, then, he dies or is slain, will you turn about on your heels? But he that turns about on his heels can in no wise harm God ﷻ - whereas God ﷻ will requite all who are grateful [to Him].

Muhammad ﷺ is only an apostle. If you, as a newly converted Muslim, see something special in him and think that he is immortal, you are mistaken. Will you then turn about on your heels and change your path? Will you harbor doubts about your path and return to the path of pre-Islamic ignorance that you were on? Will you trade that beautiful garment which Islam has tailored for you? rather, that beautiful social order which Islam has determined and made available for you, and retrograde back to the old order?

9. Two duties of the Imam after the passing of the Prophet ﷺ: The explication of the religion and harmonizing it with the needs of society

So, the Prophet ﷺ has now passed on; he is, after all, mortal. He lived for sixty-three years. There have been prophets who lived shorter lives that that; and those who lived among their people for shorter periods of time. For example, the prophet John ﷺ lived a shorter life, as did the prophet Jesus ﷺ, although he did not die [but was taken up by God ﷻ and remains alive and in a state of occultation], but at all events, Jesus lived for a shorter period of time among the people to whom he was sent There are many more examples of such prophets. What, then, is that society to do now that it has lost its prophet? This society has two needs after the passing of their prophet. Pay attention, for the meaning and purpose of the institution of the imamate is contained in these few sentences. The first is to open this "book" and to read it and understand it and assimilate it into the framework of his mind; and the second is to coordinate it with society's needs. The founder of the religion comes and proclaims the teachings and tenets of the new dispensation, and even establishes the new social order based on these teachings and dispensation. However, these new thoughts must simmer and settle into the marrow of society. That is not to say that the new teachings are raw relative to reality. No: they must simmer and cook and find their rightful place in the minds of the denizens of the new society. [The principles of] the creed must be interpreted, explicated, and specifically stipulated, and allowed time to take their rightful place in the nooks and crannies of the everyday lives of the citizenry. This is the function of that person who is most knowledgeable in the teachings and tenets of the religion.

The social dispensation of Islam requires an interpreter and an explicator. Who is that interpreter and explicator? The Imam. At this point, let me add that one thing that I strictly avoid is getting into sectarian disputes. If someone who was a non-Shī'a came up to me and protested against this policy of mine, and asked, "Sir, what are the conditions which one must fulfill in order to be able to be vested in this position, and what are your reasons for such conditions?" I would not answer him, as I even believe that this kind of discussion is not licit [under present circumstances]. What we should do is to state what the Shī'a believe; and if there is someone among the audience who does not believe in it, then that is fine: let him not believe in it. The other discussion which is a debate to prove the claims of the Shī'a correct or incorrect is another matter altogether, and that is a discussion for a whole other venue. The subject of our discussion is on account of the fact that we are all Shī'a and all believe in the tenets of Shī'a Islam. Therefore, there is no reason for me to prove what attributes the Imam must have and what conditions the Imam must fulfill in order to be able to be vested in his position. I am simply stating the beliefs and claims of the Shī'a and explicate and comment upon some of the issues that I believe might arise concerning the subject at hand in the minds of the audience or at least, in various books which have been written on the subject.

Thus, the factor that brings about the need for the institution of the Imamate, i.e. for the series of people who are considered to be the continuity of the institution of prophethood and who are to take to the helm of the ship of state after the passing of the Prophet ﷺ, consists of society's need for the interpretation, explication and propagation of the tenets and teachings of the religion. This is what society stands in need of. If the Eleven Imams ؑ had not followed in the wake of the Prophet ﷺ – from whom there is a whole hadith report corpus which is extant, thank God ﷻ, to this day – and if there did not exist their interpretations and commentary and explications of the ordinances of this religion, we would not have had Islam at our disposal in its present form. These Imams ؑ play a very effective and important role in the progress of Quranic culture, inclusive even of non-Shī'a sacred jurisprudence and teachings.

It is true that Muhammad b. Ismāīl al-Bokhārī has not narrated a single hadith report from Imam Ja'far as-Sādiq ؑ in his famous hadith compendium which consists of about seven or eight thousand hadith reports. It is also true that they do not relate any subject matter from the Shī'a and do not relate any hadith reports from Imam Sādiq ؑ or Imam

3. The Meaning and Purpose of the Imamate

Bāqir ﷺ or any of the other Imams, and that no traces of these can be seen in their words or books or in their hadith report compendia. But the presence of Imam Sādiq ﷺ in a given period – in any period where such a one as Imam Sādiq ﷺ lives – the level of culture of that era is raised and improved. This is natural.

What role does a great scholar and thinker and theologian play in the intellectual and cultural development of a nation? Even if much of the intellectual progress that is made as a result of such a person is not attributed to him by the culture at large, he nevertheless places his unmistakable mark on the progress of that society. Again, this too is natural.

Shaykh Muhammad Abu Zahrā,[43] the contemporary Egyptian scholar, who is a truly unbiased and great man who is highly informed, states in a book which he has written concerning Imam Sādiq ﷺ that all of the scholars of the Islamic sciences (such as the science of hadith or sacred history, Quranic exegesis and commentary, sacred jurisprudence, and the rest of them), go back to Imam Sādiq ﷺ as their original source and it is he who is the one from whom they have derived [the most] benefit. Therefore, Imam Sādiq ﷺ has had a decisive influence on the teachings of Shī'a Islam directly, and on the teachings of Sunni Islam indirectly. All of the other ten Imams ﷺ had a similarly positive influence on the societies and cultures of their respective times with respect to their understanding of Islam.

Of course, the farther we get from the start of the Cycle of the Imamate and the closer we get to its terminus, this factor becomes weaker. This is particularly the case with respect to the first element of the imamate, i.e. the interpretation and explication of the religion, the closer we get to the ending of the Cycle of the Imamate and the imamates of the Ninth to the Eleventh Imams ﷺ. Conversely, the second element which we have not discussed yet is strengthened as the first one is weakened.

---

[43] Muhammad Abu Zahra (1898–1974) was an Egyptian public intellectual and an influential Hanafi jurist. He occupied a number of positions; he was a lecturer of Islamic law at Al-Azhar University and a professor at Cairo University. He was also a member of the Islamic Research Academy. His works include Abu Hanīfa, Malik and al-Shāfi'ī.

This has to do with the needs and demands of the time. Thus, when Islamic society lost its prophet, and lost its "Warner" – as the Quran puts it – and its revolutionary leader, and the founder of its new social order, it stood in need of a series of pillars to hold it in place for at least a minimum period of time [like training wheels or like a cast]. This is so that the religion which has been brought by the Warner can take root and [grow as intended, and] become perfected with the [proper] interpretation and explication [which is its due]. This in turn is so that everyone [over a period of several generations and not just the initial one] understands all of its teachings and how they apply to their own generation and society and culture. This is the first purpose and duty.

The second is that this nascent society needs a leader. The Commander of the Faithful states in one of his sayings that, "Every society stands in need of a leader."[44] This is an integral part of our thesis and way of thinking. We do not believe [as the Marxists maintain] that there will come a day where societies will run themselves without the need of a leader; to the contrary, people stand ineluctably in need of a leader. After the passing of the Prophet ﷺ, there needs to be someone at the head of the Islamic society to continue managing and administering the train that the Prophet ﷺ set in motion. There needs to be someone who, like the Prophet ﷺ himself, has a strong arm for taking the reins of society in hand and guiding it to its intended destination. Nor is the presence of such leaders at odds with the freedom within Islamic society. If we pay closer attention, we will see that there is no conflict whatsoever. The leader of society guides the society through its progressive stages and brings about and ensures the conditions which are necessary for such progress to be made. Society needs a political leader as well as spiritual and intellectual guide whose function it is to interpret and explain its sacred scripture and sources of law. Now the question as to what kind of a person such a leader should be, and whether it is necessary for him to be the most knowledgeable and most just person within that society or not – these are questions that pertain to sectarian discussions and disputes and to the bailiwick of fundamental or creedal theology (*kalām*), and we are not

---

[44] Sermon 40 of the *Nahj al-Balāgha*.

about to spend our limited time on discussing such matters, which are a subject for another day.

10. The incumbency on the Imam of taking back the office of leadership

What happens if this leader, who is the true leader of that society, is prevented from carrying out his leadership function and duties? If such a ruler is ousted from office, may he then opt to continue with the first duty and function which we discussed, and continue to interpret and explicate the teachings of Islam? In doing so, can he take the position that "now that we have been prevented from carrying out our political leadership duties, let others take on this role and administer society"? May he unburden himself from the burden of this duty with such an act of magnanimity? Well, may he not do such a thing?? Or is there a third possibility: that he may do so if the [overarching] interests [of Islam] so dictate, and that he mayn't do so if they forbid such an act? It is our contention that he mayn't do so [regardless]. We believe that the person who has been chosen by the Prophet ﷺ as being the most suitable person and appointed to and vested in the office of the leadership of the community and introduced him to the people as his successor, stipulating to them that it is incumbent on them to obey him – it is incumbent on such a person, in our opinion, to struggle to retain this right and duty should it ever be taken away from him. He has no choice in the mater. This is because this is not a right that was given to him with an option of his taking or leaving it.

I might offer you a pear and ask you to enjoy eating it; and you might counter by thanking me, but saying that eating a pear does not strike your fancy right now, [and that would be fair enough]. But there might be a time when – God ﷻ forbid – you have fallen ill and you are prescribed some medicine to take. In such a situation it would make no sense for you to say that "No, I don't feel like taking that medicine right now". The response to that would be, "Too bad!" They might try to persuade you and sweet-talk you into it at first, if it is serious, and then, failing that, they might restrain you and force it down your throat for your own good. Our situation is not dissimilar to this one: a healthy nascent

Islamic political order which has just gone through an Islamic revolution stands in need of a certain medicine. Such an Islamic society does not have the right to refuse to take its medication. Nor does the person who is the keeper of this medicine and who keeps it in his sleeve have the right to say, "Well, OK then, now that you don't want to take your medicine, I will go and sulk and not talk to you anymore. It's on you; and serves you right: go and die for all I care!" No, it is not like this. It is not as if it is a personal matter. To the contrary, he will try to take back that right; he will do what he can to administer the medicine to the patient. Unless he sees that if he puts too much pressure on the patient, that he is in such a frail state that this might cause the patient's death. True: in such a situation, he will withhold his curative activities until such a time that the patient has come out of his critical or near-death condition. When the patient is no longer in a critical condition, they will at first attempt to administer the medicine to him by some trick or other, concealing it in his food, for example; and if that does not work, they will administer it to him by force. This is how it is with the Imamate as well.

11. The transference by the Prophet ﷺ of two prophetic functions to the commander of the faithful and to the rest of the Imams ؑ after him

What I am about to say is what we Shī'a believe generally; it is not the opinion or belief of a specific person. We believe that the person who was vested by God's command in taking on two of the functions of the Prophet ﷺ after his passing was the Commander of the Faithful, these functions being the function of the interpretation and explication of the teachings of the religion, and the function of the leadership of the political affairs of the community. Do not ask me for the reasons for this [as to why it was Imam Ali ؑ and not anyone else to whom the transfer took place], as this has been more than amply addressed in books and in past talks and tribunes; this is not the subject of our discussion.

The Imamate's meaning and purpose is two-fold: firstly it is in order to ensure that the scripture and teachings and tenets of the religion are properly interpreted and explicated; and secondly, that the newfound Islamic political order continues to be administered and led in its divinely-

3. The Meaning and Purpose of the Imamate

intended trajectory and direction; that the reins of society are in the hands of one who will steer it in the same direction that the founder of the social order intended. These are the two primary duties of the Imam.

These two duties and functions were assigned by the Prophet ﷺ himself to the Commander of the Faithful,[45] and after him, to the other Eleven Imams ؑ. Both Shi'a and Sunni *hadith* reports have related the Prophet ﷺ as saying that "There will be Twelve Imams ؑ after me."[46] What is meant here, of course, is the conception of the Imam as we stated earlier, i.e. as a leader who is the successor to the political office of the Prophet ﷺ and who is at one and the same time one who has full knowledge of the Quran and who acts as its interpreter and exegete *par excellence* [i.e. who is also a spiritual guide and a doctor of the sacred law]. And what is meant here, of course, is the conception of the Imam as we stated earlier, i.e. as a leader who is the successor to the political office of the Prophet ﷺ and who is at one and the same time one who has full knowledge of the Quran and who acts as its interpreter and exegete *par excellence* [i.e. who is also a spiritual guide and a doctor of the sacred law].

---

[45] On many occasions, the last of which was the fateful Final Sermon which the Prophet ﷺ delivered at the Pond of Ghadīr or Ghadīr Khumm.

[46] "There will be Twelve Caliphs after Me": The reports which appear in this class of *hadīth* are numerous to the point of being *mutiwātir* (reports whose soundness is beyond a reasonable doubt), and they appear in all of the authoritative Sunni books (as well as in the books of Shī'a *hadīth*, of course), including those of the *sahīhayn* (of Bokhārī and Muslim), the *musnad* of Ahmad b. Hanbal, the *sunan* of Dāramī, the *sunan* of Beyhaqī, and the *mustadrak fī sahīhayn* of Hākim-e Neyshāpurī. The text varies slightly in each report, but the meaning is exactly the same. We will translate the one which appears in the *sahīh* of Muslim (related by Jābir b. Samara):

> "This religion will last until the Day of Resurrection, or until such a time that twelve caliphs [other versions have 'Imāms'; the meaning is the same in this context: leader; ruler], all of whom shall be of [the clan of] Quraysh, shall rule over you."

In the *Sahīh* of Bokhārī the report appears as follows, "There shall be twelve *amīr* (rulers) [over you]". Other versions have it slightly differently: "My successors will be twelve in number, just like the chieftains of the Banī Isrā'īl, all of them from Quraysh [and according to one version of this *hadīth*] from Banī Hāshim." (Muslim, *al-Sahīh*, Vol. VI, p. 2; al-Bokhari, *al-Sahīh*. Chapter XV of "Kitāb al-Ahkām". Ahmad b. Hanbal, *al-Musnad*, Vol. I, p. 397, Vol. V, p.86; Ibn Kathīr, *al-Bidāyah*, Vol. VI, p.245; al-Qunduzī, *Yanabi' al-Mawaddah*, p. 373.)

In other words, we can say that the Imam has two basic functions: the first being intellectual or theoretical, and the other being political and practical. The Imam holds the helm of the ship of state in one hand, and with the other, he explicates the theological basis of the creed and the rational and scriptural bases of the sacred law (*maktab*). In doing so, he steers society in the direction intended for it by the Islamic dispensation. The Prophet ﷺ stated that these people to whom these dual duties have been assigned, that these Imams, shall be twelve in number. In some of the hadith reports – and these are numerous within the Shi'a report corpus – these Imams ؑ are mentioned by their names and honorifics and specific attributes; and this is correct, of course, [as an instance and example of a prophecy on the part of the Prophet ﷺ Muhammad]; nor are there any objections to this from the point of view of a historical researcher.

These are the Imams ؑ that have been named by the Prophet ﷺ, and these are the Imams ؑ [in whom we believe and to whose wisdom and guidance we defer (see the following page)]:

So, up until now, we have understood the reason these twelve noblemen were appointed by God ﷻ through His prophet to the office of the Imamate and what their duties are and what is expected of them by God ﷻ. These are the matters we have examined so far.

12. Attributes of the true Shī'a: Understanding the duties of the Imam and following in his footsteps

The true Shī'a is one who understands this objective. Allow me to tell you something: even if we live to be a hundred years old but do not understand the purpose of our Imam, and do not follow in the footsteps of the Imam, we do not deserve to be called a Shī'a. Of course others might refer to us by that title, that is their prerogative and right and kindness and that is up to them; but it would not be based on our actions and what our hands have sown. If we do not know what their path was and what they intended to accomplish and what direction they intended society to take, so that we in our turn do not know what direction to take, then that is what will come of this ignorance. If we do not know where they intended to go, this is tantamount to saying that we do not know where *we* are headed, because we are their followers. And if we do not know this, we are not followers (Shī'a).

13. Attributes of the Shī'a who lived during the Time of the Imams: Living the Life of the Faithful and Engendering Faith

I will, God 🕮 willing, talk about what it meant to be a Shī'a during the time of the Imams 🕮 in one of the upcoming days of my talks; and I think that if we understand what it meant to be called a Shī'a at that time, it will be a cause of shame for most of us. It was not only a matter of performing the ritual devotions, fasting during the month of Ramadan, and so on – these things make their appearance in the hadith report corpus, and rightly so; but they are not the principle elements, which existed in those Shī'a and which are unfortunately absent in most of us today. In those days, the Shī'a understood and felt what the purpose and function of his Imam was and what the Imam's path was and where he was being led, and what his duties were; and he would choose his path accordingly. This is why this great characteristic of Islam existed in those days, that those who are truly faithful (mu'min) support each other. The characteristic of engendering faith and increasing the number of the faithful is something that existed in that society, but which is absent in ours. The same is true of living the life of the truly faithful. They lived as the truly faithful, died as the truly faithful, and engendered faith and increased the number of the faithful.

After the Fourth Imam (Imam Sajjād 🕮) was vested in the office of the Imamate, that is after the tragedy of Karbalā, the faithful disappeared or became lame and began to harbor misgivings about their faith, even though they had not lost their beliefs. The hadith reports tell us that "the people apostatized" after the tragedy of Karbalā. Did they mean by this that they lost their faith in God 🕮? No. Nobody lost their faith in God 🕮. Did they deny the prophethood of the Prophet 🕮? No; no one did that either. Did they change their minds about the imamate and the guardianship-type regency of Ali b. Abī-Ṭālib 🕮? Not in the least! As far as their beliefs were concerned, they believed, like you and I, in the imamate and guardianship-type regency of Ali b. Abī-Ṭālib 🕮. The same people who were in Madina around Imam Sajjād 🕮 all believed in the imamate of Ali b. Abī-Ṭālib ﷺ and of Husain b. Ali. Madina was the center of the Shīʿa. But at the same time, there is a hadith report about that great man and true Shīʿa who made a great sacrifice, Yaḥyā b. Umm al-Ṭawīl,[47] which reports him as coming to the congregational mosque in Madina and turning to the weak-kneed Shīʿa of the likes of us and saying,

$$\text{إِنَّا بُرَآءُ مِنكُمْ وَمِمَّا تَعْبُدُونَ مِن دُونِ اللَّهِ كَفَرْنَا بِكُمْ وَبَدَا بَيْنَنَا وَبَيْنَكُمُ الْعَدَاوَةُ وَالْبَغْضَاءُ أَبَدًا حَتَّىٰ تُؤْمِنُوا بِاللَّهِ وَحْدَهُ ﴿٤﴾}$$

> [60:4] "Verily, we are quit of you and of all that you worship instead of God ﷻ: we deny the truth of whatever you believe; and between us and you there has arisen enmity and hatred, to last until such a time as you come to believe in the One God ﷻ!"

He tells the Shīʿa and to those who profess to be the friends of Ali b. Abī-Ṭālib ﷺ that which the prophet Abraham ﷺ said to the idolaters and the worshippers of the false gods of his time. He said that he disavowed friendship and any relationship with them and that this friendship has been replaced with enmity and hatred. He told them that the front of us three (there were three of them present) with the leadership of Imam Sajjād ﷺ is distinct from the front of you pseudo-Shīʿa. Until what time? Until "such a time as you come to believe in the One God ﷻ!" Someone in the crowd said, "O Yaḥyā b. Umm al-Ṭawīl, but we [all] believe in [the one] God ﷻ!" They knew what he was saying. The report continues: "And these [three Shīʿa] reproduced themselves". The Shīʿa in Imam Sajjād's circle gathered round and increased in number daily, until they became hundreds and then numbered in the thousands. They fought with the enemies of the Shīʿa in Madina, Kūfa, Bākmarāʾ [in the environs of Kūfa], and in Basra. They also fought in Morocco and in the other areas which were populated by the Shīʿa, and killed and got killed, and rose up in

---

[47] One of the boon companions of Imam Sajjād ﷺ who was martyred by the Umayyads on account of his being a Shīʿa. His arms and legs were severed from his body before he was put to death.

righteous insurrection against the forces of illegitimate authority and tyranny, to the point where at the time that the Eleventh Imam, Imam al-Askarī ﷺ passes from the earthly plane, Madāin, a city right beside the caliphal throne, has become a Shī'a center. Thus, these Shī'a engendered and gave birth and created other Shī'a like themselves...[48]

---

[48] The audiotape stops at this point.

4. The 250-Year-Old Warrior

[God ❁ the All-Knowing and All-Wise has stated in His Sacred Writ:]

$$\text{رَبَّنَا عَلَيْكَ تَوَكَّلْنَا وَإِلَيْكَ أَنَبْنَا وَإِلَيْكَ الْمَصِيرُ ﴿٤﴾}$$

[60:4] "O our Sustainer and Lord of Providence! In Thee have we placed our trust, and unto Thee do we turn: for unto Thee is all journeys' end.

$$\text{رَبَّنَا لَا تَجْعَلْنَا فِتْنَةً لِلَّذِينَ كَفَرُوا وَاغْفِرْ لَنَا رَبَّنَا إِنَّكَ أَنتَ الْعَزِيزُ الْحَكِيمُ ﴿٥﴾}$$

[60:5] O our Sustainer and Lord of Providence! Make us not a plaything for those who are bent on denying the truth! And forgive us our sins, O our sustainer: for Thou alone art, almighty, truly wise!"

$$\text{رَبَّنَا إِنَّكَ مَن تُدْخِلِ النَّارَ فَقَدْ أَخْزَيْتَهُ وَمَا لِلظَّالِمِينَ مِنْ أَنصَارٍ ﴿١٩٢﴾}$$

[3:192] "O our Sustainer and Lord of Providence! Whomsoever Thou shalt commit to the fire, him, verily, wilt Thou have brought to disgrace [in this world]; and such evildoers will have none to succor them.

$$\text{رَبَّنَا لَا تُزِغْ قُلُوبَنَا بَعْدَ إِذْ هَدَيْتَنَا وَهَبْ لَنَا مِن لَّدُنكَ رَحْمَةً ۚ إِنَّكَ أَنتَ الْوَهَّابُ ﴿٨﴾}$$

[3:8] "O our Sustainer and Lord of Providence! Let not our hearts swerve from the truth after Thou hast guided us; and bestow upon us the gift of Thy grace: verily, Thou art the [true] Giver of Gifts.

$$\text{رَبَّنَا وَآتِنَا مَا وَعَدتَّنَا عَلَىٰ رُسُلِكَ وَلَا تُخْزِنَا يَوْمَ الْقِيَامَةِ ۗ إِنَّكَ لَا تُخْلِفُ الْمِيعَادَ ﴿١٩٤﴾}$$

[3:194] "O our Sustainer and Lord of Providence! Grant us that which Thou hast promised us through Thy apostles, and disgrace us not on Resurrection Day! Verily, Thou never failest to fulfil Thy promise!"

O our Sustainer and Lord of Providence! [I beseech you] by [the right and station of spiritual proximity to You which] Muhammad ﷺ and his [Purified and Immaculate] Progeny ﷺ [have], to grant us that which Thou hast promised the true believers (*muʾminīn*), and grant us the self-transcendence and self-perfection which Thou hast envisioned for human beings!

[God ﷻ the All-Knowing and All-Wise has stated in His Sacred Writ:]

$$\text{وَوَهَبْنَا لَهُ إِسْحَاقَ وَيَعْقُوبَ نَافِلَةً ۖ وَكُلًّا جَعَلْنَا صَالِحِينَ ﴿٧٢﴾ وَ جَعَلْنَاهُمْ أَئِمَّةً يَهْدُونَ بِأَمْرِنَا وَأَوْحَيْنَا إِلَيْهِمْ فِعْلَ الْخَيْرَاتِ وَإِقَامَ الصَّلَاةِ وَإِيتَاءَ الزَّكَاةِ ۖ وَكَانُوا لَنَا عَابِدِينَ ﴿٧٣﴾}$$

[21:72] And We bestowed upon him Isaac and [Isaacs son] Jacob as an additional gift and caused all of them to be righteous men, [21:73] and made them Imams ﷺ who would guide [others] in accordance with Our behest: for We inspired them [with a will] to do good works, and to be constant in prayer, and to dispense charity: and Us [alone] did they worship.

1. Two functions of the Imam: The explication of Islam and the political leadership of society

I stated that the reasons for the Imamate and the rationales which necessitated the Cycle of the Imamate in the history of Islam – and perhaps in the history of all [of the monotheistic] religions are two things. The first is the interpretation and explication and systematization of the creed and religion of Islam. The second is the continuation of the path of the Prophet ﷺ and Warner, [and the securement of the values and objectives of the dispensational order revealed through the Prophet ﷺ], and guiding Islamic society towards those values and objectives. There were two factors which caused the Prophet ﷺ to appoint an Imam [as his successor]; this was the subject of our discussion yesterday.

So again: the imamate is necessitated in order that the Imam carries out two functions: the first is the interpretation and explication and systematization of the creed and religion which God ﷻ has revealed to humanity through His prophet and which has been adopted as the basis of the social and dispensational order of society. This first function also includes the harmonization of this dispensation with the various instances of social issues which arise. These new thoughts must simmer and find their rightful place in the minds of the denizens of the new society. Generally speaking, the creed must be interpreted and explicated for future generations of the nascent Muslim society. So, think of instances from the life of Imam Sādiq ﷺ which you are aware of as examples of this, where he would teach and provide new insights into the tenets, ordinances, creedal beliefs and ethics of Islam to people who had come from the far corners of the Islamic world to quench their thirst for knowledge about their religion. In one sense, the insights were not about anything new in that all the teachings were based in the two sources of the Quran and the Prophetic *Sunna* or paradigmatic example and way of life. However, the point of the matter is that much of the more allegorical aspects of these teachings, as they appear in their original sources, stand in need of interpretation and explanation, and that interpreter and explicator is the Imam.

The other function and duty which the Imam has is the continuation of the path of the Prophet ﷺ. What does this mean? What it means is that the Prophet ﷺ brings about the new social order on the basis of the principles of Islam, taking the reins of the political leadership of society in his hands, and guides this society to the objective of human individual and social self-transcendence. Just like a skilled caravan-master who is intimately familiar with the warps and woofs of the journey; i.e. the objectives of growth, perfection, transcendence, and material and spiritual progress. Once the Prophet ﷺ passes – for he is mortal, like everyone else – he must be followed by an Imam who continues these same functions [with the exception of the bringing of any new law – it is the continuation of the same dispensational order that is his task]. This is his second function. It is a valuable concept which can be used for resolving many problems. I believe that if the Shī'a had resorted to and stressed the importance of this [two-fold] rationale, that we would have resolved many of our problems and convinced our adversaries of the rightfulness of much of our claims.

2. The duty of the Imam: to struggle to actualize his two functions

I referred to something in passing yesterday which I will touch on again briefly today, for the sake of continuity. This is an almost marginal discussion but one which is necessary at the same time. That is the question as to what the duty of the Imam is in the event that he does not have [or is deprived of] the opportunity of performing these two duties. In other words, if the ruling powers of the time of a given Imam do not allow him to explicate and systematize [the tenets and teachings of] the religion [of Islam], does this relieve the Imam of the burden of duty [that was placed on his shoulders by the Prophet ﷺ, and therefore, by God ﷻ]?

4. The 250-Year-Old Warrior

To be clear, we do not want to tell the Imam what his duties are; no: [the more specific formulation of the question might be], what do the principles and teachings that we have at our disposal from their own words tell us about this matter? What do they themselves tell us about their own duties? And similarly, if the ruling powers and social conditions preclude the second function and duty from being performed, i.e. that he is prevented from being able to take the reins of the political leadership of society in his hands, and to guide society to the prophetic objective of individual and social self-transcendence and perfection – then what is the Imam's duty with respect to this issue?

It is very clear that the duty of a responsible person – let alone an Imam – here is to try, to the extent of his abilities and to the extent that it is in his power, to remove the obstacles and arrange the necessary groundwork for him to be able to continue to carry out his duties. We can see that this is precisely what they did with respect to their duty of interpreting and explaining the ordinances and teachings of Islam. [For example, the ruling powers placed restrictions on] Imam Sajjād ﷺ [such that he] was not in a position to hold teaching sessions in the congregational mosque in Madīna as did the Imams ﷺ before him, Imam Hasan ﷺ and Imam Husain ﷺ. After the tragedy of Karbalā and the Battle of Harra,[49] Imam Sajjād ﷺ was in no position to follow in his father and

---

[49] The Battle of al-Harra was fought between the Levantine army of the Umayyad caliph Yazīd I (r. 680–683) led by Muslim ibn Uqba and the original core of the Muslim community, the Ansār and Muhājirūn, who had risen up in insurrection against the tyrant Yazīd who had massacred the grandson of their Prophet ﷺ of Imām Husain ﷺ and his House and loyal supporters in the plain of Karbalā. The battle took place at the lava field of Harrat Wāqim in the northeastern outskirts of Medina on 26 August 683. Before Yazīd's army reached Mecca, it stopped to subdue Madīna. Yazīd had ordered his commander to allow for his troops the free killing and pillage and rape of the Muslims of Madīna for three days, and this order was duly announced and carried out, such that countless Muslims were murdered and thousands of virgins were raped, leaving hundreds of unmarried women giving birth to hundreds of fatherless infants.49 Among the dead who were counted were seven hundred elders from among the *muhājirūn*, *ansār* and *mawālī*, out of a number of around ten thousand, which also included seven hundred *hāfiz al-qurān* (those who knew the Quran by heart). On the fourth day, Yazīd's commander extracted pledges of fealty from the survivors, telling them "to pledge that you are [nothing more than] war booty which is the special share

uncle's footsteps with respect to the *form* in which the Islamic teachings were explicated and propagated. However, we see that this did not prevent him from continuing this function in a different way. He did so in the form of composing supplications and psalms in which he expressed that which he wanted to express. These psalms were collected into a compendium which is known as the *Sahīfaᵗ as-Sajjādīya*.⁵⁰ This compendium survived the vicissitudes of those most turbulent times and was therefore available for the use of the followers of Imam Sajjād ﷺ, as it is available for our use today.

Similarly, if the Imam is prevented from [taking to the helm of the ship of state and] moving society in a forward direction, that is, if he is marginalized and relegated to the fringes of society and the mainstream of public discourse [and his right to the political leadership of society is usurped from him], and he is prevented from succeeding the Prophet ﷺ and being vested as the leader of his ministry and community, what is the

---

of the Commander of the Faithful Yazīd, and that he has the right to do what he will with you, your property and with your children!" And if anyone refused to pledge allegiance under these terms, his head would be severed "by the command of the Book of God ﷻ and the *Sunnaᵗ* of the Prophet ﷺ". And when the heads of those who had refused were flung in front of Yazīd back in Damascus, he quoted the poetry of the poet of the idolaters who fought the Prophet ﷺ until the bitter end: "Would that my forefathers who died in the Battle of Badr were present now to see the woeful state of the Khazrajites (a tribe loyal to the Prophet ﷺ of God ﷻ), so that they would take joy [on this occasion] and say, 'O Yazīd, Well done!'. . The following sources were used for this footnote: *Tārīkh Al-Tabarī* Vol. 3, Vol. 4, 372-379, 309-356, Vol. 19, The Caliphate of Yazīd b. Muʿāwiya; Al-Athīr, Ali ibn. Vol. 3, 282-299, 310-313; Al-Dhahabi, Muhammad bin Ahmad, *Tārīkh al-Islam*, Vol. 5. P. 30; Ibn Kathir, Ismail bin Umar, *Al Bidayah Wal Nihayah* Vol 8:170-207, 219-221 & 223; & as-Suyuti, Jalaluddin, *Tarikh al-Khulafa*, p. 165), Wikipedia has this to say about Yazīd: that the opinion of a minority of "scholars" notwithstanding, most Islamic scholars during the Abbasid Caliphate regarded Caliph Yazid I as a tyrant who was directly responsible for three major historical atrocities in standard Islamic history: The Karbala massacre of the Hashimite caravan of Husain ibn Ali, the pillage and plunder of the city of Madinah (by Yazīd's general Ibn Uqbah al-Murri) in which over 10,000 Muslim citizens were slaughtered and Muslim women were indiscriminately raped, and the siege of Mecca in which Yazīd's commander Ibn Numayr ordered his troops to catapult fireballs to the shrine of the Kaaba.

⁵⁰ Ably translated by William Chittick as *The Psalms of Islam*.

Imam's duty in this case? Is it the case that the Imam is like the rest of us who, when given a responsibility which we cannot or do not want to carry out, we say, "Well, we were not able to carry out that responsibility" [and might follow that sentiment up with a verse from the Quran]".

ا يُكَلِّفُ اللَّهُ نَفْسًا إِلَّا وُسْعَهَا ۚ لَهَا مَا كَسَبَتْ وَعَلَيْهَا مَا اكْتَسَبَتْ ۗ رَبَّنَا لَا تُؤَاخِذْنَا إِن نَّسِينَا أَوْ أَخْطَأْنَا ﴿٢٨٦﴾

[2:286] God ﷻ does not burden any human being with more than he is well able to bear: in his favor shall be whatever good he does, and against him whatever evil he does.

[So that if a task is too burdensome, it is something that was not meant for me, which is why] we demur from accepting its responsibility. Does the Imam do the same thing? Is he like those lazy elementary school students who look for any excuse not to do their homework? Is the Imam like someone who, having come back home from school and seeing that he has used up the last page of his workbook or seeing that his pen has run out of ink, uses this as an excuse not to do his homework? Is that how it is? When confronted with their own realities, do the Imams ﷺ say, "Well, God ﷻ had told us to explain His religion to the people and to set the policies of the Islamic community such that it will be in keeping with his dispensation, and will move in the direction which He intended; but hey, there is nothing that we can do in this situation, so we'll sit this one out!" Like those who are sitting things out in our own time.[51] Is this how the Imam would act? Certainly not. In such a situation, the Imams ﷺ duty is to bring all of his efforts and powers to bear on whatever progress he can make in carrying out his duties and objectives. [After all,] it is possible that he might be able to seize the reins of power and guide society to where God ﷻ has intended as its leader.

---

[51] Reference to the "quietist" doctors of religion whose apolitical position held sway in the seminaries at Qom and Mashhad in the days leading up to the revolution. Alas, the first forty years of the revolution have not been able to put much of a dent in this mentality, it being so deeply ingrained.

Is there an example of such a thing? If we were to limit ourselves to selecting a single clear example, which you are aware of and can relate to. An example of this can be seen in the behavior of the Commander of the Faithful during the forty nights after the Prophet's passing. Everyone has heard the tale which appears in various books in our hadith report corpus, and it is surely true, that for forty nights after the Prophet's passing, the Commander of the Faithful [Imam Ali] ﷺ would pay visit to the houses of [certain] Companions of the Prophet ﷺ and Quran [reciters] and those who had a love for [and proper understanding of] Islam, and it is also related that he would even take [his wife, Lady Fāṭima ﷺ] the daughter of the Prophet ﷺ with him. That is, he would appeal to both the emotional as well as to the intellectual aspects [having to do with the matter at hand or the crisis of leadership that the community was faced with], so that he might be able to gather around him a steely core of supporters whose support he could rely on in the event of an insurrectionary movement, so that the sapling of Islam would still be able to take root.[52] The purpose of Imam Ali's ﷺ nightly visits was to see if people would pledge allegiance to him so that he could take back his right from a minority who was out for its own specific interests – for the people gathered at the Saqīfa were a minority who had garnered the consent of the majority of the population by a sleight of hand scam or con (*bā neyrang va tardasti*); in order to position himself at the head of the community in order to be able to implement the duties which the Prophet ﷺ, God ﷻ and the Quran had assigned him and appointed him to carry out.

3. Two duties of the Imam concerning Islam and society

So, to sum up what we have said up to this point so that we can move on to today's subject matter, is that the Imams ﷺ have two duties: one relates to the religion of Islam and the other relates to society. These are the two wings with which the Imam soars on the horizons of [the institution of] the imamate. One has to do with thought, and the other with action; one has to do with theory, the other [applies those theories] to reality. One is

---

[52] See Tabresī's *Ihtijāj*, 1:81.

when the Imam holds the Quran in his hand [and preaches its teachings], and the other is when he takes the reins of society in hand [and applies the Quran's teachings]. The Imam is tasked with these two duties. If at any given time there are adversaries and forces of usurpation and injustice who prevent the Imam from being vested in his rightful place, then the Imam is duty-bound (*bāyad*) to exert a tireless effort and engage in an exerted struggle in order possibly to regain these two divinely-appointed offices and functions, and to continue the path which God ﷻ the Sublimely Exalted has determined for him. This was a recap of what we have already said.

4. The way of the Imams: Brothers in arms or appeasers?

Here is where we arrive at the cardinal point of our discussion. As I have already said in the first and second day of our talks, our subject matter is about the question of how the Imams ﷺ – whom we know by name – lived their lives. How did they transact their social lives? Were they all some appendage in the governmental apparatus of the usurper powers of their day, as is the claim of the prattlers and drivel-mongers of history and their contemporary counterparts who follow the path of what tendentious historians have averred? Were the Imams ﷺ the kinds of people who fell in lockstep with [the marching orders of] the ruling powers of their day and [conformed their behavioral patterns] to the contours of their respective social conditions? Put it this way, were they like [our obsequious and compliant] court-allied clergy (*mullā-ye darbārī*) who would on occasion be the subject of the caliph's snipes and wrath? Are those the kinds of people our Imams ﷺ were? Did they acknowledge and accept [the legitimacy of] the reigns of the ruling powers of their day in practice, such that their relations with their own followers (*shīʿa*) was one of an aristocratic superior's to his underlings, like that of a master [to his servant] or a high religious official or an arch-bishop [would have with an ingratiating member of his flock]? Is this [what we are supposed to believe] the lives of our Imams ﷺ consisted of?? Is *this* how our Imam Ṣādiq ﷺ lived? Or were their lives different? The lives of the Imams ﷺ was a life full of exerted effort, endeavor, striving, and conflict. But that is not the subject of our discussion.

5. The 250-Year-Old warrior

At this point I would like to proffer a thesis which I have arrived at, which I will attempt to demonstrate for you gentlemen in the following few days, God 🌺 grant, to the point that it will no longer be a claim on my part but will be an established belief. Based on the research which I have carried out concerning the lives of these great noblemen, our thesis is that with the minor exception which I shall explain in due time, their lives – from the start of the history of the imamate until the day of the martyrdom of the Eleventh Imam, Imam Hasan al-Askarī 🌺 (in this period of approximately 250 [lunar] years) – were lives of struggle and lives wherein they waged *jihād* (struggle for the sacred cause of Islam) [against the usurping and illegitimate ruling powers of their day]. These men were a group of *mujāhidīn* (warriors engaged in the sacred struggle for the divine cause of Islam). This is our[53] claim.

Now if we were to take the approach that the people have been habituated to, which is to accept things on faith and without any good reason, and without themselves thinking about the matter at hand, then all of us must accept this [thesis]. Why? Because when each and every one of you recite the Zīārat[54] Amīnullāh[55] (which is one of the most creditable *zīārāt*), when you address each of the Immaculate Imams 🌺 while reciting the *zīārat* and pay your homage and respect to them, you recite [the following line]:

---

[53] Recall that Ayatollah Khāmeneī was a student of Imam Khomeini's in the 1960's in Qom prior to the latter's exile.

[54] Zīārat: 1. The act of making pilgrimage to a pilgrimage site, usually a shrine of a prophet, imam or *imamzāda* (the progeny of an imam); 2. A liturgical form of supplication or ritual prayer recited specifically during one's pilgrimage to a sacred shrine or location, but also on any other occasion. Zīārat Amīnullāh is a leading case in point.

[55] The Zīārat Amīnullāh is a highly esteemed *zīārat* as it is cited in all books of *zīārat*. It is narrated on the authority of Jabir ibn `Abdullah al-Ansari on the authority of Imam al-Bāqir 🌺 that Imam Sajjād 🌺 made pilgrimage to the shrine of Imam Ali 🌺 and composed it while he wept at the sepulcher.

4. The 250-Year-Old Warrior

$$\text{أَشْهَدُ أَنَّكَ جَاهَدْتَ فِي اللَّهِ حَقَّ جِهَادِهِ وَ عَمِلْتَ}$$

Verily, I bear witness that you waged *jihād* (struggled) for God's sacred cause as it ought to be striven for.

Thus, if we were to want to accept the matter based on scriptural proofs or "on faith" (*ta'abuddan*), [the significance of] the *jihād* which is [referred to] in this *ziārat* must perforce be accepted [by us], and the image of the Imams ﷺ which is presented [to the general public] should be one of a Warrior Imam (*imām-e mujāhid*), and one of an Imam whose life was a life full of exerted effort and endeavor and striving and conflict in God's cause. In other words, it should be the opposite of that which we imagine presently. If we were to [approach the issue from the vantage of rational historical proofs and] not to bring detailed historical evidence and [their] sources to bear, but to survey [these sources] cursorily, we would again have no choice but to accept this thesis instantly and without hesitation.

6. The martyrdom of the Imams ﷺ as the general reason for their being warriors

I have mentioned this matter in passing on many different occasions over the past years, but unlike now, I had not carried out any detailed research. When we look at our Twelve Imams, except for the Twelfth who is alive – and may God ﷻ save his blessed existence from evil-wishers and place us among his friends and helpers – all of the other Imams ﷺ were either martyred while they were in prison, or in the field of battle, or at the hands of a conniving and treacherous enemy. All of them. Is it not true that you have heard the hadith report from the Imams ﷺ themselves saying, "There is no one among us [Imams] who either has not been murdered [by sword] or poisoned".[56] And so I ask you: What kind of a person would a powerful governmental order put to the death by sword or poisoning? Would it be anyone other than one who is engaged in an active struggle against it? Someone who poses an [existential] threat to it? Someone who – in the words of the Abbāsid caliph al-Mansūr – is a bone stuck in the throat of

---

[56] Bihār al-Anwār 27:217.

the governing order, preventing it from being able to breath? There are several reports from this caliph to this affect concerning Imam Sādiq ﷺ. Is the case other than this? And so, Imam Sādiq ﷺ must be martyred; must be poisoned; because he is a warrior and a bone in the throat of the caliph.

Even if we were to ignore the specific facts and details of the lives of the Imams, the general statements which I have in mind about them and will report to you presently, God ﷻ willing, will suffice to convince you that the Eleven Imams ﷺ died the death of warriors who were engaged in the sacred struggle for the cause of Islam. This is because they were murdered; [and] because Imam Mūsā b. Ja'far, the Seventh Imam, was sentenced to life in prison. If the Seventh Imam were not martyred in prison, or if it were not the case that he passed away in prison, and would have lived for another twenty years, they still would not have released that nobleman from the dungeon they kept him in. For if they wanted to release him, they would not have imprisoned him in the first place. Because all three of these Imams, Imam Bāqir ﷺ, Imam Sādiq ﷺ and Imam Sajjād ﷺ were each exiled on two different occasions. Imam Reza was exiled. Imam Jawād, Imam Hādī ﷺ, and Imam Hasan al-Askarī ﷺ were all either imprisoned or suffered exile several times. Because our last three Imams, Imam Jawād, Imam Hādī ﷺ, and Imam Hasan al-Askarī ﷺ were put to death while they were still young. Imam Jawād was put to death when he was twenty-five, Imam Hādī ﷺ when he was thirty-two or -three, and Imam Hasan al-Askarī ﷺ when he was twenty-eight.

Why would a ruling order put to death a twenty-five or thirty-two-year-old man who is the Lord of the House of the Prophet ﷺ [of his generation] and who has such a large following of devotees who consider every word and deed of his to be divinely inspired? What possible gain could they achieve by his murder? Can it be anything other than the case that their murders must have been expedient for them and served their interests in some way? – an interest that far exceeded the interest of keeping him alive and thereby keeping his followers subdued? For if that is the case, there must have been a danger in their being alive which threatened the status quo which far exceeded the discontent and ire of the people which would result from their murder.

4. The 250-Year-Old Warrior

These are just some general points which if you take into your consideration should be sufficient to convince a fair and unbiased person that Imam Sādiq ﷺ and Imam Kāẓim ﷺ [and all of the other Imams ﷺ] were engaged in the waging of a *jihād* for the cause of Islam. In addition to this, I will of course also be presenting to you in the next few days the details of their relationships with the ruling powers, with the court-allied doctors of religion, and with their own followers and devotees.

I delivered a talk about this same subject some time ago, and the title of the talk was "Imam Husain's Brothers in Arms". In other words, Imam Sādiq ﷺ was Imam Husain's Brother in Arms, he was in [the same] field of battle as Imam Husain ﷺ. Imam Kāẓim ﷺ, Imam Jawād ﷺ, and Imam Riḍā ﷺ are Imam Husain's Brothers in Arms: they are fighting shoulder to shoulder in [the same] field of battle with Imam Husain ﷺ. How is it that whenever there is talk of Imam Husain ﷺ, people immediately cite Imam Sādiq's example? When someone says that Imam Husain ﷺ acted in such and such a way, someone else invariably says, well then why did Imam Sādiq ﷺ act in this [*other*] way, if what you say is true? Strange... How can Imam Sādiq ﷺ act in a way that is contrary to Imam Husain ﷺ? Did Imam Sādiq ﷺ act in a way that is contrary to Imam Husain ﷺ, or is it you who are as blind as a bat and have not understood [the truth of the matter]? Imam Sādiq ﷺ fought shoulder to shoulder with Imam Husain ﷺ [in the same spiritual battlefield]; they are brothers in arms fighting the same enemy; the same hand which martyred Imam Husain ﷺ also martyred Imam Sādiq ﷺ, but in two [physically] different fields of battle. This is the key point. If I were to put an end to my presentation at this juncture, this amount should suffice to convince a fair-minded and unbiased mind of the veracity of the matter, even if he was hearing it for the first time. But this notwithstanding, we will, of course, continue with our presentation of further details.

7. What is meant by the *Jihād* of the Imams

Our focus will mainly be on the eight Imams ﷺ from Imam Sajjād ﷺ to Imam Hasan al-Askarī ﷺ, but we must preliminarily know what is meant by the *jihād* of the Imams ﷺ and what we mean when we say they were *mujāhidīn* or warriors. It is important that I explain this to you properly.

[Because] when we say that Imam Sādiq ﷺ was a *mujāhid* and waged a *jihād*, someone in the audience immediately raises an objection. Of course, the gentlemen who are gathered here are too noble and considerate to do so, and will not even do so in private after the talk is over; but those who are not in the audience raise these kinds of objections. And it is precisely *because* they are not in the audience that they do so. "Where did Imam Sādiq ﷺ wage *jihād*, sir?" they ask. "We never once saw him [= read about him] hold[ing] a sword in his hand. We never once herd tale of him [fighting] in the field of battle, sir!" From the kinds of questions which I have heard concerning this matter, I feel that the word *jihād*, which is a technical term [which has a very specific meaning in the Quranic lexicon] has not been properly understood. This is the subject of the preamble which I mentioned: defining the precise meaning of the word *jihād*.

8. Two mistaken definitions and one correct definition of the word *Jihād*

There are two mistaken definitions and one correct definition of the word *jihād*. The two mistaken definitions are opposites of each other: each has deviated from the true definition in opposite directions. We know that the word *jihād* has been used frequently in the Quran, and that it appears many times more frequently in the hadith report corpus;[57] and that *jihād* is a religious obligation of the religion of Islam. The way in which the word *jihād* is used in the Quran differs from its usage in [the science of] Shī'a sacred jurisprudence (*fiqh*). In Shī'a sacred jurisprudence, the word *jihād* is used in accordance with magisterial consensus and usage by the magisters of the sacred law in a specific and limited sense, and we see that this is especially the case in the centuries after the Occultation,[58] i.e. from the fifth Islamic century forward. But this is not the case in the Quranic usage, where its usage does not have an analogue in Shī'a sacred jurisprudence (*fiqh*).

---

[57] See footnote #3 on page 20 for a definition of hadith.
[58] See footnote #39.

9. A mistaken Definition: *Jihād* defined as any type of struggle whatsoever

One of the two deviant definitions of *jihād* is when it is defined as being tantamount and synonymous with the word "struggle"; and that *jihād* in God's cause means "struggle" in God's cause in its pure form or sense. And in order to give this meaning currency, [those who define *jihād* in this way] say that anything that one does in God's cause is a struggle and a *jihād*. Assume, for example, that you "struggle" out from under your warm bed covers and "struggle" to leave your toasty home and forge out to work in the dawn of a cold and rainy morning. You "struggle" to reach into your pocket and "struggle" to get the car keys out. Getting the frozen car door open is a "struggle". Everything is a "struggle", from turning the switch to pulling out of the driveway, negotiating the heavy Tehran traffic, all the way to when you finally arrive at your place of work and find a parking spot next to the Tehran Grand Bazaar. May God ﷻ reward you!!!

You then grace your shop or your office with your presence and take a seat, and talk to such and such an apprentice or administrative assistant or client, each of which you carry on a conversation with and "struggle" with from dawn till dusk so that you can eke out a living. So you are engaged in a "struggle", but because – so the story goes – you are doing all this so that you can earn a living that is licit according to the criteria determined by the sacred law and dispensation, so that you can put food on the table that is earned in a legitimate and *halāl* way, so that you can give your firstborn his due share of oranges and kebabs and allow him to feast on a roast turkey, then therefore, your "struggle" is actually a *jihād*! Well, isn't it? Isn't it a struggle? Is it not toil? Does it not take its toll? It is all of this and a struggle to earn a [licit] living. This is why they say that earning a licit living is a form of *jihād*.[59] They call this *jihād*, such that all works great and small are a *jihād*, as long as they are done for the sake of seeking God's pleasure and good graces.

They say, "Sir! Islam defines *jihād* as [22:78] striv[ing] hard in God's cause with all the striving that is due to Him. That is the Islamic definition of *jihād*". Struggle 'with all the striving that is due to God' when

---

[59] A hadith to this effect appears in Shaykh Koleynī's *Kāfī*, 5:88.

you work for your living, when you work to increase your knowledge, when you live life and are with your friends, [live life to the fullest]. Whatever efforts you make are efforts 'in the Way of God ﷻ'". This is an interpretation of *jihād* which exists in the minds of some people, which is why they consider themselves to be warriors [in the Path of God ﷻ] (*mujāhidīn*). They say, "Sir! We too are engaged in waging a *jihād*!" And in order that you do not express your surprise at his characterization of themselves as sacred warriors when they say this, they quickly follow it up by saying that "Sir! You are engaged in waging a *jihād* also! The fact that you opened the door to your store this morning and sat down to make a living is being engaged in waging a *jihād*!" This is a wrong interpretation, and it is one that is very wide of the mark.

We do not deny that the word *jihād* means "struggle" in God's cause in its pure form or sense and is derived from the *jadhr* or triletteral root *ju-ha-da* or *ja-ha-da*. There is no doubt about that. However, if the lexical meaning of the word was as broad as that, there would not be a need to apply a separate word for [the concept in order to distinguish it from the wider sense of "struggle"]. Thus, performing the daily ritual devotions and fasting the month of Ramadan and making the Hajj pilgrimage and paying the *zakāt* poor due and all of the other Islamic acts of ritual and devotion are all *jihād* if we go by this [overly broad] definition. Why would there be a need to put a different name on these activities? Why would they invent another name for no purpose at all? Therefore, *jihād* does not mean "struggle" in God's cause in its pure sense. Rather, *jihād* is something that is distinct from the ritual acts of devotion and making the Hajj pilgrimage and paying the *zakāt* poor due and from [the ordinances having to do with the moral stewardship of the community (*ahkām-e nizārati*) such as] *al-amr bi'l-ma'rūf wa an-nahy an il-munkar* [which is a pillar of the religion and which refers to the imperative to enjoin the doing of that which is right and to forbid the doing of that which is wrong]. Moreover, it is different from all of the other obligations which are imposed on the believers by Islam's dispensational order. *Jihād* is a religious imperative and duty (*farīda*) and a word [that represents this religious obligation] in counter-distinction from other words [which represent different duties]. This [too] is certain.

4. The 250-Year-Old Warrior

Thus, circumscribing such a wide compass to the word *jihād* in Islamic culture, i.e. in the culture of the Quran and the hadith report corpus, is a great mistake; a very great mistake. So this makes for one interpretation which is false.

10. A Second mistaken definition: *Jihād* defined as armed struggle

The second mistaken definition is the opposite position of the first mistake, and this is when we are told that the Quran and hadith report corpus define *jihād* as an armed struggle, or when one goes out to a field of battle with sword in hand and stands before an enemy, and when swords are drawn and there is a fight to the death. This interpretation is also mistaken. It is true that Shī'a sacred jurisprudence defines it and uses it in this limited sense – which definition and usage is problematic in our view – but irrespective of this, this is not the way the word is used in the Quran; and I have numerous examples from the Quran to demonstrate that the word is not used there in this limited and narrow sense, i.e. with reference to a specific enemy. That is not to say that the word does not also cover this narrow sense and usage. Certainly, that is *also* a Quranic usage of the word. It is the height and summit of *jihād*, but it does not fulfill the entirety of the way the word is used in the Quran. Rather, *jihād* takes on different shapes and forms, which is why this second interpretation is also mistaken.

I shall now refer to one of the examples of this wider usage for those who like to accept things based on evidence and proffered proofs. In the *sūra* of The Disavowal (*barā'a*) the seventy-third *āya* states:

يَا أَيُّهَا النَّبِيُّ جَاهِدِ الْكُفَّارَ وَالْمُنَافِقِينَ وَاغْلُظْ عَلَيْهِمْ ۚ وَمَأْوَاهُمْ جَهَنَّمُ ۖ وَبِئْسَ الْمَصِيرُ ﴿٧٣﴾

> [9:73] O Prophet ﷺ!! Strive hard (*jāhid*) against the deniers of the truth and the hypocrites, and be adamant with them. And [if they do not repent,] their goal shall be hell – and how vile a journey's end it is!

It is a certainty [on which there is scholarly consensus] in both Sunnite as well as Shīʿa sacred jurisprudence [and historiography] that the Prophet ﷺ never engaged in armed conflict against the hypocrites. Hence, his sacred struggle (*jihād*) took a different form. At the same time, this struggle is referred to in this Quranic verse as a "*jihād*". Therefore, [this narrow and limited usage is countermanded by this example and it is established that there is a wider Quranic usage for the word].[60]

11. The correct definition of *Jihād*: struggling against an Enemy

What seems to us to be the true interpretation of the word *jihād* is that it consists of a struggle against an enemy – whomsoever that enemy might be – in any of the various possible ways and means that are available [for engaging in this struggle]. To put it in other words which also incorporate the etymological meaning of "struggle", we can say that *jihād* consists of a struggle to move close to an objective which involves an engagement with an enemy. A struggle which does not entail engaging an enemy [in whatever form] cannot be called a *jihād*. If we were to choose a Persian equivalent in this narrow Quranic technical sense, it would be the word "*mobāreze*" (a fight), adding the proviso that the word "fight" should not be construed only in its physical form.

If someone slips under his covers and becomes all warm and cozy and then thinks to see what problem he can work on, and then recalls that the problem of whether the seven heavens are made of gold or silver or some other color has not been solved, and so he ponders on this "problem" and even gets out of bed to look up some facts in reference books, and actually succeeds in solving this problem; this is not referred to as *jihād*; this is not a "fight". Or suppose that a scientist researches an esoteric problem in chemistry or biology or physics or math that is not vital – or suppose that it is vital, even; something that will be useful to numerous people – and manages to solve the problem. This is not referred to as *jihād* either, just as it is not referred to in Persian as a *mobāreze* [or in English as a "fight"]. The Einsteins of the world and those who carry out the

---

[60] It seems there is a typographical error at this point in the text; but it is clear that this is what is meant.

4. The 250-Year-Old Warrior

highest levels of scientific research are not referred to as fighters or warriors (*mobārez*). Why? Because the act of research and discovery which is brought about by way of the mind or by the hands or by whatever other means, has been undertaken for the purposes of attaining to some intellectual or ideological objective and has not been accomplished for the purposes of fighting an enemy. Thus, this too is not referred to as *jihād* either, just as it is not referred to in Persian as a *mobāreze* [or in English as a "fight"].

[The work of] a benefactor who funds the construction of a school or a house or a hospital is not referred to as a *jihād*; it is an act of benevolence, but it is not a *jihād*. Why? Because there is no opposite number in the equation to act as an adversary and enemy and hindrance against the person or persons who are carrying out the task. It is of course a laudatory act, but it is not a *jihād*. Saying one's prayers is also a laudatory act, but it is not a *jihād*. Is that clear? I want the meaning of *jihād* to become perfectly clear so that when I say that the Imams ﷺ engaged in a *jihād* you will know exactly what I am talking about.

But then we can also have the case of a scholar who goes and researches a matter which involves engaging an enemy. Assume that an enemy tries to instill a certain ideology in the minds of people which advances his heinous self-interests. For example, the Marwānid Umayyad caliph Abdul-Malik instilled the ideology of predeterminism and predestinarians into the minds of his subjects in order the better to take advantage of them and to make them more submissive and complacent. What this means is that whatever God ﷻ wills will be realized without any interference on the part of His servants and creatures, and that these have no free will whatsoever to determine their future destinies. This ideology was first propagated [in the dominions of Islam] by Mu'āwiya b. Abī-Sufyān, and was later promulgated among the people by his worthy student, the Marwānid caliph Abdul-Malik. Their aim in doing this was to ensure that their subjects would be raised as predestinarians. In other words, so that they should compose verses such as these [which were composed by the great 14th century lyric and mystic poet Hāfez of Shīrāz]:

رضا به داده بده وز جبین گره بگشای

که بر من و تو در اختیار نگشادست

> Be content with your lot and don't be such a malcontent,
> For the door of free will has not been opened
> to the likes of you and me

Why do you fight against Abdul-Malik and cause trouble for the Umayyad governmental order? What is the point? Isn't it obvious that nothing will happen unless and until God ﷻ wills it? Nor will He change His mind on account of our efforts and struggles. It is God ﷻ who has appointed Abdul-Malik to the position of authority which he enjoys and made him who he is! It is God ﷻ who has decreed that you be his subject and carry the weight of the burdens he places on your shoulders!! These are the kinds of cathexes which they instilled in the people so that Abdul-Malik could sleep at ease in his kingly palaces.

Now the intellectual *jihād* under such circumstances would consist of a scholar picking up a pen and proving that this kind of thinking is fallacious. This is a form of authorship, as was that earlier one on the part of the research scientist, but this latter one is engaging in a *jihād* whereas the former is not. Why? Because the former did not involve a conflict with Abdul-Malik while the latter does.

12. Financial *Jihād*

Another example has to do with spending money. Many people spend money [on things which enrich the commonwealth such as] digging wells and waterways, building schools and mosques and hospitals, and so on. But we stated that no activity can be considered a *jihād* unless it also involves engagement with an adversary. But at the same time there are those whose munificence and spending *is* considered to be a *jihād*. For example, take the situation where Imam Sādiq ﷺ [is engaged in a *jihād* and] needs money. Or Zaid b. Ali wants to go to Kūfa and lead an insurrectionary movement and needs financial support and sponsorship. At this point a woman reaches into her headwear and pulls out a gold coin and gives it to him to spend [on his cause]. This is *jihād*. But the hundreds of thousands of gold coins which were given to feed the poor of the

4. The 250-Year-Old Warrior

caliphal capital Damascus and the poor of Madina were certainly generous benefactions, but they were not a *jihād*. These two acts should be made distinct so that they are not confused with each other.

13. The poetic *Jihād* of Kumayt

When Kumayt b. Zaid[61] composes an ode before Imam Sādiq ﷺ, he is engaging in a *jihād*. The poems of Da'bal[62] are a form of *jihād*. But the poems of many poets who composed poetry extolling the unicity of God ﷻ and praising the Prophet ﷺ are not *jihād* because Abdul-Malik had no problem with poetry that praised the prophet and extolled God's unicity because he claims to be the Prophet's successor. But when Kumayt b. Zaid composes an ode in praise of Imam Sajjād ﷺ, it is a form of *jihād* because its contents lampoon Hām b. Abdul-Malik and Abdul-Malik himself, the caliph of the day. In those same days, there were many poets who composed poetry in praise of the Prophet ﷺ, but it was not considered to be a form of *jihād* because the contents of the poems were politically neutral. And this is why the poetry of Kumayt b. Zaid and Da'bal Khazāī are *jihādi*, because they are politically motivated and politically engaged.

At that time, Imam Sādiq ﷺ gathered several thousand Dīnārs (gold coins) from various sources and gave them to Kumayt. So you can see how the difference is applied. Performing the ritual prayers can be a form of *jihād* in one context, and is not *jihād* in another; donating money and acting as a benefactor can be a form of *jihād* in one context, and is not *jihād* in another; and the same is true of composing poetry, writing a book or essay, and spending one's time on research and in thought. Even walking [to and from a place] can be a form of *jihād* in one context, and not be *jihād* in another.

---

[61] The 8th-century Shi'ite poet who was a contemporary and companion of Imams ﷺ Sajjād ﷺ and Bāqir ﷺ and Sādiq ﷺ and who was martyred at the behest of the caliph. He is buried in Kūfa in present day Iraq.
[62] The 9th-century Shi'ite poet who was a contemporary and companion of Imams ﷺ Kāzim ﷺ, Ridā ﷺ and Jawād ﷺ. He too was eventually martyred by the Abbāsids.

14. Armed *Jihād*

Of course, a very clear example of *jihād* is when it takes the form of armed conflict [in God's cause]. In other words, it is the kind of *jihād* which Imam Ali ﷺ and Imam Husain ﷺ engaged in, and the kind for which Imam Hasan ﷺ laid the preliminaries for [and was ready to engage in had he not been abandoned in his mustering of the army by the people of Madina, Kūfa, and elsewhere]. All armed conflicts [in God's cause] are considered to be *jihād*, but not all *jihād* consist of armed conflict.

15. The correct meaning of *Jihād*

Thus, if we are to compose a correct definition of *jihād*, we should say that the Islamic conception of *jihād* consists of a struggle against reactionary forces who are against human progress, transcendence and perfection, i.e. who are against Islam and the Quran in all of the various forms that this struggle can take. More importantly, there are various degrees of *jihād*, some of which are more noble and honorable and exalted, and have greater rewards [in God's eyes], and some are less so; but all of these forms of conflictual struggle are referred to as *jihād*.

16. All of the acts of the Imams ﷺ are a form of *Jihād*

So now that we have defined the meaning of *jihād* (which is neither the restricted meaning of armed conflict, nor is it the over-broad definition of all acts done in God's cause that we discussed first, but that *jihād* requires that there be a conflictual struggle in its purpose), then we can very easily accept the fact that the Imams ﷺ were all engaged in a struggle that was *jihādi*. There will no longer be any room for questions such as the one we mentioned as to when Imam Sādiq ﷺ unsheathed a sword, because we have now demonstrated that according to our definition it is not necessary to unsheathe a sword or to engage in armed combat in order to engage in *jihād*. Rather, it suffices Imam Sādiq ﷺ to sit and think and issue orders or set out a tenet or principle for his followers to obey or abide by. This suffices us to think of Imam Sādiq ﷺ as a warrior (*mujāhid*).

5. The Four Phases of the Imamate

[God ﷻ the All-Knowing and All-Wise has stated in His Sacred Writ:]

$$رَبَّنَا آتِنَا فِي الدُّنْيَا حَسَنَةً وَفِي الْآخِرَةِ حَسَنَةً وَقِنَا عَذَابَ النَّارِ ﴿٢٠١﴾$$

[2:201] O our Sustainer and Lord of Providence! Grant us good in this world and good in the life to come, and keep us safe from suffering through the fire.

$$رَبَّنَا لَا تُزِغْ قُلُوبَنَا بَعْدَ إِذْ هَدَيْتَنَا وَهَبْ لَنَا مِن لَّدُنكَ رَحْمَةً ۚ إِنَّكَ أَنتَ الْوَهَّابُ ﴿٨﴾$$

[3:8] O our Sustainer and Lord of Providence! Let not our hearts swerve from the truth after Thou hast guided us; and bestow upon us the gift of Thy grace: verily, Thou art the [true] Giver of Gifts.

$$رَبَّنَا لَا تُؤَاخِذْنَا إِن نَّسِينَا أَوْ أَخْطَأْنَا ۚ رَبَّنَا وَلَا تَحْمِلْ عَلَيْنَا إِصْرًا كَمَا حَمَلْتَهُ عَلَى الَّذِينَ مِن قَبْلِنَا ۚ رَبَّنَا وَلَا تُحَمِّلْنَا مَا لَا طَاقَةَ لَنَا بِهِ ۖ وَاعْفُ عَنَّا وَاغْفِرْ لَنَا وَارْحَمْنَا ۚ أَنتَ مَوْلَانَا فَانصُرْنَا عَلَى الْقَوْمِ الْكَافِرِينَ ﴿٢٨٦﴾$$

[2:286] "O our Sustainer and Lord of Providence! Take us not to task if we forget or unwittingly do wrong!" "O our Sustainer and Lord of Providence! Lay not upon us a burden such as Thou didst lay upon those who lived before us!" "O our Sustainer and Lord of Providence! Make us not bear burdens which we have no strength to bear! "And efface Thou our sins, and grant us forgiveness, and bestow Thy mercy upon us! Thou art our Lord Supreme: succor us, then, against people who deny the truth!"

O our Sustainer and Lord of Providence! Our Hearts are filled with hope in Your [grace]; grant us worthy servants of yours and those who harbor hope [of your grace], then, good in this world and good in the life to come, [and keep us safe from suffering through the fire].

O our Sustainer and Lord of Providence! [I beseech you] by [the right and station of spiritual proximity to You which] Muhammad ﷺ and his [Purified and Immaculate] Progeny ﷺ [has]: our hearts and minds have become alive as a result of knowledge of Your being; therefore, do not allow us to die in a state of ignorance and a state of turning away from Your truth.

O our Sustainer and Lord of Providence! Cover our bodies and souls with the power of patience and perseverance and forbearance (*sabr*) and endurance and fortitude in the path of the realization of all that which you have determined is best for human beings

وَلَيَنصُرَنَّ اللَّهَ مَن يَنصُرُهُ ۗ إِنَّ اللَّهَ لَقَوِيٌّ عَزِيزٌ ﴿٤٠﴾ الَّذِينَ إِن مَّكَّنَّاهُمْ فِي الْأَرْضِ أَقَامُوا الصَّلَاةَ وَآتَوُا الزَّكَاةَ وَأَمَرُوا بِالْمَعْرُوفِ وَنَهَوْا عَنِ الْمُنكَرِ ﴿٤١﴾

[22:40] ...And God ﷻ will most certainly succor him who succors His cause: for, verily, God ﷻ is most powerful, almighty, and [22:41] [well aware of] those who, [even] if We firmly establish them on earth, remain constant in prayer, and give in charity, and enjoin the doing of what is right and forbid the doing of what is wrong.

1. The four phases of the life of the 250-Year-Old person

After the reign of the Most Noble Prophet ﷺ over Madina (which lasted for ten years) came to an end after his passing, a new chapter opened in the life of Muslim society, and that new chapter was the imamate. The turn had now come for the society which this most worthy prophet of God ﷻ had established to gallop towards fulfilling the values and objectives which he had determined. But problems arose which either prevented or slowed the progress of society; problems which you have heard of and are more or less familiar with; and these were problems which arose as a result of the events which took place at the Saqīfa;[63] the issue of the political maneuverings of a group of people whose love of and commitment to Islamic values was less that the necessary threshold, [which led them to] conspire and make [secret] arrangements which resulted in what the Commander of the Faithful referred to 26 or 27 years later, addressing an aphorism to a member of the tribe of Banī Asad when he was returning from a war campaign:

[64].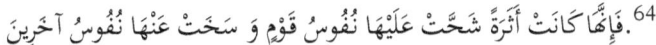

---

[63] The Saqīfa was a portico of the Banī Sā'ida where the Ansār (the clans of Yathrib/Medina who had entered into Islam and were its "Helpers") had gathered immediately upon the death of the Prophet ﷺ in order to determine who was to rule their city. It became the scene of the first manifestation of a carefully planned plot according to which six chieftains of Quraysh were to succeed, one after another, in taking the reins of leadership of the community after the Prophet ﷺ's passing. While Ali was seeing to the burial of the Prophet ﷺ and while his burial shroud was not yet completely dry, Omar pledged allegiance to Abū-Bakr, and the two of them together made most of the rest of the community fall in line, often by force of arms or the threat thereof. See Williams, Blake Archer, *Creedal Foundations of Walīyic Islam*, Chapter Seven.

[64] Part of the 162nd Sermon of the *Nahj al-Balāgha*. Here is the paragraph from which the excerpt was taken: "O brother of Banu Asad! Your girth is loose and you have put it on the wrong way. Nevertheless, you enjoy in-law kinship and also the right to ask, and since you have asked, listen. As regards the dominance over us in this office [of the leadership of the Islamic community] although we

"[... it was an act of appropriation by] some who became covetous for it, while others relinquished it through their generosity." The issue of the Saqīfa and the usurpation of [the office of] the succession (*khilāfa*) and the prevention of Ali for a quarter century from being able to administer the Islamic society at a critical juncture – to use the words of the Commander of the Faithful – has been expressed in two sentences. Firstly, it was a selfish act which strove to monopolize [that office] for [the] worldly self-interests [of the perpetrators]; a group eagerly reached for it, wanting [the authority of] the governance [of society] for themselves, and seized power in an unjust act of usurpation. And secondly, another group relinquished it through their generosity.

2. Imam Ali's Two Options after the Usurpation of the Caliphate

Imam Ali was faced with two issues. One of these was the usurpation of the right to the caliphate or to the rightful succession to the office of the leadership of society, which was a very great injustice. It was a great injustice to Imam Ali personally, but it was also a great injustice to Islamic society more generally, and to humanity at large. If a great man such as Imam Ali is prevented from occupying the office of leadership of a society based on a divinely sanctioned social order, a great injustice is committed against such a society, and not just to the person of Imam Ali, because failing this, society is precluded from being able to attain its [proper progress in its intended process of] self-transcendence and perfection. It is always the case, that the reigns of the wicked and undeserving commit grave injustices not only against the people of their own time, but against humanity as a whole. Every step that is taken either moves humanity in a forward direction towards its progress or prevents humanity's progress and prevents it from being able to soar. This is why the fact that Imam Ali was prevented from taking the reins of power in his hands by his rivals was an injustice committed against humanity at

---

were the loftiest in lineage and the strongest in relationship with the Messenger of God, it was an act of appropriation by some who became greedy for it, while others relinquished it through their generosity. The Arbiter is God and to Him is the Return on the Day of Judgement."

5. The Four Phases of the Imamate

large. And it is very difficult for a man such as Imam Ali ﷺ to countenance an injustice against anyone and against humanity at large, and to keep his peace and to do nothing. This is something that one cannot even imagine him doing, knowing how he fought against injustice so valiantly all his life. This is one side of the coin.

On the other side, there is something which Imam Ali ﷺ is for, and for which the Prophet ﷺ was commissioned from on high, and which is the engine that drives humanity to its intended self-transcendence and perfection, and that is Islam and the Quran. Imam Ali ﷺ saw that a conniving politically motivated minority had taken control of a decisive majority of the populace of the Islamic community. This minority had seized their way of thinking and had diverted it from the direction which it should have been going. Imam Ali ﷺ further saw that if he were to rise up in righteous insurrection against those who have usurped his right under such conditions, a civil war and fratricide would ensue, and the enemies to the death of Islam – the Abū-Sufyans and his ilk who ruled Mecca before the triumph of Islam and who were live coals under the ashes of those battles – would take advantage of this civil war and welcome this opportunity to destroy Islam forever.

And so, Imam Ali ﷺ was at a fork in the road. One tine of the fork is to temporarily tolerate the injustice which has been committed against him and against society and humanity at large and be prepared for [the possibility or eventuality that] the people will not be one hundred percent Muslim, although they will be 90% or 80% Muslim – or whatever percentage which you can determine for yourselves. And another tine in the fork is for Imam Ali ﷺ to prepare himself for [the possibility that] Islam will be destroyed; that the Quran will be lost; and that the nascent Islamic social order will be obliterated. [Faced with such a choice], Imam Ali ﷺ would never consent to this second option. This is why Imam Ali ﷺ chose to remain silent for 25 years. He chose to accept the lesser and more expedient of two evils; for between two important matters, one must always decide upon the one which is more important. If the choice is between a condition where one option results in 100% against, and the other results in 50% against, then in this second option there is still room for 50% to be in favor. Thus, while Imam Ali ﷺ cannot countenance a reversal into a situation of 100% unbelief and infidelity to Islam, he *can* [and must] tolerate a damaged and incomplete Islam. So, he kept his peace for 25 years.

Of course, some ignorant people who profess to be the friends and supporters of Imam Ali ﷺ make untoward accusations against him at this juncture, which he does not deserve in the least, including the accusation that he chose to seclude himself in his home [and sit out the political battle] for 25 years; whereas this was not at all the case, and Imam Ali ﷺ did not sit anything out, even for a single day. It is those people whose own lives are ones which are nothing but political self-exclusion and appeasement who characterize Imam Ali's ﷺ reticence and quietude as one of self-exclusion and political appeasement, whereas it was not at all like this. We have said this on repeated occasions. At the time when [things had already started to unravel and fall apart with the death of Uthmān, [and where] the people had gathered around Imam Ali ﷺ, [asking him to become their leader, so that perhaps they could salvage what was left of the community], Ali ﷺ told them that just as he acted as a consultant to the rulers during those 25 years, that he preferred to remain in the same capacity as the second in command [given the conditions that the people had brought about, and given the fickle support that he was expecting to receive against the civil war which was brewing which was centered in Damascus with Muʿāwiya at its head]. Thus, Imam Ali ﷺ was the second in command during those 25 years. He was consulted on every important issue, and all-important decisions were taken after having consulted him, including decisions having to do with waging war and peace. Imam Ali ﷺ was a prominent member of society with an important voice, and such a member does not have the right to seclude himself from society's affairs. What do these people mean, anyway, when they say that Imam Ali ﷺ chose to seclude himself? Does it mean that he stayed at home and did nothing but come to the mosque for the congregational prayers, and then went back home to mind his own business? Is *that* really how it was? No; that does not describe Imam Ali's ﷺ life [during those years]; he did not seclude himself. He was only excluded from the highest office of society. At the same time, of course, he had specific enemies who were intent on marginalizing and isolating him from society altogether. But Imam Ali ﷺ did not tolerate [the desires of] these enemies; he was on the stage of society [and engaged in its concerns].

3. The first phase: 25 Years of expedientiary cooperation

Twenty-five years passed and Imam Ali ﷺ did not fight or resist (*mobāreze nakard*) the ruling powers of his day. This was the only time during the 250-year history of the imamate where we see that an Imam did not fight or resist [the ruling powers] in a way other [than engaging in physical battle]. He promulgated [the religion], talked about [the preeminence of] his own merits [and right for investiture in the office of the leadership of society] and that it was he who was deserving of this office [and not anyone else]; but he did not engage in a clash or conflict [with the ruling power]. This is one point. Of course, the closer we get to the end of this period and to the caliphate of Uthmān, Imam Ali's ﷺ posture gradually changes. But that having been said, I [still] do not see the form of resistance having taken shape in Imam Ali's ﷺ political posture which I see in that of Imam Sādiq ﷺ or Imam Kāẓim ﷺ. These 25 years comprise the first phase of the life of the Imams; that is, the 25 years from the beginning of the Imamate of Imam Ali ﷺ, where he does not engage in a *jihād* – I am using the word as I defined it earlier – with the enemy who holds the reins of power in hand.

Twenty-five years have come and gone, and the people have put up with the pressures of the oppressive aristocratic [nepotism] of Uthmān's reign, and they thirst for the divinely inspired governmental order of the Prophet ﷺ. Everywhere throughout the Islamic lands, from Egypt to the 'Irāq and the Hijāz itself (i.e. in Mecca and Madina), and in the territories which were under the suzerainty of the Persian empire and which are now under Islamic control, the large provinces of the Islamic dominion, the people thirsted for justice and looked to Imam Ali ﷺ to take to the helm of the ship of state in order to bring about justice through the divinely sanctioned social order. The people gathered outside Imam Ali's ﷺ house and asked him from the bottom of their hearts to take to the helm – a deep desire which had been resisted for many years. It was a passion which existed in the hearts of the people and which the ruling powers had unsuccessfully attempted to extinguish.

This is always the way it is with deep desires. Earlier I had quoted the late Āl-e Yā-Sīn that "The character of brute force and tyranny – which is a veritable tradition – has been thus from the genesis of creation, that every time pressure is brought to bear on an intellectual issue or on an intellectual current, such pressure will cause the issue or current to grow. This is a natural phenomenon." [All] material and superficial powers have unintentionally fostered the growth of whatever need and [genuine and rightful] desire and [righteous concept or] intellectual position which they have tried to suppress. This is one of the attributes of oppressive and coercive powers: that they foster and strengthen their enemies.

The Commander of the Faithful was now confronted with the gathering of a large crowd of the Muslims [of Madina] in a situation which he described in the following terms: "Nay, by Him who has split the seed and created the soul, were it not for the presence of those who are [yet] present and the establishment of the arguments [against my withdrawing from the burden of governance] by the existence of the helpers..."[65] In other words, [Imam Ali ؑ is saying that] "If I had demurred from rising up and demanding my right and if until now I did not enter into a struggle to take the reins of power in hand, it was because I could not be sure that I had a sufficient amount of backing of the people behind me to preclude the possibility of civil war and the consequent probable destruction of the Islamic community. But on that day, that is, on the day after the death of Uthmān, I saw that it is a goodly crowd and that the people are [now at long last] desirous of having me lead them; and so this is why I [ultimately chose to] take the reins of governance in hand." [Here is the relevant paragraph from the Third Sermon (known as the Shaqshaqīa Sermon) of the *Nahj al-Balāgha*]:

{"In the end, the third of them [Uthmān] stood up shrugging his shoulders arrogantly. And there stood with him the sons of his father, eating up the property of God ؒ as the camels eat up the springtide verdure, until what he had twisted became untwisted. His destruction was

---

[65] The whole paragraph of the Third Sermon is presented below in order to provide the gentle reader with the context of the quote.

complete, and his greediness made him fall to the ground. Then all of a sudden, I was frightened to see a crowd of people around me, thick as the hyena's mane, thronging towards me from every direction until [my sons] al-Hasan ﷺ and al-Husain ﷺ were mobbed and my two sides were split, gathering around me like a herd of goats. But when I took up the [reins of] government, one group broke its pledge, another rebelled, and some others transgressed, as if they had not heard the words of God ﷻ, who says: [28:83] *As for that [happy] life in the hereafter, We grant it [only] to those who do not seek to exalt themselves on earth or to spread corruption in it: for the future belongs to those who are [ever] wary [lest their actions provoke] God's [wrath].* Nay, by God ﷻ, they have heard these words and comprehend them, but the world is sweet in their eyes and they are pleased by its gaudiness. Nay, by Him who has split the seed and created the soul, were it not for the presence of those who are [yet] present and the establishment of the arguments [against my withdrawing from the burden of governance] by the existence of the helpers, as also [for] the fact that it is not pleasing to God ﷻ for those who know better [to stand] idly by and to watch the fullness [of the oppression] of the oppressor and the hunger of the oppressed, I would have thrown back its [the caliphate's] rope on its shoulder and made its last [incumbent] drink from the cup of the first one, and you would have found that your world is as distasteful to me as the dripping from the nose of a goat."}

4. The second phase: The phase of the establishment of Islamic governance

The second phase of the life of the Imams ﷺ started [with the start of Imam Ali's ﷺ caliphate whereat the people of Madina and Egypt and Kūfa and other parts of the Islamic world pledged their allegiance to him]. This was the second of the four phases of the imamate, which is the phase where Imam Ali's ﷺ right is returned to him and the phase wherein the divinely sanctioned social order or the social order that is truly Islamic is restored. And Ali's governmental order was, of course, a revolutionary one, like that of the Prophet's. The gentlemen here present who are familiar with the words which have some currency in the new culture understand what I am saying. We do not have the opportunity to define what we mean by the word 'revolutionary', or what the attributes and functions of a 'revolutionary' government are, and what the criteria are of determining whether or not a government is or is not revolutionary. These are discussions which are necessary, but which are not presently a part of our presentation.[66]

As we just stated, Ali's governmental order was a revolutionary one; a governmental order which brings about fundamental changes in its target society. The society governed by Uthmān and that governed by Imam Ali ؑ are so different that they defy comparison [on fundamentals]; one cannot say of the latter that it is a reformed version of the former. No; it has gone through a basic and fundamental transformation, [and has upset the vested interests of the *status quo ante*] which is therefore why it also has enemies.

Who are its enemies? Everyone whose [interests] are upended by the revolution and who have been damaged by it. In other words, the reactionary elements of society: the powerful interests who strove to hold on to the reins of power, and the moneyed and aristocratic classes who had become accustomed to feed off the teat of the state like leeches and vultures whose interests were secured under the aegis of the previous caliphs at the expense of the prejudicial treatment of others; those people who had an aura of sanctity under the aegis of the *ancient regime* even though they did not do any work, but for whom this new order had no respect or value whatsoever. The likes of Rabī' b. Khusaym and the companions of Abdullāh b. Mas'ūd, Abdullāh b. Umar and the like – people who are the sons and progeny of the notables of society who have both witnessed the Prophet ﷺ personally and have narrated hadith reports about him; and in the case of the latter, one who is also the son of the second caliph. A great deal of value is placed upon these things in the Uthmānid court, whereas no value is placed upon them in Ali's. These included 'Amr b. 'Ās and his ilk who tried to get as much benefit for themselves as possible by expending the least possible effort; and the mullahs and [court-allied] doctors of religion who used the ignorance of the powers that be and doled out religion to the people like it was an

---

[66] Cf. Chapter Two of the present book.

5. The Four Phases of the Imamate

[artificial] product, for which task they were richly rewarded by the caliphs in bygone times. When these so-called scholars are confronted with the infinite knowledge and wisdom of Imam Ali ﷺ, they naturally realize they cannot maintain their former positions and hence became his enemies [in the hope of returning society to the *status quo ante*]. There are many examples of these types, such as the likes of Ka'b al-Ahbār, Abū-Hurayra, Mu'āwiya, 'Amr b. 'Ās, and their retinues, as well as many other kinds of groups. Thus, a revolutionary governmental order will have many problems to contend with. These enemies made numerous problems for it and agitated against it with their propaganda and even drew swords against it. Why? Because of the crime that it is a revolutionary order [which has deprived them of their ability to sustain their injustices]. They made fun of it and set up straw men for it in an attempt to distort its true character. These are the kinds of issues which a revolutionary order such as that of Imam Ali's ﷺ was faced with.

Imam Ali ﷺ brought these five years [of his reign] to a close,[67] and there is much to say about the historical details of these five years. Imam Ali ﷺ was succeeded by [his son] Imam Hasan, who also spent six months amid these intense problems and in the eye of a storm, after six months of which he came to a realization. Recall that at the beginning of his reign, Imam Ali ﷺ had said that, "Were it not for the presence of those who are [yet] present and the establishment of the arguments [against my withdrawing from the burden of governance] by the existence of the helpers, as also [for] the fact that it is not pleasing to God ﷻ for those who know better [to stand] idly by and to watch the fullness [of the oppression] of the oppressor and the hunger of the oppressed, I would have thrown back its [the caliphate's] rope on its shoulder and made its last [incumbent] drink from the cup of the first one." Imam Hasan ﷺ realized that he did not even have "the presence of those who are [yet] present and the establishment of the arguments [against {his} withdrawing from the burden of governance] by the existence of the helpers" – that he did not have "helpers" present in a sufficient number

---

[67] Or rather, it was brought to a close for him by Abd al-Rahmān Ibn Muljim, the Khārijite who martyred the Imam while he was praying the *fajr* or dawn ritual devotions in the congregational mosque at Kūfa.

[to ebb the tide of the civil war that had raised its head in the Levant and its capital Damascus and was heading south to Madina]. Imam Hasan's story is simply summed up in the foregoing, and that's it. He found himself in a very tight spot; a dire strait from which no human being can come out of unharmed, but which Imam Hasan ﷺ was able to pass through unharmed.

5. The third phase: The phase of the preparation of a covert organization for bringing about insurrection

The explanation of the peace [which Imam Hasan ﷺ waged with Mu'āwiya] is highly detailed as well and is outside the bounds of our present discussion.[68] When Imam Hasan ﷺ saw himself situated in the dire straits which he was in, he took a bold and innovative step; and it was this step which became the beginning of the third phase of the Imamate or the phase of resistance. What was the nature of this innovation? It was an innovation which, [upon seeing that the forces of illegitimate governance (*tāghūt*)[69] had gained the upper hand], moved the battle between the forces of righteousness and those forces, i.e. the battle between the Quran and the forces of Abū-Sufyān, and of Ali and Mu'āwiya, *sub rosa*. Up until this point, all of the battles of this war were fought in the open and in the conventional style of imprecating each other and drawing swords on each other and fighting to the death. But [seeing that things could not continue in that vein in his favor,] Imam Hasan ﷺ changed the calculus of the war in his favor [from one that was a conventional war to an asymmetrical war fought underground]. In other words, he drew a cloak over the faces of those among the population who were his true supporters. Do not get me wrong: this did not mean that he disarmed them of their swords or changed their minds and resolve; rather, what he did was to change the field of battle. He prevailed upon them to

---

[68] See http://en.wikishia.net/view/Peace_Treaty_of_Imam_al-Hasan_(a); Abidy Qurrat al Ain, *Imam Hasan and Caliphate*, Ansarian Publications available from https://www.al-islam.org/imam-hasan-and-caliphate-qurrat-ul-ain-abidiy/terms-peace-treaty; and Ayati, Ibrahim, *A probe into the history of Ashura*, Islamic Seminary Publications available from https://www.al-islam.org/probe-history-ashura-dr-ibrahim-ayati/chapter-8-peace-treaty-imam-hasan.
[69] See footnote #25

5. The Four Phases of the Imamate

understand that it was not possible to go up against Muʿāwiya in the conventional field of battle [and triumph over him]; and that the strategy that was to be adopted, therefore, was to go underground [to be able to wage a successful asymmetrical war against him and his forces]. This was the instruction which his noble father, the Commander of the Faithful, had given to him and to his select and faithful and trustworthy boon companions several years earlier.

Up until very recently I was under the impression that the innovation of turning Shīʿa Islam into an underground movement of organized partisans [during the Imamate of Imam Hasan ﷺ] was an innovation that was due to Imam Hasan ﷺ himself; and I had my reasons and historical evidence for this belief, based on the book *al-Fitnaᵗ al-Kubrā* (*The Great Sedition*) by the great Egyptian writer Shaykh Radī Āl al-Yā-Sīn. However, just recently, during these few days of the month of Muharram in which I have been coming here to deliver these talks, I suddenly realized that this [act] was undertaken in obedience to instructions given him by Imam Ali ﷺ. Ali ﷺ ordered his close companions and the good people [= leaders] who were gathered around him in a single solitary sentence which was laden with meaning and portent, that, after his passing, and when the forces of the *tāghūt*[70] gain mastery over you, you must act in such and such a way. You must adopt stealth as a tactic of your resistance; you must resort to the use of precautionary dissimulation (*taqīya*) (to use the words used by the Commander of the Faithful and the Imams ﷺ of his progeny who followed in his wake). I will discuss the issue of precautionary dissimulation in detail towards the end of my talks, so that you will know exactly what its nature is; because the greatest distortions have taken place concerning this word [and tenet of Shīʿa Islam].

So this is what Imam Hasan ﷺ did: he changed the field of battle and sharpened the swords of the forces of resistance and filled the hearts of its warriors with enmity and rancor against the forces of reaction and the anti-revolutionaries, i.e. against Muʾāwiya; and not necessarily with the person or individual known as Muʿāwiya, but with Muʿāwiya's Way;

---

[70] See footnote #25 on page 42.

and not against the Levant [and its capital, Damascus, which is where Muʿāwiya had his self-declared caliphal capital], but with anywhere where Almighty God ﷻ was not worshipped; and not with overt and patent [instances of] *shirk*,[71] but with covert instances of it; i.e. that poison which is ostensibly alluring and sweet and tasty which is placed in one's throat – the struggle against this.

Certain notables went to Imam Hasan ﷺ in Madina and suggested to him that "O son of the Prophet ﷺ, come to Kūfa where we will depose and kill its [Muʿāwiya-appointed] governor or run him out of town, so that you can enter the town and take over its governance". When this occurred, Imam Hasan ﷺ, who had firsthand experience of the adage that "A true believer does not tread the same [mistaken] road twice", and who saw that the path was dangerous and would not end well, responded negatively to the delegation. He told them that they should not appear in the field of such battles and that they should come back to themselves, first to work on themselves, and then to work on increasing their ranks. To strengthen themselves by donning a robe made of the true teachings of Islam and armor made of the Quran, and then go to [the field of the

---

[71] *Shirk*: 1. assigning partners alongside or as co-equals to God ﷻ; idolatry; polytheism; 2. paying obeisance to anything other than God ﷻ; 3. fidelity (*tawḥīd*) and Infidelity (*shirk*) to the Exclusivity of God's Providential Lordship in the Social Order; 4. Believing that there are other factors that have any affect or impact on one's fate other than one's actions or the actions of other elements which God's will allows for various reasons to have a part in one's individual and collective providence. Ayatollah Khāmeneī juxtaposes *shirk* against the primary creedal tenet of Islam which is *tawḥīd*: "*Shirk* is the act of assigning someone or something alongside God ﷻ or in His stead as the voice of one's conscience and acting on their instructions [in lieu of living within the guidelines of the divine dispensation] and obeying them and being devoted to them [rather than to God ﷻ and to His Way]; it is the act of submitting to and handing over the reins of the control of the trajectory of one's own life to anyone or anything other than God ﷻ. And *tawḥīd* is the exact opposite of *shirk*. It is the negation of all of those idols and objects of worship and resisting the lure and draw of their power and not submitting or surrendering to them. It is the act of severing any desire for obeying them or seeking their help; and, finally, of self-surrendering oneself with all one's being to God's will and focusing one's will exclusively on the struggle to exclude and banish the will of anything or anyone other than God's from one's life and from the life of one's community."

5. The Four Phases of the Imamate

asymmetrical] battle and fight against the enemies of the Quran. But strike him before you appear before him, [he said,] and before he is aware of your presence.[72] Imam Hasan's followers (*shī'a*) paid heed and understood; and that is what is interesting in that the Shī'a of those days understood what Imam Hasan ﷺ was asking of them, whereas the Shī'a of today fail to understand [his and Imam Ali's ﷺ strategy], and are still unable to interpret his words. This is where the *jihād* of the Imams ﷺ started; this was the beginning of the Third Phase, which I will describe briefly.

This phase started in the 41st year of the Islamic calendar; that is, from the time of Imam Hasan's Peace. After Imam Hasan ﷺ issued the order to his followers, organized cells (*tashkīlāt*) began to be formed in Kūfa, which was one of the centers of Shī'a Islam, in Madina, which was another Shī'a center, and in the various towns and villages and hamlets surrounding these cities and throughout the various territories of Islam in which these two centers had branches. Of course I need to clarify that when I say organized Shī'a cells (*tashkīlāt-e shī'a*) and Shī'a parties (*hezb*), one should not immediately think of well-equipped organized cells and party branch offices and headquarters, like we have now in the 20th century, with a central committee and a rank and file operating underneath them [in a formal hierarchical fashion]. There is no call to jump to such conclusions. Rather, what we mean by this is that there was a specific leader at the head of the organization who was the Imam; a group of select [followers] who understood the Imam's words well and acted on them; and a larger group which comprised the mass of the Shī'a who listened to and obeyed the instructions of their Imam. As far as the select were concerned, there was no need for there to be a letter of instruction issued by the Imam at every juncture concerning the details of their activities. It was not like that; rather, the select followers having comprehended the general direction and objectives and guidelines and marching orders, knew how to act accordingly. This was how Imam Hasan ﷺ was able to build up his Shī'a base during the remaining nine years of his life.

---

[72] This was the Persian way of the early 1970's of describing asymmetrical warfare – a concept for which no word existed in Persian at the time.

Again, it is not necessary for it to be written in the annals of history that the Shīʿa reconstituted itself; because it had nothing [to begin with]. I am a little concerned about getting bogged down in introductory matters – even though some of these matters are necessary – otherwise I would explain why this matter that I am stating has not been stated explicitly in books of the history of the period. Because this matter should have been stated as clearly as I have presented it in the history books; so why wasn't it? There is a mystery to it; there is a reason as to why it has not been stated so explicitly in history books. That is because it is a covert [organization and party apparatus that we are speaking about]; so what is there to write about?

Would it make any sense for Muhammad Taqi Lisān al-Mulk Sepehr, who was a court allied historian, to write in his *Nāsikh al-Tawārīkh* history that during the time of Nāsir al-Dīn Shāh there existed a covert organization. Or, for example, Riḍā Qulī Khān Hidāyat, who wrote another [history] – I'm thinking of the *Tatamme-ye Rowzat os-Safā* – that in his *History* it should be written and recorded that Yes, an underground party was engaged in covert activities against His Royal Highness Nāsir ad-Dīn Shāh, and their leader was such and such, and they did the following things, and so on. Is such a thing even possible? It would make no sense [on account of the innate secrecy of the subject matter]. Because there could be no access to determine the nature of the organization [by virtue and definition of its secrecy]. And besides, even if they *did* have access to such secrets and they *did* write such histories, then they would no longer be [known as the great historians] Muhammad Taqi Lisān al-Mulk Sepehr and Riḍā Qulī Khān Hidāyat, because the "Khān" title and the such and such "al-Mulk" title were on account of the fact that they were court allied and court approved historians whose job it was to hide such things and cover them up. This is the case for the majority of the historians of Islam, with little exception. The historian would sit next to the ruler and write for his pleasure and in his interests. So how could such historians write matters having to do with the Shīʿa with the clarity and vividness which I read today as it has reached us in the Shīʿa hadith report corpus, and which I am able to glean in the nooks and crannies of lost histories? It [= such an expectation] would make no sense.

5. The Four Phases of the Imamate

Verily, Imam Hasan ﷺ was the one who started the whole [covert network] movement, and he initiated it in an interesting way, and started building the people [who comprised the Shī'a support base]; the same people who were not able to resist the pressure of being in the front line on the side of Imam Hasan ﷺ against Mu'āwiya, and were not able to muster a sizable army which could be relied on to go to war against Mu'āwiya's forces. These same people had gone through such a transformation that ten or twelve years later, each and every one of them stood up against Mu'āwiya in the Hujr b. Adī affair[73]. Hujr was not a single person and did not rise up in insurrection on his own and was not

---

[73] Hujr bin 'Adi al-Kindi was known as Hujr al-Khayr. His Kunya was Abu 'Abd al Rahman b. 'Adi b. al-Harth b. 'Amr b. Hujr. He was given the nickname (i.e., *laqab*) of Akil al-Mirar. He was the king of the Kindis. It was said that he was the son of 'Adi b. Mu'awiya b. Jubla b. 'Adi b. Rabi'a b. Mu'awiya al-Akramin. Hujr was a notable companion from the Companions of 'Ali and his son al-Hasan, peace be on them. He was a lord from the lords of the Muslims in Kufa.

Hujr and his brother Hani' b. 'Adi came to the Prophet ﷺ, may Allah bless him and his family. In his book 'al-Isti'ab', b. 'Abd al-Bir al Maliki said: "Hujr was among the excellent Companions, and his age was less than their old ones." In his book *Usd al-Ghāba fi Tamyiz al-Sahāba*, Ibn al-Athīr has mentioned him with words similar to these ones. In his book 'al-Mustadrak', al-Hakim has described him as: "the monk of the Companions of Muhammad, may Allah bless him and his family." Hujr worshipped (Allah) to the extent that when he made ritual impurity, he performed the ritual ablution; when he performed the ritual ablution, he prayed. He performed one thousand rak'as a day. His religious piety was apparent, and his supplication was accepted.5 He was among the chosen reliable figures. He preferred the hereafter to the life in this world to the extent that he subjected his life to killing, refusing to renounce his Imam. He had a high social position. Hujr was in the army that conquered Sham (The Levant), and in the army that conquered Qadisiya (a city in Iraq). He took part in the Battle of the Camel headed by 'Ali. He was the commander of Kinda at the Battle of Siffīn, and the commander of the left wing of the army at the Battle of al-Nahrwān. He was the brave man who defeated al-Ḍahhāk b. Qays in the western part of Tadmur. It was he who said: "We are the children of war and appropriate for it. We start it and end it. We have known it (i.e., war) and it has known us." Mu'āwiya b. Abu Sufyan killed Hujr and six of his companions at Marj 'Athra twelve miles away from Damascus in the year 51 A.H. Up till now, Hujr's grave is apparent and famous. There is a firm dome on it. old marks can be seen on the dome that is beside a wide mosque. Hujr's companions who were killed with him are in his shrine. We will mention them one by one. Ziyad b. Abīh demolished Hujr's house in Kufa. (See al-Islam.org for the rest of the article.)

abandoned to die the lonely death of a martyr. Rather, there were a number of people who fought in the mountain valleys and summits and caves and on the highways and in their dungeons and were martyred at the hands of Mu'āwiya's henchmen, such as Rushīd Hajrī and 'Amr b. al-Hamaq and his wife, and many others. These are all the products of the intellectual and spiritual training camps of Imam Hasan ﷺ. Who was the last of these? Do you know his name? The last person whom Imam Hasan ﷺ shot out and who exploded like an artillery shell which he flung at the chest of the enemy; do you know who that was? The last person is his brother [Imam] Husain ﷺ b. Ali, the hero of Karbalā.[74]

Shaykh Āl-e Yā-Sīn or Sayyid Sharaf al-Dīn states in the introduction to the book [*Sulh al-Hasan* (Hasan's Peace)] that Imam Hasan ﷺ would instruct each and every one of his followers individually like a lieutenant who calls each of his soldiers to his presence and instructs them on their individual duties and responsibilities. Imam Hasan ﷺ would do the same using the language of the Quran and the language of history. Eventually he pointed to Imam Husain ﷺ and said, "Your responsibility is the heaviest burden of all, and it is up to you to carry out the big job," which Imam Husain ﷺ did indeed carry out. This is where the first hero of Karbalā, according to the opinions of both Shaykh Āl-e Yā-Sīn and Sayyid Sharaf od-Dīn, is Imam Hasan, and the second hero is Imam Husain ﷺ, for it was Imam Hasan ﷺ who laid the groundwork and set the scene for Karbalā.

I do not have the time [to elaborate], but my thought is that if I am to deliver a talk on the night of Tāsūā and on the night of Āshūrā, that I will talk about the situation of Imam Husain's uprising and what his motivation was for doing what he did.[75] Of course, I have repeated this before, and it is not something new which I am saying in Tehran; rather, I talked about this very topic two or three years earlier, where some of you gentlemen were also present. There is something on my mind which I mentioned at that time, and that is that if it was clear to you why Imam Husain ﷺ rose up in righteous insurrection, you would also understand why Imam Hasan ﷺ made his peace with Mu'āwiya, and what he did with

---

[74] See footnote #30 on page 38.
[75] See Chapter Four of this book.

5. The Four Phases of the Imamate

[the opportunity afforded by] the peace. Imam Husain ﷺ rose up in righteous insurrection in order to revivify [the teachings and values of] the Quran and in order to bring to fruition a matter which was religiously mandated and obligatory which it was not possible for the Prophet ﷺ to accomplish; and his uprising was able to accomplish that categorical obligation (whose explanation would require a lot of time, which we do not have). It is through this [act of Imam Husain's] which we realize for what act Imam Hasan ﷺ trained his followers and adherents, including Imam Husain ﷺ, who was a follower of Imam Hasan ﷺ (recall that Imam Hasan ﷺ was the Imam to whom Imam Husain ﷺ deferred). Thus ended the third phase of the Imamate. What did it end with? With the Event of Āshūrā.[76]

6. The fourth phase: The phase of organized resistance against the ruling authorities, and the expansion of true Islam

After the Event of Āshūrā occurred, the Umayyad rulers were at first very happy and even drunk with the thought that they had at last uprooted their problem. They spread the word everywhere that the enemies of the government and of Yazīd had been routed; and this was their own belief as well. For it was very clear [to them]: the best and brightest of the Quran reciters [those who knew the Quran by heart and could explain the context and meaning of its verses] from the Hijāz, Iraq, from greater Persia, from Yemen and the Levant and other Islamic provinces had been distilled down to 72 people, who had been massacred in half a day [at the Battle of Karbala, on Āshūrā, or the 10th of Muharram in the year 61 AH (October 10, 680 CE)]. So the matter was finished; the whole problem was uprooted.

Until now, Mu'āwiya would tell Ibn Abbās, the Prophet's and Imam Ali's ﷺ cousin, to "Recite the Quran, but do not explain its meaning". He would tell him that he could recite the Quran but that he was not allowed to interpret its meaning. This was because the practice of Quranic recitation is something that existed, so that its interpretation could exist also. My guess is that Mu'āwiya stood on ceremony with Ibn

---

[76] See footnote #30

Abbās, for the latter was not anyone whom the likes of Mu'āwiya would need to be concerned about. If Mu'āwiya knew Ibn Abbās at all, there was no reason for him to fear him, as he posed no threat and was an ordinary citizen like everyone else. I have much to say concerning Ibn Abbās: I have no respect for him; not even a little. Ibn Abbās is the grandfather of al-Manṣūr, whose progeny ruled over the Islamic world for over 500 years as the Abbāsid dynasty. The same Abbāsid dynasty who stole and squandered the money of the public treasury, who insulted [the memory of] Imam Ali 🌹 and rebelled against him; the same dynasty who is named after Ibn Abbās' father Abbās. This is the lineage of Ibn Abbās; therefore, there is nothing there for Mu'āwiya to fear; rather, it was Imam Husain 🌹 whom he feared. So now there was no longer any Husain 🌹 [left to fear]. Or any Abu'l-Faḍl, or any of the other men of the Banī-Hāshim [House; the House of the Prophet 🌹]. All those best young men who were better than a thousand wise sages, and who were nobler than them and closer to God 🌹 than them. All these were massacred on the plain of Karbalā. Men such as Habīb b. Mazāhir and Muslim b. 'Uwsaja and other great men who had turned Kūfa into a base of resistance against the enemies [of Islam] were no longer alive [to cause Yazīd and the Umayyads any trouble]. Yazīd's youth and ignorance also played a role in his feeling of jubilation; for if Mu'āwiya himself was still around, he would probably still harbor some fear. But Yazīd was drunk; drunk on youth and power and wine and did not understand. For how can one who is inebriated have any understanding?

They believed that they had uprooted the problem which the institutions of prophethood and of the Imamate and Shī'a Islam posed for them, and that there was no longer anyone else who could pose them any [serious] problems. The likes of Hujr b. 'Adī had been killed off previously, and the rest had been massacred at Karbalā, so that no one else remained. This is what they believed; but suddenly they saw that they were mistaken. Firstly, because there were people such as Lady Zaynab[77] from among the progeny of the Prophet 🌹 who transformed Kūfa on one

---

[77] Her Eminence Lady Zaynab: the august sister of Imam Husain 🌹, who survived the massacre of the Plain of Karbalā and lived to tell the tale and spread the word, which she did with courage and eloquence.

5. The Four Phases of the Imamate

occasion, and the foul and corrupt court of Yazīd in Damascus on another. And among those who survived the massacre was Imam Husain's son, Ali [Imam Sajjād ﷺ], who goes to the pulpit in Damascus and tells the truth about the events, asserts his own right [to the office of the leadership of the community], reminding the people of the virtues of Islam. He does this in the center of Yazīd's power before the people of the Levant who have lived under the yoke of Umayyad tyranny for forty years and know nothing of the meaning of true Islam, using the same pulpit which Yazīd had used to deceitfully declare his succession to the Prophet ﷺ.

When Yazīd saw these words emanating from a youth who was utterly alone and laboring under the burden of the loss of his father and whole family, he realized that his jubilation was premature, and that the House of the Prophet ﷺ and the followers of Ali were alive and well. If you read the *Luhūf*[78] (Sighs of Sorrow) of Ibn Tāwūs [on the subject], you will see that it was not only Lady Zeynab who delivered a powerful oratory, but that there were several other women who also did the same, including Umm Kulthūm, Sakīna, and Fātima ﷺ (Imam Husain's daughters), all of whose oratories have been recorded by Ibn Tāwūs in his *Lohūf*. These were the kinds of women which comprised the House of the Prophet ﷺ. They were the kinds of women who engendered real men. [And so, when Yazīd saw these], he realized that these are the kinds of women who will give birth and raise men whom they will send [to avenge the murder of the Master of their House] and that these men will be the end of him. But what could he do about it? Could he arrange for another Karbalā to deal with them? No; the time for that too had passed. My belief is that if Yazīd knew what kind of trouble these womenfolk of the Prophet's House were capable of causing him, that he would have ordered 'Amr b. Sa'd and Shimr to kill off the womenfolk at the same time and make a clean break of it. But it is not God's Way that executioners and those who are God's enemies understand things well; there are certain things which they do not understand. God's Way is for that which is good and true and just (*haqq*) to prevail and be sustained. I have said this before,

---

[78] *Luhūf* is a book by Sayyid Ibn Tāwūs, a Shia jurist, theologian, and historian. It is a kind of Maqtal al-Husain narrating the Battle of Karbala, the death of Husain ibn Ali, and subsequent events.

and I will repeat it again: that for every day that passes, the good and true and just (*haqq*) gets one step closer to its intended objective.

Those short-sighted and ignorant people believed that the good and true and just (*haqq*) was weakened by every passing day, but this was not the case. Rather, *al-haqq*[79] becomes stronger and brighter and more established by each passing day, getting closer and closer to the [ultimate] goal [or télos and eschaton]. This is God's Way, and this is, in fact, the way in which the world has been created:

﴿ مَا خَلَقْنَاهُمَا إِلَّا بِالْحَقِّ وَلَٰكِنَّ أَكْثَرَهُمْ لَا يَعْلَمُونَ ٣٩ ﴾

[44:39] none of this have We created without [an inner] truth (Asad); [or: except for just ends (Yusuf Ali)]: but most of them understand it not.

[What this unit of revelation is saying is that nothing in God ﷻ's creation has been created other than it having a share in God ﷻ's ultimate reality (which is the good, the true, the just, and the everlasting), and having been enrolled in a process which is directed back to the eschaton and back to Him in a drawn, télosic manner.]

The Earth and the Heavens are created with *al-haqq*, in the process of *al-haqq*, and with the method of *al-haqq*. This is why the oppressor will inevitably make mistakes; and why the enemies [of *al-haqq*] will fail to understand and fail to be able to carry out their intentions. This is where Yazīd understood that he failed to understand and failed to carry out his ultimate intention.

What was he to do now that he realized that he had misjudged the situation? This is where the preliminaries of the Fourth Phase of the Imamate begin, which is the longest and most arduous of these phases. They gathered all of their resources from the four corners of the Islamic world and mustered them for their effort to snuff out the beacon of Shī'a Islam. I emphasize the word Shī'a Islam for a good reason, which is the

---

[79] *Al-haqq* is a key Quranic term which simultaneously carries the meanings of ultimate reality, truth and justice. It is also one of the Quranic Names of God ﷻ and is often used interchangeably with the word 'God ﷻ.

5. The Four Phases of the Imamate

hope that on one such occasion, a spark might fly and ignite an understanding of Shī'a Islam in your minds. I will of course define Shī'a Islam; I will explain what this meant during the time of Imam Sādiq ﷺ later.[80] The expressions *āmma* (the general populace) and *Khāsa* (the select) are used in the books, where the former refers to Sunnis and the latter refers to the Shī'a. Additionally, I shall explain the attributes of each of these during the time of Imam Sādiq ﷺ. After which we can investigate ourselves and determine whether we are one of "the general populace" or one of "the select"; and I believe that it [= this exercise] will be a cause of shame for us.

Yazīd was intent on destroying Shī'a Islam using whatever means he had at his disposal. One such method was intimidation. Intimidation is not a method that is new; it has existed from times of old; from the time that selfish tyrants and oppressors have existed and when people have stood up against them for their rights and their humanity. Now the intimidation technique which Yazīd employed is interesting. For example: Madina was the center of the unrest and revolutionary activity. It is where Ali b. Husain ﷺ lived; it is where the shrine of the Prophet ﷺ is located; it is where the Muslims who had witnessed the Prophet ﷺ personally lived, [the Muslims with the highest seniority, i.e.] the ones who had lived through the Battles of Badr and Uhud. Yazīd suddenly decided to send his troops there to wipe these people out, and it was as a consequence of this decision that the Battle of Harra[81] occurred. He said, "O my soldiers! Kill the people and have no mercy for them! Do whatever it is that you will with them!" And that is what they did. Milk-suckling babies were killed in the Battle of Harra[82]; they took babies away from their mothers and threw them furiously against walls so that their skulls would explode[83]; they took babies and threw them up in the air and held spears under them so that they would be skewered when they came back down.[84] For a long time after the Battle of Harra, mothers who would give away their

---

[80] Unfortunately, Ayatollah Khāmeneī did not return to this topic.
[81] See footnote #51
[82] Ibn Qutayba's *al-Imāma wa'l Sīyāsa*, Dīnvarī edition, 1:238.
[83] Ibid.
[84] Ibid.

daughters to their grooms-to-be would disclose that they could not be guarantors of their daughters' virginity, because of what Yazīd's soldiers did here.[85]

These are things which the world has been witness to. The Shī'a who self-identified as such in those early days necessarily went through such baptisms of fire, and dared to say that they were Shī'a. This is why when Imam Sādiq ؏ was told that a number of his Shī'a had come and were waiting at his door, he would go to the door with surprise that a number of his Shī'a had come; but then would realize, once he opened the door, that they were not his [true] Shī'a, and would become disconsolate and ask where his supposed Shī'a were? If these are my Shī'a, he would say, then where are the signs of their being Shī'a?

This was one of the ways of intimidation. Another way was to fool the people and keep their minds occupied with false thoughts. This was something else that they started. What I mean by "they" is all of the Umayyad and Abbāsid tyrants, as there is no difference between Yazīd and Abdul-Malik and Mu'āwiya [in this respect].

Blood and lineage do not change; be it sweet water or brackish
It runs the same within [God's ﷻ] creatures until the blowing of the Trumpet
[which signals the start of the Day of Resurrection]
(Rumi's *Mathnawī*)

Yazīd and Abdul-Malik are not two distinct beings. It was yesterday or the day before yesterday that I stated that when the ideology of predestinarianism was promulgated, people such as Ma'bad b. Abdullah al-Juhānī who took a stance against this ideology, were imprisoned, tortured, and killed. Their program was to fool people and to put pressure on them. They invented false religious leaders [to act as false idols]; and one of the subjects which I shall be discussing in the days ahead is the relations of the Imams ؏ to these false court-allied and -sponsored religious leaders.

---

[85] Ibid.

5. The Four Phases of the Imamate

The interpretation and explication of Islam and the Quran is a duty which started from the time of Imam Sajjād ﷺ. You know of course that these kinds of policies evolve gradually and do not come into being all of a sudden. This gradual gradient started from the time of Imam Sajjād ﷺ or from the 61st year of the Islamic calendar, and gained pace and intensity until it reached its zenith at the time of Imam Bāqir ﷺ.

It might be good for me to remind you at this juncture why [Muhammad b. Ali] Imam Bāqir ﷺ is referred to as such. It is reported in the hadith report corpus that they referred to Imam Bāqir ﷺ as Bāqir ul-'Ulūm, i.e. "the one who split [the kernel of the knowledge of all of] the sciences." Does this mean that the other Imams ﷺ did not do so as well? Was Imam Bāqir's knowledge of the sciences greater than that of, say, [his son] Imam Sādiq ﷺ, or [his father] Imam Sajjād ﷺ, or Imam al-Askari? No; [the thirst for knowledge of] all of the Imams ﷺ was quenched at the same [divine] well-spring, and all of their [natural and supernatural] knowledge was the same, and none's was any more or less than any others'. My own understanding is that the reason Imam Bāqir ﷺ is referred to as "the one who split [the kernel of the knowledge of all of] the sciences" is that it was he, [more than anyone else,] who unearthed and unveiled the truths and teachings of Islam from under layers of lies and deceptions and false images and distortions, and made the unalloyed kernels of truth available to those who hungered for it. This is another aspect of the struggle which our Imams ﷺ were engaged in.

Thus, the Imams ﷺ had two functions: one was leading the [political] struggle against the Umayyad and Abbāsid caliphal courts; and the other was the promulgation of the true teachings of Islam. It also happened that at times the caliphs would send their spies to see if the Imams ﷺ were preaching anything against the distortions which they had propagated. The Imams ﷺ would identify these spies and knew that that they were spies, and dissimulate [accordingly]. Of course, this is only one aspect of prudential or cautionary dissimulation (*taqīya*), and does not cover the entirety of the tenet, which is much broader and deeper than this. A spy or someone who had loose lips and could not keep anything to himself would come up to the Imams ﷺ and ask them about a subject which was sensitive and on which the ruling authorities had placed special emphasis. The Imam would see that it was not necessary, or expedient, for this concept to be disseminated from the auspices of the Imamate, so that the powers that be would thereby become informed that such a mentality [existed therein; and so, the Imam would dissimulate the truth on such occasions].[86]

---

[86] The audiotape stops at this point.

6. The Initial Period of the Fourth Phase of the Imamate

[God ﷻ the All-Knowing and All-Wise has stated in His Sacred Writ:]

$$\text{رَّبَّنَا عَلَيْكَ تَوَكَّلْنَا وَإِلَيْكَ أَنَبْنَا وَإِلَيْكَ الْمَصِيرُ ﴿٤﴾}$$

[60:4] "O our Sustainer and Lord of Providence! In Thee have we placed our trust, and unto Thee do we turn: for unto Thee is all journeys' end.

$$\text{رَبَّنَا لَا تَجْعَلْنَا فِتْنَةً لِّلَّذِينَ كَفَرُوا وَاغْفِرْ لَنَا رَبَّنَاۖ إِنَّكَ أَنتَ الْعَزِيزُ الْحَكِيمُ ﴿٥﴾}$$

[60:5] O our Sustainer and Lord of Providence! Make us not a plaything for those who are bent on denying the truth! And forgive us our sins, O our sustainer: for Thou alone art, almighty, truly wise!"

$$\text{رَبَّنَا لَا تُزِغْ قُلُوبَنَا بَعْدَ إِذْ هَدَيْتَنَا وَهَبْ لَنَا مِن لَّدُنكَ رَحْمَةً ۚ إِنَّكَ أَنتَ الْوَهَّابُ ﴿٨﴾}$$

[3:8] "O our Sustainer! Let not our hearts swerve from the truth after Thou hast guided us; and bestow upon us the gift of Thy grace: verily, Thou art the [true] Giver of Gifts.

وَلَيَنصُرَنَّ اللَّهُ مَن يَنصُرُهُ ۗ إِنَّ اللَّهَ لَقَوِيٌّ عَزِيزٌ ﴿٤٠﴾ الَّذِينَ إِن مَّكَّنَّاهُمْ فِي الْأَرْضِ أَقَامُوا الصَّلَاةَ وَآتَوُا الزَّكَاةَ وَأَمَرُوا بِالْمَعْرُوفِ وَنَهَوْا عَنِ الْمُنكَرِ ﴿٤١﴾

[22:40] ...And God ﷻ will most certainly succor him who succors His cause: for, verily, God ﷻ is most powerful, almighty, and [22:41] [well aware of] those who, [even] if We firmly establish them on earth, remain constant in prayer, and give in charity, and enjoin the doing of what is right and forbid the doing of what is wrong.

1. The division of the 250-Year duration of the Imamate into four phases

For the benefit of those who were not present yesterday, the summary of what was stated is that the 250-year long life of the [First Eleven] Imams ؏ can be divided into four periods of phases.

- ❖ The First Phase is the first 25 years of the caliphate, which is [the initial phase of] Imam Ali's ؏ Imamate during the caliphate of the first three caliphs, [which is the phase of expedientiary cooperation].

- ❖ The Second Phase begins with the start of the reign of the Ahl al-Bayt ؏, which is the caliphate of Imam Ali ؏, followed by the caliphate of his son Imam Hasan, which did not last more than six months. [This is the phase of the establishment of Islamic governance.]

- ❖ The Third Phase is the period of the underground political activity of the Ahl al-Bayt ؏. This starts with Imam Hasan's Peace [with Mu'āwiya] in the 41st lunar year of the Islamic calendar, and continues for 20 years until the year 61, which is the year of the martyrdom of Imam Husain ؏ in Karbalā. [This is the phase of

6. The Initial Period of the Fourth Phase of the Imamate

the preparation of a covert organization for bringing about insurrection.]

❖ [The Fourth Phase is the phase of organized resistance against the ruling authorities, and the expansion of true Islam. This phase started with the Imamate of Imam Sajjād ﷺ (after the martyrdom of his father at Karbalā), and continued until the beginning of the Minor Occultation[87] in the year 260 HQ/ 874 CE.]

These were the attributes of this phase: training a group of the truly faithful (mu'minīn) into a group of revolutionary soldiers, so that if and when it becomes Imam Hasan's turn [to lead the Imamate], that these selfless warriors would have laid the intellectual groundwork in society. Secondly, so that there would be people who would help Imam Husain ﷺ achieve what he wanted to accomplish. This third phase ends with the martyrdom of Imam Husain ﷺ on Āshūrā and begins with Imam Hasan's Peace with Mu'āwiya. Hence, these two events are the two bookends of a [preplanned] program; they are two tactics in a greater, overarching strategy; they are the beginning and end of the same act. And just as Sayyid Sharīf ad-Dīn Āmolī has stated, [Imams] Hasan ﷺ and Husain ﷺ were two sides of the same coin; and Imam Hasan's Peace and the martyrdom of Imam Husain ﷺ in Karbalā are the beginning and end of the same event. And so, Imam Husain's martyrdom put an end to this third phase.

And it is of course necessary for one who is to talk about the lives of the Imams ﷺ to talk a little about the various phases and the major events that frame them. This would include things such as Imam Ali's ﷺ life during the 25 years of the caliphates of the first three caliphs, the five years of his own reign, the six months of Imam Hasan's caliphate and the peace treaty he signed with Mu'āwiya, the twenty years which followed this which contained all of the events leading up to the Battle of Karbalā, and so on. These discussions are necessary; but I do not have anything to say concerning these things because our time is very limited and the days [which I have available] are fast coming to an end. The lion's share of my talk will be about the Imams ﷺ who came after Imam Husain ﷺ; these

---

[87] See footnote #39 on page 68.

Imams are [the ones whose lives and activities are] less well-known. A lot of work has been done on the lives of the first three Imams, and there are some good works among the mountain of material that is available, but no work of historical research has been done on the eight Imams ﷺ from Imam Sajjād ﷺ through Imam Hasan al-Askarī ﷺ. And non-historical works there are aplenty, of which specie it would be better if there were none at all. There are a lot of false impressions and misapprehensions [about these Eight Imams] which we would like to dispel and disabuse the audience of a little, or to the extent that is possible, and to present that which is true, God ﷺ grant.

2. Two actions of the Imams ﷺ in the fourth phase of the Imamate

2.1 The revivification of the intellectual basis of Islam

The Fourth Phase of the Imamate starts from the Imamate of Imam Sajjād ﷺ. There are two objectives which are to be attained in this phase. During the time leading up to this period, Islamic society had degenerated to a class-stratified society which hearkened back to the days of pre-Islamic ignorance, and its true teachings and values had been forgotten as a result of Umayyad dynastic rule and as a result of factors which predated this rule and which dated back to the intellectual forefathers of the Umayyads. So, the first objective was to revivify the intellectual basis of Islam. [Because] the tenets of Islam and its worldview had been forgotten; the sense of equality and social justice of Islam had been forgotten; and the sense of working for this-worldly gains while at the same time keeping the other-worldly objectives as priorities had been forgotten. Islam had been transformed and was in the process of further transformation in its creedal principles, in its legal ordinances, as well as in its code of moral conduct.

On one hand, Islam's principles were being forgotten; and on the other, anti-Islamic principles and values were being injected to take their place and were gaining ground. Also, I had mentioned earlier that belief in predeterminism was taking the place of belief in human free will, which is what Islam teaches. For Abdul-Malik instilled the ideology of

6. The Initial Period of the Fourth Phase of the Imamate

predeterminism and predestinarianism into the minds of his subjects in order the better to take advantage of them, and in order to make them more submissive and complacent [subjects]. He thus forbade ordinances having to do with the moral stewardship of the community (*ahkām-e nezārati*) such as *al-amr bi'l-ma'rūf wa an-nahy min al-munkar*, which are pillars of Islam, and which refer to the imperative to enjoin the doing of that which is right and forbidding the doing of that which is wrong, that which arises out of the exercise of the people's free will. It was Abdul-Malik who was the first to go up to the pulpit and threaten to sever the heads of any of his subjects who had the temerity to give him advise on how to act ethically, as was the custom of the early years of Islam. In other words, this was the first instance where dissenting opinions were officially and formally silenced. There were earlier instances of the repression of the freedom of expression – it existed at the time of Mu'āwiya and Yazīd too – but it had not operated under the cover of the law of the land. He did the same thing with respect to the issue of predeterminism and free will, making it a crime punishable by law to promulgate the belief that one's own will had a part in determining one's lot in life and one's future.[88]

In any event, these kinds of distortions had obtained in the ideological makeup of Islam. At this point, another responsibility is created for the Imams ﷺ from Imam Sajjād ﷺ forward, and that is to resist this wave of distortion and falsification. It became the responsibility of Imam Sajjād ﷺ and his progeny who were the Imams ﷺ who followed in his wake, to set up an anti-propaganda operation whose function was to reverse all of the false memes and misinformation which the Umayyad and Abbāsid authorities were attempting to brainwash the people with. It also fell on them to provide the true and authentic Islamic alternative

---

[88] This idea has stuck, so that most Sunnis are Ash'aris in terms of their theology, and Ash'arites are predeterminists. How they reconcile this with the possibility of a Day of Judgement is truly beyond my comprehension, as what is there to be judged on, if all is predetermined by God ﷻ and one has no role in one's own decision making. And with the preclusion of a court with any proper and logical standing at the Day of Judgment also goes the possibility of eternal Heaven and Hell.

against the anti-Islamic propaganda that was being disseminated by the enemies of Islam. This was their first task.

And this is that same function which everyone is aware of, and that everyone has heard how each of the Imams ﷺ had a large group of students to whom they taught [the authentic tenets and teachings of Islam]. Everyone has some idea of this function, even though I dare say that most do not know the details of this function either. For example, people say that Imam Sādiq ﷺ had four thousand students. What is generally imagined is that he would sit on a stool or raised dais and four thousand students would gather round him, and he would start to speak just as we are speaking to you now, and that he would train his students in this way. But this is not how it was. The four thousand student figure refers to the number of students which Imam Sādiq ﷺ trained over the relatively long period of the 40 years – or a little less – of his imamate. These were students who learned certain truths and then went back to the lands from which they hailed and promulgated those views among their local populations. People would come from towns near and far. There is even a report of a devotee who made himself out to be a cucumber seller [in order to be able to get passed the guards who were placed to ensure Imam Sādiq ﷺ remained under house arrest]; and he was able to ask his questions by using this ruse. Another report tells of the Imam telling someone to hurry up and come in and to close the door behind him. And yet another report informs us that the Imam instructs one of his devotees not to reveal the fact that he has come from Kūfa if he is asked, and to say that he is a local of Madīna [instead], for example – because Kūfa was the Imam's support base. Another instance is when one of the Imam's followers is putting questions to the Imam, at which point one of the court's spies enters into the room and sits down. The Imam immediately changes the subject of the discussion and carries on as if they had been discussing the new subject all along. Thus, these were the conditions under which Imam Sādiq ﷺ trained four thousand students and sent them to the four corners of the dominions of Islam. And it was not the case that al-Mansūr and the caliphs before him would give the Imams ﷺ any permission to hold lectures and teaching sessions and allow the people to freely assemble and hear what the Imam had to say. That is not at all what

6. The Initial Period of the Fourth Phase of the Imamate

Imam Sādiq's life was like; it was not a life of teaching in tranquility; and I will discuss this in the second section.

2.2 The formation and management of a religio-political party

As to the second duty of these great noblemen – when I say duty, what I mean of course is their duty before God ﷻ, and the deeds that they actually performed which we have information on that have been gleaned from the historical sources. The duty of these great noblemen was that at the same time that they were performing their first duty, which was the preservation and revivification of the teachings of Islam, they strove to put together a highly structured political movement and to gather around themselves those who were devoted to their interpretation of Islam, to put them in touch with each other, and to arm them spiritually and intellectually. In sum, their duty was to ensure that there would be a core of die-hard supporters for the cause of insurrection against the oppressors and tyrants who had usurped the office which rightly belonged to the Imams; if and when the time was ripe for such an insurrection to take place. This was a function which all of the Imams ﷺ from the Fourth Imam to the Eleventh Imam performed. It can be summed up as the formation and management of a covert religio-political party and the arming of its members both spiritually and intellectually for the day when the Imams ﷺ were to make their covert claims overt, and rise up in insurrection against the forces of the enemy. The purpose of this function was preparatory, and its goal was to ensure that their supporters would be ready for such an eventuality so that it would meet with success. This is the other function of the Imams, which alas, has not even been heard of today by the followers of Imam Sādiq ﷺ, who do not have the least amount of information concerning this aspect of their imamates. But this was and remains a reality.

I have said this before, of course; that the information which I can present to you during the timeframe of these sessions is necessarily of a limited nature. And part of this is because not all of the material that one searches for in the archives and which occurs to one's mind can be presented in such sessions, as you gentlemen would become bored with such details, or at least most of you would. These are things that are better suited for a book; things that should be written down. What I say is [merely] an outline of such a book. It cannot even be properly characterized as a summary; it is not a summary or the essence of the subject. But I hope and trust that even this limited corner of the matter which I have presented will suffice to entice the minds of the curious searcher.

This movement started from the time of Imam Sajjād ﷺ. How did it start? Yesterday we stated that only three Shīʻa remained after the Battle of Karbalā; three people who were willing to sacrifice [themselves] who had not been intimidated by what had happened at Karbalā. The hadith report which states that "The people apostatized after [the martyrdom of Imam] Husain" is attributed to Imam Sādiq ﷺ, and after that event, only three Shīʻa remained and the rest of the people went [= apostatized and fell in line with the will of the ruling powers]. Also, when the others "left", and in turn lost their faith or turned away from Islam or Shīʻa Islam, one of two conditions occurred, for they were afflicted by one or the other of these blights. The first was the blight of fear, which is a very great blight indeed. And after the tragedy of Karbalā took place, and this was followed by the disaster of Herrā and the massacre of the people of Madina at the hands of the thugs of Yazīd's army, the people thought that a ruling apparatus which does not show any hesitation or mercy towards the grandson of the Prophet ﷺ who was so dear to the people of the community would certainly not show any mercy towards themselves and their like. And because they feared that they would be imprisoned and/ or tortured and/ or killed – in different ways, depending on where they were. If they were in Madina, they could be subjected to one kind of punishment; and if they were in Kūfa and living under the aegis of Hajjāj and his ilk, they would be subjected to some other kind of cruelty – for they had seen many instances of such cruelties. They thus abandoned their support of the Fourth Imam and went their own ways. This is how some of them reacted.

For others, it was not only a question of fear; although fear was also a part of it. These people saw that if they were to live in this society, and if they were to be able to make a living with relative ease, they had to bid these thoughts and words and deeds goodbye and set them aside, and

6. The Initial Period of the Fourth Phase of the Imamate

forget that there was ever such a person as an Imam Hasan ﷺ and an Imam Husain ﷺ. They had to forget that there were certain principles and teachings, and that there were certain goals and objectives to be reached, and a certain road to be traversed. They realized that they needed to forget all these. There were economic considerations to think of, such as procuring work from the caliph's governors and local representatives; being the subject of special treatment from the authorities such as tax exemptions and other economic motivators; being honored by the authorities in public gatherings; being given a cushy job by the government or the exclusive rights to some function or resource, and so on. And so, there was this other group which consisted of people who believed that they needed to set all these things aside if they were to be able to live their lives more comfortably.

The first consideration which was fear had to do with the general population, whereas this second consideration, which was thinking about making a comfortable living and avarice for the comforts of this world had to do with a more limited number of people; with the upper echelons of society. These were the considerations which caused people to abandon the Fourth Imam, leaving only those three selfless people at the beginning of the Imam's task.

And this is why we need to pay attention to the words of the Fourth Imam, which we find in the hadith report corpus and in the *sahīfa^t as-sajjādīa*, where we will see the effect of this second way of thinking. What was the second way of thinking? Attachment to [the goods of] the world which the ruling powers unsparingly bestowed on their friends and allies and supporters. A desire for the world of comfort and prosperity which is exclusive only to them, irrespective of whether or not the majority of the people who live right next to them are the beneficiaries of this prosperity or can manage even less than to prosper. It is hitching one's wagon to the caliphal court and taking advantage of the benefits that the state bestows to those who ally themselves with it. When we look into the words of Imam Sajjād ﷺ, we see that the effect of this way of thinking among the people is felt very clearly.

3. Islamic asceticism

We see, for example, that most of the words of the Imam are about asceticism (*zuhd*). What do we mean by asceticism? It means being sparing; it means closing one's eyes to the alluring glitter of the material world. Unfortunately, today asceticism is defined for us in an erroneous way. We think that it means the closing of our eyes to each other's ways, if and when possible. If possible, not to come out of our homes; if possible, even not to work to earn one's living, and to be a burden on others. But this is not what Islamic asceticism is about. The meaning of Islamic asceticism is for the human being, who is burdened with the load of a thousand worldly attractions and lures which one's lower self and desires demand (such as carnality, the desire for social standing and praise, material comforts, the desire for earning [undeservedly] more for working less, for money and in sum, for a life of luxury without responsibility); and Islamic asceticism is the act of unburdening oneself of all these desires and hooks which claw at the fabric of your spirit in order for your spirit to be free to attain to the primordial goal. This is what is meant by asceticism. An example of Islamic asceticism is when someone who has a large income and a comfortable lifestyle is confronted with a choice between holding on to this lifestyle or sacrificing it in order to perform one's duty to God ﷻ and to live within the bounds of God ﷻ's divine dispensation and within the ordinances of the sacred law (*sharī'a*). To live in accordance with what one's conscience dictates is what God ﷻ expects of us, even if this means giving up the comforts and security of one's home and social standing and refuge; even if it means the possible loss of one's beloved wife and the children who are so dear to us – in order to preserve the higher prize of attaining and maintaining God ﷻ's good pleasure and the everlasting felicity which He has promised his devout servants in the life to come. This is the meaning of Islamic asceticism.

Imam Sajjād's ﷺ words turn our attention to this kind of asceticism. The Imam would stand before the people and, [referring to the ephemeral glitter of the material world,] would ask, "Is there no one among you who will cast aside the rotting leftover food that is stuck between your teeth?" He was referring to the shameful wealth and goods and comforts of the world, which are obtained at the expense of losing

6. The Initial Period of the Fourth Phase of the Imamate

one's religion; and whether there was to be found a single person among the people who was willing to reject these illegitimate desires and cast them toward those who are deserving of nothing more than this. Is there not a single person who will stand up and say that he or she does not want the goods and glitter and wealth and financial security of this world and the prosperity which it has on offer, and that he or she prefers God ﷻ and the Quran and one's duty before God ﷻ Is there not a single person who prefers [the guidance and leadership of] Imam Sajjād ؏ in preference to these things? And so, do with me as you will, O Yazīd! Is there not a freeman [among you] that will make such a declaration?

Imam Sajjād ؏ tells us, "Your souls have but a single value and worth, so beware so as not to sell it for anything short of that price – which is [everlasting] Heaven." Heaven is the only thing that is worth exchanging all of the toil of this life for, on account of which your soul is ground down on a daily basis; it is the only thing which you can get in exchange for all of the toil of this world, in which exchange you will not have been cheated. And so, if you encounter a situation in which you can exchange your life and soul for entry into Heaven, then make the exchange and give it up, for if you save it for another exchange, you will never get a higher price for it; this is the price of your soul [and nothing less].

4. Imam Sajjād's ؏ efforts at increasing the Shī'a population

Imam Sajjād ؏ writes a warm letter to Muhammad b. Shahāb az-Zuhrī, who was a great religious scholar of the era and who was a friend and supporter of the Imam, but who is marginalized by the ruling powers. God ﷻ willing, I will read this letter here at its appropriate time so that you will get an idea of the nature of the Imam's efforts at mustering supporters in the face of all the difficulties and strife which he was confronted with. The Imam was engaged in gathering around himself people who were independently minded and who were willing to make sacrifices, and who had understood and accepted him and his specific interpretation of Islam and rejected all other interpretations and leaders. In the hadith which we cited earlier it is stated that "Verily, the people [gradually] followed [the Imam] and multiplied [in number];" after which the Shī'a population increased and took on a more organized form. Those who were willing to make sacrifices and to pay the price gradually increased to a large number as a result of the Imam's efforts such as the warm letter to az-Zuhrī, and as a result of the unstinting efforts of those three great men who had not abandoned the Imam after Āshūrā: Yahyā b. Umm at-Tawīl, Jabīr b. Mat'am, and Abū-Khālid al-Kābolī. Later, these three heroes were identified [by the authorities] and Yahyā b. Umm at-Tawīl was massacred in a horrendous way by Hajjāj; he cut off each of his arms and legs in turn, then cut out his tongue, and eventually put him out of his misery. These kinds of barbarisms did take place [for the Shī'a]. Ultimately, it became known that it was these three heroes who were the force behind Imam Sajjād's efforts. This was [the life of] Imam Sajjād; after which the turn comes for Imam Bāqir [or the Imam al-Bāqir, if you prefer the Arabic form].

5. Imam Bāqir's taking advantage of umayyad weaknesses and the increasing of the Shī'a ranks

The situation improved slightly during the imamate of Imam Bāqir. First of all because the Umayyads were losing their grip on their absolutist control of society, because the dynasty was coming to the end of its rope. The Umayyad caliphs who were at the helm were decadent [now] and were more concerned with enjoying the pleasures of the world and satisfying the cravings of their own carnality than on statesmanship and the imperative of holding on to their power. One such Umayyad caliph who reigned during the time of Imam Bāqir was Walīd b. Yazīd, who has gone down in history as having shot an arrow through the Quran, whose lover's name can be found in the history books, and who has also composed poems in praise of wine. The weakness of the caliphal court provided a great opportunity for Imam Bāqir.

This opportunity had a second cause also, which was the increased Shī'a population during Imam Bāqir's time. Imam Bāqir, being the great grandson of the Prophet, began to promulgate the hadith reports which he had heard from his father and grandfather concerning the words and deeds of his great grandfather, the Prophet of Islam; and he educated his followers and whoever has an ear and an

6. The Initial Period of the Fourth Phase of the Imamate

open mind, about the tenets and teachings and ordinances of Islam. When the people saw that the great grandson of the Prophet ﷺ, and the grandson of the martyr of Karbalā was preaching Islam in the congregational mosque in Madina or in the Great Mosque in Mecca during the major Hajj pilgrimage, they gathered around him to hear what he had to say. In parallel with this line of preaching and purely intellectual and theoretical pursuits, Imam Bāqir ؑ also pursued the practical side of organized [resistance]. The evidence we have for this is that the caliphal authorities become sensitized to Imam Bāqir's presence and activities, which is why Imam Bāqir ؑ was called to the caliphal capital in Damascus. In one of the journeys to Damascus which Imam Bāqir ؑ undertook at the command of the caliph, Imam Sādiq ؑ who was a young man at the time, was also present, which is why the story which I will relate a little later today, has reached us from Imam Sādiq ؑ. It will be a brief telling of the story because my aim is something other than relating historical tales about the Imams ؑ.

Some people are of the opinion that the reason the caliphal authorities became sensitive to Imam Bāqir's ؑ presence and activities had to do with the Imam's intellectual activities and his dissemination and promulgation of [a particular brand of] Islamic knowledge. These people say that it was because of their envy of Imam Bāqir's ؑ preaching as the Master of the House of the Prophet ﷺ that they began to harass and intimidate him. This is actually the majoritarian position, and I have seldom come across a more wrong-footed opinion than this one concerning the lives of the Imams ؑ. It is a highly ignorant position that is bereft [of any truth or historical evidence]. Firstly, because the governing authorities had no issue with knowledge and education, because other great scholars were occupied with doing the same thing, such as Muhammad b. Shahāb az-Zuhrī and scholars of the Sunnite persuasion, who taught Islamic law and related hadith reports from the Prophet ﷺ and had students and issued authoritative juridical rulings (*fatwas*). Thus, this kind of work was not something which the authorities considered to be a proscribed activity.

As to the issue that these scholars promulgated a certain brand and interpretation of the words and deeds of the Prophet ﷺ, whereas

Imam Bāqir's ﷺ interpretations and hadith reports were of a different kind – or as we now say, for them to provide the Sunnite version and for Imam Bāqir ﷺ to provide the Shī'a one – this too was not an issue which raised the ire of the authorities because the authorities were not sectarian and were neither Sunni or Shī'a; they were not even Muslim! It was not the case that, say, Hishām b. 'Abd al-Mālik was a committed Sunnite caliph; not at all. Sectarian issues were not one of his concerns. He was, of course, highly anti-Shī'a, but his antagonism and enmity with the Shī'a was on account of the fact that the leader of the Shī'a - Imam Bāqir ﷺ – [did not concede the legitimacy of his caliphate and] wanted to put an end to him. It was due to the fact that the caliph knew that anyone who was a supporter of Imam Bāqir ﷺ and who held the same beliefs that he did and who was a Shī'a would be a fearless warrior who would bring a sword down on the crown of his head if given half a chance. This is the reason the Shī'a were despised by the authorities. For the mere act of issuing authoritative juridical rulings and promulgating the teachings of Islam were in themselves completely unproblematic for all of the caliphs. As a matter of fact, they encouraged the scholars of religion to teach and to found teaching academies; which they did. All of the intellectual material that is foreign to Islam entered into Islamic intellectual discourse at the time of the Umayyads and Abbāsids. It was during the caliphates of the Umayyads that Greek, Hindu and Persian texts were translated and took their place in the libraries of Islam. There are many historical pointers that indicate that these rulers encouraged people to engage in creedal debates. Or to put it better, that the people's minds would be preoccupied with such purely intellectual matters which were disconnected from practical concerns would be an answer to their prayers, so that they would not know what [evil mischief and injustices] Hishām and other caliphs like him were really up to. They wanted people to be preoccupied with learning and religious activities, including attending teaching sessions given by Imam Bāqir ﷺ, as long as the Imam did not also engage in pursuing the other aspect of his ministry. Let them gather around each other and talk about whatever it is they talk about, let them raise their voices in heated discussions and debates, as long as they don't talk about what Hishām was really up to. This kind of activity posed no threat to

6. The Initial Period of the Fourth Phase of the Imamate

them; and it was actually something that they welcomed and prayed for. So that wasn't the reason they were sensitized to Imam Bāqir's activities.

And there are others who say that it was because Hishām envied Imam Bāqir ﷺ. And this is a truly astonishing statement! Imam Bāqir ﷺ is the subject of Hishām's envy?? What can this possibly mean? Hishām b. Abd a-Mālik ruled over half of the civilized (*ābād va ma'mūr*) world of his time! Whereas Imam Bāqir ﷺ is just a preacher living in [far off] Madina (as the Shī'a of today characterize him). The Shī'a of today *call* him an "Imam", but the characteristics which they attribute to him characterize him as a saintly preacher and a benevolent scholar who is living in Madina who has a few people gathered around him who put questions to him, get their answers from him, and perhaps give him some money for his efforts. So then if that is what they think, what kind of room does such a life leave for envy on the part of the ruler of half the world? I can't understand this. It makes no sense for the ruler of a whole empire to envy a person whose job is teaching and preaching and researching different matters and issuing opinions concerning religious matters? What is there to envy in *that*? These are not two people on the same path and vying for the preeminence of one over the other in that path, for the occasion of envy even to arise.

That said, it should also be said, of course, that Imam Bāqir ﷺ was more preeminent than Hishām, and the people knew it, too. But so what? Let us assume that Imam Bāqir ﷺ was more preeminent. It is not as though today, the president of an advanced country claims that he is more preeminent than any of the scholars of his nation. Does Nixon (1969 – 1974)[89] envy a scientist who, say, discovered a scientific fact or solved a mathematical problem? Or if [Neil Armstrong] stepped onto the Moon and his picture was published everywhere and was placed in museums, would Richard Nixon then be envious of him?? These two are on two different paths and there is no connection between the two; and [absolute] power and everything [that goes with it] are at Hishām's command; so what kind of envy is this?

---

[89] This reference indicated the year in which the lecture series was delivered, which was in the latter quarter of 1972.

6. Imam Bāqir's ﷺ being called to Damascus was due to his being intent on forming a government

Thus, the issue of Imam Bāqir's being called to Damascus was not due to the caliph's envy, neither was it due to his preaching and teaching activities; rather it was due to the caliph having heard reports concerning the Imam which the Imam does not deny either. It has been reported to Hishām that Imam Bāqir ﷺ is of the opinion that Hishām's occupancy of the office of the leader of the community of Muslims is illegitimate, and that Imam Bāqir ﷺ believes that it is he who should be the one who occupies that office, and that Imam Bāqir ﷺ is intent on divesting Hishām from that office and himself being vested in it in his stead. Hishām knew that Imam Bāqir's followers are organizing and agitating for just this objective; for if he thought that no one was paying any attention to Imam Bāqir ﷺ, he would still not be concerned with him. For if there is someone who makes such a claim but who has no supporters and no one to pay heed to anything that he says, then let that person say whatever it is that he wants to say, as it will make no difference. But Hishām sees that this is not the case, and that the people pay heed to and believe what Imam Bāqir ﷺ is saying, because there is a logic to his words, and his ideas are backed up with reasons and proofs. He says that the Prophet ﷺ has stated that the person who is to lead the community [after him] should be the one who is most preeminent and should have the most pious concern (*taqwā*)⁹⁰ in matters of the religion, and its culture and politics. The people see that Imam Bāqir ﷺ is most preeminent in all these things and has the highest degree of pious concern than anyone else in their society. It is because the people were aware of all of this that Hishām could not tolerate it and allow it to continue, [which is why he kept calling the Imam to Damascus to question him about his concerns].

    Imam Bāqir ﷺ would have killed Hishām if he were able to do so. And so, Hishām takes the upper hand and says [to himself] that he will

---

⁹⁰ *Taqwā* (pious concern): a righteousness of character which is informed by a fear of appearing before God ﷻ on the Day of Judgement and of the everlasting consequences in the hereafter as a result of the possibility of a failure to perform well in this ultimate fateful Judgement. Izutsu defined *taqwā* as "the pious fear of Divine chastisement on the Day of Judgment" which results in "a personal 'piety' pure and simple".

kill Imam Bāqir ﷺ. Likewise, if Imam Bāqir ﷺ were able to, he would imprison Hishām and not allow him free access to the outside world, because his presence is toxic. He would dethrone him and divest him from his office and turn him into an ordinary person. But now that power resides in Hishām's hands, the tables are reversed and Hishām does the same to Imam Bāqir ﷺ. This is why he calls Imam Bāqir ﷺ to the caliphal capital at Damascus.

7. The presence of Imam Bāqir ﷺ in the caliphal capital at Damascus

The story of Imam Bāqir ﷺ and Imam Ṣādiq ﷺ has been told in terms of the details of their journey and how they made their way there. Imam Bāqir ﷺ would not have responded to the call if the matter was at the level of a simple request; because Imam Bāqir ﷺ was not one to answer anyone's call if he was not so inclined. We see that in similar instances when the caliph wants to call any of the Imams ﷺ to his court – be it in Damascus, or later in Baghdad or Sāmarrā – that he would send a letter to the governor of Madina instructing him to make the arrangements, and the governor would in turn do so by taking measures and going through protocols appropriate to the Master of the House of the Prophet ﷺ. It was either that, or, if the governor was less subtle, he would have them arrested and taken to the capital in chains and leg irons. At all events, Imam Bāqir ﷺ and his son Imam Ṣādiq ﷺ are taken to Damascus, where they are expected by Hishām, who has been informed of their pending arrival. He issues instructions that they are to be brought to his presence immediately upon their arrival, and that they are not to be allowed to go anywhere else or to have any contact with the people. He also cautions his courtesans not to fall under the spell of the [mastery of] knowledge and spiritual leadership of Imam Bāqir ﷺ and not to honor them in any way; that they should ignore them completely when they enter, so that Hishām can put questions to them and interrogate them properly.

When Imam Bāqir ﷺ and Imam Ṣādiq ﷺ were brought before the court of Hishām, all of the courtesans ignored them as they were instructed to do, so that their spirits would be broken and so that they would be 'softened' for Hishām's interrogation. And so Hishām starts to talk. Pay attention to what he says, for if the Imam rejects what he says [= the accusations levelled against the Imam], it is evident that what he says is incorrect; and if the Imam does not refute what Hishām says, then they must not have been incorrect statements [or accusations], for otherwise they would have been refuted or objected to. When someone interrogates someone else and wants to determine that person's fate and issue his verdict on the basis of the interrogation, it is only natural that if the accusations which are put to the person being interrogated are false, that the person will object and swear an oath that these accusations are false, and proffer so many reasons and proofs as to why the accusations are false. But we see that Imam Bāqir ﷺ does not refute or object to the things that Hishām has to say to Imam Bāqir; and that furthermore, the Imam even affirms and confirms them indirectly.

Among the things which Hishām said to Imam Bāqir ﷺ were the following three sentences. He said, "O Muhammad, the son of Ali! You – the sons of Ali b. Abū-Tālib and the House of Banī-Hāshim – have always been this way. Whoever's turn comes [to be the Master of your House], has broken the cane of the Muslims". Meaning that you have always sown discord among the Muslims. So here we see slogans of unity coming forth. From whom? From Hishām! What does he mean by Imam Bāqir ﷺ "sowing discord"? What he means is that the people were like so many tame sheep under my command; they did not and do not understand anything, and would move to whatever direction I commanded them. I lived in any fashion which pleased me; I raised high anyone who pleased me, and brought low anyone whom it pleased me to demean, and not a peep was issued forth from the mouths of the people. Everyone is united in liking me and in their support of me. And of course, it is clear that the people do *not* like Hishām and do *not* support him; for who can like and support a tyrant and a potentate and an oppressor? They were subdued before me, and you, Muhammad b. Ali, came and gradually enlightened them and caused a group to take a position of antagonism toward me. You caused a schism in the unity which the Muslims had in their waywardness and wretchedness. You created a new [politically active] front which is different to the path which the tame sheep who are obedient to me have

6. The Initial Period of the Fourth Phase of the Imamate

been taking. This is what he means by Imam Bāqir ﷺ having "broken the cane of the Muslims".

And "Whoever's turn comes [to be the Master of your House], has ... called upon the people to yourselves." What does he mean by "called upon the people to yourselves"? It means that you told the people and made them aware of the fact that it is *you* who merit and are worthy of being vested in the highest office of Islam, such that the people should gather around you and listen to you and position you in the office of the caliphate [or succession to the Prophet's ministry].

And the third sentence explains the previous one which I just mentioned: "And each of you believed in your own minds that it is *you* who is the [true and legitimate] Imam." What does "Imam" mean [here]? It means the caliph; the ruler. That Hishām said to Imam Bāqir ﷺ that he thinks of himself as the "Imam" means that he thinks of himself as the [rightful] leader and ruler [of the community of Muslims]. It does not mean [the office of] the Imamate in the sense of one who is so vested determines what is and what is not a [reliable] word of the Prophet ﷺ; or whether a given position is correct relative to the teachings of Islam, and so on. I explained earlier that this [particular function of the Imamate] was not important to Hishām. We shall see a little later on, when we get to the life of Imam Sādiq ﷺ, that [the Abbāsid caliph] al-Manṣūr himself suggests to the Imam that he issue *fatwas*, saying, "You should issue *fatwas* and occupy yourself with religious matters" (Ibn Shahrāshūb, *Manāqib* 4:238). But Imam Sādiq ﷺ demurred and responded negatively in a very interesting manner, which we shall get to.

Thus, Hishām was not against Imam Bāqir ﷺ fulfilling the function of an Imam in today's usage of the term,[91] i.e. an [apolitical] religious leader whose role is limited to issuing religious rulings and teaching the principles, tenets, ordinances, and modes of ethical conduct of Islam. This [apolitical aspect of the Imamate] was not an important

---

[91] Recall that these words were delivered in the apolitical or close to apolitical climate of the pre-revolutionary religious leadership of Iran. It is precisely words like these issued by Ayatollah Khāmeneī and other leaders in Imam Khomeini's movement which raised the political consciousness of the masses to the point where a spark was able to ignite an entire political revolution.

matter for Hishām to object to Imam Bāqir ﷺ on such grounds, and accuse him of considering himself to be an Imam. Hishām accepted this function for Imam Bāqir ﷺ and was perfectly fine with it. If it was not for the fact that Imam Bāqir ﷺ considered this second function to be an integral part of his office and limited himself solely to carrying out the first function, Hishām would have introduced Imam Bāqir ﷺ as the "Imam" if the question were to be put to him as to who the Imam was; just as he would introduce other [religious authorities who would fit the bill just as well, for his purposes]. The [aspect or function] of the Imamate which is unacceptable to Hishām is an Imamate defined to include political governance and sovereignty. And speaking more generally, the word Imam means ruler in its Islamic and Quranic and hadith report usage. It means one who manages the affairs of the people. [28:41] [*We destroyed them,*] *and We set them up as leaders (a'immat^{an}) that show the way to the fire [of hell]*. The word "leader" here means ruler. And: [28:5] *Yet We desired to be gracious to those that were abased in the land, and to make them leaders [of men]*. Again, the word "leader" here means ruler or sovereign. There is a hadith report related from God[92], the Lord of Providence of both worlds, in which it is stated that "I shall make suffer a people who are obedient to an oppressive imam whom I have not appointed to rule over them, even if such a person is righteous in his personal affairs." What is meant by an oppressive imam here? It means an oppressive ruler. This is because there can be no oppression in the word imam as you and I are used to using it [i.e. when its compass is limited to the first apolitical function of the Imamate]. But the word imam as it is used in the Quran, in the hadith report corpus, and in the public discourse of the early years of Islam meant ruler and sovereign; the person in whose hands the reins of state rest, and who can therefore take society in whatever direction he chooses. And so now we see Hishām telling Imam Bāqir ﷺ that "each of you believed in your own minds that it is *you* who is the [true and legitimate] Imam." This is tantamount to putting forth a claim to the caliphate.

---

[92] This is an example of a *hadith qudsī*, a sacred saying of the Prophet ﷺ that is not a part of the Quran in which God ﷻ speaks in the first person through the mouth of the Prophet ﷺ.

6. The Initial Period of the Fourth Phase of the Imamate

What I say is that the Hishām of those days understood Imam Bāqir ﷺ better than the Shīʿa of today understand him! He understood what Imam Bāqir ﷺ was after, and that this was to be the [political as well as the spiritual and theological and juridical] leader of society; That he was after the power to be able to recreate a truly Islamic and divinely sanctioned social order. Hishām knew that; but this fact is something that must be proven to the Shīʿa of today before it is believed; and even then, he might believe it or he might choose not to!

Hishām says to Imam Bāqir: "O Muhammad, the son of Ali! You – the sons of Ali b. Abū-Ṭālib and the House of Banī-Hāshim – have always been this way. Whoever's turn comes [to be the Master of your House], has broken the cane of the Muslims. Whoever's turn comes [to be the Master of your House], has ... called upon the people to yourselves. Each of you believed in your own minds that it is *you* who is the [true and legitimate] Imam." And so on until the end [of Hishām's speech as it appears in the hadīth report]. And when it came time for Imam Bāqir's turn to speak, if it was the case that he had *not* called the people to rise in righteous insurrection against the caliph and to vest himself in the office of leadership instead; and if he was not engaged in political activity and was not intent on overthrowing Hishām's illegitimate political order, then the thing that he should have done was to say something to the effect that, "Sir! Who has made these accusations against me to you?" And he can do so in whatever manner that you choose, either plaintively and piteously, like some have accused Imam Ṣādiq ﷺ of slouching down to, bless their hearts! Their response will be given by Imam Ṣādiq ﷺ himself on the Day of Resurrection. Or proudly and indignantly: "Sir! Who has had the effrontery to make these accusations against me to you? Who has slandered me? Who has had the temerity to say that I have a claim to your office? Why are you accusing me of such a thing??" Raising his voice... Isn't this how one who has been slandered would react?

Pay attention to what Imam Bāqir ﷺ does now. He begins to tell the truth about himself and his father and his grandfather and his forefathers before him and makes Hishām realize that it should be no surprise that he should have a claim to the leadership of the community. [He turns the tables around by asking,]

"You are saying that I have been putting out claims for the office of the Imamate? What, so you are saying that I should not put out such a claim and that *you* should do so?? Whereas it was by means of *us* that God ﷻ guided the first of your [lineage]? (*binā had-allāh awwalakum*)". In Islam, [investiture in the office of] leadership is based on intellectual and spiritual criteria. That person is most deserving of ruling over others who is most familiar with the principles, tenets, ordinances, and values of Islam; who is closest to the wellspring of guidance; who has comprehended the divine dispensation the best, and enacted it in his life most, and exhibited the most *taqwā* (pious concern). And it was through us that God ﷻ guided you to this way of life. Therefore, we are more familiar with it; and according to the Islamic criteria for leadership, we have a higher priority and right to lead and rule over the community than you do. So then where is the cause for surprise, Hāshim, [that you should be so surprised at hearing reports of such claims]?"

This was the Imam's response. And the Hishāms and Abdul-Maliks and their successor knew and understood full well the nature of Imam Bāqir's lineage and spiritual line. Let this much suffice us for a summary treatment of Imam Bāqir's ﷺ life.

8. The all-out struggle of the Imams ﷺ with the ruling powers from Imam Sajjād ﷺ to Imam Hasan al-Askarī ﷺ (inclusive)

This same line [of struggle and resistance] continued during the Imamates of Imam Sādiq ﷺ and Imam Kāẓim ﷺ. The synopsis of what I wanted to say in my presentations of yesterday and today is that based on the highly exacting research which we have carried out on the lives of these eight Imams, i.e. from Imam Sajjād ﷺ to Imam Hasan al-Askarī ﷺ (inclusive),

6. The Initial Period of the Fourth Phase of the Imamate

we see that all of these Imams ﷺ were engaged in a struggle of resistance against the caliphs and ruling powers of their respective times. And this is not limited to just a creedal and ideological struggle, but included a political struggle and a propaganda war, and even in certain instances, a military conflict. These Imams ﷺ also entered the field of battle; but not a lot; a little. But the propaganda war which was waged was full blown; and the political struggle was fought hard and was very serious and severe. One example of this related to the Imamate of Imam Bāqir ﷺ, who was followed by Imam Sādiq.

9. Hishām orders that Imams Bāqir ﷺ and Sādiq ﷺ be imprisoned in Damascus

Hishām became offended with the unusual and unexpected response which he received from Imam Bāqir ﷺ to the questions which he had put to him and ordered their arrest and imprisonment (Ibn Shahrāshūb, *Manāqib* 4:189). Again, it is clear that no one gets imprisoned for merely preaching the religion of Islam and explicating the finer points of its ordinances. The history books tell us that these two – father and son – continued their propaganda activities in prison, and that a number of people were drawn to their way of thinking. The ruling authorities saw that it is inexpedient for the leader of the Shī'a to be in prison where he can agitate for his cause, and released father and son. And of course, there must have been some commotion and unrest reported from Madina also. And so, they were accompanied back to Madina so as to ensure that they are not able to meet with anyone on their way back.

The story is well known up to this point. There are numerous hadith reports which report the same thing: that they were brought to Damascus, the exchange which took place with Hishām, their imprisonment, their influence on the Damascene prisoners, their subsequent release from prison, their being taken back to Madina, and Hishām's order of their anathemization, i.e. that they were to be boycotted and that no one should be in contact with them or even have any business dealings with them. The latter parts of the story are less frequently related, but the part about the anathematization and boycott are repeated more often, because it contains details which give the Imams ﷺ a miraculous quality, which is why people like to repeat it, and perhaps the gentlemen present here have heard that part of the story; where Imam Bāqir ﷺ and Imam Bāqir Sādiqﷺ are brought to the town of Madyan (on their way back to Madina from Damascus), and that the people of the town refused to open their doors to them and to let them in; because the caliph's agent had gone ahead and told everyone that these [prisoners] are the enemies of the caliph and that they are not to be let into anyone's home. At this point of the story, Imam Sādiq ﷺ climbs up to the top of a hill and shouts out and addresses the people and talks to them, and the people understand [who they actually are] and welcome them, and so on until the end [of the hadith report]. More of these kinds of incidents can be found in the life of Imam Bāqir; it is not just this one. As I stated earlier, Imam Bāqir ﷺ was imprisoned at least twice, and maybe on more than on two occasions. I know this as a certainty about the life of His Eminence.

10. Two teriods within the life of resistance of Imam Sādiqﷺ

And in this way, we reach the turn of Imam Sādiq's Imamate, where the issue becomes more critical and exacting, and takes on a greater significance. Imam Sādiq's imamate can be divided into two parts: the first part occurs during the ascendancy of the Umayyad dynasty, and the second part occurs during that of the Abbāsids.

The First Period
In the first period, Imam Sādiq's ﷺ resistance activities were very blatant and active and clear for all to see. In one hadith report we see, for example, that Imam Sādiq ﷺ makes the Hajj pilgrimage [from Madina to Mecca] during the time of the Umayyads, and that he agitates openly and publicly in Mecca before the crowds who have come from all over the Islamic world in order to make their pilgrimage. The report has the Imam saying, "O people! Know that the rightful successor to the Prophet ﷺ and to the office of rulership was our forefather Ali b. Abī-Tālib ﷺ; and after him, it was Imam Hasan; and that after him it was his brother Husain b. Ali ﷺ."[93] These are words which are harmless today, but giving voice to them in those days was dangerous. Because in those days, the people who were in

---

[93] Shaykh Koleynī's *Kāfī*, 4:466.

6. The Initial Period of the Fourth Phase of the Imamate

authority were the same people who had driven Ali b. Abī-Tālib ﷺ and Imam Hasan ﷺ and Imam Husain ﷺ to the fringes of society and marginalized them; these were their rivals, so that anyone who affirmed the right of Imams Ali, Hasan, and Husain ﷺ automatically denied the right of Mu'āwiya, Yazīd, Marwān, Abd al-Mālik and Hishām. These words expressed the most contentious issue of the day.

The contemporary equivalent of the act which was undertaken by Imam Sādiq ﷺ during the Hajj pilgrimage would be similar to a situation where a duly elected government is overthrown by a military coup and its president and main leaders are thrown in prison without any due process of law, and martial law is declared; and then for someone to break the military curfew and somehow manage to get on the air for several minutes during prime time and declare the government established by the coup leaders to be illegitimate, null and void; and to urge the people to pour into the streets and demand the restoration of their duly elected president. That is the contemporary measure of the significance of what Imam Sādiq ﷺ did on his Hajj pilgrimage.

Imam Sādiq ﷺ declared publicly to the people that, "the rightful successor to the Prophet ﷺ and to the office of rulership was our forefather Ali b. Abī-Tālib ﷺ; and after him, it was Imam Hasan; and that after him it was his brother Husain ﷺ b. Ali; and after him it was Ali b. al-Husain; and after him it was Muhammad b. Ali; and after him it is me!" He repeated this several times in different areas [of Mecca or of the Grand mosque of the Ka'ba where everyone that was gathered there had come from all different parts of the Islamic world]. And he did so with a purpose, and it is reported that he also repeated his statements towards Yemen and Yasār, and that he would repeat it wherever he was in a crowd of people. And this means that Imam Sādiq ﷺ had taken the struggle out in the open.

Imam Sādiq ﷺ also agitated for political change in private. For example, he would expel certain people from the Shī'a organization and network. The story of the friend of Ali b. Abī-Hamza is a famous one which all of you might have heard as an ordinary hadith report, but might not have made the connection between it and the other of Imam Sādiq's activities to see where it fits in the bigger picture of his life and work. [The hadith reports that] Ali b. Abī-Hamza came to Imam Sādiq ﷺ and said, "I have a friend who is a part of the Umayyad governmental apparatus and wants to be of service to you." Imam Sādiq ﷺ said that he would see him. The friend came and said, "O son of the Prophet ﷺ of God ﷻ! I want to quit my position in the Umayyad government" – it was an important position – "Do I have your permission to do so or not? Will my repentance be acceptable or not? I was employed in the government, I said things and did things and signed orders and trammeled over peoples' rights, took bribes, and feathered my own nest, and so on. Well, it stands to reason; that is what a governmental official in the Umayyad government does. But now I want to quit and return [to the fold]; can I do so or not?" The Imam said that "Yes, you may return." The friend said, "So how do I do that?" The Imam said, "The way of doing that is difficult. If I tell you how it is accomplished, will you act on it?" And the friend replied, "Yes, I will do it."

When the Imam heard this, he started to talk about the Umayyad government and the players in its governing structure as a way of laying the intellectual groundwork [of the solution] for the "friend" and how these people believe that their presence in the ruling structure is of no account, as they are ordinary people working there. Then the Imam told the friend not to think that the bad and rebellious role he played against God ﷻ's will and order was of no account. Rather, it is you and the likes of you who allow the Umayyads to become organized and strong, and who service their lanterns and fill them with fuel. How would the Umayyads be able to rule over a whole nation and usurp our right if it weren't for the fact that you and people like yourself do their accounting, collect their taxes, and wage their wars?" The Imam went on to tell the fellow that, "The way to do it is to give away everything which you have accumulated as a result of your service to the Umayyads, because they do not truly belong to you as you have acquired them through illicit means."

We will leave the story there as we are not concerned with its [other] details. The point is that Imam Sādiq ﷺ worked very openly and forthrightly during the Umayyad period. And if it were not for the fact that I have grown a little tired, I would relate a couple of other stories in this same vein – in which the Imam acts even more forthrightly – from the notes which I have made and which I have in my pocket.

6. The Initial Period of the Fourth Phase of the Imamate

The Second Period

But in the second period, i.e. during the caliphate of the Abbāsids, the nature of the resistance struggle was no longer as overt. Why? Because the Umayyad dynasty was a reactionary regime which had rotted and whose pillars were hollowed out, as the people had endured the dynasty's excesses and injustices for decades and had had their fill of them. Additionally, the governmental apparatus had become weak, and it no longer commanded the power to be able to control everything. Thus, Imam Sādiq ﷺ could engage in his agitation and political activities [relatively] freely.

But the government of the Abbāsids was a newly-founded "revolutionary" government; and as they themselves claimed, a group of revolutionaries were at the helm. These were the old comrades of Imam Sādiq ﷺ with whom they jointly fought the Umayyad power, and who had themselves come to power now. The Abbāsid [caliph] al-Mansūr and his brother Saffāh were people who sat with Imam Sādiq ﷺ and Muhammad b. Abdullāh b. Hasan and Abdullāh b. Hasan, and Dāwūd b. Ali and many others and conspired to come up with different ways to start the Hāshimite revolution to overthrow the Umayyads. Al-Mansūr had a personal relationship with Imam Sādiq ﷺ and Imam Bāqir ﷺ and received financial support from them. But it so happened that when Abū-Muslim of Khorāsān [the leader of the anti-Umayyad revolution] came to the scene, he was allied more with the House of Abbās than with the Ālid House; and that is why it was the Abbāsids rather than the Ālids who ascended to power to replace the rotted-out shell of the Umayyad regime.

The Abbāsids are fresh onto the scene, so they are vigilant and keen to maintain complete control. And secondly, they know Imam Sādiq ﷺ and the Shī'a and are familiar with their characteristics, because they have worked hard together against the Umayyads. And this is where the issue of precautionary dissimulation (*taqīya*) comes in; that is, the Shī'a tried to conceal their project of resistance as much as possible, but this fell short of cutting it off altogether. For Imam Sādiq ﷺ, there is no difference between Mansūr and Saffāh on one hand, and Hishām and Abd al-Mālik on the other; both regimes are oppressive, and so they are the same in this [decisive] respect. And so, this is why Imam Sādiq ﷺ continues his political activities, but this time under the cover of precautionary dissimulation (*taqīya*) and keeping al-Manṣūr distracted in a way that only Imam Ṣādiq knows how. The chapter on the life of Imam Ṣādiq is itself a very long and detailed chapter.

11. The Āshūrā Movement: the mother of all Shī'a movements

We stated that Imam Sajjād, and his son, Imam Bāqir, and his grandson, Imam Ṣādiq, were three leaders who succeeded each other, each of whom continued the resistance struggle, which became increasingly difficult for each generation. In the earlier period, there were still some people who had witnessed the Prophet personally, or who had witnessed Imam Ali personally and had seen up close the way in which he ruled and had tasted the sweetness of its fruits. In Imam Husain's entourage there were people who had fought in the battles of Ṣiffīn and Jamal and Nahrawān. There were even those among them who had seen the Prophet himself, and had heard the words of the Prophet about Imam Husain with their own ears. But in the period of Imam Sajjād, Imam Bāqir, and Imam Ṣādiq, these kinds of people were almost all gone and those who were still alive such as Jābir b. Abdullah were few and far between.

But the resistance struggle of these three great Imams springs from the epic event of the Battle of Karbalā; this seminal event from the morning till the dusk (*asr*) of Āshūrā which, though brief, was the mother of all of the struggles of the Shī'a which came after it. Husain b. Ali was another of Imam Hasan's progeny who rose up in insurrection against the Abbāsid caliph al-Hādī and was martyred in the environs of Fakh; Muhammad b. Ibrāhīm b. Ismā'īl b. Tabātabāī was the eponymous progenitor of the Tabātabāī branch of the descendants of the Prophet; and Ibrāhīm b. Abdullāh b. Hasan was another of Imam Hasan's progeny who rose up in insurrection against the Abbāsid caliph al-Manṣūr and was martyred in the environs of Kūfa. All of these heroes who rose up in righteous insurrection against the Abbāsid oppressors did so several generations after the tragic event of Karbalā, but they all maintained that their insurrectionary movements were in order to seek revenge for the blood of Imam Husain and his 72 companions which was shed on the

6. The Initial Period of the Fourth Phase of the Imamate

plain of Karbalā. This battle lasted half a day gave rise to all of the Shī'a movements which followed in its wake throughout the length of history; and if it not be an exaggeration, to all movements which champion human values throughout history, even if they are not Shī'a. The events of this half-day are full of passion and portent for the Shī'a, and if we are able to talk about Imam Bāqir ﷺ and Imam Sādiq ﷺ today, after fourteen hundred years, it is because of the events which took place in this half a day. The talks which we are giving, the gatherings which we hold, and the sermons which we deliver are all due to the benefits which derived from the events which took place in this half a day. We gather together and talk about Imam Bāqir ﷺ and the followers of Husain ﷺ and the progeny of Husain ﷺ in the name of the day of Āshūrā.

7. The Political Life of Imam Sādiq

[God ﷻ the All-Knowing and All-Wise has stated in His Sacred Writ:]

$$\text{رَبَّنَا آمَنَّا بِمَا أَنزَلْتَ وَاتَّبَعْنَا الرَّسُولَ فَاكْتُبْنَا مَعَ الشَّاهِدِينَ ﴿٥٣﴾}$$

[3:53] O our Sustainer! We believe in what Thou hast bestowed from on high, and we follow this Apostle; make us one, then, with all who bear witness [to the truth]!"

$$\text{رَبَّنَا لَا تُزِغْ قُلُوبَنَا بَعْدَ إِذْ هَدَيْتَنَا وَهَبْ لَنَا مِن لَّدُنكَ رَحْمَةً ۚ إِنَّكَ أَنتَ الْوَهَّابُ ﴿٨﴾}$$

[3:8] "O our Sustainer! Let not our hearts swerve from the truth after Thou hast guided us; and bestow upon us the gift of Thy grace: verily, Thou art the [true] Giver of Gifts.

O our Sustainer and Lord of Providence! [I beseech you] by [the right and station of spiritual proximity to You which] Muhammad ﷺ and his [Purified and Immaculate] Progeny ﷺ [have]: awaken our hearts and sharpen our minds (both of which have become degraded and stupefied) with the whip of Your divine teachings and ordinances, with Quranic revelations, and with Islamic truths and realities.

O our Sustainer and Lord of Providence! [I beseech you] by [the right and station of spiritual proximity to You which] Muhammad ﷺ and his [Purified and Immaculate] Progeny ﷺ [have]: Now that You have opened our eyes to that which is true and real and just and everlasting (*haqīqat*), and have acquainted our hearts with the crystalline wellspring of Your true teachings, do not allow our hearts to be afflicted with carnal desires and pride and selfishness and vainglory and the love of the pleasures of this world; do not allow our hearts to die in such a state of ignorance and a state where we have turned away from Your truth.

O our Sustainer and Lord of Providence! Just as you have chosen and exalted our Imams ﷺ and the Purified and Immaculate noblemen of the House of the Prophet ﷺ to be your vicegerents on Earth, help us who claim to love them and to be their followers to get to know their true characters better, and to follow them more closely.

وَلَيَنصُرَنَّ اللَّهُ مَن يَنصُرُهُ ۗ إِنَّ اللَّهَ لَقَوِيٌّ عَزِيزٌ ﴿٤٠﴾ الَّذِينَ إِن مَّكَّنَّاهُمْ فِي الْأَرْضِ أَقَامُوا الصَّلَاةَ وَآتَوُا الزَّكَاةَ وَأَمَرُوا بِالْمَعْرُوفِ وَنَهَوْا عَنِ الْمُنكَرِ ۗ وَلِلَّهِ عَاقِبَةُ الْأُمُورِ ﴿٤١﴾

[22:40] ...And God ﷻ will most certainly succor him who succors His cause: for, verily, God ﷻ is most powerful, almighty, and [22:41] [well aware of] those who, [even] if We firmly establish them on earth, remain constant in prayer, and give in charity, and enjoin the doing of what is right and forbid the doing of what is wrong.

1. The plethora of information on Imam Sādiq ﷺ comingled with misleading information

There is a lot of material available concerning [the life of] Imam Ja'far b. Muhammad, known as the Imam as-Sādiq ﷺ. And there are as many misleading and distorting matters and false methods and ways of life reported about him in the hadith report corpus as there are true and accurate and enlightening reports. Yesterday and the day before, we

7. The Political Life of Imam Sādiq

already discussed to some extent Imam Sādiq's ﷺ social and political environment, and I want to continue that discussion that follows in the hope of shedding more light on Imam Sādiq's ﷺ role.

2. The necessity of intellectual activities prior to and during the resistance struggle

It is clear for those who are inclined to examine social matters methodically that political activities and decisive struggles must take place under conditions where a sufficient quantum of intellectual agitation laying the groundwork for such activities has already taken place. If a group of like-minded people who share specific political objectives begin to attempt to implement a specific political program which they have in mind under conditions where not even the bare minimum of the requisite preparatory intellectual activities has taken place, it is obvious that such a program will not meet with success. We have been witnesses to these kinds of failures in history, more or less. First of all, the people must be prepared to have the [intellectual] prerequisites for accepting [a given political agenda]; and before that, they must have the requisite political consciousness for such an acceptation. After which the mindset and ideology of such a group's political agenda must be made clear for the people up to the minimum threshold that is necessary, so that it is necessary for preliminary cultural and intellectual agitation and political information and propaganda to be disseminated both prior to and during the implementation of such an agenda.

3. The beginning of the Shī'a intellectual movement with Imam Husain ﷺ

When the cycle of the Imamate and [*de jure*] reign of the Eight Imams ﷺ started, i.e. with the Imamate of Imam Sajjād ﷺ, conditions were very unfavorable. Of course it should not be forgotten that prior to Imam Sajjād's ﷺ imamate, during the imamates of Imams Hasan and Husain ﷺ i.e. in the twenty year period between the martyrdom of Imam Ali ﷺ and the event of Karbalā, intellectual propagation activity did take place to a large extent on the part of the Shī'a. Sacrifices were made, each of which were considered to be a means by which the Shī'a worldview and the mindset of the Shī'a Imams ﷺ was represented. People such as Hujr b. 'Adī and others like him had valiantly sacrificed their lives for Shī'a Islam, and the murder and martyrdom of the great personalities who were the Companions of the Commander of the Faithful, such as 'Amr b. al-Hamiq al-Khazāī, and Rushīd al-Hajarī, and Hujr b. 'Adī and his retinue and aides, all of whom formed the vanguard of the resistance movement, each caused a huge movement to be set in motion in the Islamic society of the day which had relapsed into a deep sleep. This change in political consciousness and awakening was effected to a large extent through two main activities: by means of Imam Hasan's preaching in the congregational mosque in Madina, where he talked and made the people aware of the true nature of Islam, thereby undermining the distorted Umayyad narrative; as well as by the call of people like Hujr, Rushīd and 'Amr b. al-Hamiq who shouted out to the people [in support of the cause of Imams Hasan ﷺ and Husain ﷺ and the Ālid House]. These activities had fostered an alternative narrative to the one being disseminated by the ruling powers; but this was not sufficient.

The propagation of this alternative narrative took place in two ways: the first was by giving expression to social realities and giving voice to issues whose discussion was necessary, and explicating [the Shī'a] ideology. These tasks were led by Imams Hasan ﷺ and Husain ﷺ, who were the leaders of the movement and who were the grandsons of the Prophet ﷺ, and whose intellectual [and creedal] positions were trusted by the people. And the second way was by the politico-religious agitation of people like Hujr, Rushīd and 'Amr b. al-Hamiq which they proclaimed aloud to the people, and whose Shī'a identity was sealed with the blood that they shed as martyrs in the cause of Shī'a Islam. These two propagation activities had taken place, but these were insufficient. What were they not sufficient for? For an organized movement on the part of the House of the Prophet ﷺ which was to achieve success in rising up in insurrection and taking to the helm of the ship of state.

4. An analysis of Imam Husain's insurrectionary movement

The question might be posed at this juncture that if such activities were insufficient, they why did Imam Husain ﷺ rise up in insurrection?

7. The Political Life of Imam Sādiq

Unfortunately, I cannot go into this issue at this time because the issue of the rationale behind the martyrdom of Imam Husain ﷺ would require at least an hour or more to explain. My own opinion on this issue is that Imam Husain ﷺ did not travel [from Madina to Kūfa] solely for the purposes of [bringing about his investiture in the highest office of] governance, as some maintain, such that when he sees that this objective is unobtainable and that he is in danger of being killed, he becomes intent on returning [safely back to Madina]; nor is it the case that others have imagined, namely, that he came solely for the purposes of bringing about his own martyrdom. It was neither of these. It was not solely for governance because it is clear from His Eminence's behavior that he was counting on martyrdom as well (*hisāb-e shahādat rā ham karde [būd]*); it is very clear that he had given thought to the bloody future [= massacre and martyrdom] which awaited himself and his companions. It was solely for the purposes of bringing about his own martyrdom because he himself stated that he was going [to Kūfa] in order to right what was wrong and to bring about social justice (*iqāme-ye haqq*) and to fulfill the religious imperative to enjoin the doing of that which is right and to forbid the doing of that which is wrong (*al-amr bi'l-ma'rūf wa an-nahy min al-munkar*). Furthermore, the contemporaneous understanding of the followers or *shī'a* of the Imam about this move was nothing other than that His Eminence the Imam was engaged in an attempt to bring about a [political] order which was [truly] Islamic.

Therefore, it was something other than those two options, which if I were to leave the detailed discussion of the matter for another time and to encapsulate its essence for you gentlemen in a single sentence – albeit one which is a summary statement and necessarily somewhat ambiguous – I would have to say that Imam Husain ﷺ initiated his movement in order to fulfil [an ordinance having to do with the moral stewardship of the community (*ahkām-e nizāratī*) which is] a religious obligation (*wājib*) which had hitherto not been fulfilled up to that time in the Islamic community, and [which was a religious obligation (*wājib*)] which the Prophet ﷺ himself was unable to perform. [The nature of] this religious obligation (*wājib*) is such that even the Prophet ﷺ himself who is a Warner and a Bringer of Glad Tidings, i.e. who is the progenitor and originator of the Islamic Revolution and is its leader, could not undertake it. [Its nature is such that] someone other than the Prophet ﷺ himself had to undertake it; someone who was the continuation of the Prophet's being, and who moved in the same path and direction as him; and that person is Husain b. Ali ؑ.

5. Imam Husain's principle objective: the revival of the Prophet's Islamic revolution

What was that religious obligation (*wājib*)? It consisted in the renewal of the Prophet's Islamic revolution after the inception of the forces of reaction. It was the [attempt at] putting the train of the Islamic social order back on its tracks, after its having been derailed [with the *coup d'état* at the Saqīfa of the Banī Sā'ida]. With the action that he took, Imam Husain ؑ demonstrated that whenever the train of the Islamic social order is derailed and the values and ideals of the Islamic revolution forgotten, that this is how one must act, and that this is the way the train is brought back on its tracks. And this was naturally something which the Prophet ﷺ could not perform himself, because reactionary forces do not arise during the time of the leader of the revolution, but do so only after his passing.

Thus, Imam Husain's issue was not that of taking back the right of the House of the Prophet ﷺ, which had been usurped by illegitimate forces; this was the responsibility whose burden lay on the shoulders of Imam Hasan's progeny, from the Fourth to the Twelfth Imams ؑ. It was the responsibility of each of these great noblemen to move the cause of the revolution forward if and when they had the opportunity to do so, and to restore the Islamic social order which had been destroyed and lost, back to its original condition.

6. Two responsibilities of Imams Sajjād and Bāqir ؑ: The explication of authentic Islam and creating a well-equipped following

What were the responsibilities of Imams Sajjād and Bāqir ؑ? We mentioned these yesterday. These two Imams ؑ felt the weight of responsibility and worked for two things: to interpret and explicate the authentic meaning of Islam, and to harmonize its principles [and values with the needs of the respective societies of their day]; the same principles [and values and objectives] which had been forgotten by society. And secondly, creating an ordered and well-equipped following by means of which it would be possible to bring about an insurrection and to unseat the usurping and illegitimate ruling power and to take back the right of the righteous to provide direction to Islamic society. We saw that Imams Sajjād ﷺ and Bāqir ﷺ were active in this path, some examples of which I presented to the honorable gentlemen here present during yesterday's session.

7. Imam Sādiq ﷺ continues his father's methods

Imam Sādiq's imamate is a continuation of the methods of his father and grandfather, Imams Sajjād ﷺ and Bāqir ﷺ. Ultimately, there is the fact that during his imamate, an attribute arose within Islamic society which had not arisen previously, which was that the Imam lived during a historical period in which the Umayyads House, the old enemy of the Banī-Hāshim (i.e. the Ālid House), was in decline and at the nadir of its powers. Thus, the final phase of the decline of the Umayyad dynasty is the beginning of the blooming of Imam Sādiq's activities. We stated yesterday that these activities of Imam Sādiq ﷺ were covert and vigorous and decisive. That Imam Sādiq ﷺ would stand in the midst of crowds in the House of God ﷺ [in the Grand Mosque of the Ka'ba], and before crowds in Mina and Arafāt [during the Hajj pilgrimage] and forthrightly issue slogans which contained the kernels of the teachings of authentic Islam. We mentioned that he would say that it was he who was the [legitimate] ruler of society; and that the legitimate ruler before him was his father Imam Bāqir ﷺ, and so on back to the most preeminent forefather of the Imams ﷺ of the House of the Prophet ﷺ. And we mentioned also that these kinds of slogans and this kind of discourse were the kinds of talk which the Umayyads were most sensitive to and feared. As a consequence of the activities and political agitation of Imam Sādiq ﷺ and his followers, the situation changed and the people became aware of the crimes of the Umayyads and they came to know who their enemy was, as a result of which a movement sprang up which uprooted the Umayyads and a fresh House and dynasty came to power known as the Abbāsids; after which the situation changed.

8. The Reason for the inability of Imam Sādiq ﷺ to form a government after the fall of the Umayyads

Before we proceed any further, a question remains, which is why the Banī-Hāshim (i.e. the Ālid House) failed to take to the helm of the ship of state in the wake of the fall of the Umayyad dynasty? Why was it that it was the Abbāsids acceded to power [rather than the Ālids]? This is a legitimate question and one which should be asked, but if one looks into the lives of the Shī'a Imams, and particularly into the lives of Imams Bāqir ﷺ and Sādiq ﷺ, one will reach the certain conclusion that the conditions which needed to obtain in order for these revolutionary leaders to accede to power did not obtain during their lifetimes. The people had not been completely prepared and were not ready for leaders such as Imam Bāqir ﷺ and Imam Sādiq ﷺ to take to the helm of the ship of state. In point of fact, the uprising which was led by Abū-Muslim of Khorāsān and whose effects spread throughout the whole of the dominions of Islam was a premature uprising. I give a high probability that if this uprising had taken place 20 or 30 years later, that Imam Sādiq ﷺ or his son Imam Kāzim ﷺ or one of the other Imams ﷺ of the House of the Prophet ﷺ would have acceded to power; but the insurrection was premature [as it happened], and the people were not ready for it.

Let us also note that when Imam Ali ﷺ accedes to power 25 years after the passing of the Prophet ﷺ from the earthly plane, Imam Ali's ﷺ predecessors, that is, the third caliph, and before him, the second caliph, have brought about such a change in the [cultural and political] landscape of the community in the 22 years or so of their caliphates that the people are unable to digest [the revolutionary ideals of] Imam Ali ﷺ. We see people who were among the close companions of the Prophet ﷺ drawing their swords on Imam Ali ﷺ.[94] Internal differences arose and gave rise to

---

[94] Reference to Talha and Zubayr, who instigated the first internecine war of Islam which came to be known as the Battle of the Camel, based on the fact that it was centered on the camel which Āisha was riding, who was the person who encouraged these two erstwhile Companions of the Prophet ﷺ to rebel.

civil wars which burnt the whole edifice of Islamic society to the ground, such as the Battle of the Camel, the Battle of Siffīn, and the Battle of Nahrawān. These arose as a result of the preliminary requisites [of the accession of Imam Ali ﷺ to power] not being in place. My belief is that the reason the Commander of the Faithful stated that "were it not for the presence of those who are [yet] present and the establishment of the arguments [against my withdrawing from the burden of governance] by the existence of the helpers, as also [for] the fact that it is not pleasing to God ﷻ for those who know better [to stand] idly by and to watch the fullness [of the oppression] of the oppressor and the hunger of the oppressed, I would have thrown back its [the caliphate's] rope on its shoulder and made its last [incumbent] drink from the cup of the first one, and you would have found that your world is as distasteful to me as the dripping from the nose of a goat;" – that were it not for this fact, that he would still not have accepted being invested in the office of the caliphate; I believe he said this because he knew that the situation was not ripe [for the kind of rule that he would want to impose]. The prematurity of the [political] conditions were just as evident during the imamates of Imam Bāqir ﷺ and Imam Sādiq ﷺ, which were coincident with the blooming of the anti-Umayyad movement at the end of that dynasty's dynastic reign.

9. The consolidation of Abbāsid power makes Imam Sādiq's task more difficult

The enemy of the House of the Prophet ﷺ changed and yesterday's friends who had now acceded to power had become today's enemies. The same people who used to gather around with Imam Bāqir ﷺ and Imam Sādiq ﷺ and Muhammad b. Abdullāh b. Hasan and Ibrāhīm b. Abdullāh b. Hasan to plot the overthrow of the Umayyads, i.e. Mansūr and Ahmad as-Saffāh and Dāwūd b. Abī-Abbās and other well-known names of the House of Abbās, these same spineless cowards tortured and imprisoned Imam Sādiq ﷺ and Muhammad b. Abdullāh b. Hasan and Ibrāhīm b. Abdullāh b. Hasan and the Shaykh or Elder of the House of Abī-Tālib, i.e. Abdullāh b. Hasan. Thus had the political positions shifted.

When a fresh political order accedes to power, the political struggle becomes much more difficult. Up until now, Imam Sādiq ﷺ had to deal with the Umayyads, whose injustices were well known and were repeated in the marketplaces [of every town and city throughout the realm of Islam]. The people had suffered through many a long year [and indeed decades] of their injustices and oppression; they had had their properties confiscated by them, and had had a taste of their whip. Ḥajjāj b. Yūsuf[95] had instituted persecutions and mass executions; but now the "revolutionary" Abbāsids were at the helm – a House whose official attire was black in color which was supposed to signify their supposed grief and mourning for the tragedy of Āshūrā. So this context should be borne in mind. I fail understand why those historians who have researched Imam Ṣādiq's life and concluded that he was a quietist fail to take these conditions into account. Why can they not understand the nature of the situation which Imam Ṣādiq ﷺ was in?

The Abbāsids claimed that the black clothes which they wore and which was the official color of their attire was the mourning attire for the tragedy of Āshūrā (Ibn Shahrāshūb, *Manāqib* 3:300). This was the symbol that the Abbāsids used to accede to power; the same black attire which Imam Ṣādiq ﷺ characterized was "the attire of the People of Hell". Imam Ṣādiq ﷺ is reported to have said, "I know that these people have donned the Robes of Hell, and that they have forced the people to do the same."[96] This was what the Abbāsids' black attire [really] represented. So, truly, what is Imam Ṣādiq ﷺ capable of doing when faced with [the extent of the evil duplicity of] this ruling power, given the paucity of the number of his supporters? And with the vast majority of the ignorant masses who have fallen for the empty hype and pseudo-revolutionary slogans of the Abbāsids, whose fresh forces are intimately familiar with the secrets [of the tactics and strategy] of the Ālid House. Is he to be expected to rise up in insurrection against this newly established power?? Is such a thing at

---

[95] Abū Muhammad al-Ḥajjāj ibn Yūsuf ibn al-Ḥakam ibn ʿAqīl al-Thaqafī (Ta'if 661 – Wasit, 714), known simply as al-Hajjaj ibn Yusuf was perhaps the most notable governor who served the Umayyad caliphate. A highly capable though ruthless statesman, strict in character, a harsh and demanding master, he was widely feared by his contemporaries and became a deeply controversial figure and an object of deep-seated enmity among later, pro-Abbasid writers, who ascribed to him persecutions and mass executions.

[96] Shaykh Koleynī's *Kāfī*, 6:449.

all realistic and practicable? Abū-Ja'far al-Mansūr even knew the number of Imam Sādiq's Shī'a. Ahmad as-Saffāh knew the areas from whence letters containing financial support would arrive for Imam Sādiq ۩, and which villages and hamlets were his supporters. And it was only natural that he should know these things, because it was only yesterday that they were brothers in arms who fought in the same front against the Umayyads.

10. The Intellectual Efforts of Imam Sādiq ۩ for the Dissemination of Shī'a Islam and the Training of the Shī'a Cadres

Imam Sādiq ۩ had to come up with an innovation. He first needed to start his [teaching and] propaganda activity anew and to prepare the intellectual grounds [for the ultimate goal of the accession of the Imams ۩ to political power] by telling the truth about the usurpation of the caliphate by the enemies of the Ālids who nevertheless impudently claimed to be championing their cause. Imam Sādiq ۩ had to first make people aware of the fact that these claimants to power were, like the usurpers before them, liars and dissolute and debauched profligates. Secondly, he needed to promulgate the Shī'a ideology among the people; the ideology which Shī'a Islam lived and died by. And thirdly he needed to train the followers which he had into elite cadres who were capable of managing the insurrection that was to come if and when the time became ripe for it.

These were the things Imam Sādiq ۩ was preoccupied with. The first priority was the matter of raising peoples' awareness, because there were still people within the Levant (which was the seat of the erstwhile Umayyad power) who did not consider the Ālid house to have any privileged status within Islam, and some of whom did not even consider them to be Muslims [thanks to the unrelenting Umayyad propaganda apparatus]. Are you surprised, then? The Umayyad propaganda had worked, such that the people believed not only that Ali ۩ was not a Muslim but that he was the enemy of Islam! It is clear that when the Abbāsids acceded to power, that they would not defend their enemies, the Ālids, from the onslaught of decades of relentless propaganda and lies.

Thus, rectifying this massive disparity was Imam Sādiq's first task: to enlighten the sworn enemies of the Ālid House: the people who celebrated the tragedy of Karbalā, and who had sworn solemn vows to do something or give something away in order to seek the pleasure of God ﷻ (*nadhr*) if Husain b. Ali ؈ were to be killed.

Pay attention to the kind of propaganda which was being disseminated in those days against the House of the Prophet ﷺ. It is by becoming aware of such information that the role and Islamic responsibilities of Imam Sādiq ؈ will become clear for you.

11. A Hadith Report about the Negative Effects of Umayyad Propaganda against the Ahl al-Bayt ؈

I came across a hadith report in my notes where a contingent from [the tribe of] the Banī-Awad came to Hajjāj b. Yūsuf's court, the governor of the 'Irāq during the caliphate of Abd al-Mālik al-Marwān [at that time], i.e. a few years after the tragedy of Karbalā, or about thirty years after Imam Ali's ؈ martyrdom. All these years had passed since his martyrdom, but because Imam Ali's ؈ name was a Shī'a slogan, [the Umayyad propaganda apparatus] had worked relentlessly [to vilify] his name. And so a contingent of this population who were known for their enmity with the House of the Prophet ﷺ and who raised their womenfolk [and children] to harbor rancor toward the Ālids came to Hajjāj. The leader of the contingent entered into Hajjāj's presence; and because they were staunch supporters of the Umayyads and enemies of the Ālids, they allowed themselves some latitude to talk freely with such a ruthless governor.

The tribal elder started to talk with sharp words to Hajjāj, who responded to him in a like manner, saying things like 'mind your own business', 'be quiet', 'what in hell are you talking about', and things of this nature. So the man turned to Hajjāj and asked "Why do you talk to me in such a derogatory manner, O commander? The Quraysh are the highest of the tribes of the Arabs, and the tribe of Thaqīf is another great Arab tribe" – which Hajjāj was a part of – "and there is no superlative virtue in these two tribes which we too are not in possession of. So why do you talk to me in such a derogatory manner?" To which Hajjāj responded, "We

7. The Political Life of Imam Sādiq

have not heard of any of the virtues of your tribe. What are they?" Thus, the tribal elder began to list the virtues of his tribe.

Now pay close attention to the things which he lists as virtues, and you will see the kinds of characteristics and attributes which were considered to be virtues during the time of the Umayyads. He said, "There has never once been an instance of the disparagement of Uthmān" – the third caliph – "in any of our gatherings." Hajjāj replied that "Truly, this is indeed a virtue."

The elder continued, "There is not a single rebel against the ruling powers in our tribe, or anyone who is against the ruling order." Hajjāj again replied that "Yes, this is also a virtue." Did you pay attention to the beginning of the hadith report? These are the "*superlative* virtues" [of the tribe].

The tribal elder continued, "In all of the battles which Abī-Turāb waged against his enemies, there has only been a single person from our tribe who fought on his side." The use of the epithet "Abī-Turāb" instead of the title "Commander of the Faithful" is a sign of a lack of due respect for Imam Ali ﷺ. "...there has only been a single person from our tribe who fought on his side, and that person is no longer looked upon with any favor or respect by the people of our tribe. Hajjāj again replied that "Yes, this too is a virtue for you."

The tribal elder continued, "It is a custom of our tribe for anyone who wants to marry, to ask his intended bride whether she is fond of Abū-Turāb, and whether Abū-Turāb's name has ever been used by her in any favorable context. And if that woman responds in the affirmative, then the marriage will not take place, because this is considered to be a great crime." Hajjāj again replied that "Yes, this is also a virtue."

The elder continued, "There has never been any son born to any member of our tribe who has been named Ali ﷺ or Hasan ﷺ or Husain ﷺ, nor any daughter who has been named Fātima ﷺ." Hajjāj again replied that "Yes, this is also a virtue." Notice that [the nature of the "virtues"] continue to degenerate as the hadith report progresses. The report ends by mentioning some details which are worthy of note and of our attention.

The elder continued, "When Husain b. Ali was making his way from the Hijāz to the 'Irāq, a woman made a solemn vow [to do something or give something away in order to seek the pleasure of God 🕊] (*nadhr*), that if Husain 🕊 were to be killed in this journey, she would sacrifice ten camels [and distribute the meat to the indigent as a way of gaining God 🕊's good pleasure]. And after Husain 🕊 was killed, the woman remained faithful to her pledge." These were the "virtues" that the society of that day held in esteem. Hajjāj again replied that "Yes, this is also a virtue."

The elder continued, "One of the people of our tribe was told to disavow and anathemize Ali 🕊. He said that he would, and that he would imprecate and put a curse on Hasan 🕊 and Husain 🕊 too!" Hajjāj said "By God 🕊, this is a virtue."

The dissemination of information is critical. [Thus,] the [Abbāsids] who came to power with slogans which were against the atrocious Umayyad regime had to fall from the people's favor to something less than the credit-worthiness of an average person. It is not possible to imprecate an average person, but Ali 🕊 and Hasan 🕊 and Husain 🕊 had to be demonized to the point where ordinary people imprecated them because they were the cause of the insurrections which the Umayyad regime faced; because it is their names and their teachings which are the beating heart of that part of Islamic society which is alive. Thus, it is imperative that they fall from grace.

The elder said, "Now that you have heard what we are about, also pay heed, O Hajjāj, to the Commander of the Faithful Abd al-Mālik's judgment about us, who told us that 'You are the closest of those who are close to me; and that after the Helpers (*ansar*) of the time of the Prophet 🕊, you are [my] helpers'." Hajjāj said "I agree that this too is a virtue."

Do you imagine that when al-Mansūr the Abbāsid accedes to the throne that he will feel sorry for Imam Hasan 🕊 or Imam Husain 🕊, or for the Commander of the Faithful 🕊, so that he will try to rectify these misconceptions and disabuse the minds of the people of the false wall of propaganda which has been erected against them by the Umayyads? This is the same al-Mansūr who would curse Ali's name in public while he was sitting on the *minbar*[97] while he was the governor of MadinaMadina. This is the same al-Mansūr who disparaged Imam Hasan 🕊 before a group of

---

[97] *Minbar*: the Islamic form of a pulpit or dais consisting of an elevated sitting area reached by a short flight of stairs.

his revolutionaries and mentioned the [supposed] high number of Imam Hasan's wives, giving rise to this virulent false meme.[98] And the gentlemen who repeat this vicious meme are the followers (*shīʻa*) of al-Mansūr, not the followers of Imam Ali ﷺ; the Mansūr who holds rancor in his heart for the sons of Imam Hasan ﷺ and Imam Husain ﷺ; and the same Mansūr who has fought in the same front with these people [against the Umayyads], who has seen their courage at first hand, who has seen their willingness to sacrifice themselves with his own eyes, and has seen how the people are drawn to them – do you think this Mansūr will make any effort to disabuse the people of the tissue of lies which have been erected like a veil before them, and to join the ranks of their followers? No, he will do no such thing. Rather, he will pick up where the Umayyad propaganda machinery left off. And consequently, the situation of the Shīʻa during the reign of al-Mansūr became [as dire] as its situation during the reigns of Abdul-Malik and Marwān and Hajjāj and Ziād b. Abīh and Abdullāh b. Ziād and the other Umayyad despots.

Who is left to rectify these lies? Imam Sādiq ﷺ must begin that same process of the dissemination of true information and to disabuse the people's minds of the false information with which they have been fed, which is a process which was started by Imam Sajjād ﷺ, starting a party base from scratch and work on building a core of dedicated believers who can in turn work on others with the ultimate objective of preparing an underground organization which is capable of rising up in insurrection to seize the reins of power when the time is right and the opportunity presents itself. The essence of the nature of this movement can be heard in the words of Imam Sādiq ﷺ which are repeated from the pulpits in the sermons which everyone has heard. These same points which I have just stated can be found quite distinctly and explicitly.

12. The Paucity of the Number of True Shīʻa during the Time of Imam Sādiq

The hadith report which I just read appears in Shaykh Koleynī's *Kāfī* (2:242); and there are several reports in this same vein. I stated to you

---

[98] Wilferd Madelung has dealt with this false meme in one of the appendices to his landmark work, *The Succession to Muhammad*, Cambridge UP, 1997.

gentlemen in the first couple of days that what I have to say is just a small representative sample of the mountain of material that is available. I am talking about the mountain of material which I have gathered, not of the entirety of the material that is out there in the books [of hadith scripture], which is a lot more.

A man comes up to Imam Sādiq ﷺ in Madina and makes suggests to him that he should rise up in insurrection [against the ruling powers]. It is the era of the reign of the Abbāsids. He says, "Sir! Why do you not rise up in insurrection and seize the reins of power? Why do you not do that which you should be doing?" Imam Sādiq ﷺ tells him to accompany him to the outskirts of Madina; it seems that perhaps it was not secure to talk [in his own home]. The two of them leave and arrive at a place where they make their ritual devotions. After the prayers have been offered, the man says, "I saw Imam Sādiq ﷺ turn to me suddenly and, pointing to the sheep which were in our vicinity, said, 'If I had as many [loyal and reliable] supporters as the number of these sheep, I would rise up in insurrection [as you suggested].'" The man then says, "I counted the number of sheep and there were seventeen of them."

This is the state that the Shī'a party had fallen to after the accession to power of the Abbāsids. Thus, Imam Sādiq ﷺ had to work on building his base, and carving people out of the stones which the enemy has laid in his path. And so he started. For the first ten years, the matter remained covert and hidden. The Abbāsids had issues which they had to deal with. There were enemies in the Levant and in Yemen which they had to fight. So they had bigger problems to deal with than dealing with Imam Sādiq ﷺ. Consequently, some latitude was afforded to the Imam. These several thousand hadith reports which have reached us are from those ten years. And after al-Mansūr was rid of his more immediate problems, he realized that the political agitation that the Ālids were engaged in during the reign of the Umayyads was being played out again under his nose. He was aware of the methods that they used, and knew what their program was, as he had worked with them before personally. He knew what they were up to, and he knew that it is through these very tactics of raising the people's awareness and political consciousness that great revolutions are made. He knew that it was in these teaching circles that men of steel were born. And that is why he felt he had to deal with Imam Sādiq.

Imam Sādiq ※ was alone for a long time. Once he was exiled to Hayra [near Najaf in Iraq], and another time, he was exiled to another town in Iraq, whose name I cannot recall right now. [There is a report of someone who says that] he went to Hayra and stayed there for three days, but was unable to meet with Imam Sādiq; which is an indication of how tightly he was kept under guard. And there are similar stories, such as the story of the cucumber vendor, and others like it, which are plentiful. This is because the Abbāsids had cottoned on to the fact that the political agitation and education regimen had started in earnest.

Some of the Imam's time was spent in this way, and some of it on matters having to do with the way in which his followers were organized and creating important programs. The other important matter had to do with fostering intellectual growth...[99]

13. The insurrection of Zaid b. Ali from the perspective of the Imams

Some people criticize and denigrate Zaid b. Ali b. Husain severely and mercilessly. This is the same Zaid concerning whom the Most Noble Prophet ※ stated, "There will come a person from among my progeny who will be martyred; and anyone who is martyred with him in that battle will be raised above the shoulders of [others of God ※'s] creatures and will enter Heaven before others". And then there are ignoramuses who know a little Arabic who have the temerity to criticize and denigrate [the memory of] Zaid b. Ali. Zaid b. Ali is the same person concerning whom [his father] Imam Sajjād ※ has stated, "When God ※ gave this child to me, I opened the Quran and saw the following verse come up: [9:111] *Behold, God ※ has bought of the believers their lives and their possessions, promising them paradise in return, [and so] they fight in God ※'s cause, and slay, and are slain.* I then understood that this was the child which the Prophet ※ had referred to, which is why I named him Zaid." Because the Prophet ※ has said that his name was Zaid. Imam Sajjād ※ says that when

---

[99] An error in the tape recording occurs at this point.

this verse appeared, another verse also appeared – His Eminence opened the Quran twice – and that is how he knew that it is the same child to which the Prophet ﷺ had made reference. And there are many other examples in a similar vein concerning Zaid.

14. Imam Sādiq's position concerning Muhammad b. Abdullāh's insurrection

Zaid's uprising occurred during the latter phase of the Umayyad Dynasty. Another warrior who rose up in insurrection, this time against the Abbāsids, was Muhammad b. Abdullāh b. Hasan b. Hasan b. Ali b. Abī-Tālib ؏, known as an-Nafs az-Zakīya (the Pure Soul). Imam Sādiq ؏ provided much aid to this man. [Yet,] he too has been the subject of much severe criticism in our books and religio-historical discourse. If I have time, I will relate the hadith reports in which Imam Sādiq ؏ talks about Muhammad b. Abdullāh where the uninitiated would be led to believe that the Imam was against Muhammad b. Abdullāh's uprising and provide an explanation of their true meaning. We should not dismiss that hadith report [as unsound], but it has been misinterpreted.

Abul-Faraj Esfahānī relates in his book *Maqātil al-Tālibīn* (1:170) that Muhammad b. Abdullāh b. Hasan sent word to Imam Sādiq ؏ to pay him a visit at his home as he had some [urgent] business he needed to discuss. When Imam Sādiq ؏ arrived, Muhammad b. Abdullāh said, "O son of the Apostle of God ﷺ, I intend to attempt a *coup d'état*. Are you willing to work with me [on achieving this goal] or not?" The word used is *bay'at* [which is usually translated as giving a pledge of allegiance but] which means "working together" (*hamkārī*) [in this context]; [thus:] "Are you willing to pledge an oath of mutual cooperation or not?" The Imam replied in the negative [with something to the effect of, "I beg pardon from not being able to enter into such an arrangement" (the Arabic is not given, and the Persian is idiomatic)]. Now that I am looking at the situation after the passage of 1300 years, I see that the Imam should indeed have been pardoned from getting involved in this affair, because if Imam Sādiq ؏ had entered into Muhammad b. Abdullāh's group, there would be no such thing as Shī'a Islam today. It was necessary for the Imam to keep himself

7. The Political Life of Imam Sādiq

intact in order to ensure that tens of other uprisings would occur after that of Muhammad b. Abdullāh's.

Muhammad b. Abdullāh said, "O son of the Apostle of God 🌸, I understand." His understanding was the same as mine. When he saw that the Imam demurred, he didn't accuse him of acting [too] conservatively or of fearing for his life; because he knew that Imam Sādiq 🌸 was the composer of the following verse of poetry:[100]

> *I strike a bargain concerning my soul [only] with God,*
> *For there is nothing among the entirety of His Creation which is worthy of its exchange.*

The language of poetry is the most expressive [form of] expression. And if I have time, I shall say a sentence or two concerning the poetry and poets and bards of that era. Imam Sādiq 🌸 proclaimed his message with the language of poetry to all of his followers and Muslims of his day, as well as those of times to come. He says that he strikes a bargain about his soul [only] with God 🌸. In other words, his soul is at the ready [for the ultimate sacrifice, as long as the price is right, i.e. as long as it is truly in God 🌸's cause]. And Muhammad b. Abdullāh knows Imam Sādiq's personality and that he is not one who is concerned about the possibility of his death. And that is why he said that he understood.

Abul-Faraj tells us that two of Imam Sādiq's sons were present at that meeting. One was Mūsā b. Ja'far [the Seventh Imam, Imam Kāzim], and the other one was Abdullāh b. Ja'far. When Imam Sādiq 🌸 stepped out of the house, Muhammad b. Abdullāh turned to the Imam's sons and said, "Go with your father; I no longer expect you to cooperate with me (*bay'at*) [in this regard]". What do you think he means by the sentence "I no longer expect you to cooperate with me"? Let us proceed to the rest of the hadith report, where it becomes clear that they [Imam Sādiq's two sons] had already made such a pledge. Thus, what it means is that Muhammad b. Abdullāh was relieving them of the commitment to which they had sworn a solemn oath. And [what this tells us is that] Mūsā b.

---

[100] Ascribed to Imam Sādiq 🌸 in Ibn Shahrāshūb, *Manāqib* 4:275.

Ja'far and Abdullāh b. Ja'far had made this pledge in the presence of their father, Imam Sādiq ﷺ. Now the question becomes, would Mūsā and Abdullāh do such a thing without the permission of their father? You might or mightn't allow for this possibility in the case of Mūsā b. Ja'far, but [at all events,] *I* do not. [I believe that it must have been] with Imam Sādiq's nod of approval (*bā ishāre-ye imām būde ast*).

Muhammad b. Abdullāh turned to the Imam's sons and said, "Go with your father; I changed my mind about you two." When Imam Sādiq ﷺ was walking in the street, he heard footsteps behind him. He turned around and saw that it was his two sons. He asked them, "Why did you leave?" And they told him that Muhammad b. Abdullāh had relieved them of their commitment and told them to leave too. At this point, Imam Sādiq ﷺ tells his sons to go back to Muhammad b. Abdullāh, because the reason he made his excuses was not because he feared for his life, but because of an overarching reason which made such a commitment inexpedient. With this, Imam Sādiq ﷺ sent his two sons back to Muhammad b. Abdullāh.[101] This is stated in Abul-Faraj Esfahānī's *Maqātil at-Tālibīn*, a book that is highly regarded by Sunni and Shī'a [scholars] alike. Imam Sādiq ﷺ helped these [kinds of movements] and gave them his approval. There are numerous other tales [such as these, but] the repetition of them would be tiresome, as well as being repetitive. In other words, they would only be acting to affirm the same point which this hadith report provides; and a single instance should suffice an unbiased and fair-minded person. We thus see that one of Imam Sādiq's ﷺ activities was to maintain close contact with these radical revolutionary groups and movements [in the post-Umayyad era as well].

15. Evidence of Imam Sādiq's not intervening to prevent insurrections against the oppressor Caliphs

I will relate another of Imam Sādiq's activities which has reached us by way of a hadith report which appears in the noble book *Wasāil ash-Shī'a*, which is a renowned book which is accepted and referred to by all [Shī'a] scholars and historians of sacred history. The hadith report appears in the

---

[101] Abul-Faraj Esfahānī, *Maqātil at-Tālibīn* (1:170)

thirteenth chapter of Book 3. Imam Sādiq ﷺ says, "Let the freedom fighters of the House of the Prophet Muhammad ﷺ enter into the critical phase [of their insurrectionary activities]; I will cover their costs." Generally speaking, what do those people who believe that Imam Sādiq ﷺ was against armed conflict against the ruling powers of his time, say to the hadith report which I just cited, of which there are numerous examples, another of which I will also be discussing? I ask you to really ponder this point, because you might arrive at a conclusion which I have been unable to arrive at. [Our hadith report corpus tells us that anti-regime elements] are constantly coming up to Imam Sādiq ﷺ and asking him why he does not rise up in insurrection against the Abbāsid order. One such report was the report narrated by Sadīr Sirafī, which I read earlier. The report about the seventeen sheep. When these people come up to him and urge him to rise up in insurrection, what should the Imam say if he is against such a thing? Is he supposed to raise his voice at these people and say, "What in Hell are you talking about? What kind of talk is this?? Is that what you think our function and responsibility is?? What I want to do is [to be left in peace so that I can] conduct my lessons and relate the hadith reports of the Prophet ﷺ [which I have heard from my father and forefathers before him]! What kind of talk is this that you are giving voice to??" Is that not the case that if the Imam is against this kind of activity, then that is the kind of response that we should expect of him? But this is not how Imam Sādiq ﷺ responds. The Imam asks how many brothers in arms he has at his disposal; and when his interlocutor gives him a number, the Imam proves to him that he is mistaken, and that he does not understand the complexity of the task at hand and the overall situation, and that the number of men that are available are insufficient to the task. All of these kinds of hadith reports point to the fact that Imam Sādiq ﷺ is ready to carry out such an uprising, but that he does not see the preconditions as having been met.

What are your thoughts about these hadith reports? Have you thought about this issue? And if you have not, then you should: it is an issue which demands our attention!

16. Imam Sādiq's position with respect to the caliphs of his time

Another matter which it is necessary for me to mention concerning Imam Sādiq's life is how he related to the caliphs of his time. This is a matter which is the subject of much discussion; and I did touch on the matter briefly in the first couple of sessions, but I did not go into a detailed explanation, so I am not sure that everyone has understood it properly. And some of you might not have been present.

There are several hadith reports [about this subject]; as far as I have been able to tell, there are maybe five or six of them, the gist of all of which is that the Abbāsid caliph al-Mansūr called Imam Sādiq ﷺ to his presence, or it might have been that Imam Sādiq ﷺ went to his court himself, at which point al-Mansūr started to speak in an inappropriate and insulting manner to the Imam, who responded, "O Commander of the Faithful! [The prophet] Job ﷺ was afflicted [with difficulties] and he exercised patience and forbearance. Josef was given [a goodly amount of] God's ﷻ blessings, and he praised the Lord and thanked Him. And you are the progeny of the same line [of prophets], so exercised patience and forbearance!"[102] In other words, be more tolerant of the faults which you see in us. In some of these hadith reports, it is related that al-Mansūr becomes angry and dismisses the Imam in anger. In others it is related that a kindness overcomes him, and that he embraces the Imam and kisses him. There are a few of these kinds of reports. But the task before us is to look into the matter and examine the nature of the hadith report.

The first point that I have to say about these several reports is that the [initial] narrator is Rabī', [who was al-Mansūr's] chamberlain. Thus, Rabī' is someone whom Mansūr has searched high and low among those closest to him and chosen to act as his chamberlain and to manage his ongoing affairs. He is someone whom Mansūr took with him even when he made the Hajj pilgrimage to Mecca; this fact appears in the hadith report corpus. He was also with Mansūr in Baghdad and in Hayra. The initiator of the hadith report is none other than Mr. Rabī'! What can this be likened to? Let us use an analogy from everyday life and leave the lofty

---

[102] Allāma Muhammad Bāqir Majlisī (d. 1110/1698), the *Bihār al-Anwār* (Oceans of Light), 47:193.

7. The Political Life of Imam Sādiq

places to themselves. Let us suppose that you have an enemy who is bent on your destruction and is constantly engaged in a feud with you; and that you feel the same way about him. And your friends and followers are also in a feud with this person, on account of their friendship with you. Let us further suppose that you are in prison, or in another town, or are otherwise preoccupied or at all events are not present. Now this enemy, seeing your absence, starts to pick up your friends one at a time by saying things like, "Why are you carrying on a feud with me? Your master was just here the other day, throwing himself at my feet and kissing them, saying how sorry he was, and how mistaken he was, and how he was one of my sincere friends and supporters." How much credence would you give to such words?

Rabīʿ, the chamberlain of Mansūr, who is trusted by him implicitly, reports that Imam Sādiq ﷺ came and said such and such a thing, after which Mansūr said so and so. Except that in order for the Shīʿa to believe what he has to say and in order that they repeat his lie from one generation to the next, he inserts a few virtues and merits of Imam Sādiq's; but he chooses virtues which do not affect Mansūr's situation one way or another. For example, he would say that Imam Sādiq ﷺ entered the court and that he saw that the Imam's lips were moving, and that as soon as he entered, Mansūr suddenly got up and embraced him, even though he was angry just before the Imam came into the room. And that he later asked, "O son of the Apostle of God ﷺ, what were you murmuring when you entered?" And that the Imam replied, "Prayers." [In this way], the Shīʿa immediately think that Imam Sādiq ﷺ knew a prayer which changed Mansūr's mood with respect to their Imam, and do not pause to think that it is the coward Rabīʿ who, under the guise of some praise, has committed a great slander against Imam Sādiq ﷺ and convinced the Shīʿa of a great lie.

What is even more interesting [is that Rabīʿ has been able to pull this ruse off despite the fact that,] because, as it is said, that liars have short memories, Rabīʿ's has reported the way in which Imam Sādiq ﷺ enters into Mansūr's presence in three different ways which are mutually contradictory, because one cannot say that this event took place on three different occasions; for how can there possibly be three different incidents which are so similar to each other, but yet have fundamental differences? [Such that,] in one report, [Rabī'] relates that Imam Ṣādiq ﷺ said this particular prayer, and in another that he said a different one; and that in one report the Imam said such and such to him before, and in another, he said the same thing to him after such and such an event; and the same contradictions exist about Manṣūr's words and deeds. It is not possible to have so many contradictions concerning a single event [and for one to be able to rely on any single version of the various versions of the event being reported]. Thus, the first point about these kinds of hadith reports is that we must pay close attention to the person who has initiated the narration of the report.

17. Hadith reports which relate clashes between Imam Ṣādiq ﷺ and the caliphs

Another point to consider about these hadith reports is that there are a number of reports which paint a picture [of the relationship of Imam Ṣādiq ﷺ with the caliphs of his day] which is the exact opposite of the other group [which we just mentioned]. [Namely,] there is a group of hadith reports which portray Imam Ṣādiq ﷺ as a tame and submissive and incapable person who is obedient and subservient [to the caliph] and whose highest interests are to ensure his own material comforts, and who is afraid of even a single lash of Manṣūr's [enforcer's] whip. [In these reports,] Imam Ṣādiq ﷺ wails and moans when he is told that Manṣūr has called him to his presence, but then hangs his head and proceeds obediently and then acts meekly and obsequiously in the manner [that everyone has heard about], humbling and humiliating himself before Manṣūr.

Another group of hadith reports portray the same Imam Ṣādiq ﷺ before the same Manṣūr – not a different one – as a brash and presumptuous person who is looking for any excuse to clash with the caliph, calling him a "tyrant" (*jabbār*). Or, for example, one such report will relate the tale of Manṣūr putting a soft question to Imam Ṣādiq ﷺ in order to provide the Imam with an opportunity to provide a response which puts the Imam in a good light, thereby garnering the Imam's favor; but that the Imam sees through this ruse and answers in a way that

7. The Political Life of Imam Ṣādiq

demonstrates that he has seen through the caliph's ruse and that he knows that this attitude of the caliph's is to soften the Imam up rather than to resolve any differences between them, [which are fundamentally unresolvable in any case].

Thus, Manṣūr said, "O Father of Abdullāh! What is [the nature or purpose of] this fly which lands on me?" What he intends to elicit is a response with a tone which is in the vicinity of something like, "Ah, yes... the fly is one creature among all of the various creatures which God 🕮 has created.... It is a vexatious creature... It serves such and such purposes... The Prophet 🕮 has said such and such a thing concerning the fly..." This is the kind of response which such a question is intended to elicit. Manṣūr's point is to preoccupy Imam Ṣādiq's mind with these kinds of issues, and at the same time to demonstrate his [mock] respect for the Imam by virtue of the fact that he, the caliph, seeks the guidance of the Imam in certain matters. The Imam's response [which typifies this group of hadith reports] is: "[The fly has been created by God 🕮] in order to humble tyrants [such as yourself]!"[103] In other words, Imam Ṣādiq 🕮 is calling [this brutal] caliph a helpless wretch to his face!

This is a representative sample of this other group of hadith reports, of which there are many. I have made notes of some of these, but I shall not read them now, as they are not suitable for recitation in such a gathering and tribune, but are more suitable for scholars who are interested in the minutia of historical research.

Now which of these two [opposing portrayals] is true? You and I will open Allāma Muhammad Bāqir Majlisī's *Bihār al-Anwār* (Oceans of Light), only to see a hadith report of the first kind on one page, and one of the other kind on another. In the same book. What Allāma Majlisī's intention was, was to collect all of the hadith reports which the Shīʻa had reported through the ages in one book, and this is a project which he succeeded in doing.[104] And so, it is up to us to separate the wheat from the chaff in this compendium; the fault does not lie with Allāma Majlisī, who is merely the compiler and not the critical editor of the collection, which

---

[103] (Ibn Shahrāshūb, *Manāqib* 4:251).
[104] The *Bihār al-Anwār* collection is printed in one hundred and ten quarto volumes in its new Tehran edition.

contains all manner of reports about the life of all of the Imams, many of which contradict each other. And it is the *Biḥār al-Anwār* collection which is the major source of reference for people such as myself who carry out work of historical research in this field. The *Biḥār al-Anwār* collection contains the report which I mentioned yesterday or the day before where Imam Sajjād ﷺ tells Yazīd that he is his humble servant; just as it contains the passionate epic poem of Imam Sajjād ﷺ wherein he addresses Yazīd, stating, "We shall not compromise with you and make amends with you even for a single day; you want to kill us, and we want to kill you!" (45:175). Thus, the responsibility to sort these reports out falls on your and my shoulders.

So now which of these [reports] are true? Is it the ones which portray the Imam as humbling himself before the Pharaoh of the Age, or the ones which portray the Imam as the sons of Imam Ali's ﷺ [who is known for his courage and uncompromising moral stance against the enemies of Islam]? Imam Ṣādiq ﷺ tells us himself. When Mansūr orders Imam Ṣādiq's house to be burned to the ground – and it is obvious that he would not issue such an order concerning the house of a scholar who supported him – the Imam said, "I am the son of that Ancient House." [By making this statement, it is as if the Imam is saying,] "You burn down my house and think that by doing so you will be able to destroy me, or that this will induce me to surrender my will to yours. But I am the son of one whose House is the most deeply-rooted in this community, such that we are positioned in the very depths of this community." And he was right, of course. The blood of Imam Husain ﷺ and Imam Ali ﷺ course through Imam Ṣādiq's ﷺ veins. The blood of Imam Ali's ﷺ wife, Her Eminence Lady Fāṭimaᵗ az-Zahrā ﷺ, and the blood of the Prophet ﷺ himself course through his veins. So why would he submit to injustice?

Which of these two portraits is the true one, then, in your opinion? It is your decision. [But it seems to me that it is a case of] what the logicians would say is a proposition that is 'self-evident' and which does not stand in need of another reason. My suggestion, therefore, for those who can read and understand Arabic, and allow themselves on the basis of this alone to slander and disparage the reputation and posterity of Imam Ṣādiq ﷺ after the passage of a millennium and some centuries in favor of the intellectual heirs of the Manṣūrs of the world, that they should moderate their slander and defamation, and their spreading of aspersions. [The great 13th century Iranian lyric and civic poet] Sa'dī says [in his *Būstān* or *Rose Garden*], "Someone insulted me, but I did not hear his insult; it was like an arrow which was flung which missed me. [Now] you have picked up this arrow and are thrusting it into my side." At one time, long ago, some insults were said about Imam Ṣādiq; and now you have picked up these insults and have carried them [back] throughout the course of history in order to thrust them into Imam Ṣādiq's body?? Is that a good thing? Is that even right? Is that what it means to be called a dedicated follower (*shī'a*) of Imam Ṣādiq?!

Why is it that you make judgements when you do not understand what it is that you are passing judgements about, and when you do not have the intellectual wherewithal to make such evaluations? The source for all of these hadith reports which I have been reading is available: it is none other than the *Behār ol-Anwār*. What do you say about these hadith reports? Do you say that it is [an instance of the Imam practicing the Shī'a tenet of] precautionary dissimulation (*taqīya*)? I shall define *taqīya* [in due course]; but no, it is not a case of *taqīya*; *taqīya* is not like this. I shall discuss this subject as a side-issue in one of my talks.[105] But let me just say this briefly now, because I fear that I might not have time to discuss it in full later.

18. A preamble regarding precautionary dissimulation (*taqīya*)

Imam Ṣādiq ﷺ has said, "I exercise precautionary dissimulation (*taqīya*) in everything other than in drinking wine and in wiping my hands over my feet [as part of the ritual of ablution prior to prayer] (*mas'h*)."[106] This is one of those hadith reports which is not understood by a large number of people, i.e. they get stuck on the meaning of these two words. There are some matters which are not subject to precautionary dissimulation or concerning which one cannot dissimulate in this [religiously sanctioned] way. Some hadith reports report these as being two in number, and others

---

[105] See Chapter Ten.
[106] Shaykh Koleynī's *Kāfī*, 2:217.

report them as being three. Thus, it is evident that it is not [either] two or three, but [that these were being used as particular instances and not as absolute values, and that] there are criteria at play [for the general rule]. What the hadith report states is that in the event that I were forced to drink wine, I would not do so, and I would not resort to precautionary dissimulation (*taqīya*) [as a way of preventing harm to my person which would arise as a result of such a refusal]. What does it mean to say that "I would not resort to precautionary dissimulation"? What it means is that if I were to be told that I would be killed if I didn't drink wine, I would say, "Then kill me." And why is this the case? Because it is the Imam [who is speaking]; and the Imam is the exemplar [of the community], and Shī'a Islam does not want to have a drunk as an exemplar. This is a question of leadership. And this is what Imam Sādiq ﷺ takes into consideration and is sensitive to and rightly insists on [as a principle of] his religion and the religion of his forefathers before him: "Precautionary dissimulation (*taqīya*) is [an integral part of] my religion and of the religion of my forefathers" and "Anyone who does not practice precautionary dissimulation (*taqīya*) does not practice [an important and inseparable part of] Islam".[107] But at the same time he says that he will not resort to precautionary dissimulation when it comes to the matter of drinking wine, even if it means that he will be risking being put to death.

My contention is that because Imam Sādiq ﷺ is the leader who must take a stance against the illegitimate power (*tāghūt*) of his day and is an exemplar of the teachings of the Quran, he cannot allow himself to be abased and humiliated [before the supreme representative of this illegitimate power], and allow this humiliation and ignominy to be carried [in the minds of his detractors as well as his supporters] for thirteen centuries. This contradicts [the dignity of the station and] the office of the Imamate. And so, there is no call for resorting to precautionary dissimulation in such situations. And this is in addition to the fact that precautionary dissimulation is something that is essentially different from what these people imagine it to be.

---

[107] Allāma Muhammad Bāqir Majlisī, *Bihār al-Anwār* (Oceans of Light), 64:103.

7. The Political Life of Imam Sādiq

19. Two blows struck by Imam Sādiq ﷺ to Mansūr after his martyrdom

Imam Sādiq's imamate came to a close with his passing from the material plane, whereas Mansūr failed to find a pretext to put the Imam to death. He was not able to find an opportune moment to do so because of the extent of Imam Sādiq's political support, which he had garnered as a result of his organizational skills in organizing the resistance movement. He had gathered so many dedicated and devoted followers around himself in MadinaMadina as well as throughout the territories of Islam as a result of his retelling of all of the hadith reports about the Prophet ﷺ and all of his exemplary interpretations of the Quran and its teachings, that the caliph finds that he is powerless to put an end to him in any overt way, which is why Mansūr has him poisoned. But in addition to all of these blows which Imam Sādiq ﷺ dealt to the caliphal court and its power apparatus, Imam Sādiq ﷺ strikes two other blows to al-Mansūr by way of precaution in the last moments of his life.

19.1 The recommendation of weeping for him [= for his martyrdom] in Mina

The first of these is that he does not allow his murder to remain concealed. His death has been advertised as ostensibly occurring while he was [asleep] in his bed; so that the people say that Ja'far b. Muhammad 'died'; they do not say that he was murdered. Imam Sādiq ﷺ does not allow this matter to remain covered up. He sets aside a sum of money, asking that his followers and supporters – and Muslims more generally – weep for him [= for his martyrdom], from the time of his death until seven years hence, whenever they are gathered together for the Hajj pilgrimage ritual ceremonies.[108]

Now the House of the Prophet ﷺ was always against doing such things. They would not weep at the loss of their loved ones, or if they did, they wept briefly and did not hold mourning ceremonies for years to come. The question thus arises as to why Imam Sādiq ﷺ would ask his friends and supporters to weep for him for seven years? [The answer is

---

[108] See Shaykh Saddūq's *Man lā Yahḍarhū al-Faqīh* (4:244), and Shaykh Tūsī's *Tahdhīb* (9:144).

that] firstly, arranging mourning ceremonies for Imam Ṣādiq ﷺ acts to rejuvenate certain issues concerning him: What did he die of? What illness had he contracted? And then someone would whisper in someone else's ear that he did not die but was murdered. And secondly, Imam Ṣādiq's purpose was to teach his followers that the tears which they shed for him are of the same kind as the tears which Imam Sajjād ﷺ shed for forty years for Imam Ṣādiq's great grandfather [Imam Husain].

Why is it that a long and sustained series of mourning events occurred in the House of the Prophet ﷺ? One such event is the mourning of Her Eminence Lady Fāṭima ﷺ, the Prophet's daughter, who wept in a special way which laid the foundations for the enemies [of the House of the Prophet ﷺ] becoming afraid of her weeping. The second mourning event is the mourning of Imam Sajjād ﷺ who would weep at various occasions for the martyrdom of his father, Imam Husain ﷺ. The slaughtering of a sheep at the hands of a butcher becomes an occasion for Imam Sajjād ﷺ to break down and weep; and his having wept in such an unexpected manner becomes an occasion to say things which could not otherwise have been said. These also became the occasion for Imam Sajjād ﷺ to stipulate that his followers enter into a state of ritual mourning; and his followers understood this.[109] The *Tawwābūn* (those who turn in repentance) who were the first insurrectionary movement after the massacre of Karbalā came to Imam Husain's ﷺ gravesite and wept the same kind of tears. Their coming together [to express their repentance at having abandoned the Imam in his time of need] became the occasion for them to band together and form a resistance and an insurrectionary movement, which turned into the core of the movement which ultimately caused the downfall of the Umayyads in the 'Irāq. And the third mourning event is the tears which Imam Bāqir ﷺ stipulated should be shed in a highly calculated and exact way. All this is in the context of a Shī'a population which is aware of the fact that the House of the Prophet ﷺ was not known for holding long and sustained mourning ceremonies. [This made them ponder the question as to why things had changed so dramatically and tragically for the worse.] This was the first blow.

---

[109] Allāma Muhammad Bāqir Majlisī, *Bihār al-Anwār* (Oceans of Light), 46:108 & 111.

19.2 Depriving Manṣūr of any pretext by assigning several heirs and successors in Imam Ṣādiq's last will and testament

The second blow to Manṣūr is that Imam Ṣādiq ﷺ does not allow his enemy to know the identity of the Imam's successor, which he keeps as a secret. Immediately upon hearing of Imam Ṣādiq's death, Manṣūr sends a missive to the governor of MadinaMadina instructing him instantly to kill any successor which Imam Ṣādiq ﷺ might have stipulated, before such a successor is given the opportunity to become "a bone stuck in the throat" of the Abbāsid power apparatus, just as Manṣūr had described Imam Ṣādiq ﷺ as being. Assigning an heir or heirs is not problematic in itself: any father who is close to passing from this world to the next will assign his sons as his heirs. But Manṣūr is familiar with the logic of this House and realizes full well what the stipulation of an heir and successor mean. What it means is that the heir is responsible for taking up and continuing the work of his father and forefathers, and that their followers (Shīʿa) must obey him. There were certain things which the Umayyads did not fully understand, but Manṣūr is very familiar with this House and understands the significance of this matter, which is why he ordered any heir which had been stipulated to be destroyed.

The forces of the governor of Madina came to Imam Ṣādiq's house, asking who Jaʿfar b. Muḥammad had stipulated to be his heir and successor. They were told that his last will and testament was available for them to inspect. When they opened it and read it, they saw that he had stipulated five heirs and executors, one of which is Manṣūr himself! Together with his two sons, and two other people. Thus, Manṣūr was confused as to whom he should kill(!) And so this was the second blow which Imam Ṣādiq ﷺ struck to Manṣūr 'from the grave', so to speak.

20. Imam Kāẓim's ﷺ way

Imam Ṣādiq ﷺ passed and Manṣūr was faced with [the seventh Imam] Mūsā b. Jaʿfar, [known as Imam Kāẓim ﷺ]. At the beginning of his imamate, Imam Kāẓim ﷺ was preoccupied with seeing to the affairs of his father and with the continuation of his father's path; and of course, he did so covertly and *sub rosa*, as it were. Thus, Manṣūr was not able [to find an excuse to kill Imam Kāẓim] and [consequently] predeceased him. Manṣūr was succeeded by his son al-Mahdī, who was succeeded by his son al-

Hādī, who was succeeded by Hārūn, al-Hādī's brother and al-Mahdī's other son. The reign of these three Abbāsid caliphs which falls in the middle [of the Abbāsid dynastic range] is somewhat different [in terms of their quality]; each has their own unique characteristics, of course. Al-Mahdī ruled in one way, and al-Hādī in another, and neither had the attributes of al-Mansūr – neither in terms of the depth of their experience, nor in terms of their maturity. But Hārūn was a prominent individual and a very powerful and quick-witted and clever caliph.

The era is the era of the success of Imam Kāzim ؑ, who is able to attain to many successes throughout these few years and to gather a [substantial] following. Two or three uprisings take place during these years, one of which is the uprising of Husain b. Ali (another of Imam Hasan's progeny), the Martyr of Fakh, who was aided in his efforts financially and intellectually (but not physically or in actual battle) by Imam Kāzim ؑ. The quelling of Husain b. Ali's uprising set the cause of the resistance back yet again. He was one of the notables of the House of the Prophet ﷺ, the *Ahl al-Bayt* ؑ, whom the people of today have not understood and whom they have given themselves the permission to ignore and wipe clear from their consciences. Whereas the Prophet ﷺ has something to say about Husain b. Ali, the Martyr of Fakh. Abul-Faraj Esfahānī relates in his book *Maqātil at-Tālibīn* that the Prophet ﷺ is reported to have said that "One of my progenies who is named Husain b. Ali will be martyred in the environs of Fakh" (p. 289); and: "The brothers in arms of Husain b. Ali ؑ will be compensated the rewards of two martyrs" (*ibid*). The Prophet ﷺ had prophesied Husain b. Ali's ؑ martyrdom. Now martyrdom was not a prospect that weighed heavily on the members of the House of the Prophet ﷺ, all of whom were prepared for such an eventuality. But this [prophecy] relates specifically to Husain b. Ali, the Martyr of Fakh. Such hadith reports have not been related by the Prophet ﷺ concerning the other martyrs [in his cause and in the cause of his House]. This was [the stature of] this great man who rose up in righteous insurrection [against the forces of tyranny and oppression] who was an obedient devotee of Imam Kāzim ؑ, and who hailed from [the noble lineage of] the House of Hāshim and the House of [Imam] Hasan.

Imam Kāẓim ﷺ gradually developed the groundwork for armed conflict and a coup to the point where superficial contradictions begin to appear. Perhaps one will arrive at a different conclusion upon a deeper study of the subject, for my research into the life of Imam Kāẓim ﷺ have not yet been quite perfected (*kāmel-e kāmel nīst*). I don't want to imply that my knowledge of the life of Imam Sādiq ﷺ is 100 % [either], but only that I have studied the life of Imam Kāẓim ﷺ less. What I have been able to glean so far is that Imam Kāẓim ﷺ was in the habit of or was able to express things more forthrightly and in a way that was less veiled. Maybe it was the social exigencies of his times which necessitated this. [In other words, maybe it was because] the people [= the Shī'a] had a greater need for reassurance from the center of the power of the Imamate and the supreme [office of the] leadership of the Shī'a. Thus, perhaps it was the case that the Shī'a rank and file [needed the encouragement of and] were encouraged by the greater forthrightness of tone which Imam Kāẓim ﷺ adopted with the Abbāsid caliph Hārūn, and the general raising of the tone of enmity and rancor in the resistance struggle between the Imam and the caliph. [Perhaps it was the case that] news of the [bold and daring] way in which Imam Kāẓim ﷺ interacted with Hārūn reached the Imam's followers, who were buoyed and boosted by such news. And it was a time when Hārūn was still new to his office.

21. Imam Kāẓim's insistence on his right to the caliphate in Hārūn's presence

The hadith report which I am about to discuss is one which you have heard frequently; but one must know the reason (*jahat*) [for the statement] and why [the Imam] chose to take this particular direction or orientation (*jahat*) with respect to this issue. When Hārūn was passing through Madina on his way to Mecca to make the Hajj pilgrimage, he stopped at the Prophet's shrine. In order to justify the legitimacy of his reign, he addressed the Prophet ﷺ in the following terms: "Greetings of peace, O cousin [of mine]!" After all, the caliphate is passed down from cousin to cousin, not to distant relatives! It is very clear; very natural; as cousins are so close. I don't know if you know this – that the House of Abbās (or the Abbāsids) have a lineage like the House of Ali (or the Ālids).

What we maintain is that Imam Kāẓim ﷺ was designated to the Imamate by [the Immaculate and Divinely guided act of the designation to succession by his father] Imam Ṣādiq ﷺ, who in turn was so designated by Imam Bāqir ﷺ, and so on all the way back to Imam Ali ﷺ who was so designated by the Prophet ﷺ himself. Well, the Abbāsids had conjured up a similar sort of chain of succession for themselves. They would say that al-Manṣūr inherited the caliphate from Abdullāh b. as-Saffāḥ (Abul-Ās), who inherited it from his brother Ibrāhīm the Imam, who inherited it from his father Muhammad, who inherited it from his father Ali, who inherited it from his father Abdullāh, who inherited it from his father 'Abbās, who inherited it from the Prophet ﷺ! This is the kind of chain of succession which they had conjured up for themselves and they believed that in this way, they were the ones who had the greatest right to the caliphate and the greatest priority to the Imamate; this is the narrative which they disseminated.

In order for him to prove this and to establish it further in the minds of his subjects, Hārūn would address the Prophet ﷺ by saying, "Greetings of peace, O cousin [of mine]!" Now Imam Kāẓim ﷺ happened to be in the shrine at the time, and as soon as he heard Hārūn say these words, he retorted in a loud voice, "Greetings of peace, O father [of mine]!" In other words, he immediately cut him down to size and 'put him in his place' (*zad tu dahan-e Hārūn*). In other words, what he was in effect saying is that if you, O Hārūn, lay claim to your office on the basis of your kinship with the Prophet ﷺ, and the fact that you are his cousin; then if that is indeed the criterion[110], what about my right and my claim, which is far greater than yours, being his son!

---

[110] Which of course it is not. Islam came to rid the world of hereditary kinship. The succession of the Twelve Imams ﷺ in Shī'a Islam which, granted, mostly (but not always) also involves a father to son succession is not *based* on the filial relationship, but on divine designation, which also happens (usually) to be from father to son. This was also the case for the prophets of the Old Testament.

22. The boundaries of the Fadak Lands as described by Imam Kāẓim ﷺ to Hārūn

Hārūn knew that the House of the Prophet ﷺ is and will remain a thorn in his side. He had also come to know Imam Kāẓim ﷺ, so he was thinking of ways of deceiving him or tricking him into submitting to him or into accepting the legitimacy of his reign. This state of affairs is nothing new and existed between al-Manṣūr and Imam Ṣādiq ﷺ as well. And there was a very interesting story which I had intended to relate this evening, but which slipped my mind, unfortunately. I will not tell that story, but this one.

One day Hārūn met with Imam Kāẓim ﷺ. The details of where this meeting took place and under what conditions is not known; we just know that they met somewhere. Hārūn asked Imam Kāẓim ﷺ how it would be if I were to return the Fadak lands back to you [= to your House]. He had come up with a good idea, because the first of the slogans of the Shīʿa and their first demands for the restoration of justice revolved around the issue of the Fadak lands.[111] In order to demonstrate that the caliphate does not belong to those who have seized power and taken it in hand, the Prophet's daughter [Lady Fāṭima ﷺ] stated, "You have usurped our Fadak [lands]." What does this mean? It means that you are usurpers and oppressors. And an oppressor, in turn, cannot be a successor to the

---

[111] Before his conversion from Sunni Islam to Shīʿa Islam, the great English historian Ḥāmid Algar described the issue of Fadak in the following terms: "After the death of the Prophet ﷺ, his daughter Fatima asked for the arable lands near Fadak (a small town near Medina) to be assigned to her as a legacy from her father, since in his lifetime the Prophet ﷺ had used the produce of the land for the upkeep of his wives. Abu Bakr refused, citing the words of the Prophet ﷺ: "We prophets bequeath no legacies; what we leave behind is charity (*sadaqa*)." See al-Baladhurī, *al-Futūḥ*, ed. De Goeje (Leiden, Netherlands, 1886), pp. 29-33. For the Shiʿi tradition, Fadak is a symbol of unjust denial." The fact that the so-called hadith report cited by the first caliph was an obvious fabrication was not yet proven to him Fadak was usurped by the caliph who refused to give it back despite Lady Fāṭima's legitimate claim to it, based on a spurious claim concerning what the Prophet ﷺ had supposedly said. See *Islamic Beliefs and Practice: Definitive Responses to 40 Salafi Objections* by Reza Muhammadi; Translated and Annotated by Blake Archer Williams, Lantern Publications, 2021.

Prophet ﷺ and the ruler of the Islamic order, as the successor (*khalīfa*) is the embodiment of justice [in such an order].

So this was a Shī'a slogan which lasted for some time. But it aged and wore thin and no longer served its purpose. Its efficacy was at its peak when those who had usurped Fadak were in power; once that person has gone, and those who had inherited that usurped property were also gone, it no longer had any efficacy as a slogan that acted to restore justice. Which is why we do not see Imam Husain ؑ making any mention of it at Karbalā. After all, it was not as if it was Mu'āwiya who usurped Fadak, so that it could be used to motivate or justify an uprising against him. But a few too-clever-by-half caliphs thought that it might be a clever move to return these lands to the Ālids in order to subdue them. One such caliph is Umar b. Abdul-'Azīz, who is, I believe – though I am not 100% certain of this – one of the [most prominent] duplicitous liars within [Islamic] history, not unlike Anūshīravān the Just!

Imam Sādiq ؑ stated [concerning Umar b. Abdul-'Azīz] that, "This man will become the caliph, and then he will die. And when he dies, the people of Earth will cry for his loss whereas those who are in Heaven will curse him."[112] Because he was an imposter and a dissembler. One of the supposed virtues of Umar b. Abdul-'Azīz is that he had returned Fadak [to its rightful owners]. Bless his heart! What a magnanimous gesture, to return some arable land [to the House who has been designated by God ﷻ to be the leaders of the community of the faithful]. Of the thousands and hundreds of thousands of acres of arable land which he has stolen or taken by brute force from various people, he has returned one! How nice. And at a price, no less. At the price of buying the silence of the Ālids. Hush money, so to speak. Another one of these too-clever-by-half caliphs was Hārūn or-Rashīd who asked Imam Kāzim ؑ how it would be if he were to return the Fadak lands [to their rightful owners]. He wanted to exchange the Fadak lands for the insurrectionary slogans of the Ālids; so that he could say "What are you going on about now; didn't I return the Fadak lands to you?" Now let us see what kind of response Imam Kāzim ؑ gives.

---

[112] Allāma Muhammad Bāqir Majlisī, *Bihār al-Anwār* (Oceans of Light), 46:251.

7. The Political Life of Imam Sādiq

The hadith report which I am reading is taken from Ibn Shahrāshūb's *Manāqib*. "*Kāna yaqūl...*" It is clear that Hārūn tried this on more than one occasion [as this is the continuous form of the past tense conjugation of the verb]. Hārūn had repeated on several occasions to Imam Kāzim ﷺ that "Sir, we would like to return the Fadak lands to you! Will you give me your permission to do so?" But the Imam would demure and say, No; I do not want the Fadak lands." The caliph kept on insisting, but the Imam would not accept. Until Hārūn's insistence became urgent, imploring and urging Imam Kāzim ﷺ to accept; at which point the Imam said, "Alright. I am ready to accept the Fadak lands back from you. But I will only accept them as they are defined by their true boundaries." Thus, the caliph said, "What are the true boundaries of the Fadak lands?"

Well, the Fadak lands are the arable lands near Fadak, which is a small town near Madina, whose boundaries are indeterminate. The Imam said, "If I specify the true boundaries and limits of the Fadak lands, you will change your mind about giving them back to us." To which Hārūn replied, "Upon my word by [the right which] your ancestor [= the Prophet ﷺ] [has over me], I *will* return them!" Imam Kāzim ﷺ said, "The first limit of Fadak is Aden." The farthest southwestern corner of the Arabian Peninsula. Hārūn's face lost its color. "What are you saying?" he said. "Does Fadak go all the way down to there??" The Imam continued, "Its second limit is Samarkand." This was the northeastern limit of the Abbāsid empire at the time, at the northern boundary of Greater Khorāsān, which is in the hands of the Russians today [1972; it lies in present day Uzbekistan]. Hārūn's face turned dark. The Imam continued: "The third limit is Tunisia." That is, the western-most limits of the dominions of Islam at that time. Hārūn's face turned black and he blurted out involuntarily, "Woe!" And the Imam said, "And its fourth limit is Arminiya."[113] The north-western limit of the dominions of Islam at that time.

When Imam Kāzim ﷺ said this, Hārūn said, "Nothing is left for us! So come and sit in our place." Imam Kāzim ﷺ said, "I told you that if I specified the true limits of the Fadak lands, that you would change your

---

[113] Arminiya is being used in a wider sense so as to include under it the whole district situated between the Kur and the Caspian Sea (*EI*1).

mind about giving them back to us." What does this mean? It means that once upon a time, Fadak was the slogan of the Shī'a, you imbecile! Today, the Shī'a slogan is governance. The right to govern is ours and you have usurped it. Hārūn understood this. That which the Shī'a of Imam Kāẓim ﷺ do not understand now and must be force-fed if they are to come to understand it, Hārūn understood back then, 1,300 years ago. [The hadith report continues]: The decision to murder Imam Kāẓim ﷺ was made on that very day. Hārūn threw Imam Kāẓim ﷺ into one of his dungeons, sentencing him to life imprisonment; nor was he able to be content with this sentence and that Imam Kāẓim ﷺ should be able to live out his life in a dungeon. [Which is why he had the Imam poisoned in his cell.]

23. The Condition of the Shī'a during the Imamate of Imam Kāẓim

The condition of the Shī'a during the Imamate of Imam Kāẓim ﷺ was such that they frighten Hārūn. Do you not believe me? When they brought out Imam Kāẓim's body from the prison [in which he was kept and in which he was martyred], at first it was being carried by four pallbearers on a plank of wood. But how did it [the procession] end? You have heard this story many times. It ended in a large crowd being gathered to pay their respects, with the Imam's body being carried in an expensive burial shroud in a funeral procession with a [significant] presence of the people. And where did this take place? In Baghdad, under Hārūn's nose. Have you not heard from the mouths of the elegists that a number of Imam Kāẓim's friends came up to Sindī b. Shāhak – the infamous jailer – asking [permission] to see their Imam. Where did these people come from? They were residents of Baghdad. The Shī'a had gained a foothold in Baghdad as a result of the efforts of Imam Ṣādiq ﷺ and Imam Kāẓim ﷺ after him. Did you not know, for instance, that one of the great scholars of the Shī'a intellectual world was the grandson of Sindī b. Shāhak? His name is [Maḥmūd b. Ḥusain b. Sindī b. Shāhak, known as] Kashājam, Sindī b. Shāhak's grandson! Sindī b. Shāhak's wife is also a follower (Shī'a) of Imam Kāẓim ﷺ - either she was, or became – and she trained offspring [to be Shī'a], one of whose sons is none other than the great Shī'a scholar Kashājam.

Shī'a Islam had gained a foothold in Baghdad and was spreading; and it was this groundwork and socio-political context which forced Hārūn to call Imam Sādiq ﷺ from Madina to Khorāsān where he was right next to him and where he could keep a close watch over him; and to ostensibly make him his heir apparent in an effort to lower his standing in the eyes of his followers. And Shī'a Islam's popularity and support continued to grow through the Imamates of Imam Jawād ﷺ, Imam Hādī ﷺ, and Imam Hasan al-Askarī ﷺ, during whose Imamates the Shī'a were at the height of their powers and endurance as a religio-political organization. And this is the reason why Imam Jawād was murdered at the age of 25: to deprive him of the opportunity to reach the age of 65 like Imam Sādiq ﷺ. His son, Imam Hādī ﷺ, is murdered at the age of 42, and his grandson, Imam Hasan al-Askarī ﷺ, is murdered at the age of 28. And [all three of these Imams] were either in prison or in exile [or house arrest] during the 28 or 42 years [of their Imamates]. Imam Hādī ﷺ had been sentenced to long prison terms on numerous occasions, during which time the Shī'a were under extreme pressure and were being severely suppressed. And while the resistance struggle was ongoing, it was not possible to carry out a successful attempt at an uprising or coup.

24. The Imperative to Seek Forgiveness for [One's] False Appraisals [of the Character] of the Imams

So this is how our Imams ﷺ were, my brothers. What have we been saying? Where [= how far afield] have we been?? Let us seek forgiveness from these great men in our history and from these luminous visages in the history of humanity, and not just in the history of Islam. Let us seek forgiveness for what we thought about them until now! Let us seek forgiveness for the false appraisals and hasty judgments about them which were made either in ignorance or because of some bias or latent agenda. Let us [repent and] seek forgiveness for the wrong way in which we thought and talked about and judged Imam Sādiq ﷺ. We laid [the blame for] our own weaknesses and sloth and seeking the path of least resistance squarely on the shoulders of Imam Sādiq ﷺ, doubling the onus of our sins. This is not how Imam Sādiq ﷺ lived. I know this for a fact, but do not force it on you. Those of you who can carry out the task of research [into these historical concerns] should do so; and those who cannot, should ask someone who is unbiased and fair to carry out such research so that some of the dust of the misunderstandings and superstitions and distortions can be polished away from the images of these brilliant sources of light in history. Because the understanding that we have of the lives of our Divine Guides is inadequate and will not do.

25. All of the Imams ﷺ are Imam Husain's Brothers in Arms

As I have said, all of the Imams ﷺ are Imam Husain's Brothers in Arms. All of their hearts are in the same place, and all of them are warriors fighting in the same front, having given up the pleasures and comforts of this world and the sense of security, wealth, and social standing, and like their forefather Imam Ali ﷺ fought against the front of those who chose the way of the world and the pleasures and comforts which it offers. This story has been told from the time of Imam Sajjād ﷺ and has been the frontispiece of the resistance project of the Shī'a Imams ﷺ since the time of Imam Sajjād ﷺ, who would stand before the people and, [referring to the ephemeral glitter of the material world,] would ask, "Is there no one among you who will cast aside the rotting leftover food that is stuck between your teeth?" He was referring to the shameful wealth and goods and comforts of the world which are obtained at the expense of losing one's religion. Is there nobody who will [join our cause and the cause of the Prophet ﷺ, which was the whole purpose of his ministry and] jettison this life of bitter humiliation [of bending to the will of tyrants and oppressors], and the senseless and short-sighted way of taking the path of least resistance, and throw it in front of those who are content with such a life and nothing more? Is there not a single freeman to be found? Imam Bāqir ﷺ said, "Yes, I am such a freeman." And Imam Sādiq ﷺ said "I am such a freeman," as did Imam Kāẓim ﷺ and all of the other Imams, who proved that they are such a freeman, together with all of their Shī'a. These were all inspired by Imam Sajjād ﷺ, who in turn was inspired by Āshūrā. And today we revere the memory of Āshūrā, but have no reverence for what the act of Āshūrā represented; even though every word and every action which took place on that august day can and should be a source of inspiration for all of us.

8. The Imams' Politicism and their Militant Actions

[God ﷻ the All-Knowing and All-Wise has stated in His Sacred Writ:]

$$رَّبَّنَا عَلَيْكَ تَوَكَّلْنَا وَإِلَيْكَ أَنَبْنَا وَإِلَيْكَ الْمَصِيرُ ﴿٤﴾$$

[60:4] "O our Sustainer and Lord of Providence! In Thee have we placed our trust, and unto Thee do we turn: for unto Thee is all journeys' end.

$$رَبَّنَا لَا تَجْعَلْنَا فِتْنَةً لِّلَّذِينَ كَفَرُوا وَاغْفِرْ لَنَا رَبَّنَا ۖ إِنَّكَ أَنتَ الْعَزِيزُ الْحَكِيمُ ﴿٥﴾$$

[60:5] O our Sustainer and Lord of Providence! Make us not a plaything for those who are bent on denying the truth! And forgive us our sins, O our sustainer: for Thou alone art, almighty, truly wise!"

$$رَبَّنَا إِنَّكَ مَن تُدْخِلِ النَّارَ فَقَدْ أَخْزَيْتَهُ ۖ وَمَا لِلظَّالِمِينَ مِنْ أَنصَارٍ ﴿١٩٢﴾$$

[3:192] "O our Sustainer and Lord of Providence! Whomsoever Thou shalt commit to the fire, him, verily, wilt Thou have brought to disgrace [in this world]; and such evildoers will have none to succor them.

رَبَّنَا لَا تُزِغْ قُلُوبَنَا بَعْدَ إِذْ هَدَيْتَنَا وَهَبْ لَنَا مِن لَّدُنكَ رَحْمَةً ۚ إِنَّكَ أَنتَ الْوَهَّابُ ﴿٨﴾

[3:8] "O our Sustainer! Let not our hearts swerve from the truth after Thou hast guided us; and bestow upon us the gift of Thy grace: verily, Thou art the [true] Giver of Gifts.

وَلَمَّا بَرَزُوا لِجَالُوتَ وَجُنُودِهِ قَالُوا رَبَّنَا أَفْرِغْ عَلَيْنَا صَبْرًا وَثَبِّتْ أَقْدَامَنَا وَانصُرْنَا عَلَى الْقَوْمِ الْكَافِرِينَ ﴿٢٥٠﴾

[2:250] And when they came face to face with Goliath and his forces, they prayed: "O our Sustainer! Shower us with patience in adversity, and make firm our steps, and succor us against the people who deny the truth!"

وَلَيَنصُرَنَّ اللَّهُ مَن يَنصُرُهُ ۗ إِنَّ اللَّهَ لَقَوِيٌّ عَزِيزٌ ﴿٤٠﴾ الَّذِينَ إِن مَّكَّنَّاهُمْ فِي الْأَرْضِ أَقَامُوا الصَّلَاةَ وَآتَوُا الزَّكَاةَ وَأَمَرُوا بِالْمَعْرُوفِ وَنَهَوْا عَنِ الْمُنكَرِ ﴿٤١﴾

[22:40] ...And God ﷻ will most certainly succor him who succors His cause: for, verily, God ﷻ is most powerful, almighty, and [22:41] [well aware of] those who, [even] if We firmly establish them on earth, remain constant in prayer, and give in charity, and enjoin the doing of what is right and forbid the doing of what is wrong.

1. Hadith reports claiming that the Imams ﷺ were appeasers are forgeries

A matter remains to be pointed out from yesterday's discussion before we can proceed to today's discussion. In discussing the various aspects of the lives of the Imams ﷺ we arrived at the subject of the nature of their

8. The Imams' Politicism and their Militant Actions

relations with the caliphs of their respective eras, pointing to the distortions and falsifications of parts of the early history of Islam. And we saw the skill with which hadith reports were falsified in order to serve a specific purpose; and how a narrative was constructed wherein the leaders of the Shī'a (and especially Imam Sādiq ﷺ, the founder of the Shī'a religio-legal rite) were depicted as being obsequious and servile to the rulers of the day, in order to deceive the Shī'a of the generations to come to desist from their political activities and resistance struggle. When we looked into these kinds of hadith reports, we found that most of them were narrated by Rabī', al-Mansūr's chief of staff; someone who had been selected by al-Mansūr from among all of his entourage to be his intimate friend and confidant. In other words, he was someone in whom al-Mansūr had complete trust; and this fact clarified many issues for us.

2. Giving preference to reports of the courage of the Imams ﷺ to those which report the opposite

We then investigated hadith reports concerning Imam Sādiq ﷺ which reported stories which were the opposite of the other group of reports, and we said that there can be no doubt for a historian and even for a non-specialist who is somewhat familiar with the Islamic worldview who encounters the contradiction between these two sets of reports, that it is the ones which report the courage of Imam Sādiq ﷺ, the son of Imam Husain ﷺ, and Imam Ali ﷺ, which are the ones which properly represent Imam Sādiq's true character, who was someone who was fully aware of the teachings of Islam, was the founder of the Shī'a rite, as well as being the leader of the resistance movement. And we concluded that we should not, therefore, entertain the possibility, even for a moment, that Imam Sādiq ﷺ behaved in an obsequious and servile manner, as this is not something that is worthy of an ordinary Muslim, let alone that of the leader of Muslims, and the leader of a group of Muslims, no less, whose identity is based on the righteous claim that Islam can only properly be viewed through the lens of the interpretation and explication of their Imam; and that such obsequious and servile behavior was in no way compatible with the character of such a leader.

Thus, we can rest assured about this issue, and I am personally satisfied [of the falsity of those slanderous hadith reports], having researched the lives of the Imams ﷺ [in some depth]. My own curiosity has been quenched in this regard, and I am convinced that whoever carries out any research into the matter – and the more research, the better – will invariably reach the same conclusion that these reports were forgeries which were produced by the multi-century old Abbāsid reign, who had no choice but to forge these; just as any other [usurper] regime would similarly have no choice but to come up with such insidious deceptions, so that even today, after the passage of a thousand years, Imam Sādiq's behavior with respect to al-Mansūr spreads aspersions and doubts in the minds of the Shīʿa with respect to their own Imam. You can see that it has been a successful policy to date, too. This was a synopsis of yesterday's discussion, which we brought to bear with various exhibits and evidence, of course.

I hope that these words are still fresh in your memories and that you will not remain content to keep it there, but will repeat it and suggest it [as an alternate position] to those who are convinced of the veracity of the first group of hadith reports; because it is entirely possible that they might not have paid attention [to the logical discrepancies which are innate to their view]. It is an important subject: a huge distortion, and the falsification of an [important] truth, and the transformation of a given orientation to its opposite, which is a grave historical injustice to humanity. It is a crime in principle, over and above the fact that [it is a crime to us personally as] we are Shīʿa and we have love and affection for our Imams ﷺ.

[Until one researches the subject], one will not countenance anyone's saying that a tyrant who has gone down in history as being so-and-so "The Just", was not just at all. When we look into the life of Anūshīravān "The Just", we see that his was no different than the lives of his father and his son and all of his ilk throughout history, which was filled with injustice and oppression and brutality and inhumane behavior. If his name has gone down in history as Anūshīravān "The Just" as a result of his programmatic pretense and deceitfulness, it will no doubt be difficult for you to accept the fact that he was not just without first

8. The Imams' Politicism and their Militant Actions

carrying out some research into the matter. I have heard some people react to this, saying that one should not say that Anūshīravān was not just. They don't like to hear this said about him. It is as if they are Anūshīravān's progeny! They think of this as a crime. But then, how is it that you do not think it a crime when Imam Ṣādiq ﷺ is accused of carrying water for the Pharaoh of his age? This is the same Imam Ṣādiq ﷺ whom you yourselves say is the founder of the Jaʿfarī [Shīʿa] religio-legal rite. This is the same Imam Ṣādiq ﷺ whom you yourselves say that if Islam is not interpreted the way that Imam Ṣādiq ﷺ interpreted and explicated it, that it is not even Islam, properly so called; not that it is a false Islam, but that it should not properly be characterized as Islam as such; that it is not true Islam. And I would agree with you. This is the same Imam Ṣādiq ﷺ whom we believe to be the embodiment of the Quran – *kāna halqaᵗ al-qurʾān* – a Quran which separates [people] into two [distinct] fronts:

الَّذِينَ آمَنُوا يُقَاتِلُونَ فِي سَبِيلِ اللَّهِ وَالَّذِينَ كَفَرُوا يُقَاتِلُونَ فِي سَبِيلِ الطَّاغُوتِ فَقَاتِلُوا أَوْلِيَاءَ الشَّيْطَانِ ﴿٧٦﴾

> [4:76] Those who have attained to faith fight in the cause of God ﷻ, whereas those who are bent on denying the truth fight in the cause of the powers of evil.

Does it not bother you to see the leader of this first group being characterized as one who carries water for the leader of *those who are bent on denying the truth* and for those who *fight in the cause of the powers of evil*? Does this not surprise you? Is this not an injustice and a crime? Can there be a greater distortion than this? A greater sin? At any rate, let the gentlemen here present consider this [= the dissemination of the falsity of these slanders] to be their [religious] duty. This was [a summary of] a subject which we have already talked about.

I have of course repeated on several occasions from the first of Muharram [i.e. from the beginning of the lecture series] that what I am presenting is not a compressed summary of my research but selections from it. Because it is not possible to summarize the material, as there is so much material and so much evidence to consider, that it is not possible to summarize it in a couple of sessions or in two to four hours. And this is even more the case in an environment where our people have been accustomed to hear sermons on the kinds of subjects which are usually delivered from the pulpit, and who get bored as soon as a modicum of critical thinking is expected of them.[114]

3. Veins of active resistance in the lives of the Imams

Another subject remained [from yesterday], and that is that from the time of Imam Sādiq ﷺ onward, we see a phenomenon in the lives of our Imams ﷺ in the hadith report corpus which is their leadership role in the faction of active resistance [against the ruling powers]. One of the issues is the issue [of the involvement] of the sons and posterity (*imāmzāda*) of the Imams; but this is a matter which we shall not enter into for the time being. It is a separate subject which I will go into if time permits, even if only briefly.[115]

The insurrections which arise under the aegis of the progeny and posterity of the House of the Prophet ﷺ requires a separate discussion, i.e. one that goes into the details of the insurrections of leaders such as Yahyā b. Abdullāh, Yahyā b. Zaid, Zaid b. Ali b. al-Husain, Muhammad b. Abdullāh Mahdh, Ibrāhīm b. Abdullāh Mahdh, Husain b. Ali the Martyr of Fakh, Ibrāhīm b. Ismā'īl Tabātabāī, and other great men. But there are other currents, references to which are fragmentary or brief, and which require a close attention to detail if one is to be able to elicit [the subject matter from them]. It would seem that the Imams ﷺ carried out a campaign of active resistance in parallel with their teaching and propagation activities. I cannot be sure of the exact nature of the activity or how extensive it was, but I have no doubt that such activities existed.

There is a hadith report [in] which [the narrator] states: My father entered Imam Sādiq's house with Mu'allī b. Khanīs and, without the Imam having said anything to them [by way of preliminaries] or without him

---

[114] *Chenān-che yek zarre masā'il-e tahqīqī dar ān bāshad, kesek mīshavand.* It would seem that at least in this respect, the revolution has failed to change anything! (Although it has been highly successful in many other very important respects, of course.)

[115] See Chapter 9.

8. The Imams' Politicism and their Militant Actions

having asked them any questions, said, "*shafī allāhu sudūrakum wa adhhab ghayẓa qulūbakum wa adā lakum man 'aduakum*". ["God ﷻ has healed your hearts; God ﷻ has removed the animus from your hearts [by] making you vanquish your enemy."] My take on this hadith is the following: the Imam has sent two people on a mission which involved a physical clash; and that there is the possibility of the Imam's two agents having been killed [in the conflict], while at the same time, the possibility of the mission's success also exists. One of these two people is Mu'allī b. Khanīs, a close companion of Imam Sādiq's, who remained faithful to the Imam until his death.

Mansūr's governor entered Madina in order to identify Mu'allī b. Khanīs, whom he called [to his presence] within the first few days of his arrival there. Again, my take is that Mansūr had sent this governor [Dāwūd b. Alī] for the specific purposes of purging Madina [of elements of his opposition]; to identify the friends and close associates of Imam Sādiq ؑ and those whom they had identified as Shīʻa resistance fighters, and to destroy them. The first person of interest to the governor is Mu'allī b. Khanīs, who is an active resistor as well as an intimate companion of Imam Sādiq's ؑ. This is public knowledge, in addition to which Mu'allī b. Khanīs is the person who handles Imam Sādiq's financial affairs and a person through whom much of the Imam's affairs with his followers are managed. The governor called Mu'allī b. Khanīs and told him, "You must tell me the name of Imam Sādiq's close companions."

Mu'allī b. Khanīs replied, "I will not."

Dāwūd b. Alī said, "You must, and if you do not, I shall kill you."

Mu'allī b. Khanīs said, "Upon my word of honor with God ﷻ, if the list of the Imam's companions were under my foot, I would not raise it so that you could pick it up. And you say that I should [willingly] tell you their names??" He didn't say he didn't know, because that was not an avenue that was open to him, as it was known that he knew the names.

Dāwūd b. Alī said, "I shall kill you!"

Mu'allī b. Khanīs said, "Very well, then kill me."

And so Mu'allī b. Khanīs was martyred at the hands of Dāwūd b. Alī (Ibn Shahrāshūb, *Manāqib* 4:225). Dāwūd was one of the pillars of the Abbāsid dynasty and one of the leaders of the revolution which brought them to power. This was [the fate of] Mu'allī b. Khanīs, after whose martyrdom Imam Sādiq ﷺ came and formally complained to Dāwūd b. Ali, [was rebuffed, and Dāwūd b. Alī was subsequently cursed by the Imam and met his doom soon thereafter (*ibid*)]. The story of Imam Sādiq ﷺ and Dāwūd b. Alī, Mansūr's governor [of Madina], is one of the sweet stories within the history of Islam. This was the situation of Mu'allī b. Khanīs.

Mu'allī b. Khanīs enters Imam Sādiq's house accompanied with one other person. It appeared as though the Imam had sent these two people on a mission – although this does not appear in the hadith report but is only my interpolation. It is possible that these two might lose their lives in this mission. As soon as he sees these two men, the Imam realizes that the mission has been successful and starts to talk without their saying anything or giving a report. He said, "God ﷻ has healed your hearts; God ﷻ has removed the animus from your hearts [by] making you vanquish your enemy. God ﷻ has given you one of "the two best things". In the lexicon of Islam, going to war against the enemy is one of "the two best things".

$$ \text{قُلْ هَلْ تَرَبَّصُونَ بِنَا إِلَّا إِحْدَى الْحُسْنَيَيْنِ ۖ وَنَحْنُ نَتَرَبَّصُ بِكُمْ أَن يُصِيبَكُمُ اللَّهُ بِعَذَابٍ مِّنْ عِندِهِ أَوْ بِأَيْدِينَا ۖ فَتَرَبَّصُوا إِنَّا مَعَكُم مُّتَرَبِّصُونَ ﴿٥٢﴾ } $$

> [9:52] Say: "Are you, perchance, hopefully waiting for something [bad] to happen to us - [the while nothing can happen to us] save one of the two best things? But as far as you are concerned, we are hopefully waiting for God ﷻ to inflict chastisement upon you, [either] from Himself or by our hands! Wait, then, hopefully; behold, we shall hopefully wait with you!"

This is Islam's logic. In war, one of "the two best things" obtains for those who fight: either they will achieve victory, or they will achieve martyrdom at the hands of the enemy. Death is meaningless to one who fights in the cause of God ﷻ, for his or her death is not an ordinary death. He will have died at the hands of the enemy, which is an instance of

8. The Imams' Politicism and their Militant Actions

martyrdom, which is the greatest honor that a Muslim can achieve. Thus, one achievement is victory, and the other is martyrdom. When the Imam said that they had returned [from their mission unharmed] he told them that they had achieved one of "the two best things". And what was the one best thing? Victory. Thus, it is clear that they had been sent and had come back from battle. After the Imam utters these words, he says, "If the other case had obtained and you had been martyred at the hands of the enemy, you would have been in the highest stations in Heaven."

The point of interest for me in this hadith report is the fact that the narrator is the son of one of these two agents. [But despite this,] he does not say, "My father and Mu'allī had gone to such and such a place..." nor does he give the identity of the enemies they engaged or the reason for the battle or when the Imam had sent them on their mission. These are left out of the narrative. Why? Because of precautionary dissimulation (*taqīya*). At this point, a form of such a practice should enter your minds so that you understand the nature of precautionary dissimulation. What is going on is the resistance organization's need to maintain secrecy and to maintain information on a "need to know" basis; which is why the son is not privy to the information as to where his father had been. [Rather, what we are seeing is the case of] a father who has been filled with joy from what the Imam has told him, and who then turns to his son and tells him what the Imam had said to him. Or perhaps it is the case that the son was with his father when they entered the Imam's house and heard what the Imam said at first hand; or that his father had mentioned the words of the Imam elsewhere, and that the words had made it back to him. But the son is not to know the identity of the enemies they engaged or the reason for the battle or when the Imam had sent them on their mission, because of the organizational need for secrecy's prompting precautionary dissimulation (*taqīya*). And when we pay close attention to these kinds of situations, we see that there are numerous examples of them.

4. The harsh treatment of the Imams ﷺ by the caliphs as reason for the militant nature of their activities

Another aspect of the militant nature of the activities of the Imams ﷺ is their harsh treatment at the hands of the caliphs and their henchmen. I had mentioned earlier that Imam Sādiq ﷺ was said to have four thousand students. What is generally imagined is that he would sit on a stool or raised dais and four thousand students would gather round him, and that he was free to start to speak just as we are speaking to you now, and that he would train his students in this manner. But this is not how it was. The four thousand student figure refers to the number of students which Imam Sādiq ﷺ trained over the relatively long period of the 40 years – or a little less – of his imamate; students who learned certain truths and then went back to the lands from which they hailed and promulgated those views among their local populations. These students would wait to be given permission [by the authorities who were keeping the Imam under guard or house arrest] to enter, and would perhaps not be able to glean more than a hadith or two from a given visit; or they would not be given permission to enter at all and would have to return, disappointed. Thus, these were the kinds of conditions under which the Imams ﷺ lived, which is a far cry from the comforts of life which we are used to having nowadays.

Now allow me to draw your attention to this hadith report which has been related concerning Imam Kāẓim ﷺ in Ibn Shahrāshūb's *Manāqib* (4:311). It boils down to two words; and you are free to make of these two words what you will. It states, "Mūsā b. Ja'far entered a village in the Levant disguised as a fugitive and encountered a Christian Monk in a cave." It is a famous hadith report which I have personally heard related several times in the past, except it is [usually] related from the point *after* which I just now stopped. In other words, I had not heard the hadith report being related from its beginning to the point where I stopped. So that when I came across it [= the beginning portion that is usually omitted], it was very new to me. [The hadith report] is [usually] related from this point forward; which is that Imam Kāẓim ﷺ encounters a Christian monk, engages him in a conversation, and catches him out on a point of their argument, whereupon the Monk [admits the error of his ways and] enters into Islam.

But what about the beginning of the report? The beginning tells us that our very own Imam Kāẓim ﷺ was wondering in the mountains and villages of the Levant in disguise or as a fugitive until he reached the mouth of a cave. We [usually] only think of Imam Kāẓim ﷺ as being the Portal of [God ﷻ's grace, by means of which our] Needs [are met] (*bāb ul-hawā'ij*), so that our needs are met, or so that we are able to put food on the table, and the like. But listen, my brothers! This Portal of Grace has spent a portion of his life as an unknown fugitive in the hills and valleys of the Levant! Forget about his having served [long] prison terms, because they have comingled his serving time in prison with certain other words which deprive him of his original grandeur and glory. This is Imam Kāẓim ﷺ we are talking about: what was he doing in the Levant?? What had driven him to [seek refuge in] the mountains? Why should he be a fugitive from the law? Why should he have to travel incognito? Now it is up to you to justify this. It is your call. But to put it succinctly, know that these kinds of incidents can be found in the lives of our Imams ﷺ. This is the first point.

5. The important subject of the clash of the Imams ﷺ with the court-allied Scholars of Religion and poets

The matter I wanted to talk about today is not unrelated to yesterday's subject matter insofar as it is another aspect of the lives of the Imams ﷺ. The day I first mentioned the revolutionary activity of the Imams, I said that we would look at the subject from several angles: one of these is the way in which these Divine Guides related to the caliphs and the powers of the caliphal courts; another aspect is the way in which they related to their followers, and the third is how they related to the court-allied scholars of religion and poets, the intellectual and cultural leaders of the Islamic society of those days. This is a very large and important subject which we must understand. It is a subject matter which falls under the rubric of research into the lives of the Imams ﷺ and how they transacted their lives. This is the subject of today's discussion, and I hope that the state of my health and my chest, as well as your state of well-being, allows us to finish the subject today and not to postpone a part of the discussion to tomorrow. And I would appreciate it if you would bear with me if I do happen to bore you a little, as I think that we can all benefit from the subject under discussion.

6. The Scholars of Religion: the intellectual and cultural leaders within the history of Islam

The first thing to be done is to see the extent to which that I have said about the court-allied scholars of religion and poets is true. I said that these were the intellectual and cultural leaders of the Islamic society of those days. From after the time of the second caliph [Umar b. al-Khattāb] ...[116] This is how hadith reports were created. The people wanted to see everything from the perspective of the wellspring of the Most Noble Prophet ﷺ and leader of Islam. Or if the Prophet ﷺ had mentioned an interpretation of a certain verse of the Quran, the people preferred to understand that verse in the way in which the Prophet ﷺ had explained it. They would say that the Prophet ﷺ understood the Quran better than they did, and that if he stated that such was the meaning of a certain verse, then that is what its meaning was. I used a verse of the Quran which is explicit and clear, and which anyone who knows the Arabic language can readily understand. Nonetheless, if there is a certain verse of the Quran concerning which there was a commentary or exegesis from the Prophet ﷺ himself, the people undoubtedly preferred to understand it in light of what the Prophet ﷺ had said about it, and preferred this to their own understanding.

Now extrapolate this to every other matter. If something was related and it was stated that it came from the Prophet ﷺ himself, the people would accept it unconditionally. If there were hadith reports from the prophet concerning how one is to live one's life, the people would naturally accept it and incorporate its teachings in their lives as part of the exemplary model of the Prophet ﷺ of Islam. And similarly, if something was related and it was stated that it came from the Prophet ﷺ himself, concerning somebody which stated that he was a good person and would go to Heaven, or that he was a bad person and would end up in Hell, then the people would accept these statements unconditionally also.

This matter of unconditional acceptance is not a mistaken attitude, [based on the following verse and others like it]:

---

[116] There is a gap in the audiotape at this point.

8. The Imams' Politicism and their Militant Actions

$$\text{وَمَا آتَاكُمُ الرَّسُولُ فَخُذُوهُ وَمَا نَهَاكُمْ عَنْهُ فَانتَهُوا ۚ وَاتَّقُوا اللَّهَ ۖ إِنَّ اللَّهَ شَدِيدُ الْعِقَابِ ﴿٧﴾}$$

[59:7] accept [willingly] whatever the Apostle gives you and refrain from [demanding] anything that he withholds from you.

What this resulted in, however, is that the scholars of religion and historians of sacred history, the *muhaddithūn*, became the intellectual and cultural leaders of Islamic society and determined its orthopraxy. Under such circumstances, the possibility of taking undue advantage of this situation presented itself to the ruling powers of the day, and particularly to the more unscrupulous ones. If a ruler who has attained to power by usurping it using criteria and moral standards which were based on the paradigm of the pre-Islamic era of ignorance rather than on Islamic standards and criteria, were to be able to procure the sympathies and services of some of the intellectuals and religious scholars, then this could make a significant difference to [the legitimacy and longevity of] his reign; because the people look up to the doctors of religion in order to determine how they should live. And these sympathies and services could be procured either by financial incentives, or, failing that, by threats of brute force, or by family ties, previous friendships, and the like. Thus, usurpers and oppressors can benefit greatly from the services and alliance of such scholars; and of course, legitimate powers can also benefit from their services.

7. Mu'āwiya puts the court-allied scholars of religion to use

Mu'āwiya was quick to understand this matter which I just stated and which you have affirmed. He felt that he needed to gather a few of these skilled historians of hadith around his court. But skilled in what sense? In the sense of Abū-Dharr and Salmān? But Abū-Dharr would never compromise his values for Mu'āwiya's sake. As a matter of fact, if he were able, he would bring his sword down on the crown of Mu'āwiya's head! You have all heard of Abū-Dharr's clashes with Mu'āwiya, and if you haven't, you should make a point to look them up. And as for Salmān the

Persian, who was the second caliph's governor for Madā'in province, he writes a letter to the caliph when Umar is at the height of his powers, refusing to address him as the "Commander of the Faithful" as the caliph had demanded he be called by everyone.[117] He addresses him as: "O Umar". His letter is full of subtle insults in a way that only Salmān the Persian can pull off, without the use of swear words. His letter is full of scorn and disdain and contempt, and plainly indicated his alignment as a loyal partisan of Ali's, just as he was during the time of the Prophet ﷺ when Ali ؑ had the Prophet's backing. He writes such a letter to Mu'āwiya, who is not even in the same league as Salmān. Neither Salmān nor Abū-Dharr can get along with Mu'āwiya, nor can the likes of Ammār b. Yāsir and the rest of Ali's hardcore supporters. So what is a poor caliph to do? He has no choice but to go looking for lesser known personalities which he can employ in his service, and which he can then make a legend for and make famous by way of deception with money and brute force and the power of propaganda, presenting these so-called scholars as great Companions of the Prophet ﷺ; the plan being for the people to eventually buy into the meme that anyone who wants to hear what the Prophet ﷺ said about a given subject should refer to these court-allied "scholars" of the religion.

Who are these so-called scholars? One of these is Ka'b al-Ahbār, who had never even seen the Prophet ﷺ. And this is something that is truly strange! Ka'b al-Ahbār was a Jewish rabbi who became a Muslim during the reign of the second caliph. He is considered one of the great and honorable narrators of hadith reports of the Prophet ﷺ in Mu'āwiya's court, even though he had never heard a single hadith report from him. Another one is Abū-Hurayra; someone who has related so many so-called hadith reports from the Prophet ﷺ that it is estimated that even if he was in the company of the Prophet ﷺ night and day, he could not have had the opportunity to generate so many reports about him! Abū-Hurayra was not an important personality during the time of the Prophet ﷺ. He gained a modicum of respect for himself during the reigns of the first two caliphs,

---

[117] This is a title that is reserved exclusively for Imam Ali ؑ by the Shī'a.

8. The Imams' Politicism and their Militant Actions

and by the time of Muʻāwiya's reign, had become a renowned and "great" *muhaddith* or historian of sacred history, and an honored man of the cloth.

Furthermore, Abū-Hurayra was a student of Kaʻb al-Ahbār. I read this recently in a book by Hāshim Ma'rūf al-Husainī – which was not a bad read – but I have not researched the matter personally, nor have I carried out extensive research in this field. Hāshim Ma'rūf al-Husainī says that Abū-Hurayra was a student of Kaʻb al-Ahbār. [So the logic is that] even though Kaʻb al-Ahbār had never seen the Prophet ﷺ and even though Abū-Hurayra had seen him and had been in his company, but because the latter was a skilled and knowledgeable scholar and had a lot of information concerning the history of bygone eras, Abū-Hurayra spent some time apprenticing under the tutelage of this experienced veteran Jewish rabbi in order to perfect his trade! These are the kinds of people who Muʻāwiya gathers around himself in his court. Muʻāwiya values worthless people. "A fly which you personally set loose to fly, soars like a hawk [in your eye]." Unfortunately, when one looks into the hadith reports in the Sunni hadith report corpus, ones sees that a large number of them have been originated by Abū-Hurayra; and only a very small fraction are originated by Abū-Dharr or Salmān or Miqdād or Ammār, or by the companions who were close to the Commander of the Faithful Imam Ali ﷺ, who were the great Companions of the Prophet ﷺ. Abū-Hurayra has originated much more hadith reports in the Sunni hadith report corpus, and this is Muʻāwiya's doing.

What is Abū-Hurayra's role here? What are the duties of the likes of Abū-Hurayra [in the caliphal courts]? If I were to sum it up, I would have to say that their function was to prepare the groundwork for Muʻāwiya to rule over the people with peace of mind [i.e. with no concerns about the legitimacy of his reign or of his actions]. This task was brought about through various means. Verses of the Quran are misinterpreted and the misinterpretations are credited to the Prophet ﷺ. Or hadith reports are forged wherein the Prophet ﷺ is alleged to have praised the virtues of Muʻāwiya, and Muʻāwiya's father, and the Umayyad House. Or indirect means can be resorted to, which for me are even more interesting.

8. Examples of hadith report forgeries

Pay attention to these couple of hadith reports which go back to Abū-Hurayra and his ilk. One is obliged [to satisfy oneself] with taking [but] a sampling. It is imperative that you get to know this type of hadith report; for when you have gotten to know the type, you will recognize those which are in a similar vein. "Ka'b al-Ahbār came across someone" – like a rider on a horse in the desert – "and asked, 'Where are you from?' The person said, 'I am from the Levant.' As soon as he said this, Ka'b al-Ahbār said, 'Ah, I believe you must be one of the members of the army concerning which there is a hadith report from the Prophet ﷺ which states that seventy-thousands of its troops will enter Heaven immediately and without an evaluation of their Book of Deeds'". Ka'b al-Ahbār reckons that this person might be someone who is one of Mu'āwiya's soldiers or one who is close to him, and that if this is the case, that he will relate this supposed hadith report to him, so that he will know that Ka'b al-Ahbār is doing his duty in every time and every place and in every corner of the world.

The man became confused and asked what army it is whose seventy-thousand troops will enter Heaven immediately on the Day of Judgement without their Book of Deeds being subjected to any evaluation. If he was a true Muslim, he would know that everyone's Book of Deeds are subjected to evaluation on the Day of Judgement, even those of the prophets. As a matter of fact, it makes no sense to say that one can enter Heaven without his or her Book of Deeds being subjected to an evaluation.[118] Islam is all about being accountable for one's words and deeds and the Hereafter is all about [being rewarded or punished in] due measure. So how could they possibly enter Heaven without any accounting of their deeds?? But he was from The Levant and the people of The Levant were of a much higher station to pay attention to and understand these things.[119]

---

[118] For this would undermine the entirety of the moral order of Creation.

[119] Recall that the Levant was the province which Mu'āwiya was the governor of during the reign of Uthmān, and whose people were loyal to Mu'āwiya and followed his example when he started the first Islamic civil war against Imam Ali's ﷺ caliphate after Uthman's death.

8. The Imams' Politicism and their Militant Actions

The man asked, "And me too? Who are these people, seventy-thousands of which will enter Heaven immediately on the Day of Judgement without their Book of Deeds being subjected to any evaluation?"

Ka'b al-Ahbār said, "They are the people of Homs."

And the man said, "Alas, I am not from Homs."

Ka'b al-Ahbār said, "Perhaps you are one of those people upon whom Almighty God ﷻ looks upon with His mercy twice per day."

The man asked, "Which people would those be?"

Ka'b al-Ahbār said, "They are the people of Palestine."

Not, of course, the people of today's Palestine, who are subject to God ﷻ's daily kindness and mercy, but the people of the Palestine of those days, who fell in line behind Mu'āwiya and made up the rank and file of his army. This was one [blatant] example of a [forged] hadith report.

Here is another example, whose originator is 'Amr b. Ās.[120] Do you laugh at the fact that 'Amr b. Ās is a narrator of hadith reports about the Prophet ﷺ? But 'Amr b. Ās is a companion of the Prophet ﷺ! How were the people of those days to know that the hadith reports narrated by 'Amr b. Ās are a pack of lies? It is because you know who 'Amr b. Ās is, and you know the true nature of his personality that you are surprised at the fact that he has narrated hadith reports. Therefore, do not be surprised, for in addition to his being a narrator of hadith reports, 'Amr b. Ās was also the leader of the Friday congregational prayers in Egypt during the time of the caliphs prior to Imam Ali's ؑ caliphate. People deferred to 'Amr b. Ās as their prayer leader and prayed behind him and would consult him on religious matters, considered him to be a legitimate source in matters of governance, and would ask him about matters having to do with the Quran. And 'Amr b. Ās was of course also a significant chess piece in Mu'āwiya's court in the game of injustice, iniquity and oppression against the justice of Ali b. Abī-Tālib ؑ. Here is the hadith report:

I heard this personally from the Prophet ﷺ, who said that the people of the House of [Ali b.] Abī-Tālib are no kindred (*awlīā*) of mine. Here the word *walī* [singular of *awlīā*] is not used in the sense of a friend.

---

[120] The audience laughs at the mention of this infamous man's name.

Rather, here it is used in the sense of one who is attached and in the same [spiritual and creedal and intellectual] front [as the Prophet ﷺ]. [What the hadith is attempting to convey is that] the people of the House of [Ali b.] Abī-Tālib are not attached to the Prophet ﷺ in any significant sense.

Allow me to read another hadith report for you, which in my mind is the most interesting and most devious of the lot. And there are a lot of these kinds of reports which try to do something indirectly in order to pave the path of the Muʿāwiya's of the world and to help them rest easy at night in their beds. The report is taken from Bokhārī's *Sahīh*, which is considered by Sunnis to be the most authoritative collection of hadith reports in their hadith report corpus.

عن عبد الْوَارِثِ عن الْجَعْدِ عن ابى رَجَاءٍ عن بن عَبَّاسٍ عن النبى (صلى‌الله‌عليه‌وآله‌وسلّم) قال: من كَرِهَ من اَمِيرِهِ شيئا فَلْيَصْبِرْ فانه من خَرَجَ من السُلْ طَانِ شِبْرًا مَاتَ مِيتَةً جَاهِلِيَّةً

[Whoever is unhappy about anything [which issues forth] from his ruler, let him exercise patience and forbearance, for anyone who disobeys his ruler has died the death of the days of pre-Islamic ignorance].

Well, if Muʿāwiya were to rule as a caliph, he cannot spend the money of the public treasury in the way it should be spent [according to the ordinances and teachings of Islam, and still see to his own selfish desires]. If he does so, no money will remain for him to spend on the Abū-Hurayra's and Kaʿb ol-Ahbar's and the ʿAmr b. Āṣ's and the Ziād b. Abīh's of the day whom he surrounds himself with in order to secure his position. So he must perforce not spend this money on what by rights belongs to the people, so that he can spend it on what he believes props up his own legitimacy. Therefore, the problem of inequality, favoritism and class stratification is an intrinsic and ineluctable and natural part of the governments of Muʿāwiya and his ilk. If Muʿāwiya distributes the public purse evenly and ensures that everyone receives their fair share of the treasury's money, then no one would remain in his court, as his courtiers have been retained with [excess and undue] compensation. Which is why

8. The Imams' Politicism and their Militant Actions

inequality, poverty and class stratification are engendered, which in turn cause turmoil and discontent in the people and provoke them into rising up in righteous insurrection against Mu'āwiya's regime; which is an eventuality he cannot abide. So what is he to do? He forges hadith reports of the Prophet ﷺ such as the following – and there are hundreds of them – مَنْ كَرِهَ مِنْ أَمِيرِهِ شيئًا فَلْيَصْبِرْ "Whoever is unhappy about anything [which issues forth] from his ruler, let him exercise patience and forbearance (*fal yasbir*)." Why should one "exercise patience and forbearance"?

By the way, note how the word *sabr* (patience and forbearance and longanimity) is used. Let those among our friends who were at the Engineers' Islamic Association last night pay attention to the way [the meaning of] this word has been distorted. We defined the word *sabr* briefly last night. Now compare that definition with how the word is being used here. فانه مَنْ خَرَجَ مِنَ السُّلْطَانِ شِبْرًا مَاتَ مِيتَةً جَاهِلِيَّةً "for anyone who disobeys his ruler has died the death of the days of pre-Islamic ignorance". And this is the continuation of the word of the Prophet ﷺ narrated by Ibn 'Abbās – let [the consequences of] the sin [of his forgery] fall on his own neck! Anyone who strays a foot afield from the aegis of the established and ruling power does not die the death of a Muslim. Well, it is clear to everyone how useful and valuable this hadith report is to Mu'āwiya. How much do you think he paid Ibn 'Abbās in compensation for this forgery? How many billions of dinars should he have received from Mu'āwiya so as not to have come out the loser in the deal? In any event, this is a situation which arose in the earliest years of Islam [after the passing of the Prophet ﷺ]; but this is not the aspect which I want to focus on.

Forged hadith reports fill all of the horizons of Islamic society. And while Mu'āwiya was seeing to this, others thought it opportune to inject their own thoughts and tendencies into [the minds of] the people under the guise of Islamic teachings. One such group were the Jews who strove to implant their own Torahic myths into Islam by this method, which process eventually produced a body of hadith literature which came to be known as the *isrāīliāt* [or Judaic accretions]. [These were] Judaic [influenced] hadith reports which Jews such as Ka'b al-Ahbar and others like him forged and fed to the people. The horizons of Islamic society became filled with forged hadith reports reporting words which the

Prophet ﷺ was alleged to have said, supposedly narrated by the earliest Companions of the Prophet ﷺ, which praised those who were unworthy of praise and denigrated those who were worthy of praise. These forgeries permeated Islamic society, creating a [pseudo-Islamic] environment in which the culture developed.

9. All of the oppressors utilized the services of the court-allied clergy

Using the authority of the clergy is not a phenomenon which is exclusive to Muʿāwiya, nor is it limited to the oppressive rulers of Islam; it has existed from the beginning. Anyone who has studied the history of religions knows that the clergy are one of the elements which have been embedded and institutionalized in the power structure of oppressive and despotic powers who wanted to usurp the rights of the people for themselves. This is a phenomenon which can be seen in all of the ancient civilizations of the world, inclusive of those of India and China, as well as those of western Asia such as the Egyptian civilization and those of northern Africa, and those of the Middle East such as those of Chaldea, Assyria and Babylon; and not least, those of the Iranian civilizations, the most prominent example being the religion of Zoroaster. Religious elements acted to an extensive degree as guarantors of social stratification and class inequalities. Whereas [such differences which are artificially created and maintained by] brute force can only be sustained for so long. It is only by means of a [false] spiritual element that the people can be primed to carry the throne of the mindsets of the despots throughout history on their bare shoulders and not to cast them onto the ground; it is only by means of a [false] spiritual element that such tyrannies can be sustained: an element which is utilized in the name of religion in order to convince the people of the justness of such class differences and inequalities.

In ancient India, if someone from the lower classes [an Untouchable] touched a Brahmin, his hand would have been cut off; and if he so much as looked at a Brahmin, he would be blinded. But no one was unsatisfied with this arrangement because they believed that such an arrangement was God ﷻ's will, and that one must submit to the will of

God ﷻ. So what can bring such a social condition about other than [false] spiritual and intellectual elements? Thus, this problem obtained before Islam and the time of Muʿāwiya as well. Like all of the despots before him, Muʿāwiya put this element to use; and it is only natural that those who followed him and continued his line would not lose the opportunity to take advantage of this valuable asset. In the era of the eight Imams ʿa from Imam [Ali b. al-Husain] as-Sajjād ʿa, [the Fourth Imam], on down to Imam [Hasan b. Ali] al-Askarī ʿa [the Eleventh Imam], [inclusive], which we are discussing, this element has raised havoc of an unprecedented proportion within Islamic society and with respect to these Imams ʿa and their followers. You will have to look up and read about the specifics yourselves, as I will only have time to touch on a small portion of this large subject.

10. Muhammad Zuhrī: A prominent example of the court-allied clergy

There was a famous cleric by the name of Muhammad b. Shahāb az-Zuhrī during the Imamate of the Fourth Imam, Imam Sajjād ʿa. He is also known as Muhammad b. Muslim az-Zuhrī. Also, some people refer to Zuhrī as Zoharī, but Zuhrī is the correct pronunciation. Muhammad b. Shahāb az-Zuhrī was a highly knowledgeable and erudite scholar of religion. This is confirmed by the content of the letter which was written by the Fourth Imam to him, which I will read for you, God ﷻ willing. Muhammad b. Shahāb az-Zuhrī is someone whose knowledge and scholarship was not questioned by anyone of his era. Furthermore, he had great love and respect for the progeny of the House of the Prophet ﷺ, and loved Imam Sajjād ʿa from the bottom of his heart.

It would seem – and this is not something that I am certain of, but a probability – that when Imam Sajjād ʿa and his young son Muhammad b. Ali [Imam Bāqir ʿa] were taken to Damascus in handcuffs which were chained to neck-yokes and made to appear in the court of the caliph; it would appear that the person who said that Imam Sajjād ʿa is a son of the Prophet ﷺ and that the chains should be released from his neck-yoke, was Muhammad b. Shahāb az-Zuhrī. Thus, he was someone who had affection for the people of the House of the Prophet ﷺ and related hadith reports [which he had heard] from them. But nevertheless, this gentleman is one of the religious elements embedded in the ruling apparatus of Abdul-Malik and his sons, who played this role during the Imamates of Imam Sajjād ﷺ and Imam Bāqir ﷺ. And this is where we can see how valuable this love and affection for the members of the House of the Prophet ﷺ can be. Muhammad b. Shahāb az-Zuhrī has affection for the members of the House of the Prophet ﷺ, but he stands in opposition to the Fourth Imam. And today, when the Shī'a evaluate Muhammad b. Shahāb az-Zuhrī, they do not dare to feel pity for him or to ask God ﷻ to forgive him, because they have read the harsh words in the letter which Imam Sajjād ﷺ wrote to him. Unless Zuhrī had repented afterwards and changed his position and joined the ranks of the Shī'a behind Imam Sajjād ﷺ; which is something that I am not aware of, if he had done so. But [failing this], he stands in opposition to Imam Sajjād ﷺ, even though he feels affection and love for him. And this is where we can understand how hollow love and affection can also be a valuable asset. The function of Muhammad b. Shahāb az-Zuhrī and his ilk during the caliphate of Abdul-Malik b. al-Marwān was to provide a religious rationale to justify Abdul-Malik al-Marwān's political apparatus and the social order which he had inherited from Mu'āwiya the son of Abū Sufyān, [the Prophet's greatest arch enemy].

  Allow me to read a hadith report which Zuhrī has narrated. One of the rebellions which occurred, which was not a Shī'a insurrection but one which was nonetheless against the caliphal authority, was the one which was led by Abdullāh b. Zubayr. This Abdullāh b. Zubayr is not an acceptable character; he is a very bad person. His emotional and intellectual makeup is wicked, and his religious position went against that of Imam Ali's ﷺ and Imam Husain's. Nevertheless, he rebelled against Yazīd, and after him, against al-Marwān, and after him, against Abdul-Malik b. al-Marwān. And this rebellion was successful to a degree in that he was able to seize control of Mecca, as well as certain parts of the Hijāz, and, for a time, he had control of Kūfa as well, which had been seized with the aid of his brother Mas'ab. Abdul-Malik b. al-Marwān's power was limited solely to the Levant [or greater Syria, inclusive of Palestine and Trans-Jordan].

8. The Imams' Politicism and their Militant Actions

The pilgrimage month of Hajj had arrived, and the people were getting ready to make the Hajj pilgrimage to the House of God ﷻ, [the Ka'ba], where Abdullāh b. Zubayr was the ruler, who is not an ideal person, but who is beyond comparison with Abdul-Malik, who is the son of Marwān, who was driven out of Madina into exile by the Prophet ﷺ. The enmity of Marwān and his House with the Prophet ﷺ and with the Quran and with Islam is one which all the Muslims are aware. So, so much for Abdul-Malik b. al-Marwān and his Islamic reputation.

But Abdullāh b. Zubayr is the son of Zubayr, the Prophet's cousin. And while it is true that Zubayr [ultimately rebelled and] fought against Imam Ali ﷺ [in the Battle of the Camel], that nevertheless, when he was killed in that battle, Imam Ali ﷺ took up Zubayr's sword in his hand and said, "How great were the number of the layers of opacity which were removed from the visage of the Prophet ﷺ by this sword!"[121] This is the kind of personality which Zubayr had within Islamic history. Thus, Abdullāh the son of Zubayr and Abdul-Malik the son of Marwān are beyond comparison. Additionally, Abdullāh b. Zubayr is someone who has some knowledge of Islam, has heard hadith reports from the Prophet ﷺ, and is the son of the Prophet's cousin. He has a limited understanding of Islam and is an abstemious, religious person; whereas Abdul-Malik is an offensive, licentious, atrocious, blood-thirsty voluptuary and drunkard; so there is no comparison between the two.

So what about the prospect which looms for Abdul-Malik now that the people of the Levant are about to make their pilgrimage to Mecca, whereat they will enter its revolutionary environment and see the ruler of the rebellion and become familiar at first hand with him at their own popular level, after which they will take up political positions which are against Abdul-Malik. Is that a favorable prospect for him? No. So what should the people do instead that would be good for Abdul-Malik? They should refrain from travelling to Mecca in this year when Abdullāh b. Zubayr is its ruler. And how, pray, is this feat to be accomplished? Is such a feat even possible?? After all, it is nothing less than the Hajj pilgrimage, which is a religious imperative (*wājib*) [if one has the financial

---

[121] Allāma Muhammad Bāqir Majlisī's *Bihār al-Anwār* (Oceans of Light), 32:200.

wherewithal, and] the people have the wherewithal to do so and want to make the pilgrimage. And so, the religious element must be put to use, because it is situations such as these that are out of the hands of all of the pillars of Abdul-Malik's court, be they the generals of his army, all of his various powerful governors, or the various statesmen and courtiers who surround his throne. But who *can* help in this situation? His Eminence and Grace, Meister Zuhrī, the great holy man, the holy of holies! This is his province and his bailiwick; and it is up to him to prevent the people from travelling to Mecca. So what does he do? He narrates a hadith report. But wait, the Prophet ﷺ has never uttered the words which he now needs to relate. Well, never mind that; he will make up a forgery; it is not so difficult for the likes of him. And that is exactly what he does. Now listen to the hadith report.

"The Prophet ﷺ said, 'The people have no right to release their commitments and make their way to anywhere other than to three mosques, which are equal to each other in terms of their virtue. The first is the Sacred Mosque [in Mecca], the second is the Prophet's Mosque in Madina, and the third is the Sacred House [in Jerusalem]." Why go to Mecca when you can go to the Sacred House in Jerusalem which is in your own back yard, and the pilgrimage to which has equal rewards to the pilgrimage to the Sacred Mosque in Mecca. The emphasis is on the Sacred House in Jerusalem, which is why the hadith continues: "The Sacred House in Jerusalem is like the Sacred Mosque in Mecca." And if someone objects that the Sacred Mosque in Mecca is where the Ka'ba is located, whereas the Sacred House in Jerusalem does not house the Ka'ba, they will respond that it too has a Ka'ba. Is there not a stone there, upon which the Prophet ﷺ set foot on his Night Journey (*isrā'*) from Mecca to Jerusalem and his subsequent ascension (*mi'rāj*) to Heaven? That stone is the same as the Ka'ba; go and circumambulate *that* stone! This was Zuhrī's plan, whose ripples continue to be felt to this day.

11. Abdullāh b. Umar in the service of Mu'āwiya's objectives

These kinds of issues existed from the time of Imam Sajjād ﷺ, and before his time also. Such as the activities of Mr. Abdullāh the son of Umar, [the second caliph]. Abdullāh b. Umar refused to pledge allegiance to Imam

8. The Imams' Politicism and their Militant Actions

Ali ﷺ, but pledged fealty to Hajjāj b. Yūsuf for fear of his life, and pledged fealty to Hajjāj's foot, at that![122] And what is strange is that Abdullāh b. Umar was one of the people who occasionally claimed to be an enemy of Muʿāwiya, but Muʿāwiya had recognized his type and knew that he could easily take advantage of him. Abdullāh b. Umar and Muhammad b. Shahāb az-Zuhrī and other religious scholars after their times during the Imamate of Imam Bāqir ﷺ were all at the service of the fiendish ruling powers of those times, so that the Quran was utilized in the service of the devil; and "God ﷻ" was used in the service of oppression and of His enemies; a method which continued up to the time of Imam Sādiq ﷺ.

12. The ascetics welcome al-Mansūr the Abbāsid

The time of Imam Sādiq ﷺ, which is the time of the intellectual blooming and glory of the Shīʿa, also happens to be the time of the greatest activity of these court-allied scholars of religion. Imam Sādiq ﷺ was exiled from Madina to Hayra, where Mansūr is located, who feels safer with Imam Sādiq ﷺ close by. When Mansūr entered Hayra, all of the religious personalities and ascetics and scholars of religion from the environs of Hayra came out to welcome him. Those who were in the ʿIrāq came out to welcome him, and some who were farther afield released their daily commitments to come over and welcome him too; such as [Abū-Ishāq Ibrāhīm] Ibn Adham, who is one of the mystics which today we unfortunately consider to be a saintly personality and who is respected and revered. [Whereas these were in fact] lackeys in the pay of Mansūr and other Abbāsid and Umayyad caliphs.

This is the kind of situation which prevailed during the time of the Imams ﷺ. This is the preliminary matter to the discussion at hand. And as far as the question of what [exactly] the role of these [court-allied men of religion] was is concerned, it is a long and detailed discussion which does not lend itself to this kind of presentation, because the subject is so vast that it will not be exhausted no matter how much time we spend on it.

---

[122] Ibn Abī'l-Hadīd, Commentary on the *Nahj al-Balāgha*, 13:242.

13. The Imams' harsh response to the court-allied men of religion

So now, the question which can be posed is, how did the Imams ﷺ relate to these court-allied men of religion? This question goes to one aspect of the lives of the Imams ﷺ. And it is when we consider their relationships to these people that we realize how true and close to reality the position is which holds that the Imams ﷺ played the role of militant soldiers and chivalrous warriors during the times of their respective governments. And conversely, how deluded and unjust is the claim of those nonsense-mongers who claim that the Imams ﷺ were conservative, apolitical appeasers who were only interested in their own comfort and safety; and how far afield of the historical realities such claims are. Let us proceed now to see how the Imams ﷺ dealt with these men. There is a lot of material available about this subject. I shall read a hadith report which has been narrated by Imam Sajjād ﷺ, and another shorter one which has been narrated by Imam Bāqir ﷺ. I shall read this second one first.

14. Imam Bāqir's harsh words to ʿIkrama

[The context is that] Imam Bāqir ﷺ was on the Hajj pilgrimage. I believe that Hishām b. Abdul-Malik was also on the Hajj pilgrimage; or that any [other] Umayyad caliph who is present for the Hajj pilgrimage had made the pilgrimage with his entourage, which includes his court-allied clerics, ʿIkrama being among them. ʿIkrama was a student of Ibn ʿAbbās; and the hadith books of today [within the Sunnite hadith report corpus] are full of hadith reports which have been narrated by him. And of course the Shīʿa do not include any of his reports in their corpus, praise God ﷻ. It is our Sunni brothers in faith who have retold hadith reports which he has related. ʿIkrama is a petty courtier of the Umayyad caliphal court, and if you ask me, a student of Ibn ʿAbbās cannot be expected to amount to anything more than this: such a person will ultimately ally himself with the court of the ruling power. [Ibn ʿAbbās] himself was a courtier of Muʿāwiya's court, and so it is only fitting that his student would be a courtier of Abdul-Malik's court.

ʿIkrama does not know Imam Bāqir ﷺ, who was a young man at the time. He saw that a man was walking ahead whom the people honored

8. The Imams' Politicism and their Militant Actions

and deferred to, and that the majesty and grandeur of the House of Knowledge and Piety was clearly visible on his face. He thus thought to himself that he should go and see who this person was. When he approached the man, he saw that he did not know him. He asked around as to who this person was in whom he saw such majesty and grandeur, and was told that he was Muhammad b. Ali al-Bāqir ﷺ, the son of Imam Sajjād ﷺ. Then he recognized him; well, these people know these things. The student of Ibn 'Abbās grew up with the people of the House of Banī-Hāshim. Oh, so *this* is Muhammad b. Ali. He wants to meet him; to have a chin-wag with him, so that he can show off his erudition. [To say things like] "O Muhammad b. Ali, what [stories] do you have to report from your ancestor [the Prophet ﷺ]?" [And follow it up with,] "Ah, yes. I, too, narrate that report." The purpose being to open up a conversation, which might perchance lead to a friendship; so that he would have the friendships of both Muhammad b. Ali as well as that of Abdul-Malik's. That is what he had in mind when he approached the Imam.

But as soon as he drew near to the Imam and wanted to start talking, his hands and legs began to tremble, and a tremor took over the whole body of this obsequious and fawning and worthless man who was not endowed even with a truly human character, let alone with the character of a man of true learning and piety; a man who has sold his personality and his humanity to the ruling powers of the day and who has no self-worth or independence of character [left]. When this man came face to face with Imam Bāqir ﷺ, who was a mountain of stability and assiduity, his legs began to shake and he was not able to maintain his balance and threw himself into the Imam's arms, as if he had thrown himself to the Imam's feet. The Imam held him up and then sat him down, after which he was gradually able to find his words.

He said, "O Muhammad b. Ali, O son of the Apostle of God ﷺ! I have seen many great scholars of religion. I have apprenticed with Abdullāh Ibn 'Abbās and [other renowned] Companions of the Prophet ﷺ and sages; but the presence of none of these men had the effect of putting me in a swoon and causing me to tremble and lose my balance. How is it that I lost [control of] myself in your presence?"

What do you think Imam Bāqir ﷺ said to him? Do you think that he [made small talk and engaged in social niceties such as] "Not at all; I am not worthy of such profuse praise; you are a most honorable person, and I would be eternally grateful to you if you would give my regards to Mr. Abdul-Malik; perhaps you would be able to do us the service of resolving any differences there might be between us and the honorable caliph..." And so on. Is that how Imam Bāqir ﷺ responded to this man? No; he said, "Woe to you, you petty-servant to the Syrian nation! Woe to you, O worthless slave! You are nothing but a little slave and we are in the House in which God ﷻ has allowed His name to be hallowed and glorified [in peace]! Here is the House of the Teachings of Islam; it is where the Quran has descended from on high, you worthless slave! Do you then expect not to tremble [in its presence]??" (Ibn Shahrāshūb, *Manāqib* 4:182).

15. Two hadith reports concerning Zuhrī's allegiance to the caliphal court

But now to proceed to the hadith report concerning Imam Sajjād ﷺ. You must know Muhammad b. Muslim az-Zuhrī; who is of course someone other than Muhammad b. Muslim ath-Thaqafī, the great magister of the Quranic sciences (*faqīh*) who was a student of Imam Sādiq's. I have noted down two hadith reports which I have taken from Ibn Sa'd's *Tabaqāt* which are about Muhammad b. Shahāb az-Zuhrī and which provide insights into the man's social and intellectual condition; so that you can get an idea of the kind of person who is Imam Sajjād's interlocutor. Firstly, I should say that his learning and intellectual standing was accepted by all [of his contemporaries], inclusive of all of the magisters (*fuqahā*) and historians of sacred history (*muhadithūn*). There is no doubt about this, and wherever you come across the name of Muhammad b. Shahāb az-Zuhrī in books of hadith, *rijāl*[123], and historiography, his name is

---

[123] The science of *fiqh* is divided into the two sub-disciplines of *riwāyat -al-hadīth* and *dirāyat- al-hadīth*. The former is concerned with the chain of custody and the probity of the custodians within the chains of the transmitted text, and the latter is concerned with the text itself. *Riwāyāt-e hadīth* is further divided into the disciplines of *Ilm al- rijāl*, which is the science of the systematic evaluation of the

8. The Imams' Politicism and their Militant Actions

accompanied by praise. So much concerning his scholarly aptitude and station.

But what was the situation [of his personal allegiances] and what was his position with respect to the caliphal court? Let us go over these two hadith reports, so that you will get a feel for the kind of person who is being addressed by Imam Sajjād ﷺ in the letter which he wrote to him.

It is reported that Muhammad b. Shahāb az-Zuhrī stated, "We were loath to write down hadith reports and matters of knowledge and learning until the rulers forced us to do so." Notice the extent to which the Islamic rulers loved knowledge and learning, and how they loved to preserve the words of the Prophet ﷺ and the teachings of Islam that they forced Muhammad b. Shahāb az-Zuhrī and scholars like him to commit their knowledge to writing! And to ensure that they wrote books, because this was something that was necessary [for the preservation of the religion].[124] "We realized that when the rulers told us to write hadith reports and to commit our knowledge to writing, that no one would disagree with us in this matter any longer. Our minds having rested assured, and we started writing hadith reports and books." This was the

---

character and reliability of the custodians in the chain of custody, and *ilm-e mustalah-e hadīth*, which is the science of the evaluation of the nature and qualities of the chain of custody itself, including its continuity or discontinuity, the number of different chains of custody for a given *hadīth*, and other criteria which are used to evaluate and categorize the authenticity and probative force of the hadīth based solely on its chain of custody. The objective of this science is to arrive at decisions as to the acceptability of the *ahādīth* as bases for the derivation of secondary laws and codes of conduct. *Ilm al-Rijāl* (the science of *rijāl*) is a major branch within the science of *hadīth*. It is the science of the study and classification of the history, character, and trustworthiness of narrators of *hadīth* reporting. Books within this specialty compile biographical data on the narrators of hadith reports and classify them in accordance with the soundness of the character of the narrators in order to ascertain and rank them in terms of the reliability of their reportage. This information is in turn used to ascertain the integrity of the chain of custody within a given provenance title (*sanad*).

[124] Ayatollah Khāmeneī is being facetious, of course. For the true attitude of the early caliphs to the preservation of Islamic scripture, see Blake Archer Williams, *Creedal Foundations of Walīyic Islam*, Chapter 7, 7.17 The Systematic Falsification of Hadīth Reports; & 7.18 Abu-Bakr and Omar Burn Hadīth Reports.

first hadith report, which gives you a vignette into az-Zuhrī's relations with the rulers.

The second report [reads]: "From Muʻammar" – it is a hadith report from the Sunni corpus – It states that "We believed that there were a lot of hadith reports from az-Zuhrī available to us." The reports which we related from az-Zuhrī seemed to us to be very numerous. "Until Walīd b. Abdul-Malik" – the bloodthirsty Umayyad caliph – "died. After his death we saw the notebooks and books and scrolls of Muhammad b. Shahāb az-Zuhrī being brought out from Walīd's palace! It then became evident for whom his knowledge and learning and writing was in the service of!" Muhammad b. Shahāb az-Zuhrī's books and writings were at the service of the caliphal court, and entered onto the personal bookshelves and library of none other than Mr. Walīd! And Mr. Walīd kept these books in safe keeping for times when he needed to access a hadith report in order to get one up on the people. This is the character of Muhammad b. Shahāb az-Zuhrī! And I have with me other material in this same vein which I had brought to be able to read from, but it seems that this is no longer necessary.

16. Muhammad b. Shahāb az-Zuhrī takes a lashing from Imam Sajjād's admonishments

Now you should know that this Muhammad b. Shahāb az-Zuhrī has genuine feelings of affection for Imam Sajjād ﷺ and truly has not acted in a treacherous way toward the Imam. In other words, fairness dictates that we also mention that he has not passed on any reports about Imam Sajjād ﷺ to the caliphal court. That said, we can also add that allegiances are not exclusively determined by the passing of reports; Zuhrī does more than pass on the occasional report: he is at the service of the governing apparatus of the Umayyad and Abbāsid courts, so there is no need for him to pass on reports. And the Imam knows that he will not be generating a report, so he writes a letter to Zuhrī with the following content and in the following tone: "This is a letter which Imam Sajjād ﷺ has written to Muhammad b. Shahāb az-Zuhrī in which Muhammad b. Shahāb az-Zuhrī is admonished by the Imam." The book from which I am reading the letter,

8. The Imams' Politicism and their Militant Actions

Tuḥaf ul-Uqūl,[125] is compiled by Ibn Shuʿba al-Harrānī. The letter starts like this:

"May God help you and me to pass the trials and tribulations of life with honor." The Imam first says "you and me," and then changes to "and to have mercy on *you* from the fire [of Hell]." In other words, the Imam is implying that Muhammad b. Shahāb az-Zuhrī is destined for the fire of Hell given the condition that he is presently in, which is why he stands in need of God's mercy. [The letter continues,] "You are in a state the condition of which is such that anyone who sees you in such a state should feel sorry for you." What condition is that? Is he not the foremost men of letters of the nation? Is he not the man whose slight hint or indication has more weight within the social order's governing apparatus than the explicit [commands] of the [viziers and other] pillars of the political order? He does not want for wealth or social position and status; yet, the Imam says that he is in a condition in which people should feel sorry for him and take pity on him. "God's blessings weigh heavily on your shoulders. God has given you a healthy physique and a long life. These are blessings from God. God has concluded his *Hujjat* or conclusive argument [in the case that is being prepared] against you [for use on the Day of Judgement] (*i'timām-e Hujjat*)." It is possible that an ordinary person who works at the pleasure of the caliph and is serving his interests not be subjected to too much punishment by God, because he might not know better. But what about you? What about someone with your degree of knowledge and learning? God's argument against you has been completed so that you have no excuse. "You have read and understood God's sacred writ, and are aware of its ordinances and prohibitions. God has taught you the Way of the Prophet and his paradigmatic example. And with every blessing which He has bestowed onto you, He has placed a burden of responsibility on your shoulders." O ye who are aware! O ye who understand! O ye who have knowledge! For every quantum of knowledge and intelligence and awareness which you

---

[125] *Tuḥaf al-ʿuqūl fī mā jāʾa min al-ḥikam wa l-mawāʿiẓ min ʾal al-rasūl* (Arabic: تُحَفُ العُقول في ما جاءَ مِنَ الحِكَمِ وَ المواعِظَ مِن آلِ الرَّسول) is a hadith book written by Ibn Shuʿba al-Harrani, the hadith scholar of 4th/10th century.

have acquired, you have taken on a mission and responsibility onto your shoulders. "And he has made you subject to being held to account [for your thoughts and words and deeds and failures to act], telling you that if you are thankful; if you recognize the blessing which you have been given, and recognize the Giver of those blessings, and made appropriate use of those blessings – which is the meaning of being thankful: recognize the blessing, recognize the Giver of those blessings, and making appropriate use of those blessings – then God ﷻ will increase His blessings on you.

So far, these are the preambles of the letter. The Imam goes on to state: "On the morrow of the Resurrection when God ﷻ holds you to account and asks you the cause for which you expended His blessings, and in what way you benefitted from and used the awareness and information and *Hujjat*[126] which you attained, what will your response to Him be? Do not imagine that God ﷻ will accept your excuses, or that He will forgive your faults and errors. That is not the way it will be. Far be it from that!" Rather, you will be held accountable for the smallest of your mistakes and the least of your failures to take responsibility for your duties; God ﷻ will not overlook these things as easily as you might think. "God ﷻ has taken a covenant with those who have knowledge in his sacred writ and dispensation that they have a responsibility to explicate and annunciate the truth, and not to hide anything from the curious eyes of the people; and these are your duties, O Ibn Shahāb az-Zuhrī, given that you are one of the scholars of the religion!" God ﷻ's has concluded his *Hujjat* or argument [in the case that is being prepared] against you [for use on the Day of Judgement]. The Quran has instructed you not to hold back and hide the truth, and that you have a duty to give expression to that which you know to be the truth. But you have failed to do so. Why did you fail in your duty? At this point the Imam points out az-Zuhrī's shortcomings and failures to act and failures to recognize his responsibilities. Pay close attention now.

---

[126] *Hujjat*: the clear and perfect embodied evidence of and unimpeachable authority for all truth on Earth and therefore the conclusive argument and evidentiary proof against all falsehood on the Plain of Assembly on Judgement Day.

8. The Imams' Politicism and their Militant Actions

"The least of your failures and sins is that you have modulated and dampened and eliminated the revulsion of the oppression of an oppressor by your association with him, for if you had not positioned yourself among his ranks and in the front of the oppressor, he would fear for [the possibility of] the people rising up against him." But you got close to him and became intimate with him and thought of him as being a part of your [crowd] or of you as being a part of his, thereby quenching people's horror and revulsion of him [and of his unjust actions], and providing him with assurance and peace of mind, and the ability to sleep in peace at night. Your quenching of the people's horror and revulsion of him is the least of your sins, and paved the way for his continuing his waywardness and oppression and enmity [with the people and with God ﷻ's dispensational order]. "Whenever he called you, you unhesitatingly complied, saying, 'Yes, sir! No, sir! Three bags full, sir!' Whenever he needed you, you complied and went along like a tame and servile and obedient sheep, and did whatever it was that he wanted of you. O Ibn Shahāb! I fear for you that on the Day of Resurrection, you will be among the rank of sinners and of those who carry the weight of their sins against Islam and the Quran and the Muslim peoples upon your shoulders. And that you will be asked to answer for all of the things which you had attained as a consequence of your providing aid and succor to oppressors." Do you imagine that God ﷻ will not ask you about your social status and your abilities and spiritual capacities; and about the fact that when you entered the Sacred Mosque [in Mecca], that people would whisper among themselves that Ibn Shahāb az-Zuhrī has entered [the sanctuary]? [Do you imagine that] the social standing which you have been given is free and does not come at a price? You have attained to your station [of honor within a false social order] by affirming [the iniquities and oppression of] an oppressor; do you think, then, that God ﷻ will not hold you to account for any of this??

"You took whatever was given to you, irrespective of [the question as to] whether or not it [rightly] belonged to you." You took whatever money or gift or honorarium which you did not deserve whenever someone offered you these things. The caliph sent you a hundred thousand dinars and you think that therefore, that money is yours; but it isn't, you unfortunate and miserable wretch! In the hamlets and villages throughout the Umayyad dominions, there are people who go to bed hungry and spend their nights in hunger, and a hundred thousand dinars would not be given to you as a gift [in the ordinary course of events]; but because the caliph granted it to you, you accepted it and honored it [= the fact that it was given to you by the caliph]. "And you became intimate with someone and accepted money from someone who has not given even a penny [of that which belongs] to the people [back to them]." You have chosen to keep the company of one who does not give to others what is their rightful due, O Muhammad b. Shahāb az-Zuhrī! What are you doing??

"And when you became his intimate associate, you were yet unable to dissuade him from the error of his ways and to bring him back to the Straight Path." You reconciled your conscience by telling yourself that you will associate with him so that in this way, you will be able to guide him aright, heedless of the fact that if Abdul-Malik were to follow the path that you had in mind for him, he would no longer be Abdul-Malik [the Caliph]. And that if he were no longer Abdul-Malik [the Caliph], that he would no longer be in need of an abject groveler and a pitiful, servile wretch such as yourself. When Abdul-Malik is no longer Abdul-Malik [the Caliph], he will stand in need of Imam Sajjād ﷺ, not of [a wretch like] you O Muhammad b. Shahāb az-Zuhrī! So you went to reform him and put him back on the straight and narrow, did you? Is that even in the realm of possibility? It is not as if Abdul-Malik can change. He is no more capable of changing that a tiger can change his stripes, you *simpleton*!

"And you chose to befriend one who is the enemy of God ﷻ". What does this mean? Pay attention to the meaning of friendship and enmity. Do you think that Muhammad b. Shahāb az-Zuhrī truly acted in friendship toward Abdul-Malik? No, he did not. I am certain that this was not the case. Why should he have any affection for Abdul-Malik? It is his interests which drove him into Abdul-Malik's arms. But the Imam says that he befriended him. What does he mean by this? It means that he entered into Abdul-Malik's ranks; that he is in the same *front* as him, despite the fact that he has no affection for him, or that he might even curse him in his heart; but he is in the same front as him *in practice*. I ask

8. The Imams' Politicism and their Militant Actions

you: was Muhammad b. Shahāb az-Zuhrī in Abdul-Malik's front or in Imam Sajjād's? Is it anything other than the case that he was in Abdul-Malik's front? For if it were otherwise, the Imam would not have written him this letter and would not have addressed him in such a tone. But at the same time, there can be no doubt that he loved Imam Sajjād ﷺ deeply, even though he had positioned himself in the ranks of Abdul-Malik's supporters. But that kind of love and friendship, which does not result in anything and which cannot be depended on for anything, is worthless. Friendship means standing and fighting in the same front [and for the same values and ideals].

"Did you not understand, O unfortunate wretch! that when these people called you to come to them, that they cared nothing for God ﷻ and Islam and the Quran and the Way of the Prophet ﷺ, and that they were not concerned about whether or not the truths and ideals [of Islam] would or would not be lost; but that they were after something else?" They wanted you to be the axel of their mill wheel, so that they could spin the millstone of their oppressions; a spindle without which their millstone could not spin and the gristmill could not run to produce the flour for their bread. Muhammad b. Shahāb az-Zuhrī! You are that very same spindle around which the millstone of the oppressions of the Umayyads turns. Notice the great and central importance of the role played by az-Zuhrī and the likes of him. "They used you as a bridge over which they passed to reach their iniquities. You thus became a ladder with which their oppressions were elevated; and you became someone who called [them] to [continue] their oppressions, having become a wayfarer on their path." So you are with them; you are of them; you are on their path. Don't fool yourself, saying that you are Muhammad b. Shahāb az-Zuhrī and that you are a scholar of religion, whereas he is Abdul-Malik the Umayyad caliph, and that you are a friend and supporter of Imam Sajjād ﷺ. No. You too are a part of them; you are just another individual who is a part of that caravan which is headed towards Hell.

"They entered doubts in the hearts of the scholars of Islam by means of you [and your kind]." The doubt that is referred to here is the doubt that arises from the question that 'If this path is wrong, then why did [the great] Muhammad b. Shahāb az-Zuhrī follow such a path?' And the question that follows on its heels, which is, 'Why should I, too, not follow that path?' What a perilous responsibility it surely is! They used you in order to draw to themselves even those who are knowledgeable in the religion! But you have not cottoned on to the fact that you are being used, because of your ignorance and floundering heedlessness. This is the sentence that I had referred to, which talks about the role religious authorities have played in the service of [false and oppressive] political orders throughout history. The truths which we are just now arriving at were spoken of thirteen centuries ago by the Fourth Imam: "They attract the hearts of the ignorant to themselves by means of you [and people like you]." They attract people toward themselves and draw them after themselves. This is your role, O Muhammad b. Shahāb az-Zuhrī!

Let this suffice us then; the hadith report [of the letter] is long and continues on, [but let this much suffice our purposes]. [So that is the role of the court-allied clergy and] this is the role of Imam Sajjād ﷺ and the other Immaculates: to stand up against them and against their alliance with the objectives of false and oppressive governments. Can you still maintain that Imam Sajjād ﷺ was a quietist who cloistered himself up in his home and [did nothing but] weep and cry? Why did Imam Sajjād ﷺ write this letter?

Another piece of my talk for today still remains which I would like to express, as I want to move on tomorrow from the discussion of the court-allied clergy and poets to another important topic.

17. The Imams' utilization of their Shī'a warrior-poets

Another issue is the issue of the poets. The poets play just as important and sensitive a role in their own right and province as the court-allied clergy do in theirs. Poets have always played a role in every society. It has always been the case that the poets have played a fundamental role in any community that is purposive and which is intent on heading in a given direction. If memory serves, it seems to me that I had talked briefly about the role of the poets in society in this same forum a couple of years ago. A huge responsibility lies on the shoulders of poets in each era. They are not cognizant of what great sins are being committed by those poets who spew nothing but nonsense, which is in fact an indirect acceptance if not

8. The Imams' Politicism and their Militant Actions

affirmation of the false and unjust policies which prevail in the world today, and which have always prevailed throughout its history. These poets do not know the extent of the crime that they are committing when they reduce the level of a culture's vision to nothing but sexuality by composing lurid and immoderate and uncouth poetry and lyrics. This is the greatest crime that can be committed in this field. The poets, and especially the young poets, should know that the instrument of their trade is a very sharp and incisive one. The form of modern poetry is much more incisive and penetrating and expressive than the classical molds. I have an interest in modern poetry and its expressive forms; I am referring, of course, to those forms which are based on certain rules and criteria; not some of the nonsense which passes for "poetry" nowadays.

If a poet – be it a contemporary one or one in bygone eras – proceeds to use his sharp and penetrating skills on issues which are not the first priority of the nation, then he has committed the greatest of sins. And this has always been the case. But there are several types of deviance which occur in poetry. It used to be the case at one time that a poet's deviance was that he composed his poetry for the sake of receiving a reward or for financial gain. And it was usually not the case that those who were not wealthy would give money to such poets. But if they were able to do so, poets would compose poems for them as well, even if they happened to be a beggar. If the 11th century poet Onsorī knew that his local grocer would provide him with the riches which he so desired, he would have composed his odes for him.

> I heard that Onsorī's urn stands were of silver
> And that his serving utensils were of gold[127]

We see that Onsorī, one of our past poets, had urns of silver and serving utensils that were made of gold. Well, [it is clear that] he was willing to compose his poetry for whomsoever gave him these things. It is just that in those days, there was no one other than Sultān Mahmūd to give him such things. And Sultān Mahmūd would bestow such gifts to him

---

[127] Khāqānī (12th century).

unhesitatingly, and Onsorī, in his turn, would compose odes for him. This was one kind of deviance, which of course became less common in later eras. And there is another deviance which we are witness to today, but this enters into the subject of [social] deviance, which I do not want to get into as it does not pertain to our subject.

Poets were numerous during the time of the Imams ﷺ. Generally speaking, the Arabs were more skilled at poetry than the Persians. In the days when Persian poets could hardly cobble together a couple of couplets, the Arabs were busy composing odes of the highest aesthetic value which still shine like jewels in the crown of Arab letters, i.e. the *mu'allaqāt-e sab'* were composed in those days and were hung from the crown of the Ka'ba. The Arabs have a longer history of poetry than we do. The Arabic language and culture have a brilliant history in this respect. And so, there were many poets who composed all sorts of poetry. Much of the population composed poetry: men, women and children.

Two types of people benefitted from the instrument of poetry: one was Abdul-Malik, and the other was Imam Sajjād ﷺ; Hāshim, or Imam Sādiq ﷺ; Hārūn or Imam Kāẓim ﷺ. The ruling powers started to expend money in order to leverage the power of poetry [in their favor]. In the midst of the hullabaloo and ruckus which the ruling powers had raised by their sponsorship of poetry and poets, in which money was given and made in order to paint white as black and black as white, the Imams ﷺ were not idly standing by. They gathered around them a number of sharp-tongued poets whose poetry was like the whip of the spirit, and gave large prizes as incentives to those among their Shī'a who had these abilities.

I became aware of this facet of the Imams' lives while researching an unrelated subject; and [once I came across the matter,] I had no choice but to delve into the subject and investigate to see how the amounts which were paid as incentives by, say, Imam Bāqir ﷺ and Imam Sādiq ﷺ, compared with the amounts paid by Imams ﷺ Jawād ﷺ, Hādī ﷺ, and Askarī ﷺ. I saw that Imam Bāqir ﷺ and Imam Sādiq ﷺ – the earlier Imams ﷺ – were in financial difficulties, which is why their generosity towards the poets among their following was very small. There are a few hadith reports in the *Bihār* collection where Imam Bāqir ﷺ is quoted as saying that his father Imam Sādiq's gifts and grants were [variously] seventy dirhams, and fifty dirhams, and the like. There are perhaps five or six such hadith reports which describe these gifts as being very paltry (63:61-63). But in the same era, we read about Kumayt b. Zaid al-Asadi, the great Shī'a poet and warrior, composing an ode and being given one hundred thousand dirhams by either Imam Bāqir ؑ or Imam Sādiq.[128] This is how it was back them: [the poets were like TV advertising spots and] the Imams ؑ relied on them [to spread the word of truth and to counter the wall of lies which the Umayyads and Abbāsids had erected around and against them]. And this was because the propagation of information by way of poetry and poems was very important and effective [in those days]. And one of the reasons for this is that poetry caresses the strings of the instrument of the mind and has a deep and lasting effect on people.

18. The Imams ؑ reprimand court-allied poets and encourage Shī'a poets

There were two groups of poets, one group was allied with the caliphal court, and the other was comprised of the Shī'a or followers of the Imams ؑ. Additionally, there were also some who were hypocrites and who played their roles accordingly. The poet Kathayyir came to Imam Bāqir ؑ and the Imam said to him in a chiding tone, "[How is it that you claim to be our friend and yet] you compose poetry in praise of Abdul-Malik?" Kathayyir was lost for words and didn't know how to respond, as he didn't want to admit his sin. He started to apologize instead, saying: "O son of the Apostle of God ؑ! I didn't praise him very well" – he wanted to hoodwink the Imam – "I didn't characterize him as 'the Imam of Guidance'"; in other words, he didn't submit that Abdul-Malik was the Divinely-Guided Imam as he claims to be, which is rightly an office that is exclusive only to Imam Bāqir ؑ. Rather, he characterized him in terms such as 'O [Valiant] Lion' and so forth. "And a lion is a kind of dog;" – he is trying to justify his actions to the Imam – "I called him a 'Viper of the Field of Battle'; which is [nothing but] a [lowly] reptile". "I called him a 'Sun' and a 'Moon'; and these are [nothing but] solid [inanimate] matter; so there should be no issue with the kinds of things which I have said."

---

[128] Ibn Shahrāshūb, *Manāqib* 4:197.

Note the subtlety of the error that has taken place. He is either mistaken or is pretending to be mistaken, whereas the pretense to error is problematic in itself. Do you think the Imam was not aware of what you had composed, you petty fool? Do you think the Imam does not know that you have characterized Abdul-Malik as 'a lion'? That is what he has heard, and that is what he objects to. You should not be saying *anything* about the man, let alone words of praise. You should not be in his service and in his pay; and you should not be helping him to further his agenda! Granted that you did not characterize Abdul-Malik as 'the Imam of Guidance'; but you should not call him 'a lion' either.

"The Imam smiled." In other words, he was saying 'I understand what you are saying'. It is evident. He then turned to Kumayt and said, "Now *you* recite [one of your poems], O poet of ours! Let you recite, O poet of truth and justice!" At which point Kumayt commenced to recite his famous long ode called *The Hāshimīāt*, which is revolutionary from top to bottom.

Kumayt is the same person whom the ruling authorities wanted to arrest for these same poems of his. Kumayt was on the run from the authorities for twenty years and he would say that he had carried his cross over his shoulders for twenty years. The authorities pardoned him for a while, and then executed him on a minor trumped-up charge. When he entered the [Governor's] court at Kūfa, they made a pretext and told their Turkish slaves to take him out and cut him into small pieces. They obviously didn't want him around, so they cut him up with their swords into little pieces. His son relates, "As soon as my father fell to the ground, I went over to him and heard him say with his dying breath, 'O God ﷻ! [I have been killed for the sake of] the House of the Prophet ﷺ! O God ﷻ! the House of the Prophet ﷺ! O God ﷻ! the House of the Prophet ﷺ!' He was saying that he knows why they killed him, and that it was because he fought in the cause of justice and of defending the truth.

Thus, there were these other kinds of poets also. It was a very noble thing for poets to do during those days where taking sides with the wrong party and front could cost them their lives; and that is what the Shī'a poet-warriors did.

19. The role of weeping and redemptive suffering in the growth of Shī'a Islam

Di'bal al-Khuzāī was one such poet. Today is the day of Āshūrā, and so we must spend more time in remembrance of the glorious event of Karbalā, to talk about its significance to humanity, and to weep at its tragic [and senseless loss of life]. Any human being cannot help but [be moved and to] weep at [the sadness of] this [tragedy], because it is the story of the honoring of humanity. It is the story of human virtue [of an unprecedented and highly exalted scale]. And anyone who understands and values human virtue better, is more moved by this great historical event. I am not advocating that we should weep until we swoon, and not even know what we are weeping for. No; that is worthless and meaningless. Rather, a weeping that is informed by the realities of the events and is endowed with a deep understanding of them is a merit and a sign of virtue. And weeping was a factor which was used by the Imams for furthering the cause of true Islam and the cause of the truth. I am not talking about the situation that prevails nowadays, which has been subject to distortion; but that is the rationale in Shī'a Islam behind weeping for the tragedy which occurred in the Plain of Karbalā. Weeping is a motivator; it shows the truth and moves people to action. It makes the heart more supple and makes the revolutionary person more sensitive [to the realities of the world and the need to bring about change for the good].

And then there are those who are ignorant [to the truth of what Imam Husain stood for] and who are well fed and who shed tears as a kind of cathexis or a way of releasing their mundane sorrows. Those tears are not shed for the sake of Imam Husain or his cause or his values. They are more a result of their unpaid bills and rent and the fear of going hungry. I am not talking about those kinds of tears. I am talking about the tears which are shed by those who are aware of the intellectual and spiritual teachings of Shī'a Islam. That is what I support. May God have mercy on those who shed these kinds of tears.

20. The passion of Imam Husain ﷺ as told by Di'bal al-Khuzāī in the presence of Imam Reza ﷺ

Di'bal al-Khuzāī came to the presence of Imam Reza ﷺ during the time that the Imam was still residing in Madina and the Abbāsid policy [of wanting to keep him close by for monitoring purposes] had not yet forced the Imam to emigrate to [Marv, which was the caliphal capital at the time, and which was located in] Khorāsān. And of course, that is a story in itself, [but a story for another day].

Di'bal al-Khuzāī is a great poet and a great promulgator of Shī'a Islam, a favorite of the Eighth Imam, and a pillar of Shī'a Islam in his own time. The Imam said, "O Di'bal! Do you not have a poem to recite?" The Imam is a connoisseur of poetry. When Kumayt recited one of his poems for the Imam, the Imam corrected him on a point in such a way that the great poet responded by saying, "You are more of a poet than I am!" The Imam knows his poetry. And furthermore, and more importantly, the ode is about the Imam himself: about his thoughts and ideas, about his way, and about the caravan which he has following in his train. Therefore, His Eminence asks, "O Di'bal! Do you not have a poem to recite, so that I can listen to it and take pleasure in doing so?" Di'bal said, "Yes, I do, O son of the Apostle of God ﷺ. I have a poem at the ready. Should I recite it?" And when the Imam told him to recite his poem, he started to recite the long ode which he is famous for and which begins with a couplet about the tragedy of Karbalā and the day of Āshūrā, and which is addressed to Lady Fātimaᵗ oz-Zahrā ﷺ, the august daughter of the Prophet ﷺ of Islam. Here is the first couplet of the ode:

O Fātima ﷺ! Did you ever imagine that your son, Husain ﷺ, would one day fall naked and unclothed under the scorching sun on the sands of the plain of Karbalā?
Did you ever imagine that they would martyr your son on the banks of the Euphrates without allowing him to quench his thirst?

In the ode, the poet speaks to the daughter of the Prophet ﷺ. Why? The usual commentaries say that it is because she is Imam Husain's mother, and that she is the first person who feels the loss of her son and who would

8. The Imams' Politicism and their Militant Actions

weep at the death of her son. But I do not think that is the reason because it is not a matter of feeling loss and weeping. I think there is a different reason. Is it not the case that Di'bal is a Shī'a revolutionary and that Imam Reza is the leader of this revolutionary movement? And is it not the case that the ode is all about recalling the memory of the greatest revolutionary leader of Shī'a Islam – Imam Husain ﷺ – and the memory of one of the past leaders of the Shī'a movement and the events of the past? Is that not the case? So if this is the case, what we have is a case of one revolutionary (Di'bal al-Khuzāī) singing the elegy (*marthīa*) of another revolutionary (Imam Husain); and his aim is to provoke emotions. So he must address the ode to Lady Fātima^t az-Zahrā ﷺ, because it was she who initiated the Shī'a revolutionary movement. Lady Fātima^t az-Zahrā Fātima^t is the first Shī'a revolutionary, which is something which I had mentioned to you earlier. And so Di'bal addresses Lady Fātima ﷺ, saying, "O Fātima ﷺ! Did you ever imagine that your son, Husain ﷺ, would one day fall naked and unclothed under the scorching sun on the sands of the plain of Karbalā?" When you started on your Path and saw the great trials and tribulations ahead, did you ever imagine such a thing, O Fātima ﷺ? "Did you ever imagine that they would martyr your son on the banks of the Euphrates without allowing him to quench his thirst?" And that they would throw his body down onto its scorching sands?

Arise O Fātima ﷺ and shed tears, for the Stars of Heaven are strewn on the desert floor;
The Stars of Heaven are the sons and daughters and little children of Fātima ﷺ!

What heart-rending event is Di'bal referring to? Around the time when the sun is setting, when the final arrow of the quiver of justice, i.e. Imam Husain ﷺ himself, enters the field of battle and goes up against the heart of the enemy and is slaughtered, suddenly all of the womenfolk of his contingent realize that Husain ﷺ has died. They want to see if they can help him, but the enemy forces come and set the tents of the womenfolk on fire, and the daughter of Imam Husain ﷺ heads toward the desert.

The Stars of Heaven are the sons and daughters and little children of Fātima ﷺ!

La hawla wa la quwwata illa bi'llāhi'l-'Alī al-Azīm

There is no might or power other than with God ﷻ, the Most High and Most Supreme.

9. The Revolutionary Sons of the Imams

[God ﷻ the All-Knowing and All-Wise has stated in His Sacred Writ:]

$$\text{وَقَالَ مُوسَىٰ رَبَّنَا إِنَّكَ آتَيْتَ فِرْعَوْنَ وَمَلَأَهُ زِينَةً وَأَمْوَالًا فِي الْحَيَاةِ الدُّنْيَا رَبَّنَا لِيُضِلُّوا عَن سَبِيلِكَ ۖ رَبَّنَا اطْمِسْ عَلَىٰ أَمْوَالِهِمْ وَاشْدُدْ عَلَىٰ قُلُوبِهِمْ فَلَا يُؤْمِنُوا حَتَّىٰ يَرَوُا الْعَذَابَ الْأَلِيمَ ﴿٨٨﴾}$$

[10:88] "O our Sustainer and Lord of Providence! Verily, splendor and riches hast Thou vouchsafed, in the life of this world, unto Pharaoh and his great ones-with the result, O our Sustainer, that they are leading [others] astray from Thy path! O our Sustainer! Wipe out their riches, and harden their hearts, so that they may not attain to faith ere they see the grievous suffering [that awaits them]!"

$$\text{وَلَيَنصُرَنَّ اللَّهُ مَن يَنصُرُهُ ۗ إِنَّ اللَّهَ لَقَوِيٌّ عَزِيزٌ ﴿٤٠﴾ الَّذِينَ إِن مَّكَّنَّاهُمْ فِي الْأَرْضِ أَقَامُوا الصَّلَاةَ وَآتَوُا الزَّكَاةَ وَأَمَرُوا بِالْمَعْرُوفِ وَنَهَوْا عَنِ الْمُنكَرِ ﴿٤١﴾}$$

[22:40] ...And God ﷻ will most certainly succor him who succors His cause: for, verily, God ﷻ is most powerful, almighty, and [22:41] [well aware of] those who, [even] if We firmly establish them on earth, remain constant in prayer, and give in charity, and enjoin the doing of what is right and forbid the doing of what is wrong.

1. The important and misunderstood matter of the revolutionary sons and posterity of the Imams

One of the subjects within [the study of] the life of the Imams ﷺ which requires further research is the matter of the revolutionary sons and posterity (*imāmzāda*) of the Imams ﷺ and the leaders of the insurrections which occurred during the reigns of the Umayyad and Abbāsid dynasties. It is a highly important issue and a difficult one, which we hope to cover today and to arrive at a conclusion, God ﷻ grant.

You should be aware, as a preliminary point of the discussion, that – to the best of my knowledge – that from the time of Imam Bāqir ﷺ to the time of Imam Hādī ﷺ and Imam Hasan al-Askarī ﷺ, during each generation of this time period (which lasted for approximately two hundred years), one or another of the sons of the Imams ﷺ would gather a group of followers and rise up in armed insurrection against the ruling caliphal authority. These *imāmzādahs* or sons of the Imams ﷺ were either the sons of Imams Hasan ﷺ and Husain ﷺ, or, to the best of my knowledge, were the sons and posterity of Imam Sādiq ﷺ. These insurrections would invariably be crushed, sooner or later, for reasons which are specific to the social conditions of the respective eras. I will touch upon some of these conditions in some cases. There is also a general consideration, and specific reasons in one or two cases, which I shall also discuss.

2. Two positions regarding the revolutionary Imāmzādahs

The question has always obtained for the Shʿīa in the eras after the occultation as to whether the armed insurrections of the sons and posterity of Imam Hasan ﷺ and Imam Husain ﷺ were something that was right and proper, or whether they were mistakes [in the light that historical hindsight can shed on these events].

9. The Revolutionary Sons of the Imams

2.1 The position asserting the rightfulness of the insurrections of the Imāmzādahs

Some are of the opinion that these insurrections were rightful and that they were correct actions [to be taken at their respective times]; but not in the sense that *all* of them were correct, but that one or two of them, or a specific number of them were correct and even necessary, and that failure so to act would have put them outside of the pale of Shʻīa Islam. For example, one of the creedal principles of the Zaidīya, who came to believe in the Imamate of Zaid [b. Ali b. al-Husain], is that the Imam is someone who must necessarily rise up in armed insurrection [against the false ruling powers] and that a person's failure to do so disqualifies him from candidature from the office of the Imamate. It was because of this belief of theirs that this group of the Shʻīa did not accept anyone as their Imam after [the martyrdom of] Zaid, who was the son of the Fourth Imam, Imam Sajjād ﷺ.

Nor did they accept the Imamate of Imam Bāqir ﷺ; by which I do not mean to imply that there was a group of Shʻīa contemporaneous with him who did not accept his Imamate, as there was no such thing as the Zaidīya at that time, as this was a sect which came into being later. They thus did not accept the Imamate of Imam Bāqir ﷺ, but rather, accepted the Imamate of Yahyā, the son of Zaid. Yahyā also rose up in armed insurrection in the Māzandarān region [of northern Iran, in the Caspian littoral], and his uprising was similarly quashed and he too was killed, after which the leadership of this group continued for generations of posterity to come. The Zaidīya were one such group which developed a religio-legal school or understanding (*fiqh*) of their own, as well as their own history and set of teachings and beliefs, and they [thus] became a sect among the [other] sects within Islam. This was one group.

2.2 The position asserting the wrongfulness of the insurrections of the Imāmzādahs

Juxtaposed against this group in terms of their position with respect to [the insurrections of] the *Imāmzādahs* were those who believed that these people were good for nothing extremists whose insurrections served no rightful purpose as the conditions of the time were not conducive to [the success of] armed insurrections, such that one's [religious] duty was to hold one's peace. This group of people based their reasoning on the fact that the Imams ※ themselves did not rise up in armed insurrection and claimed that they submitted to and remained quietists in the face of the oppression and tyranny of the caliphs, and even claimed the Imams' impotence [relative to the power of the caliphs]; and concluded therefore that the militant actions of the *Imāmzādahs* was inappropriate. So this was another group, which unfortunately comprised the majority of the Twelver Sh'ia populace, and this mentality which amounts to a wholesale condemnation of the *Imāmzādahs* still holds sway from those days of old up to our present time.

3. The wrongfulness of the second position

When we refer back to the hadith report corpus and compare the words of the Imams ※ to the revolutionary posture of the *Imāmzādahs*, we see certain aspects of the lives of these great men which forces us to reconsider the majority popular position regarding the apolitical nature of their lives, and to demonstrate that the situation is not what the populists hold – populists who probably think of themselves as holding a superior position, no less!

The subject which we want to focus on today is the more basic question as to what kinds of people these *Imāmzādahs* were: the *Imāmzādahs* who rose up in armed insurrection against the ruling powers from the time of Imam Sādiq ※ all the way to the Imamate of Imam Hasan Askarī ※. Can they all be judged in the same way? Or are each of them unique and should therefore be evaluated individually? Or do they fall into different groups? And we should examine the lives of one or two of these *Imāmzādahs* in detail.

4. The aspersions cast by the oppressor regimes posited as the main reason for the disrepute of the revolutionary Imāmzādahs

It is first necessary for me to draw your attention to the reason for the fact that these *Imāmzādahs* have a bad reputation; for, if one takes a step back and thinks about it, there should be no reason, in the normal course of events, for people who fight in God ※'s cause and for [attempting to

9. The Revolutionary Sons of the Imams

establish and maintain Islamic ordinances having to do with the moral stewardship of the community (*ahkām-e nizāratī*) such as] *al-amr bi'l-ma'rūf wa an-nahy an al-munkar* [which is a pillar of the religion and which refers to the imperative] to enjoin the doing of that which is right and to forbid the doing of that which is wrong; and who fought in order to preserve the rights of the people – why should such people take on a bad reputation among the people for whom they fought and gave their lives? Why should the feeling arise that these were not people whom the Imams liked and were people whose actions did not enjoy the approval of the Imams? I will first state the reason briefly and preliminarily.

As is well known, one of the tactics which the tyrants and despots have used throughout history is to defame and slander the most serious of their opponents who had popular support, before the people [whose interests they served and to whom they were beholden]. This is a very common tactic which has existed from old times. In the Quran, one sees, for example, that when Pharaoh talks with Moses or with his aristocratic courtiers, he characterizes Moses as a corrupter and seditionist:

$$\text{وَقَالَ فِرْعَوْنُ ذَرُونِي أَقْتُلْ مُوسَىٰ وَلْيَدْعُ رَبَّهُ ۖ إِنِّي أَخَافُ أَن يُبَدِّلَ دِينَكُمْ أَوْ أَن يُظْهِرَ فِي الْأَرْضِ الْفَسَادَ ﴿٢٦﴾}$$

[40:26] And Pharaoh said: "Leave it to me to slay Moses – and let him invoke his [alleged] sustainer! Behold, I fear lest he cause you to change your religion, or lest he cause corruption to prevail in the land!"

When simple-minded people hear such words emanating from Pharaoh, they become impressed about the extent to which Pharaoh is interested in the preservation of the people's religion and in preventing corruption from prevailing in the land; and that it is on account of these concerns that he wants to destroy Moses and Aaron and their associates and helpers. But the more exacting among the people who know that religion is not even a word that appears in Pharaoh's dictionary or that it is a word which has no meaning within it, and that for him, the people's religion and social order is naught but the carrying out of his own self-seeking and selfish will, and that he does not care an iota for the people or their interests (because the continuity of his reign depends on the weakness of the people, and that he could not continue his reign given a strong and united populace) – it is abundantly clear for those who understand these things about Pharaoh that his wanting to destroy Moses is not because of his concern for the distortion of the people's religion at Moses' hands; rather, it is because of his fear for his own safety and well-being, and for fear of his life.

This is the kind of tactic which Pharaoh resorted to; and it is a tactic which had been used prior to Pharaoh, as well as one that was used after him. And in order to make the matter of the *Imāmzādahs* perfectly clear, I shall cite an example from relatively recent times so that it can be seen how the method employed by Pharaoh and Muʻāwiya and the other Umayyad and Abbāsid caliphs is exactly the same method which was used a few years ago in an era and place which is close to us historically and geographically, in the years 1840 or 1850 of the Christian Era, or about 150 years ago. As you know, an extraordinary resistance movement sprung up in India against British rule [at that time]. And this episode relates to a time which predates Gandhi's birth. In other words, the great Indian leader had not yet been born, and the movement which I am talking about took place 40 or 50 years before Gandhi was even born and was engendered by the Muslim population of India. This was the sector of society which ruled over India at the time, although the Mongol and Timūrid dynasty's hold on power had been weakened by the British presence, which gradually took over running the affairs of state through the East India Company.

Who were the leaders of this movement? They consisted of a few of the better-known Islamic scholars and leaders of India, including Mawlā Shāh Ismā'īl of Delhi (*Dehlawī*), who was one of the grand Ayatollahs and important scholars of India and one of the leaders of the resistance against English colonialism. This movement resisted the English arduously and much has been written about their activities. I have written briefly and incompletely on the subject[129], and I think that anyone

---

[129] The Role of the Muslims in the Freedom Movement of India by Ayatollah Khāmeneī was published in 1347 (1969).

9. The Revolutionary Sons of the Imams

who endeavors to write a monograph on the subject would be rendering a valuable service. Briefly, the British strove to destroy these great men by any means which they had at their disposal, and to quash their movement, including arrests, harsh imprisonment terms, exile, and even executions, and the like. They put these [leaders] under a lot of pressure, but the truth of the matter was that no matter how much their leaders were subjected to imprisonment, exile, and torture, their popularity would be increased in the eyes of the people, resulting in the strengthening and blooming of their resistance movement. These matters relate to about 150 years ago, or to an era that is close to our own.

The British government realized that they needed to come up with a more radical solution to their problem if they were to be able to do away with the threat that this resistance movement posed to them. A lot of thought went into this project. Eventually a decision was reached which paid relatively good dividends for the British, and this decision consisted of their spreading the rumor about the Muslim leaders of India and throughout the Islamic dominions that leaders such as Mawlā Shāh Ismā'īl of Delhi and others like him are Wahhābis.

Now the Wahhābi movement, which was a reactionary and colonialist [-aided and -abetted] movement, had just recently been inaugurated at that time. A group of Arabs who had been wound up by the enemy [= the British] had conquered the Hijāz and destroyed the shrines of the Companions of the Prophet ﷺ, as a result of which a strong wave of hatred and enmity towards them had been put in motion throughout the Islamic world; a wave which was much stronger than that which exists today, despite the fact that the Wahhābis are hated and rejected today by Sunni and Sh'īa alike. In that same book, I pointed out that Wahhābism was a reactionary and colonialist [-aided and -abetted] movement which was created for the sole purpose of inciting internecine conflict among the Muslim populations, and that it was something which no Muslim could agree with. But regardless, the people of those days held a greater hatred and enmity for the Wahhābis than you and I do today; and the reason for this is that the movement had only recently been founded, and the shrines of the Imams ؑ and *awlīā* (those who enjoy proximity to God ﷻ) or saints had only recently been destroyed. Thus, the

Muslim population of India which was majority Sunni with a minority Shʿīa population were united in their hatred of the Wahhābis.

The British thus began to spread the rumor that leaders such as Mawlā Shāh Ismāʾīl of Delhi and other great leaders like him were Wahhābis. This was one of their plans which worked for a while as a number of simple-minded souls bought into the British hype and were under the spell of its meme, believing these great leaders to be the hated Wahhābis. But gradually the truth came out and we now know, not only were these leaders not Wahhābis, but that they were *anti*-British activists, whereas the British were the lords and masters of the Wahhābis. Therefore, the Muslim leaders of India were anti-Wahhābī as well. The facts of this matter are things that are very clear for us today.

I wanted to give an you an example [of the kind of psychological warfare which the enemy has always employed], so that you will be able to relate to something concrete when considering similar kinds of memes which were being disseminated against the enemies of the Umayyad and Abbāsid tyrants during the time of the Imams ؑ and against the active and revolutionary progeny and posterity of the People of the House of the Prophet ﷺ.

The Abbāsid caliph al-Manṣūr was one of the caliphs whose reign was put under pressure by the armed insurrectionary activity of these *Imāmzādahs*. He went to the pulpits [of the congregational mosques] and other places of assembly and started to curse the progeny and posterity of Imam Hasan ؑ and the other *Imāmzādahs* of the Ālid line. Nor was he content to stop with them, but went on to curse their fathers too – cursing Imam Hasan ؑ and even cursing the Commander of the Faithful ؑ and finding baseless faults with the Imam who was at one time the subject of the prayers and well wishes of Manṣūr. And all this was in order to show these righteous revolutionaries in a bad light so as to garner their disfavor in the minds of his subjects.

Consider this a categorical principle in the critical evaluation of the lives of the *Imāmzādahs* during the time of the presence of the Imams; and always remember to bear in mind that the hadith reports which have reached us have been forged by the hands of their enemies for the purposes of denigrating their repute. This was the general matter which I wanted to mention by way of a preamble before I entered into the discussion proper.

5. The division of the Imāmzādahs into two groups
Now let us proceed to address the question of what my own opinion is concerning the revolutionary *Imāmzādahs*. I shall state this now, and I feel that I need to truncate the matter, so kindly note that I am talking in summary terms. My own opinion, given the research that I have carried out into this matter, is that the *Imāmzādahs* divide into two groups.

5.1 The Imāmzādahs whose values and priorities are centered on the lower world (*dunyā*)[130]
There is a group of *Imāmzādahs* who wanted to take undue advantage of the fact that they were the sons and grandsons and progeny of Imams ﷺ in order to arrive at lower-worldly objectives (i.e. objectives having to do with the *dunyā*). They had a certain measure of courage which they brought to bear for attaining their objectives. They would take up a sword in hand and rise up in rebellion with a number of their associates and friends, after which the ruling authorities would see that there are a number of malcontents with which they would almost invariably come to some sort of mutually beneficial arrangement, after which they would all be friends again!

There was a group of *Imāmzādahs* who weren't motivated by the desire to act in accordance with God ﷻ's will and in accordance with the ordinances of the religion and the Quranic dispensation. They were not intent on reforming the current governmental order or on establishing a just and Islamic social order. Rather, they simply wanted to replace one group of despots with another, namely, one headed by themselves. As a matter of fact, because their faith was wanting, and because their objectives were aimed at fulfilling their personal interests, if a hint of some sort of mutually beneficial arrangement was given by the ruling

---

[130] *Dunyā*: this lower world of existence. In Islamic cosmology, the material world is the "lowest of the low" (*asfal as-sāfilīn*) in the order of existence. An authoritative hadīth reports the Prophet ﷺ to have said that this world is but a dream from which one awakes upon his death.

authorities after a period of fighting, they would immediately respond favorably and make a deal and would even at times work alongside the ruling authorities against whom they had supposedly rebelled against.

The Eighth Imam had a brother named Zaid. So remember that the Zaid to whom I am referring is the brother of the Eighth Imam, and was born and lived several decades after the famous Zaid, the son of Imam Ali ؑ [Zain ul-Ābidīn, Imam Sajjād ؑ, the son of Imam Husain ؑ, who was the eponymous founder of the Zaidīya sect whose members are primarily to be found in present day Yemen]. So I repeat that there are two Zaids. Whenever I personally mention the name of the first one, who is the son of Imam Sajjād ؑ, I always follow his name with the phrase *alayhi salām*, as he is considered to be one of the great martyrs within the history of Islam. But the Zaid to whom I am referring presently is Imam Riḍā's ؑ brother. He was initially a militant revolutionary, holding a sensitive position in one of the Shʻīa resistance cells of [Ibrāhīm b. Ismāʻīl] Ṭabāṭabāī under Abū's-Sāya.[131] The peak of his militancy was reached when he conquered the city of Basra and burned down the houses of those whom he considered to be "Sunni" or antagonistic to him and his cause. Thus, at one point he ordered the houses of a number of such people burned to the ground, after which he was referred to as Zaid un-Nār or Zaid the Arsonist. Well, this was an act which was obviously wrong-footed: it makes no sense to burn people's houses down! That is not the logic of the Imams ؑ. The policy of Imam Ali ؑ when taking possession of a conquered town or village was to make sure that the women and children were not frightened or disturbed.

It is clear that this fellow knew little of the teachings of his own religion, and that he was a man out to serve his own self-interests and ambitions. It seems he just wanted to make a display of his power and to have done something just for the sake of doing it, and so he went ahead and set some houses on fire, with which act he brought the enmity of the people onto himself; after which he was arrested. It so happened that his brother the Eighth Imam was in Khorāsān at the time of his arrest. In order to make Imam Riḍā ؑ beholden to him in some way, [the Abbāsid caliph

---

[131] Sarrī b. Manṣūr Shaybānī, the military commander of the uprising of Ibrāhīm b. Ismāʻīl Ṭabāṭabāī against the Abbāsid caliph al-Ma'mūn.

9. The Revolutionary Sons of the Imams

of the time] al-Ma'mūn mentioned in passing to the Imam that "When the Umayyads captured your Uncle Zaid – referring to Zaid the son of Imam Ali ﷺ [b. Husain as-Sajjād ﷺ], unto whom be [God ﷻ's] peace – they crucified him and killed him and let his body stay tied to the wooden pole[132] [of his execution] for a long time, after which his body was burned. But I am an Abbāsid, and now that I have captured your other Zaid, who is your brother, I will not kill him." He wanted to endear himself to Imam Riḍā ﷺ by not killing his brother and by pretending to be of the same mindset as him. And it is my estimation – this is not something that appears in the hadith report but something which I simply think is likely – that Zaid was bought off by the Abbāsid ruling apparatus during his arrest and made of him a bought and paid for agent of theirs; and that Ma'mūn wanted to free Zaid under this arrangement and at the same time to ensure that the Imam does not realize that his brother has been 'turned', so to speak. It was this dual objective that Ma'mūn had in mind when he spoke to the Imam.

But the Imam immediately put a stop to Ma'mūn's words, saying, "Do not compare my brother Zaid with Zaid b. Ali!" These were two different kinds of people. My uncle Zaid rose up in armed insurrection in order to establish the governance of the House of the Prophet ﷺ Muhammad; and would have been faithful to his word if he were to attain success. In other words, his government would have been a righteous one, and one based on [the Islamic dispensational] law. He might have placed Imam Sādiq ﷺ at the head of the new governing order; but my brother is not like that. My brother is a hoodlum; a useless self-serving ruffian.

I noticed in another hadith report that after a while, Imam Riḍā admonished his brother Zaid not to cooperate with the enemies of their House and not to put his followers (sh'īa) into difficulties. It is not stated [explicitly] in the hadith report that Zaid had become a spy for al-Ma'mūn, but one is led to believe – and this is my own estimation – that Zaid was bought off and turned by the Abbāsids during his arrest, after which he

---

[132] I do not use the word "crucifix" here because the pole to which convicts were tied and left to die did not have a cross-beam to which hands were affixed; thus, they were not cruciform.

became a bought and paid for agent of theirs and worked in their interests. The details of his services are not clear, of course.

There were thus a series of *Imāmzādahs* who were like this. Our opinion of the *Imāmzādahs* in this group is the same as that of those religious leaders: we do not consider these to be the friends of God ﷻ or to be those who are destined for Heaven; nor do we consider them to be true revolutionaries. It matters not whether they are the sons and progeny of the Prophet ﷺ. That kind of mentality that "the progeny of the Prophet ﷺ are immune from the wrath of God ﷻ" is a product of none other than these spoilt brats. There is a hadith report in which Ismā'īl, Imam Sādiq's son, is reported to have asked his father whether the progeny of the Prophet ﷺ are immune from the wrath of God ﷻ; asserting that [this should be the case as] "we are of the family of the Prophet ﷺ". But Imam Sādiq ؑ responds, "Yes, we will be subject to punishment [like everyone else]; anyone who is punished by God ﷻ has committed a sin, and anyone who has sinned will be punished regardless of what his genealogy is."

I have noticed that there is some currency to the kind of thinking which holds that God ﷻ the Sublimely Exalted will not punish those who are the progeny and posterity of the Prophet ﷺ; and this is separate from the case where God ﷻ Himself mediates [so as to assure that no sin is committed and consequently] does not punish a person. Because I personally am descended from the same line [of Mohammedan prophethood], I would ask God ﷻ and would be happy if this were the case; but based on what we have read in the hadith report corpus from our ancestors Imam Sajjād ؑ and Imam Sādiq ؑ and others among the Imams, this is not the way it is.[133]

Tāwwūs [b. Kaysān al-Khulānī] came to Imam Sajjād ؑ and tells him that he troubles himself overmuch with all the time he spends in his devotions and prayers and supplications, questioning him about the

---

[133] In addition to the evidence from the hadith report corpus, there is Quranic evidence as well (in addition to the fact that the whole rational order of creation would be undermined if this were not the case): [99:6] *On that Day will all men come forward, cut off from one another, to be shown their [past] deeds.* [99:7] *And so, he who shall have done an atom's weight of good, shall behold it*; [99:8] *and he who shall have done an atom's weight of evil, shall behold it.*

wisdom of such deeds. Besides, he continues, you are the son of the Prophet ﷺ of God ﷻ, and your mother is Lady Fātimaᵗ az-Zahrā ﷺ; so, you do not stand in need of so much weeping in the middling hours of the night, and so much effort expended on prayers and ritual devotions. After he finished saying these things to the Imam, the Imam became irate. It does not say as much in the report itself, but what I mean is that the tone of the words changes, such that it is evident that the Imam is annoyed. He suddenly responds as follows: "Stop talking about my father and mother and my ancestors. Heaven belongs to the obedient". What [nonsense] are you talking about?

I believe that the kind of mentality which holds that the family of the Prophet ﷺ is immune from God ﷻ's punishment is something that has been generated and encouraged by these kinds of people; and that they would rise up in insurrection based on the love that the people had for them based on their being the progeny of their beloved Prophet ﷺ, and their "uprisings" would be stillborn, [their having come to an understanding with the authorities], and occasionally, they would [even] join forces with the enemy, like Zaid the Arsonist.

So much for this group, then. So I hope and trust that when we speak in defense of the [revolutionary] *Imāmzādahs*, that it is clear to you that we are not talking about any and all of the *Imāmzādahs* who rebelled; because it makes no difference to us in terms of [the overarching imperative of] obedience to God ﷻ whether one is the son of an Imam or not, as these are just ordinary people. It is not our intention to provide a seal of approval on the actions taken by any and all *Imāmzādahs*. Rather, there are a specific number [within that larger category] which we have in mind.

5.2 Imāmzādahs who were righteous and who sought to establish justice

Another group of the *Imāmzādahs* were those who saw that the conditions in which they lived were at variance with the tenets and teachings of Islam and the Quran, and who attempted to re-establish and maintain Islamic ordinances having to do with the moral stewardship of the community (*ahkām-e nizārati*) and thus engaged in *al-amr bi'l-ma'rūf wa an-nahy min al-munkar* [which is a pillar of the religion and which refers to] the imperative to enjoin the doing of that which is right and to forbid the doing of that which is wrong, being prompted and motivated by genuinely religious and Islamic feelings. In other words, they felt a sense of responsibility in the face of the social dissonance and discord they were witness to, and wanted to reform the problems which they were confronted with. It was not possible to reform the society of those days without resorting to the use of the sword. These were another group, of which I shall name two or three prominent examples.[134]

6. Zaid b. Ali b. al-Husain

One of these people is Zaid b. Ali b. al-Husain, who was a prominent personage within the Islamic community of his time, mention of whom has already been made. The Most Noble Prophet ﷺ has referred to Zaid [in a prophecy]. Addressing [his grandson] Imam Husain ؑ, he stated, "A man will emerge from your seed by the name of Zaid who is beloved by me and who is of my House." It is he who is very beloved by me among my posterity. This is the first hadith report [about Zaid].

In another report the Prophet ﷺ states, "A person named Zaid will rise up in [righteous] insurrection from among the progeny of Husain ؑ, and the people who are martyred fighting in his cause will be like the martyrs of the Battles of Badr and Uhud, and will enter into Heaven before the other martyrs on the Day of Resurrection". This is a second hadith report which is available.

[Our hadith report corpus tells us of] Imam Sajjād's ؑ position concerning Zaid. We stated that the matter of martyrdom of certain people within the House of the Prophet ﷺ, such as the martyrdom of Imam Husain ؑ, was well-known within Islamic society because of the prophecy which the Prophet ﷺ had made in this regard. And just as everyone knew that Husain b. Ali ؑ would be martyred and that

---

[134] Several prominent personalities within this group have already been mentioned in the previous discussions, including Yahyā b. Abdullāh, Yahyā b. Zaid, Zaid b. Ali b. al-Husain, Muhammad b. Abdullāh Mahdh, Ibrāhīm b. Abdullāh Mahdh, Husain b. Ali the Martyr of Fakh, and Ibrāhīm b. Ismā'īl Tabātabā. But Ayatollah Khāmeneī refers only to Zaid b. Ali in the continuation of the present discussion.

9. The Revolutionary Sons of the Imams

martyrdom was his historical mission; people similarly knew that person named Zaid from the progeny of Imam Sajjād ﷺ would be martyred. This was also something that was well known within the House and progeny of the Prophet ﷺ. Imam Sajjād ﷺ has stated, "When God ﷻ gave this child to me, I opened the Quran and saw the following verse come up: [9:111] *Behold, God ﷻ has bought of the believers their lives and their possessions, promising them paradise in return, [and so] they fight in God ﷻ's cause, and slay, and are slain.* I then understood that this was the child which the Prophet ﷺ had referred to, which is why I named him Zaid." Because the Prophet ﷺ has said that his name was Zaid, and because the Imam saw that the Quranic verse was alluding to the prophecy that this child would be martyred while fighting in God ﷻ's cause; that he will be sacrificed for God ﷻ's cause and in the way of His religion.

I just remembered another hadith report, but before I mention it, let me say this by way of a preamble – because this great nobleman Zaid has been slandered outrageously; I want you to be aware of the kinds of injustices which have been committed against the most respectable personalities within Islamic history, and for you to know the reasons why these injustices were committed. Because the plan of these slanderers is for us to defer to the image and paradigmatic example of an Imam Sādiq ﷺ which has been distorted by false hadith reports in which he is reported to have gone to the court of the Abbāsid caliph al-Mansūr, at which point al-Mansūr starts to speak to the Imam in an inappropriate and insulting manner, and where the Imam responds, "O Commander of the Faithful! [The prophet] Job was afflicted [with difficulties] and he exercised patience and forbearance. Josef was given [a goodly amount of] God ﷻ's blessings, and he praised the Lord and thanked Him. And you are the progeny of the same line [of prophets], so exercise patience and forbearance!"[135] In other words, the Imam asks the caliph be more tolerant of the faults which he sees in him! Thus, if there is to be a Zaid to whom people are to defer, then such a person's image and reputation must be sullied and damaged for the length of Islamic history, [so that people will

---

[135] Allāma Muhammad Bāqir Majlisī (d. 1110/1698), the *Bihār al-Anwār* (Oceans of Light), 47:193. See Chapter 7, Section 16 for a full treatment of this hadith report.

not use him as an exemplary model]. There is a need to get to know Zaid anew.

Let us now review this other hadith report, in which the Prophet ﷺ says to Zaid b. Hāritha, whose son Usāma is the very youth whom the Prophet ﷺ had assigned on his deathbed to lead the Muslim army in a campaign against Byzantium, "I love you, O Zaid! Because you have the same name as a Zaid who will be born of the seed of al-Husain ؑ and who will be martyred fighting in God ﷻ's cause." This makes the third hadith report from the Prophet ﷺ.

In any event, Zaid was born into the House of the Prophet ﷺ within such a context. He is a youth who is about the same age of his paternal cousin Imam Sādiq ؑ. Imam Bāqir ؑ was Zaid's older brother, and during the time that he was still alive, they would talk about Zaid occasionally and Imam Bāqir's eyes would well up with tears – this is the emotional side of the story – and he would say that it is as if I see him being martyred by way of his being tied to a post and being left to die in the Kunāsa district of Kūfa, where his body was left to be seen by all of the people of that town. This hadith report established the fact that Zaid's martyrdom is something that was a certainty within the House of the Prophet ﷺ, and that includes Zaid himself, of course.

7. The objectives of Zaid's uprising and the Imams' opinions of him

So now let us firstly look into what Zaid's objectives were for his uprising; and secondly, what Imam Sādiq ؑ, who was his contemporary, thought of his uprising. I would like to enter into the discussion of these two matters, and it would seem that I will not have enough time to discuss the case of Muhammad b. Abdullāh b. Hasan b. Hasan b. Ali b. Abī-Tālib ؑ, known as an-Nafs az-Zakīya (the Pure Soul).

As far as Zaid's objectives for his uprising, I shall content myself with citing a couple of hadith reports and providing my comments on them. Because these are not opinions which are based on rational constructs or abstractions but are, rather, textual in nature, or are based on the text of [hadith report] scripture; such that the task at hand involves

9. The Revolutionary Sons of the Imams

seeing what the texts within the corpus of our sacred history have to say on the subject. I shall cite two or three hadith reports from Imam Sādiq.

One report relates that Zaid b. Ali goes to [the Umayyad caliph] Hishām. The report does not provide the reason for his visit. At all events, Zaid was a person among the many people within society who had some business with this chieftain; it could be as if someone was making a call on some official or administrative business to the highest authority in charge of the governmental services of society. Because everything was referred back to the caliph [in those days] and it was the caliph who made the final call on such matters. There was less bureaucracy in those days. When Hishām saw that one of the sons and progeny of Imam Ali ﷺ was present in his court, he thought it opportune to take advantage of his presence and started to insult him. Among the insults which appear in the hadith report is that he insulted Imam Bāqir ﷺ, Zaid's brother; because Imam Bāqir ﷺ was Hishām's adversary. At this point Zaid takes offense and feels that the time of maintaining his silence is over, and the time has come to take a decisive measure.

Why? Was it only on account of a single [insulting] word? No. It was because he saw that the corrupt condition of the political order which was headed by the Umayyads who were taking personal advantage of it had reached a point where these people no longer felt any sense of restraint against openly insulting the sacred teachings of Islam – the tenets of which it was Zaid's purpose and the purpose of people like him to act to revivify. It was the fact that Hishām did not feel the need to restrain himself even before people such as Zaid, that prodded him into action. This is what Hishām's outrageous behavior indicated. Zaid was moved deeply by this and got up and left the court (Ibn Shahrāshūb, *Manāqib* 4:197). He later told some of his friends, "If I had a single person with me, I would not have held my tongue and remained quiet."

In another sentence Zaid has uttered an eternal word which is similar to the words of the Immaculate Imams ﷺ. The sentence is approximately[136] as follows: "Verily, no man has feared the cutting heat of the sword without his [also] being humiliated and broken (*dhallū*)."

---

[136] The Ayatollah is reciting the hadith report in its original Arabic from memory.

Any nation who has feared the heat of the sword has also become defeated and abject and subservient. How long am I to sit by and abide Hishām's insults to the Quran and to all I hold sacred?! Zaid uttered these words and with them decided not to take Hishām's iniquity and injustice any longer, and began to work on the preliminaries of his insurrection.

In this midst, a group of people [who were equally fed up] would go to Zaid and pledge allegiance to him. Zaid moved from the Hijāz to the 'Irāq as he felt that this move would better serve his organizational and mustering purposes, as his father's and grandfather's supporters were more plentiful there. The details of Zaid's uprising are numerous and do not bear much on the subject of our discussion. In several reports which appear in the Sh'īa corpus, the people would constantly gather around him and ask him about Imam Sādiq, just as they would gather around Imam Sādiq and ask that nobleman about Zaid. Zaid would respond by saying that "God the Sublimely Exalted has placed a *Hujjat* [137] among every nation, and in our time, the *Hujjat* is my paternal cousin Ja'far b. Muhammad [Imam Sādiq]." Zaid repeated this statement constantly and was a supporter of Imam Sādiq's.

When the people asked Imam Sādiq about Zaid – and this is my own interpretation; for I will also point to a hadith report which evinces its opposite – the Imam would say certain things which would prompt whosoever heard his words to go and join Zaid's forces and pledge allegiance to him. In one report, Imam Sādiq says, "[The Heavenly rewards of] anyone who is martyred with Zaid will be like those who were martyred with [= while fighting in the cause of] Ali b. Abī-Tālib." And Zaid's movement did not last long, of course. In other words, it was not long before he was brutally suppressed. An event occurred whose details I cannot go into right now.

---

[137] *Hujjat* or *Hujjatullāh*: the Proof [of God] [36:12] ... *For of all things do We take account in a manifest Imām (imāmin mubīn)* [who shall be called to testify and provide evidence on all matters on the Day of Judgment]. This is the meaning of the word *Hujjatullāh* or God's proof for mankind, which is one of the names given to the Imāms by the Quran: The *Hujjat* is the perfect embodiment and "clear evidence" of all truth on Earth and the conclusive argument and evidentiary proof against all falsehood on Judgement Day.

9. The Revolutionary Sons of the Imams

Zaid and his supporters entered the congregational mosque in Kūfa and took most of the town. While this was taking place, a tactical neglect enabled the Umayyad forces to hit Zaid's forehead with an arrow, felling him to the ground and martyring him. And if it were not for the fact that he was shot by this arrow, his uprising was making good progress and it would seem that his forces would have been successful in capturing Kūfa and Basra and the 'Irāq in their first offensive. At all events, their uprising was not one that was ill-thought out and unplanned; but alas, this event took place, and these kinds of accidents can occur for everyone at any time. The point is that once Zaid determined to go to Kūfa and rise up in insurrection against the Umayyad power, and once he was martyred in that cause and the people asked Imam Sādiq about his uprising and martyrdom, Imam Sādiq responded by affirming Zaid's uprising with words which were very aphoristic (*muwajjiz*) and interesting and deep, both prior to and after his martyrdom.

In another report which has to do with the period after Zaid's martyrdom Imam Sādiq is reported to have said, "May God have mercy on my uncle's soul, for he was [= his insurrectionary actions were] beneficial both for our religion as well as for our [life in the] *dunyā*."[138] He was beneficial for our religion in the sense that he promulgated the religion of Islam; he revivified the Quran; and would destroy its enemies. But Zaid was also beneficial for Imam Sādiq's lower-worldly existence, since Imam Sādiq's supporters are under extreme pressures of repression and control during the time of the Umayyads; they are living under the constant threat of being killed at the hands of the authorities, so that when Zaid rose up in insurrection, this aspect of the life of Imam Sādiq and his followers was also improved. Was that clear? In any case, these kinds of interesting things can be found in the hadith report corpus from Imam Sādiq about Zaid.

Another sentence from Imam Sādiq is where he states, "I swear upon my oath with God that my uncle Zaid is a martyr like the martyrs who were martyred fighting alongside the Prophet [in the battles that were waged against him and his nascent community by the pagans]; and

---

[138] *Dunyā*: this lower world of existence. In Islamic cosmology, the material world is the "lowest of the low" (*asfal as-sāfilīn*) in the order of existence.

are like [the martyrs] Ali ﷺ and Hasan ﷺ and Husain ﷺ." In another hadith report, the Eight Imam, Imam Riḍā, is reported to have stated, "Zaid waged a sacred battle (*jihād*) in the way of God ﷻ." You should be aware of these positions [which the Imams ﷺ have taken with respect to Zaid and his uprising]. In another hadith report, Imam Sādiq ﷺ recites an elegy for Zaid, telling of his passion and suffering and death, bringing the people to tears in their sorrow for him. I shall refer back to this and what occasioned the recitation of this elegy [later]. There are many reports concerning this subject.

But to move on to Zaid's motivations; one of the sermons of the many sermons which Zaid delivered is a lengthy one in which he stipulates his motivation as being the imperative to enjoin the doing of that which is right and to forbid the doing of that which is wrong (*al-amr bi'l-ma'rūf wa an-nahy min al-munkar*), as well as being the seeking of revenge for the blood of the martyrs of Karbalā, which is exactly the same motivation which Imam Husain ﷺ had stipulated for his own uprising: "I wanted [to practice the religious imperative and duty] to enjoin the doing of that which is right and to forbid the doing of that which is wrong (*al-amr bi'l-ma'rūf wa an-nahy min al-munkar*)" (Ibn Shahrāshūb, *Manāqib* 4:89).

In another hadith report, [Zaid] describes his motivation as being the reformation of society, saying that the reason for his uprising the reformation of the Islamic community; which again, is exactly the same motivation which Imam Husain ﷺ had stipulated for his own uprising, when the Imam stated, "Verily, my uprising was for the purposes of reforming the community of my grandfather" (Ibid). Here Zaid also says, "My desire is that I be burned in a fire and burned again, but that the task of the reformation of the community be accomplished."[139] In any event, [hadith reports about] these kinds of subjects are numerous and it would take a long time if I were to read each and every one of them.

There is a final hadith report from Imam Sādiq ﷺ about this matter which I will relate in order to cap off the subject. The report states

---

[139] Allāma Muhammad Bāqir Majlisī (d. 1110/1698), the *Biḥār al-Anwār* (Oceans of Light), 46:208.

that one of Zaid's companions came to Imam Sādiq ﷺ, who asked him where he had come from. Zaid's companion said, "Kūfa". The Imam asked what news he had of there and what was happening. His Eminence was concerned about Zaid and had not received any news from him; whereas the companion was bringing the news of the failure of the uprising and Zaid's martyrdom to the Imam. Zaid's companion said, "O son of the Apostle of God ﷺ! Your paternal uncle was killed in the congregational mosque of Kūfa," following this with the details of the event. His Eminence the Imam was deeply moved and became very sad and said, "Were you with my uncle?" When the man answered in the affirmative, the Imam asked, "And when you were with my uncle, did you manage to kill anyone yourself?" When the man again answered in the affirmative, the Imam asked, "How many men did you kill?" The man said, "Five or seven." Imam Sādiq's response consists of words which were meant to assuage Zaid's companion, and at the same time, these words give us an insight into the Imam's views. The Imam raised his hands [heavenward] and prayed, "O Lord! Make me a partner to and give me a share of the rewards of this man's [righteous] killings". Can you see what is happening? Because there can be no doubt that Imam Sādiq ﷺ [already] has a share in the rewards of those acts, because there are fragmentary evidences [dispersed through the hadith report corpus] indicating his cooperation and support for Zaid's uprising, and as we have already stated, the Imam would tune his followers in to Zaid's activities. But he wanted to let the man before him know that what he did was rightful; and that is why he said those words. There is also a report which states that the Imam took on the responsibility of administering the affairs of the families of those who were martyred in Zaid's uprising and acted as their guardian.

8. An examination of the hadith reports concerning the disapprobation of Zaid

In any event... there is a matter which I feel I need to mention at the end of this discussion, and that has to do with hadith reports which censure Zaid. There are some reports which are juxtaposed with and stand in opposition to the ones which I have just been reviewing with you which were all full of praise and approbation for Zaid and his uprising; and this second set of reports censure Zaid and his action. A number of these reports – a few of which have ostensibly solid [chains of custody in their] provenance titles (*asnād*) – have the same content. I shall state this content, and I will demonstrate to you that such a conception is counter to Islam and is a lie, [and that therefore,] it is not possible for that hadith report to be genuine.

The hadith report states that one of the companions of Imam Sādiq ﷺ argues with Zaid, telling him that his [plan to] rise up in insurrection is wrongful and inappropriate. The name of the companion referred to in the report also varies: in some versions it appears as being Zurāra, and in others as Jāhā or "Mu'min ut-Tāq" – but in any event, it varies. The companion claims that because the Imam has not risen up in insurrection, you do not have a right to do so. These kinds of words are exchanged between Zaid and the companion. That is how it is in some reports, whereas in others it is as if Zaid had laid claim to the Imamate, and the narrator tells him that he is not the Imam, and that his brother was the Imam, after whom the Imamate passed to Imam Sādiq; and Zaid refuses to accept this [reality]. According to these hadith reports, Zaid refuses to accept what the narrator is telling him and persists in his claim to the Imamate. Now I have numerous scriptural[140] evidences (*shawāhid-e naqlī*) which prove that this statement is a lie, over and above the logical reasoning (*istinbāt*) which we have [made] concerning [the text of] the hadith report. I have numerous scriptural evidences which prove that this position is a lie and that Zaid believed in Imam Sādiq's ﷺ Imamate, an example of which I mentioned earlier, and of which there are other examples as well.

This hadith report has it that Zaid claims that he is the Imam and his interlocutor contradicts him, saying that he is a *cousin* of the Imam. Among the things which Zaid is purported to have said in the report is that Zaid says to the man words to the effect of, "How can my brother's son Ja'far b. Muhammad be the Imam, for if my cousin were in fact the Imam, I would have known about it, as I am close to this House; and how

---

[140] *Naqlī* (and *riwāī*, and so on) refer to the hadith report corpus scripture rather than to the Quranic corpus or text.

9. The Revolutionary Sons of the Imams

could it be that you who are far from [the affairs of] this House know this, and I who am close to it do not know it? How is it, then, that I was not told of this – me, who am the son of Imam Sajjād ﷺ and my father – Imam Sajjād ﷺ – used to position me on his knee and place morsels of food into my mouth, and would blow on the morsels to cool them if they were hot, so as to ensure that they would not burn my mouth. How was he able to content himself with allowing me to go to Hell by not telling me that after him, his son Muhammad al-Bāqir ﷺ will be the Imam, and that after him, it will be Muhammad's son Ja'far? He did not tell these things to me whom he liked so much that he would position me on his knee and place morsels of food into my mouth, and would blow on the morsels to cool them if they were hot, so as to ensure that they would not burn my mouth; but you who are an outsider not only to the House of Hāshim but to the tribe of Quraysh as a whole have been told this, and have come across this piece of information and are knowledgeable about it; is that what you are saying?? Whereas if this was the case, they would have told me first."

They ascribe these words to Zaid, unto whom be God ﷻ's peace, which have been related by, Mr. "Mu'min ut-Tāq" or Zurāra or Muhammad b. Muslim, who ostensibly responds to those words. Whoever it is turns to Zaid and says, "It is precisely for the reason which you stated that you were not told, because you were too dear to them and so they told me and not you, as they knew that if they told you that Ja'far b. Muhammad was the Imam, it would be a point of contention between the two of you. They thus preferred to keep the news from you as you were beloved by them and they wanted to keep you in a state of blameless ignorance so that you would not go to Hell [as you would not be held responsible for your actions on this count]. But I was an outsider to whom they reasoned they would tell [the news to], so that if I disagreed and went to Hell, then so be it. But they pitied you and they did not pity me. And when His Eminence Zaid heard these words, he went silent and didn't have anything else to say in response. After which this person got up and came to Imam Sādiq ﷺ and said, "We had such and such a discussion with your uncle, Zaid. He responded in such and such a way, and we parried in such and such a way, after which he went silent." Imam Sādiq ﷺ said,

"Well done! You closed his path [of escape] from all four directions!" (Ibn Shahrāshūb, *Manāqib* 1:259).

Does this hadith report seem genuine to you? Of course, the matter of the provenance title and who the narrator is are germane and the question as to who the [original] narrator is and [who are the people who make up the links in the chain of custody of] the provenance title must be determined. But before we proceed to examine the provenance title of the hadith report, we should scrutinize the text itself.[141] If we come across a hadith report which cannot be reconciled with the Islamic worldview, [it will be rejected] without the slightest glance to the report's provenance title [and who it was that supposedly made the false statements]. The Imams themselves have stated that we are to accept anything which corresponds with the Quran, and are to reject anything that is contrary to the Quran; to throw it against the wall and not pay any attention to it.[142]

The gist of this hadith report is that a heavy dollop of favoritism obtains within the sacred law of Islam and in the lives of the Imams with respect to the life of this lower world as well as for the hereafter. The Imam shows favoritism toward his own son, withholding the truth from him, so that if he disagrees with that truth and reality, such a disagreement would not count as a sin [in his Book of Deeds]. But this favoritism does not apply to "Mu'min ut-Tāq" who is told the truth so that if he disagrees with it, he can burn in Hell, and to Hell with him! Good riddance!!

Needless to say, this is something that is completely unacceptable in Islam. All people are equal before God in Islam; and what distinguishes a person's virtuosity is the extent of his submission and devotion and servitude before God. It makes no sense for the son of an Imam to be the beneficiary of a one-sided favoritism simply by virtue of the fact that he is the son of an Imam. It makes even less sense for God to affirm this favoritism on the Day of Judgement. This is a logic that is miles wide of mark according to the ethical logic of Islam.

Furthermore, let us assume for the sake of the argument that Imam Sajjād did not inform his son Zaid [of the unfolding of the

---

[141] See footnote #130.
[142] See Shaykh Koleynī's *Kāfī*, 1:69.

9. The Revolutionary Sons of the Imams

investiture of the Imamate]. Are we then to assume that Zaid himself would not know [who his Imam is]?? After all, do the Shʿīa believe that it is necessary for there to be an Imam or don't they? So are we saying that Zaid was ignorant of the identity of his Imam? To the extent that he did not know who Imam Bāqir ﷺ and Imam Sādiq ﷺ are?? This is certainly not the case. And if he *did* know them (which he assuredly did), but did not recognize them as his Imams, then his ignorance would be a blameworthy one and not a blameless one, irrespective of whether or not he was or was not informed of these realities by his father Imam Sajjād; and his abode would therefore be in Hell regardless. Are you following me?

Therefore, this hadith report is a report whose content is very weak and is completely unacceptable. And even if we grant that its provenance title is sound, the most we would be able to do with it is to say that we cannot understand its content and so cannot accept it [as there would be nothing that would be within the compass of our comprehension to accept]. So this report is unacceptable both in terms of its own textual content which is [creedaly] problematic, as well as on account of the fact that its content are clearly contradicted by other [genuine and unproblematic] hadith reports which demonstrate that Zaid was a highly devout person who had excellent relations with Imam Sādiq ﷺ, who liked him and numbered him among his faithful followers.

9. The formation of the Zaidīya sect after Zaid's martyrdom

[And finally,] there is a small matter which should be addressed which is to respond to a question which might be posed, namely, that if Zaid was such a good person, then what are the people of the Zaidīya sect on about who think of Zaid as their Imam and leader? For Zaid is the Imam of the Zaidīya sect, after all; so what is this sect all about?? The response is that it should be borne in mind that the Zaidīya sect did not originate during Zaid's lifetime, and that Zaid never harbored any claims to the Imamate. God ﷻ the Sublimely Exalted addresses Jesus, the son of Lady Mary, [in the Quran] as follows:

وَإِذْ قَالَ اللَّهُ يَا عِيسَى ابْنَ مَرْيَمَ أَأَنتَ قُلْتَ لِلنَّاسِ اتَّخِذُونِي وَأُمِّيَ إِلَهَيْنِ مِن دُونِ اللَّهِ ۖ قَالَ سُبْحَانَكَ مَا يَكُونُ لِي أَنْ أَقُولَ مَا لَيْسَ لِي بِحَقٍّ ۚ إِن كُنتُ قُلْتُهُ فَقَدْ عَلِمْتَهُ ۚ تَعْلَمُ مَا فِي نَفْسِي وَلَا أَعْلَمُ مَا فِي نَفْسِكَ ۚ إِنَّكَ أَنتَ عَلَّامُ الْغُيُوبِ ﴿١١٦﴾

[5:116] And lo! God ﷻ said: O Jesus, son of Mary! Didst thou say unto men, 'Worship me and my mother as deities beside God ﷻ'?" [Jesus] answered: "Limitless art Thou in Thy glory! It would not have been possible for me to say what I had no right to [say]! Had I said this, Thou wouldst indeed have known it! Thou knowest all that is within myself, whereas I know not what is in Thy Self. Verily, it is Thou alone who fully knowest all the things that are beyond the reach of a created being's ordinary perception.

How can Jesus be blamed if the people consider him to be a deity [against his own wishes and intentions]? And how can Imam Ali ؓ be blamed if a certain group of people exaggerate [his virtues and attributes] and consider him to be God ﷻ? And how can Zaid be blamed if a group of people consider him to be the Imam and do not accept the Imamate of Imam Ṣādiq ؓ? Zaid is not to be blamed in this matter, just as I allow for such a possibility in the case of Muḥammad b. Ḥanafīyah; which I can talk about at another time if the occasion arises.

10. Precautionary Dissimulation (Taqīya)

The discussion which we have in mind for today, which will act as a capstone and appendix to the discussion of the lives of the Imams, has to do with the subject of precautionary dissimulation (*taqīya*) which we had promised earlier to go into in more detail. What is the pertinence of the subject to our overall discussion? Its relevance has to do with the fact that, as we stated, we see in the hadith report corpus that the lives of the Imams ﷺ were lives of a constant political struggle (*jihād*) in God ﷻ's cause, and that the way they led their lives is the exact opposite of the image that has crystalized in the imagination of our contemporaries (in contradistinction to that of the contemporaries of the Imams). And we saw that there is a unitary line from the Imamate of Imam Sajjād ﷺ to that of Imam Hasan al-Askarī ﷺ; a continuous line of nothing but constant struggle and entrenchment against the ruling powers of their days, as well as against the court-allied clergy and poets and intelligentsia.

The question arises that, If the Imams ﷺ were engaged in a constant struggle as you say, then where does the Shʿīa principle and creedal tenet of precautionary dissimulation (*taqīya*) fit into the picture? Did they not practice *taqīya*? And if you grant that they did, then how can you reconcile their *taqīya* with their constant and ongoing [political] struggle? This question has either occurred to you already; or, if it has not already done so, it would have done in time, once you gave the subject some more thought. I shall thus be addressing this inevitable question today.

The other matter which I need to mention preliminarily is that, just as we qualified our previous discussion by saying that the treatment of the subject matter will necessarily have to be cursory and selective [due to the vastness of the subject and the limitations of time], a similar qualification needs to be made with respect to the subject of *taqīya*, as this subject requires a comprehensive survey of the literature in its own right. It is possible that work has been done in this regard, but such research has not been carried out specifically with respect to the question of how *taqīya* relates to the lives of the Imam [and their political activity]; and this is something which has to be done with great care and in meticulous detail and in a comprehensive and all-inclusive manner. But our discussion of *taqīya* is, rather, a marginal one which [we offer as] an aside. There is a point that everyone should know about the matter of *taqīya* so that a unified mindset will obtain with respect to it, God ﷻ grant; so that people will not define it in any manner of their choosing. These were the two matters which I wanted to mention preliminarily.

1. The indubitability of the principle of taqīya is Shʿīa Islam

Keep the material which I will be mentioning today concerning *taqīya* in mind in the numerical order which I present them. There are a few subjects which might be separate from each other. The first matter is owning to [the reality of] the ordinance [of the creedal tenet] of *taqīya*: no one should deny the fact that in Shʿīa Islam there is a [creedal] principle called *taqīya*. Because we have seen that when two people are engaged in a discussion concerning *taqīya*, and one of them uses an incorrect definition of the principle, his or her opponent will resort to denying [the existence of] the principle itself [rather than denying its mischaracterization]. But this is a mistake, because this is a principle which we have not only in Shʿīa Islam, but in Islam more generally, and indeed, in all of the divinely-revealed religions; indeed, it is a necessary and vitally important principle. And the Imams ؑ have talked about this principle in various ways and insisted on it adamantly, all of which I shall be talking about presently; but what I ask is that once you have

10. Precautionary Dissimulation (Taqīya)

understood the proper meaning of the principle of *taqīya*, that you place the emphasis and insistence of the Imams ﷺ alongside its true definition so that you know exactly what it is that they were insistent upon. I ask that the gentlemen present not prejudge anything; in other words, now that I will be reading hadith reports where the Imams ﷺ emphasize *taqīya*, that you not associate the meaning that you have in your own minds concerning *taqīya* with the Imams' insistence on, and that you should not jump to the conclusion that the Imams ﷺ bid you to the conception of *taqīya* as you presently conceive the concept.

One of the hadith reports which affirms *taqīya* in a definitive fashion is the one which states, "*Taqīya* is my religion and the religion of my forefathers."[143] Another report which affirms this definition is the following: "Anyone who does not practice *taqīya*, does not practice Islam [either]".[144] One must resort to the practice of *taqīya*, for failure to do so leads to one's not having a correct and complete Islam. There are other reports which mention the principle of *taqīya* by name and affirm it and also provide explicit definitions, but these are but a few. There are a few of these hadith reports whose meaning is indubitable in our view. Thus, let us all be aware that in Islam and in Sh'īa Islam, and as we shall point out, in prior [adumbrations of the monotheistic] faiths, there has been an important principle named *taqīya*. This is the first point.

2. The lack of an exact equivalent for the word taqīya in the Persian language

The second point is the question as to whether or not an equivalent word for *taqīya* exists in the Persian language which can convey its meaning completely; and the answer is that I have not been able to find an equivalent term which conveys one hundred percent of the meaning of the Arabic word *taqīya*. If I say that it means *istitār* (camouflage), we shall see that it is broader than that; and if I say that it means "acting is a furtive manner", then that is again similar to *istitār*. If we say that it means creating a [furtive] organization in order to attain to a given purpose, we see that it includes this [possibility], but is again broader and deeper than

---

[143] Bihār al-Anwār 64:103.
[144] Shaykh Koleynī's *Kāfī*, 2:217.

this. But what is certain is that the meaning that is usually associated with the word is 100% mistaken.

3. The mistaken common conception of taqīya
How do people conceive of the principle of *taqīya* nowadays? What they think *taqīya* means is that when someone wants to do something or to perform a religiously obligatory act, and if it is felt that there is the threat of a danger or a loss occurring as a consequence of the performance of this act, that one can then [legitimately] refrain from performing the act in question; this is what people believe *taqīya* to be. This is very wrong. It is so wrong that if it were not for the fact of the currency that this erroneous belief enjoys among the people, I would have just given the correct definition. But because this mistaken understanding is so entrenched among the people, the explanation of the principle must be accompanied by the disabuse of its mistaken understanding at the same time.

4. An allegory clarifying the difference between the correct and mistaken conceptions of *taqīya*
It is a categorical certainty that the definition of *taqīya* which we obtain by referring to the hadith reports on the subject is not that which is commonly conceived, and that its correct definition stands in opposition to the commonly conceived view. What do we mean by this? What we mean is that *taqīya* if the performance of a [religiously obligatory] act poses a threat or a risk of harm to someone, then one must act in such a way so as to ensure that the [religiously obligatory] act is performed and that no harm comes to the performance of the act. This is how the hadith reports define *taqīya*. Now I do not mean to imply that this definition covers the entire gamut of the meaning of the word. I will now read a few [relevant] hadith reports from books of hadith as our discussion today centers around such hadith reports; but I only say this preliminarily so that you know that the meaning of *taqīya* is not limited to that which you will be hearing from the hadith report corpus. But there is no doubt that ensuring that the act in question is performed [despite the dangers posed] in such a way such that no damage is incurred in the performance of the

act itself, is in fact a part of the essential and intrinsic meaning of the word *taqīya*.

Imagine, for example, that there has been a flood, or that there are thieves at the mountain pass [which preclude your passage], so that if you were to continue your journey, you would either be drowned, set upon by bandits, or attacked by wolves. Or suppose that you get to a point in your journey where the path becomes very narrow and perilous, and that if you were to continue your journey by car at your normal speed, you would be risking your life, and so you must exercise caution.

Now where does *taqīya* fit into the picture here, both the version that is popularly conceived as well as that which appears in the hadith reports and which is conceived of and explicated by the Imams? The people would say, "Sir! Exercise precautionary dissimulation!" In what sense do they mean this? They mean that as soon as you see that there is a flood, make your way back and that there is no need to continue on your journey; head back home and rest at ease. What need is there for you to continue your journey in the face of such dangers; it is senseless to endanger yourself, as you will not get to where you wanted to go anyway. This is the popular conception of *taqīya*; but Imam Sādiq ﷺ does not define it in this way. From what we have gathered from the hadith report corpus, what he says is: "Sir! As soon as you see that a bandit or a wolf or an outlaw has cut you off from the pass, try to journey in such a way that you avoid the floodplain." In other words, continue your travel on higher ground, avoiding the floodplain. Go, and climb the mountain if you have to, but do not take the regular path [as there is danger there]. Travel in such a way that you are out of the reach of the bandit or wolf or outlaw so that they cannot harm you and prevent you from reaching your destination. In other words, go over the mountain to avoid the flood and the mountain pass, or come up with some alternative arrangement such as burrowing under or going well-equipped to deal with bandits and wolves and to remove the obstacle which they pose from your path.

You can thus see how these two definitions differ from each other, and that they are in fact polar opposites of each other in that in the first definition, *taqīya* becomes the cause of returning from one's objective, whereas in the second definition, *taqīya* causes one's progress toward one's goals. They are opposites in that it is not possible for one factor to be the cause of one's return and one's progress at one and the same time. Do you see? I thus mention this so that you can see in a summary fashion that the popular conception of the principle of *taqīya* is a mistaken one, and that it does not accord with any Quranic verse, hadith report, or valid form of reasoning and deduction with any authority. This was the summary treatment [of the subject].

5. Taqīya in the Quran and the Hadith report corpus: A correct tool for attaining to one's goals

The Quran[145] and hadith report corpus tell us that *taqīya* is an instrument or tool which enables one to reach one's goals. This is the concise treatment of the matter. What is this instrument? Does it consist of any instrument which helps one to attain to one's goals, or is it a particular type of instrument? No; it does not consist of any instrument. There are several specific instruments that are intended to remove obstacles from one's path and help one to attain to one's goals. Thus, for example, bypassing an obstacle by committing a crime is not referred to as *taqīya*. Similarly, the norms and teachings of Sh'īa Islam reject any definition of *taqīya* where the means to attaining to a given goal are contrary to the principles of the objective itself.[146] So assume, for example, that someone wants to lead the Muslim community; and that the requirements of investiture in such an office are being possessed of piety and a sound moral character; and that this person then partakes of means and methods which run counter to his piety and to the soundness of his moral character in order to attain to his overarching goal. That is, his actions go against the principles of statesmanship which have been stipulated in the Quran and Islam. This cannot be an instance of *taqīya*.

In the council which Umar had set up [to determine the identity of his successor], Imam Ali ﷺ could have easily become the next caliph by fabricating a simple lie, [answering affirmatively to the question posed to him by 'Abd ar-Rahmān b. 'Awf and] saying that yes, he would act in accordance with the precedents of the *shaykhayn* [Abū-Bakr and Umar]

---

[145] Verses 3:28 and 16:105-6 are the main verses which relate to *taqīya*.
[146] The ends do not justify the means.

10. Precautionary Dissimulation (Taqīya)

in addition to the paradigmatic example of the Prophet ﷺ and to the ordinances and teachings of the Quran; but he did not commit such a sin. This would have guaranteed him investiture into the office of the caliphate; and then he could refrain from acting in accordance with precedents set by the *shaykhayn* once he was firmly vested in office. This was something which the Commander of the Faithful could have done quite easily but did not. Why? Because in Islam, the ends do not justify the means; because one cannot use unholy means to reach holy ends. The means must be correct also, and must accord with [the values and ideals represented by] the end. Ali ؏ wanted to rule over the community in order to rid the world of lies and of the breaking of one's word and bond and of bad moral conduct, and to guide the people to the intended objective [of Islam] by way of [teaching them] the correct method [to do so]. These were the reasons why Ali ؏ wanted to rule, so it would not be correct for the means of attaining to such a goal to be a lie and a deception. That would not be right. It is also not right that we should define *taqīya* as any means which enables one to attain to his or her goals. Rather, certain specific means are what are intended [by the principle].

6. The conditions for the correct employment of Taqīya

6.1 Maintaining order and being faithful to the principles of the objective

One of the elements which enable one to attain to one's goals is maintaining order and being faithful to the principles of the objective, and never slackening in one's efforts and considerations of arriving at one's determined goal. This is one of the factors which gets one closer to one's goals.

6.2 Concealment

Another factor – I shall enumerate a couple of these, and then bring the relevant hadith reports into evidence – which gets one closer to one's goals is concealment. The companions and close aides of the Imams ؏ must necessarily conceal the nature of their path which is at loggerheads with that of the ruling powers; they cannot proclaim publicly that they are acting to overthrow the existing government and to replace it with a government of justice which can only be headed by one of the Imams ﷺ. It is certain that if they conceal their true intentions that they will reach their goal quicker. And conversely, if they fail to conceal their intentions and the ruling powers find out what those intentions are, that Mansūr, for example, finds out that such and such a person is organizing an uprising on behalf of Imam Sādiq ﷺ, which if successful would result in the death of Mansūr and the destruction of the Abbāsid dynasty; then it is evident that Mansūr would not abide such activity, and that he would respond to those who want to put an end to him by putting an end to them instead. This is obvious. Therefore, concealment is something which would allow the Imams' companions and close aides to get closer to their goals.

6.3 Getting things done by way of a hierarchic organizational structure

A hierarchic organizational structure is another element which can aid the Imams' companions and close aides to get closer to their goals which order the relationships between the Imam and his followers on one hand, and between the followers themselves on the other. If the companions and close aides of the Imams, such as Mufaḍḍal b. Umar and Muʻallī b. Khunays who live in Madina, and Zurāra b. Aʻayn who lives in Kūfa, and so and so who lives in Baluchestan, say, and Zaid b. ʻAmr who lives in Khorāsān – if all these are organized such that they each know of the others' activities and can relay the commands of the Imam to each other and support each other in their efforts to obey the Imam's commands ever more closely and to help each other not to make mistakes, and in sum, to coordinate and harmonize their activities with each other, then the efforts of Imam Sādiq ﷺ to carry the aims of Shʻīa Islam forward and to bring about a just social order will be accelerated and closer to becoming realized. Is that not the case? So this is another instrument by means of which the goal is attained: the coordination of the Shʻīa resistance movement during the time of the Umayyad and Abbāsid powers; and setting up specific relations between select Shʻīa cadres and the Imam himself; and between all of the individual members and sub-groups of the resistance between each other.

So far, we have mentioned three instruments or means: (1) Maintaining order and being faithful to the principles of the objective; (2) Concealment; and (3) Getting things done by way of a hierarchic organizational structure. And I do not intend to imply by this third category that a formal and powerful party organization was in place and was busily occupied in carrying out its activities in some corner of the globe; because all of these events have to do with a time and place that is thirteen centuries in our past and prior to our current civilization and culture. And it goes without saying that the party organizational structures of those days were not as advanced and organized and modern as that which we have today.

Briefly speaking, what existed at that time was a kind of relationship where people coordinated their activities and kept each other informed and worked together under the direction and aegis of a single leader and source of direction. This is what I meant by a "hierarchic organizational structure"; and the practice of *taqīya* applied to all three of the means which I have mentioned, which are themselves examples of the practical application of the principle. And there are numerous hadith reports concerning this subject, some of which I shall now read for you.

7. Examples of covert actions by way of Taqīya

7.1 Anonymity in communications by letter
For example, there is a hadith report which appears in Ibn Shahrāshūb's *Manāqib* concerning how the Imam related to the general populace of his following who were in touch with His Eminence, in which Ahmad b. Ishāq comes into the presence of Imam Hasan al-Askarī ﷺ and asks that the Imam provide him with a sample of his handwriting so that he can become familiar with it and recognize it, as the subject matter of their correspondence is of a sensitive nature which should not fall into anyone else's hands (Ibn Shahrāshūb, *Manāqeb* 4:433). Why does Ahmad b. Ishāq want to be able to recognize the Imam's handwriting? Because the Imam does not plan to sign his letters to Ahmad b. Ishāq; for if this was not the case, there would be no need for the latter to learn to recognize the Imam's handwriting. Say a letter from the Imam reaches Ahmad b. Ishāq al-Qomī in Qom, and it so happens that the letter falls into the hands of the

representatives of the Abbāsid caliph who controls and governs Qom. If these powers then interrogate Aḥmad b. Isḥāq, the fact that the letter is not signed gives him plausible deniability to be able to say he does not know who has written such a letter; at the same time, [if the letter reaches him securely], he will know who has written it and where it came from.

The Imam says that there is no problem with granting Aḥmad b. Isḥāq's request and provides him with a sample of his handwriting, whereby Aḥmad b. Isḥāq becomes familiar with it. But then the Imam provides Aḥmad with an explanation, saying: "Be advised that [the thickness of my quill will vary;] sometimes I will write with a thick point, and sometimes with a narrow one." In other words, pay attention to the fact that the width of my penmanship will not always be the same. This is a very small example. It is the kind of hadith report which you might read and pass over, and not realize the significance of, thinking that it is just an ordinary report about a simple act of correspondence between Aḥmad b. Isḥāq and Imam Ḥasan al-Askarī ﷺ. But this same simple correspondence reveals a special relationship that obtained during the time of the Imams ﷺ [between them and their trusted followers and lieutenants]. For if the subject matter of the correspondence between them was limited to a cordial exchange of views and asking about each other's health and about the weather in Qom and the level of the water of its river, then why would there be a need to conceal the identity of the letter's writer by his refraining from signing it? It only stands to reason that the Imam would indeed have been signing his letters if it were not for the fact that they contained instructions to Aḥmad b. Isḥāq concerning what he should and should not do in Qom; how much money he should spend on what, and how much he should pass on up to the Imam; and generally, to give instructions for the proper operation of the resistance apparatus. If it were not for these things, why would Aḥmad b. Isḥāq and Imam Ḥasan al-Askarī ﷺ take measures to conceal their tracks in the event that such letters should fall into the wrong hands? If an ordinary letter falls into the hands of the authorities, then there is no harm, no foul, as it were. But it is clear that this is no ordinary correspondence; and this in turn indicates a specific slant of the lives of the Imams ﷺ.

10. Precautionary Dissimulation (Taqīya)

7.2 A well-organized political resistance structure

The letter which I shall now read provides us with an insight into the way in which the Imams ﷺ communicated with their companions and lieutenants, as well as providing a confirmation of what we stated earlier. Its content is also of interest, and is an example of the quality of the Imams' penmanship. The letter is from Imam Hasan al-Askarī ﷺ to the people of Qom and Āvaj,[147] whose Arabic pronunciation is Ābah. The contents of the letter leads one to believe that the Sh'ia of these towns are crestfallen from the fact that their leader is surrounded by the forces of the ruling powers and thought that Imam Hasan al-Askarī ﷺ had reconsidered continuing the path of resistance of his father and forefathers as a result of all of the pressure that was being brought to bear on him by the regime. The Imam's letter gives them reassurance and encouragement about his leadership, and tells them that he is intent on continuing the path of resistance, and that the political pressures and restrictions which he has been subjected to have not caused him to reconsider his intentions and objectives, towards which he is steadily marching. This hadith report is also taken from Ibn Shahrāshūb's *Manāqib*.

In the letter Imam Hasan al-Askarī ﷺ writes: "Our intentions are solid and our resolve is firm. And our soul attains its tranquility through your well-wishes." In other words, we are confident of your loyalty and support, and believe that you too have not changed your minds or reconsidered the path [that we are on]. Notice how empowering this is for the Sh'ia of Imam Hasan al-Askarī ﷺ of Qom and Āvaj. And notice also the whole *purpose* of the empowering rhetoric. Because if the matter [of the function and ministry of the Imams] was limited to providing responsa to religio-legal question having to do with ritual and acts of devotion and providing individual private guidance, then there would be no call for this [kind of pep] talk. So let us assume that the Imams ﷺ provided such guidance to their followers like the leaders of other sects did at the time, such as the religious leaders of the Sunnite majority. But this does not

---

[147] A town between Qom and Hamedān in north-western Iran. This town, together with Qom and Rey were the three most important Sh'ia centers in Iran during the first formative centuries of the Islamic era.

accord with the Imam's saying things like "We are with you" and "We stand with you" and "We have full confidence in you and count on you." I emphasize these expressions, and because their purport might be uncertain in your minds – and because I want you to be clear on the subject – [I need you to consider] the occasion for which such words are written: can it be for anything other than a major perilous operation? Can it be for anything other than an armed struggle and battle? Can it be for anything other than the traversing of a perilous journey? The Imam continues: "The relationship and bond between you and I is strong." We are kindred [spirits] and brothers [in arms] with you [in this eternal struggle]. The Imam considers his followers and partisans to be his kith and kin, but this same Imam Hasan al-Askarī ﷺ does not consider his [blood-] brother Ja'far to be his kin; the same Ja'far who put forward a false claim to the Imam's station and office.

Then there are a few other sentences in the letter which are lengthy but not germane; but the last sentence refers to the existence of a highly organized and directed intellectual apparatus. Pay special attention to the use of the word 'true believer' (*al-mu'min*) and what it means. The Imam states that "The relationship between you [plural] and I is very close" The expression used means that we are relatives of the first order, like father and son, or like a mother and her child, or like brothers; that is the nature of our relationship. And it would seem that Imam Askarī ﷺ is relating a report from one of his forebears, who is either Imam Sādiq ﷺ or his son, Imam Kāẓim ﷺ, who has said, "The true believer (*al-mu'min*) is a brother [or sister] of other true believers as [if they were born of the same] mother and father." What this means is that the relationship and bond which exists between two [or any number of] true believers is that of full blood brothers [and sisters] (*peyvand-e barādarī-e pedarī va mādarī ast*); the nature of the bond is not even that of a step-brother [or step-sister] – that is how close it is.

Who is being referred to when the word *mu'min* is used here? Does it refer to anyone who utters the words [of the Muslim confession of faith,] "There is no deity other than Allāh ﷻ, and Muhammad ﷺ is His apostle"? There were many of those; even Mutawakkil [the Abbāsid caliph at the time of Imam Askarī's Imamate] would utter those words as well,

10. Precautionary Dissimulation (Taqīya)

as did the caliphs before him during the time of Imam Hādī ﷺ, each of which would take turns [repeating this confession] at the tribune of the caliphate, after which they would fall headfirst to the ground. Everyone said those words, so that wasn't it. Rather, it referred to those who had faith in [the Imamate of] Imam Askarī ﷺ, and who follow him on his path. And what is that, exactly? It is the partisan relationship; [the relationship of partisans and spiritual blood brothers in arms engaged in an organized armed struggle intent on overthrowing the forces of tyranny]. It is the relationship between the Imam and his partisan. This is one hadith report.

7.3 Sending secret letters

There is another hadith report which also tells of the existence of a party apparatus and a series of secret activities in the lives of the Imams, which is a highly portentous and significant report in my opinion. It would seem that it pertains to Imam Hādī ﷺ; but in any event, what is certain is that it pertains to one of the three final Imams, because from what I have been able to gather from my readings, the peak of the partisan and resistance activities of the Shʿīa occurs after Imam Riḍā ﷺ, i.e. during the Imamates of Imam Jawād ﷺ, Imam Hādī ﷺ, and Imam Hasan al-Askarī ﷺ. And it is the fact that the partisan and resistance activities of the Shʿīa peaked during the Imamates of these three Imams ﷺ that explains why they were martyred and why no latitude of action was given to these Imams, and why they were each brought immediately from Madina to the ʿIrāq, where they were forced to remain in exile and where all three of them were martyred in their youth and buried there.

Have you not heard the story of Abul-ʿAdyān? It is frequently stated in the pulpits that Abul-ʿAdyān left to bring certain monies [of the Imam's due, to Imam Hasan al-Askarīﷺ], only to find upon his return that the Imam had passed from the material plane, [at which point] Abul-ʿAdyān recognized the Lord of the Age [the Twelfth Imam] ﷺ with the signs that he had been given [by Imam Hasan al-Askarī ﷺ]. Where had Abul-ʿAdyān gone to fetch the monies [of the Imam's due]? He had gone to Madāʾin, which is smack under the watchful eyes of Baghdad, the center of the Abbāsid power, i.e. Sāmarrā. There were large numbers of Shʿīa in Madāʾin who made financial contributions to the Imam and who ran the Imam's resistance organization [there]; and the depth of their organization was to such an extent that the monies which they contributed to the Imam enabled him to help the general Shʿīa population in this vast [underground] organization. This demonstrates the power of the Imam's [resistance] activities. Therefore, the hadith report which I am about to read and comment on briefly belongs either to Imām Hādī ﷺ or Imam Hasan al-Askarī ﷺ – I think it is one of these two.

The hadith report states that the Imam gave one of his servants a piece of wood, instructing him to take it and give it to such and such a person. The servant is not a Shʿīa or partisan of the Imam's. It so happened sometimes that the ruling authorities placed servants within the household of the Imams ﷺ who doubled up as spies, so that they could keep closer tabs on the Imams ﷺ. And there are hadith reports which state, "The servants who surround us are the worst of God's ﷻ creatures." Of course, this is a context-specific statement and cannot be generalized to characterize all of their servants and retainers; it applies to the specific agents which the Imam had in mind when he made this statement.

The report characterizes the piece of wood which the Imam had given his servant to deliver to someone else as having the shape of the heel of a door. For as you might know, the doors of those days did not have hinges like ours do today. Holes would be made out at the top and bottom of the doorframe to accommodate an extension of the wood of the door at the pivot point, and these extended "heels" at the top and bottom and to one side of the door is what the door would pivot on. So the piece of wood looked like one such extension or "heel".

The manservant took the piece of wood and made his way to make his delivery. It so happened that on the way to making his delivery, the manservant dropped the piece of wood from his hand, and the wood splintered when it hit the ground, revealing several scrolls that had been secreted within it. Flustered, the manservant gathered the scrolls and brought them all back to the Imam, telling him what happened. When the Imam heard this, he started to chide and rebuke the servant. Why did you

10. Precautionary Dissimulation (Taqīya)

let the piece of wood fall from your hands? Why did you spill the scrolls? And so on.[148]

My question is: what was written on these scrolls? First of all, what sense is there in giving a written message to someone who lives in the same town as you? Can it be anything other than that these were instructions which needed to be given in some form or other, written and cryptographic? Can it be anything other than this? And secondly, if these were ordinary sentences that were written on the scrolls, why would the Imam go to the trouble of having the heel of a door emptied out in order for it to be able to accommodate the secreting of written materials within it; and have the carving out be done in a fashion where the lid is so constructed so as not to reveal its seam and the fact that it is of two pieces, and so that it would appear as a simple piece of wood?? Making some such thing is not an easy undertaking, after all. And then for the Imam not to deliver the message himself but to entrust its delivery to a servant so as not to attract attention to himself; and then for the manservant to maybe play with it as if it were a plaything and drop it, and so on. Does this not demonstrate the fact that the Imam had a non-ordinary relationship [or communication protocol] with his companions and lieutenants? So this is another aspect and dimension of *taqīya*.

8. Project nomenclature posited as scriptural proofs of Taqīya

Please pay full attention so that you understand the matter properly. You might now say that OK, granted that the Imam did indeed resort to this kind of [furtive] communication; we are not denying that. But this is not *taqīya*. *Taqīya* is something, and this is something different. Since when is this called *taqīya*? This is a question that you are entirely within your rights to be asking. But I call this [phenomenon] *taqīya* based on several hadith reports of the Imams ﷺ. So now pay attention and see if something that is the exact same thing has been characterized as *taqīya* by the Imams ﷺ or not.

---

[148] Ibn Shahrāshūb, *Manāqib* 4:427.

8.1 The Imams' stipulation that their partisans are to maintain secret communications with each other

There is another hadith report which falls under the rubric of commentaries on the following famous Quranic verse:

$$\text{يَا أَيُّهَا الَّذِينَ آمَنُوا اصْبِرُوا وَصَابِرُوا وَرَابِطُوا وَاتَّقُوا اللَّهَ لَعَلَّكُمْ تُفْلِحُونَ ﴿٢٠٠﴾}$$

> [3:200] O you who have attained to faith! Be patient in adversity, and vie in forbearance and longanimity with one another, and close ranks and remain in contact with one another, and be wary of [the just retribution of] God 🌸, so that you might attain to a happy state!

The Imam is commenting on the above verse. He says, "Be patient in adversity by means of *taqīya*; and maintain relations with the leader to whom you defer." If it was the case that this was the only sentence which appeared in the report, the maintenance of relations could be construed to refer to a spiritual relationship; or that it was referring to a relationship based on intercessory recourse (*tawassul*).[149] But because it follows the previous sentence where we are told to "Be patient in adversity by means of *taqīya*", then it is clear that the relationship with "the leader to whom you defer" is [a physical or objective] one that is secretive and systematic.

8.2 A party organization that is as secretive as a fort is strong

There is another hadith report whose meaning is very explicit and telling, and which falls under the rubric of commentaries on the following Quranic verse which is about Dhū'l-Qaranayn[150]:

---

[149] *Tawassul* is a specific type of intercessory recourse in which someone resorts to or takes recourse in various instruments that have been made available to him by God 🌸 (such as the supplications or the spirit of a prophet or saint) as an intermediary means for help in his endeavors to recommend himself to the notice and favor or mercy of God 🌸.

[150] Dhul-Qarnayn, translated as "the possessor of the two horns," is a legendary king mentioned in Chapter 18 of The Quran, Sura al-Kahf ("The Cave"). The Quran narrates the story of how Allah establishes Dhul-Qarnayn as a powerful

10. Precautionary Dissimulation (Taqīya)

قَالُوا يَا ذَا الْقَرْنَيْنِ إِنَّ يَأْجُوجَ وَمَأْجُوجَ مُفْسِدُونَ فِي الْأَرْضِ فَهَلْ نَجْعَلُ لَكَ خَرْجًا عَلَىٰ أَن تَجْعَلَ بَيْنَنَا وَبَيْنَهُمْ سَدًّا ﴿٩٤﴾ قَالَ مَا مَكَّنِّي فِيهِ رَبِّي خَيْرٌ فَأَعِينُونِي بِقُوَّةٍ أَجْعَلْ بَيْنَكُمْ وَبَيْنَهُمْ رَدْمًا ﴿٩٥﴾

[18:94] They said: "O thou Two-Horned One (Dhū'l-Qaranayn)! Behold, Gog and Magog are spoiling this land. May we, then, pay unto thee a tribute on the understanding that thou wilt erect a barrier between us and them?" [18:95] He answered: "That wherein my Lord of Providence has so securely established me is better [than anything that you could give me]; hence, do but help me with [your labor's] strength, [and] I shall erect a rampart between you and them!

When Dhū'l-Qaranayn comes to where Gog and Magog were, the people asked Dhū'l-Qaranayn to build them a dam which God ﷻ and Magog would not be able to surmount so that they would no longer be able to attack and harm them. Dhū'l-Qaranayn tells them that he will build a dam between the two mountains at the mountain pass. The word *radam* is used in another verse, which means a strong barrier or dam. So Dhū'l-Qaranayn tells the people that he will build a dam or a *radam* between them and God ﷻ and Magog. This is the Quranic verse which only relates to our discussion tangentially in so far as the Imam comments on the meaning of the word *radam* by saying that *taqīya* is a strong barrier which must be erected between the true believers and the Gogs and Magogs of the era. The name of this barrier is *taqīya*.

This sentence is followed by: "If you protect yourself with and act by taking due precaution (*taqīya*), you will be outside of their reach." And then the Imam states: "*Taqīya* is a strong fortification." When you are a part of the [underground] party organization, you will be out of their

---

ruler on earth and allows the king the freedom to do with his subjects as he pleases. Dhul-Qarnayn appears in Quran 18:83-101 as one who travels to east and west and erects a wall between mankind and Gog and Magog (called Yā'jūj and Ma'jūj).

reach and they will not be able to find you. "A barrier will have been erected between you and God ﷻ's enemies through which the enemies will not be able to burrow through in order to get to you." This refers to a secret or underground organization. So this is [yet] another hadith report [which buttresses our contention].

8.3 The office of the Bāb (Portal) for the special access of the companions of the Imams

Let me mention another example with respect to the matter of the organized resistance apparatus of the Shʿīa which I think is significant and which bears further research. In my studies of the hadith reports concerning the lives of the Imams ؑ I have come across a subject which I consider to be an example of the secret relationship which the Imams ؑ maintained with their close companions and select followers and lieutenants which demonstrates an organized resistance apparatus.

The following sentence can be found in some of the hagiographical accounts where Imam Sajjād ؑ is reported to have said, "And the Portal (*bāb*) of the Imam was Yahyā b. Umm ut-Tawīl." And the "Portal" of each of the Imams ؑ is provided, from Imam Husain ؑ through the Eleventh Imam. And this office or position is not mentioned with respect to Imam Ali ؑ or Imam Hasan ؑ. What is this *bāb*? If you look at Ibn Shahrāshūb's *Manāqib*, you will see the same thing: that one of the renowned companions of the Imams ؑ has been characterized as their respective *bāb*s.[151]

What is this *bāb* about? What I mean to say is, it is not as if the Imam isolated himself in his home and would not allow anyone in to visit with him, and that his companions would not allow people to see the Imams ؑ so that they could perchance kiss their blessed hands; so that there would be a need for a *bāb* or chamberlain through whom people needed to coordinate their access to the Imams ؑ. Is that how it was? Certainly not. Imam Sajjād ؑ lived in the midst of the people night and

---

[151] See page 15 for a listing of the names given in the fourth volume of the *Manāqib*, bearing in mind that it is doubtful that Muhammad b. Sanān was in fact Imam Sādiq's *bāb*, and it is more likely that this function was carried out by Muʿallī b. Khanīs.

10. Precautionary Dissimulation (Taqīya)

day; in the marketplaces, in the streets and alleys, in the countryside and on his travels, he was with the people. The same is true of Imam Sādiq ﷺ, whom the people were free to visit and converse with whenever he was not under house arrest or in prison or exile, of course. There was no barrier between them which would in turn necessitated the need for a chamberlain to coordinate access. So, what did these *bābs* do – these people who took their directions from the Imams ﷺ and who relayed the requests and needs and desires of the people to the Imams? They were in charge of the secret affairs [of the Imam and his interface with the resistance movement]. It is on this account that they were called *bāb*. As a matter of fact, we arrive at a point [in our investigations] where some of these people who have been described as the *bābs* (or, properly speaking, *abwāb*) of the Imams, such as Yahyā b. Umm ut-Tawīl and Mu'allī b. Khanīs [sic], are identified and recognized and are "outed" and put to death in a most outrageous and barbaric manner. You might recall that we pointed out the case of Mu'allī b. Khanīs earlier, whom we said was identified by Dāwūd b. Alī and put to death because the latter realized that this was the way to tackle the problem at its root.

Mansūr had sent his governor, Dāwūd b. Alī, for the specific purposes of purging Madina of elements of his opposition; to identify the friends and close associates of Imam Sādiq ﷺ and those whom they had identified as Shī'a resistance fighters, and to destroy them. The first person of interest to the governor was Mu'allī b. Khanīs, who was an active resistor as well as an intimate companion of Imam Sādiq's, in addition to which Mu'allī b. Khanīs is the person who handled Imam Sādiq's financial affairs and a person through whom much of the Imam's affairs with his followers are managed.

Dāwūd b. Alī called Mu'allī b. Khanīs and told him, "You must tell me the name of Imam Sādiq's close companions."

Mu'allī b. Khanīs replied, "I will not."

Dāwūd b. Alī said, "You must, and if you do not, I shall kill you."

Mu'allī b. Khanīs said, "Upon my word of honor with God ﷻ, if the list of the Imam's companions were under my foot, I would not raise it so that you could pick it up. And you say that I should [willingly] tell you their names??" He didn't say he didn't know, because that was not an avenue that was open to him, as it was known that he knew the names.

Dāwūd b. Alī said, "I shall kill you!"

Mu'allī b. Khanīs said, "Very well, then kill me."

And so it was that Mu'allī b. Khanīs did not betray the names of his partisans and was martyred at the hands of Dāwūd b. Alī (Ibn Shahrāshūb, *Manāqib* 4:225).

And then there is the case of Yahyā b. Umm ut-Tawīl who was interrogated and refused to respond to the questions put to him and was therefore massacred in a horrendous way by Hajjāj who cut off each of his arms and legs in turn, then cut out his tongue, and eventually put him out of his misery. Yahyā b. Umm ut-Tawīl was Imam Sajjād's *bāb*.

So these *bābs* were subjected to these kinds of torture and death as well; and this in itself demonstrates the fact that the persons who have been characterized as being the *bābs* of the Imams ﷺ were the key personnel within the Shī'a resistance movement; and if the enemy wanted to burrow into the resistance movement, he would do so through these key people if their identities were known to them. But the Imams ﷺ also knew which people to appoint as their *bābs*. Yahyā b. Umm ut-Tawīl would be appointed to the position so that if he was captured, he would not break under torture; or Mu'allī b. Khanīs would be appointed to the position so that if he was captured and each of his arms and legs were cut off in turn, his tongue would still remain silent. I mention these things as corroborative proofs of my thesis.

8.4 Secret aides-de-camp of the Imams

Another matter which I have thought of for a long time now is that in the hadith report corpus of the People of the House of the Prophet ﷺ, there are reports in which certain acts are ascribed to *jinns*.[152] Among these reports is the report of Sadīr Sīrafī[153] which I shall recite from Ibn

---

[152] The *jinn* are a class of supernatural creature which are endowed with free will. Their existence is affirmed by the Quran, which states that they live in the *'ālam al-ghayb*, which is a domain or dimension of being which is "beyond the ken of ordinary human perception and understanding" (Muhammad Asad).

[153] Ibn Shahrāshūb's *Manāqib*, 4:190.

10. Precautionary Dissimulation (Taqīya)

Shahrāshūb's *Manāqib*, in which Sadīr Sīrafī states that when he wanted to leave Madina, he went into the presence of the Imam ﷺ and asked if the Imam had any business which Sadīr could attend to. It would appear that it is Sadīr Sīrafī who is speaking, and that he was headed either to Khorāsān or to Kūfa. The Imam says, "No." Sadīr Sīrafī asks again whether he can deliver a letter or some such thing, to which the Imam again says, "No; Go and may God ﷻ be with you." Sadīr Sīrafī says that he left the limits of Madina, and that once he had travelled a ways – he tells how far he had travelled later on in the hadith report – when he reached such and such a place, he saw that he was suddenly confronted by a person who came towards him, gave him a letter, and said, "This is the property of your master the Imam;" and left. Sadīr Sīrafī continues his report, saying that he looked at the letter, and sure enough, it was a letter from the Imam to him in which there were certain instructions and specifications. Sadīr Sīrafī says that he later asked either[154] the Imam or the person who had delivered the letter to him who the person was who had delivered that letter with such alacrity, to which the Imam replied that there are a number of *jinn* who provide services to us.

These kinds of hadith reports in which the *jinn* perform certain kinds of tasks [for the Imams] are numerous. And note that, to be sure, we are not adamant in our denial of the *jinn* here; but the literal meaning of the word *jinn* means hidden or occulted (*penhān*), [so that] any hidden or occulted thing is called *jinn* [in Arabic]; are you following me? *Jinn* means that which is veiled or is covered and cannot be seen by the eyes [and is something which exists in a domain or dimension of being which is beyond the ken of ordinary human perception and understanding]. Why should there be an objection [to the interpretation] that this gentleman was one of the *rijāl*[155] *al-ghayb* of the Imam? [Recall that egress and entry through] the gates to the city of Madina are under strict control,

---

[154] The ambiguity is in the Ayatollah's memory rather than in Sadīr Sīrafī's recollection of the conversation.

[155] We have already explained the word *al-ghayb* (see note 159, above). *Rijāl* is the plural form of *rajal* which means man or person. Thus, *rijāl al-ghayb* translates to "people who exists in a domain or dimension of being which is beyond the ken of ordinary human perception and understanding".

and if the Imam were to give Sadīr Sīrafī a letter within the walls of the city and ask him to take it out with him, there would be the risk of Dāvūd b. Alī's men doing a body search and finding the letter and exposing the Imam's secrets. So why would the Imam 🕊 want to take such a risk [if he does not have to]? That is why the Imam tells Sadīr Sīrafī to go in peace, and Sadīr can leave for his destination knowing that he has done his duty and asked if there was anything that he could do for the Imam, and the Imam had not given him a letter which would be a heavy burden of responsibility and a possible looming menace that he would have to worry about. So he exited the city gates with peace of mind, and shortly thereafter a man who is *jinn* in the sense that he is hidden, i.e. that people do not associate him with the Imam or think of him as being related to the Imam, and who ostensibly is not a close friend or companion of the Imam but is a secret friend, exits the city gates on the quiet with the clay-sealed letter of the Imam in his possession, and delivers it at speed – for that is his job – to Sadīr Sīrafī. There was no wax sealing in those days; they sealed the letters with a special sealing clay which was impressed with a signet or signet ring to ensure its seal of privacy. The messenger's speed is such that Sadīr Sīrafī states that when he was given the letter, the clay of its seal was still moist and had not dried. Why should there be a problem for us to say [= interpret the report] in this way? There is no difficulty [that I see], and this is another point that has occurred to me which [interpretation] can act as another affirmation of the meaning which I stated.

This is the subject of the organized resistance apparatus in the lives of the Imams 🕊 and the fact that they headed such a [covert and underground] organization; and this is one of the aspects and dimensions of *taqīya*.

8.5 Characterizing Taqīya as an endeavor
One of the aspects of *taqīya* which you should be aware of is the matter of covert action. One [aspect] has to do with action, and another one with concealment or camouflage. *Taqīya* does not mean not performing something [out of fear of unjust retribution]; rather, it means the performance of an act, but performing it in such a manner so as to ensure its success [under adverse conditions]. *Taqīya* means traversing the

10. Precautionary Dissimulation (Taqīya)

distance towards a goal, except that if there is a mountain in the way [and the pass is blocked and one cannot circumnavigate the mountain due to flooding or wild predators, etc.], it means traversing the mountain by burrowing through it [or climbing over it] or taking an alternative route. Thus, at all events, it includes the performance of an action and proceeding forward.

One of the hadith reports which perfectly affirms the action-oriented definition of *taqīya* is that when the Imam defines the word *mu'min* (true believer) and provides attributes for such people, one of the attributes includes his or her being a *mujāhid* (or one who engages in a struggle or endeavor). In other words, the *mu'min* (true believer) is someone who engages in a *jihād*. This [other] report is a very good one; a very interesting one. It says that the true believer is in a constant state of struggle (*jihād*) and never quits his *jihād*. And that even if society was being administered by a just society and that if the Commander of the Faithful was at the helm of the ship of state, that the true believer would continue his *jihād* alongside the Commander of the Faithful; he would unsheathe his sword and would go and fight alongside Ali 🕊 against his enemies and against the enemies of justice. This is in the event that the government of the day is a just one; and if it is not a just one, then the true believer would do the same thing, except he would do so in a covert rather than an overt manner; he would do so while employing *taqīya*.

Thus, the tenet of *jihād* is contained within the tenet of *taqīya*, and it surprises me how some people can believe that hadith reports about *taqīya* are antithetical to those about *jihād* or are antithetical to those about the actions of the Imams 🕊. And [the problem is so pervasive that] even one of our excellent Muslim intellectuals, many of whose positions we affirm and whose explication of the religious imperative to enjoin the doing of that which is right and to forbid the doing of that which is wrong (*al-amr bi'l-ma'rūf wa an-nahy min al-munkar*) and *taqīya* in one of his books was excellent – may God 🕊 gladden his spirit – [this person] nevertheless committed an error at the beginning of the discussion of *taqīya* where he stated that "*taqīya* is an exceptional condition". Why is *taqīya* exceptional? *Taqīya* is not an exception. Rather, if we desist from [the continual practice of] *taqīya*, that would be [an instance of its] exceptionality. *Taqīya* is not desisting from an action; it *is* [itself] an action, but in another form; [under a different guise]. *Taqīya* is a continual practice; it is an action under a different guise. Why should it be an exceptional occurrence when it is always required, just as action is always necessary? *Taqīya* is not something in opposition to action; it is a form of action; thus, it is not an exceptional condition. The book which [Sayyid Ahmad] Tayyibī [Shabistarī] – may God 🌸 gladden his spirit and cause his efforts to be further appreciated – the religious imperative to enjoin the doing of that which is right and to forbid the doing of that which is wrong and *taqīya* is a very good one and is truly beneficial. And his discussion of *taqīya* is a very good one. But this sentence of his is not acceptable to us. He says that the religious imperative to enjoin the doing of that which is right and to forbid the doing of that which is wrong is a constant and continual act whereas *taqīya* is exceptional; whereas I believe that both are constant and continuous.

Taqīya is a form which *jihād* and the performance of the religious imperative to enjoin the doing of that which is right and to forbid the doing of that which is wrong takes [under conditions of oppression]. *Taqīya* is not an exception; *taqīya* and *jihād* are [in fact] one and the same thing; they are not two separate things. Anyone who thinks that *taqīya* is inaction or the absence of action has not understood *taqīya*, or if he has understood it, he does not want to act on it. Seeking the path of least resistance is a very powerful catalyst. It effects changes in many minds and alters how one imagines things to be. But this is not the way it is; *taqīya* means acting in a specific way. That is how it is. This is another hadith report which tells us that *taqīya* is conjoined with action.

8.6 *Taqīya* as misdirection or setting a false trail in order to deceive the enemy

There are a few hadith reports which look at *taqīya* from a different perspective. In these reports, *taqīya* is equated with a situation where one sets a false trail in order to deceive the enemy, which is a characterization which includes deception and taking action, but from another perspective. In the old days, a battalion or a platoon would set out on a path which they did not want the enemy to find out about. For example, if the enemy

10. Precautionary Dissimulation (Taqīya)

was encamped in front of them, they would go around them furtively so that they could attack them from their back and have the advantage of surprise. Meanwhile, the enemy has not been standing idly by so that they can be caught off guard at night with a surprise attack. They have scouts whose duty it is to see what the enemy is up to. And if these scouts see the hoof prints of a number of horses which headed in a certain direction, they will know what direction the enemy has taken, and will follow their trail until they see that the enemy has encamped behind them. Thus, they will be able to prepare accordingly.

In order to be able to maintain the advantage of surprise, they did an interesting thing in the past when preparing for night raids and surprise attacks, which occurred until recently as well. What they used to do is to take off the horseshoes of their horses and nail them on backwards (with the two prongs of the shoes facing towards the front of the horses rather than to their back) so that it would appear that the cavalry was headed in the direction that was the opposite of the direction which they had actually headed for. Thus, they would do this so that if they were headed north, for example, the enemy would think that they had headed south. This is what was called misdirection or setting a false trail.

In some hadith reports, *taqīya* is used in the sense of misdirection or setting a false trail. In other words, going in one direction but doing something so that the enemy will think that you have gone in some other direction. One such report is about the prophet Abraham, the Friend [of God ﷺ], who resorted to *taqīya* in a Quranic verse where he said that he was ill: "Verily, I am ill!" This is how Abraham practiced *taqīya*.

[Here is the full Quranic context:]

وَإِنَّ مِن شِيعَتِهِ لَإِبْرَاهِيمَ ﴿٨٣﴾ إِذْ جَاءَ رَبَّهُ بِقَلْبٍ سَلِيمٍ ﴿٨٤﴾ إِذْ قَالَ لِأَبِيهِ وَقَوْمِهِ مَاذَا تَعْبُدُونَ ﴿٨٥﴾ أَئِفْكًا آلِهَةً دُونَ اللَّهِ تُرِيدُونَ ﴿٨٦﴾ فَمَا ظَنُّكُم بِرَبِّ الْعَالَمِينَ ﴿٨٧﴾ فَنَظَرَ نَظْرَةً فِي النُّجُومِ ﴿٨٨﴾ فَقَالَ إِنِّي سَقِيمٌ ﴿٨٩﴾ فَتَوَلَّوْا عَنْهُ مُدْبِرِينَ ﴿٩٠﴾

[37:83] And, behold, of his persuasion was Abraham, too,
[37:84] when he turned to his Sustainer with a heart free

of evil, [37:85] and [thus] spoke to his father and his people: "What is it that you worship? [37:86] Do you want [to bow down before] a lie - [before] deities other than God ﷻ? [37:87] What, then, do you think of the Sustainer of all the worlds?" [37:88] Then he cast a glance at the stars, [37:89] and said, "Verily, I am ill!" [37:90] and at that they turned their backs on him and went away.

When the people of Abraham's city – which was Babel, apparently – went outside of the city walls for the festivities, and the young Abraham saw an opportunity to break the idols, he saw that if he went with them only to return early, that they would realize that he wanted to return in order to do something, and so they might prevent him from being able to return. He thus thought that it would be best for him not to go with them. But he did not simply state that he did not want to go with them because he had some business to attend to in town; because the townsfolk would then keep an eye on him. Rather, he tricked them by laying a false trail for them by saying that he was ill and so he would stay behind. And so, they left him to himself. When Abraham was thus left alone in town, he then took an axe in hand and went and smashed each and every one of the idols to pieces. This is an example of misdirection: to make like you are ill in order [to have the opportunity] to break idols.

But your and my Imam calls this *taqīya*; so now, you can define *taqīya* in any way you please. The Imamate calls this *taqīya*; that is what the hadith scripture tells us. Of course, the whole report is not about that; it is just referred to as such [in a part of the report]. This hadith report, which is the fourth report, continues after telling us to maintain our practice of *taqīya*, as follows: "Abraham said that he was ill; but he was not truly ill." He was deceiving them.

8.7 The companions of the cave
There is another report in this same vein about the Companions of the Cave,[156] who were a group of chivalrous young men who had attained to

---

[156] Companions of the Cave or 'Aṣḥāb al-Kahf were Christian believers who lived during the rule of Decius (201 – 251 CE), an ancient Roman emperor. Except one

10. Precautionary Dissimulation (Taqīya)

faith and to correct belief within the ignorant pagan society of their day. But the conditions of society prevented them from being able to practice their faith. Thus, they had held onto their faith and beliefs in the hope that a suitable opportunity would arise and that they would one day be able to manifest their faith, thereby guiding the people aright. They were waiting for a suitable opportunity, for if they were to practice their beliefs, the ignorant heavens would take it as an insult to their customs and norms and idols, then Decius[157] (*daqyānūs*) [who was the ruler of their day] would have them arrested and imprisoned and subject them to all sorts of ill treatment, thereby preventing them from being able to provide guidance when the opportunity arose. In order to prevent Decius from knowing what they were really about, they misdirected him. What did they do? They participated in the celebrations [of the pagans], because they were from the upper echelon of society and they would be invited to the festivities held by the government; and they would girt idolaters' belts (*zennār*) and attach to themselves the insignia of the religion of the ruler in order not to stand out. They would do these things so that by virtue of the cover that it provided them, they would be able to keep themselves safe for the day that the opportunity presented itself. And it so happened that this misdirection of theirs was successful and ensured that their true identity remained hidden from the authorities. And when the opportunity

---

of them who was a shepherd and had a dog, others were among the noble ones and courtiers who escaped to save themselves from the oppression of Decius and to save their faith, and moved to a cave and went to a deep sleep which lasted about 309 years. There is a sura in the glorious Qur'an named al-Kahf, in verses 8 to 26 of which, the story of these believers is mentioned. Also, there are reports about this story in Christian sources. In Shi'a hadiths, the Companions of the Cave are mentioned among the companions of Imam al-Mahdi (a). (WikiShi'a)
The story of the companions of the cave is found in the 18th surah of the Qur'an, al-Kahf (the Cave), for which the surah is named. It relates the tale of a young group of believers, who fall into a supernatural sleep in a cave, only to awaken hundreds of years later. This story mimics a story found in the Syriac homily by a Christian bishop named Jacob of Serugh (521 CE).[1] His story tells of seven young Christians in Ephesus (an ancient Greek city now situated in modern-day Turkey), who hide from an evil emperor in a cave, fall into a supernatural sleep for hundreds of years, and awaken to find that their home town has been converted to Christianity. (WikiIslam)

[157] Decius, also known as Trajan Decius, was Roman Emperor from 249 to 251.

did present itself in a public gathering where all of the various echelons of society were present, these people suddenly arose and declared their beliefs openly and explicitly.

نَحْنُ نَقُصُّ عَلَيْكَ نَبَأَهُم بِالْحَقِّ ۚ إِنَّهُمْ فِتْيَةٌ آمَنُوا بِرَبِّهِمْ وَزِدْنَاهُمْ هُدًى ﴿١٣﴾ وَرَبَطْنَا عَلَىٰ قُلُوبِهِمْ إِذْ قَامُوا فَقَالُوا رَبُّنَا رَبُّ السَّمَاوَاتِ وَالْأَرْضِ لَن نَّدْعُوَ مِن دُونِهِ إِلَٰهًا ۖ لَّقَدْ قُلْنَا إِذًا شَطَطًا ﴿١٤﴾

[18:13] [And] Behold, they were young men who had attained to faith in their Sustainer and Lord of Providence (*rabb*): and [so] We deepened their consciousness of the right way [18:14] and endowed their hearts with strength, so that they stood up and said: "Our Sustainer is the Sustainer of the heavens and the earth. Never shall we invoke any deity other than Him: [for if we did,] we should indeed have uttered an enormity!

And who knows? – I do not, as I have not investigated the matter – but it is possible that this act of theirs might have brought about a fundamental shift in the consciousness of the society of their day which ensured that the society to which they [these Seven Sleepers] awoke after many long years of being asleep was the society which they had desired and which was acceptable to them. And this shows that the action that they took brought about a change in the consciousness of the people of their society, and that they had been able to successfully guide the people to the right way and to God ﷻ's religion.

And what had enabled them to bring this about? *Taqīya*. In the sense of laying a false trail while holding on to the ultimate objective while waiting for the right opportunity to present itself. That is what I want to emphasize: waiting patiently for the right opportunity to present itself rather than giving up altogether.

9. The falsity of the definition of taqīya as 'not taking any action'

In sum, if anyone defines *taqīya* as not taking any action and giving up on attaining one's goals, this betrays the fact that such a person is not familiar with *taqīya* as it is defined in Shʿīa Islam and by the Imams ﷺ. If someone so defined *taqīya* and said, for instance, "What? Why don't you just partake in *taqīya* [and forget about it]?", then that would wreck all havoc [on the religion] because if this definition of *taqīya* is adopted, nothing would be left of the religion before too long!

10. Taqīya is intertwined with action and endeavor (*Jihād*)

Taqīya is intertwined with action and endeavor (*jihād*). Allow me to point something out that some of you might not realize. If the objective is for the identity of a group of people to remain unknown – it might be imperative, for instance, that the identity of the followers of Imam Ṣādiq ﷺ remain unknown to al-Manṣūr and his forces – then this imperative which is a means to achieving an end itself becomes an end or objective in its own right. Thus, if they are to remain incognito, as it were, then they must refrain from doing anything which might expose their identities for as long as performing such an act risks their ultimate objective. Let us assume that one of the companions of Imam Ṣādiq ﷺ, Mu'allā b. Khanīs, say, is in a public gathering at a mosque where Dāvūd b. Ali and his henchmen are present, and that Imam Ṣādiq ﷺ or Imam Sajjād ﷺ or Imam Ali ﷺ are slandered and insulted there. Well, if Mu'allā b. Khanīs stands up to defend the name and reputation of the Imams, he will have thereby outed himself as one of their followers. And he will also, therefore, have precluded himself from being able to carry out the overarching objective for which he is willing to sacrifice his very life. And so, this is where he must bite his tongue and not say a word. And this is why you will see that in some hadith reports the Imams ﷺ urge their followers that if they are being cursed, that they too should go along and join in the imprecations. Curses cause ripples in the air which dissipate and disappear. But at the same time, they also say that if you are told to turn back from the way of the Imams, that you are not to do so. That you should never give up following Ali's path and objectives.

Thus, when it comes to [the direction of] the path and the objectives which you are aiming for, which is that which you share with Imam Ali ﷺ [and all of the Imams, all of whom take their directions from the example of the Prophet ﷺ and the Quran,] then that is something that one must partake in and endeavor towards, no matter what. But when the issue is a semantic one, where the pronunciation of a word or the failure to partake in the imprecation of the Imams ﷺ could mean that the ultimate and overarching goal might be endangered, then we are told to exercise patience and forbearance.

To go back to the example of Muʾallā b. Khanīs: let us assume that he goes to the pool in the congregational mosque in Madina [where people make their ritual ablutions] and starts to make his ablutions in accordance with the Shʿīa rite's stipulations. If he wipes his wet hand over his feet once [instead of giving his feet a thorough washing as in the Sunnite rites], then everyone will know that he is a Shʿīa, and he will have outed himself again, which would be contrary to the imperative of maintaining cover. And this is why we are told to make our ablutions the way the Sunni do [if the situation necessitates our doing so], [and in short, to abide by the adage that 'when in Rome, do as the Romans do']. Because the failure to make one's ablutions in accordance with the stipulations of the Sunni rite [in certain situations] will cause the identity of a covert Shʿīa operative to be outed, and will thus endanger the greater operation. And it is the greater operation and objective that is more important than the way the ritual ablutions are made. Thus, when we are told to refrain from religiously mandated imperatives (*wājibāt*), these are imperatives which are not necessary for attaining to the [overarching] objective.

Imam Kāẓim ﷺ had an agent placed in a highly sensitive position within Hārūn ur-Rashīd's palace circle and governmental apparatus. Who is this agent? It is Ali b. Yaqtīn, by means of which the Imam is able to accomplish much. Would it not be a waste and a shame that such an important agent be outed and destroyed? Thus the Imam tells him, "My dear sir! Make your ablutions in accordance with the Sunnite rite [even] in your own home; because they are monitoring you either by way of their own agents or themselves. So do not allow them to find out that you are with us." This concerns an ordinary religiously mandated imperative

10. Precautionary Dissimulation (Taqīya)

(*wājib*), do you see? Hold your hands together [when you pray, like the Sunnis do] as this is not important [relatively], and as a failure to do so would mean your expulsion from your position within the caliphal court.

And at times Ali b. Yaqtīn would verge on making a mistake. He would become hot-headed [and forget his overarching priority]. Ali b. Yaqtīn was a close aide of the caliph, so that he was frequently in the presence of the caliph armed with his sword; it seems he was a vizier (or minister), but an important one. At one point, Imam Kāẓim ﷺ had been arrested and brought to the caliph's court, where Ali b. Yaqtīn was standing over Hārūn. As soon as the Imam entered the court chambers, Ali b. Yaqtīn's hand went for the hilt of his sword with the intention of drawing it and putting an end to Hārūn. But Imam Kāẓim ﷺ saw Ali b. Yaqtīn's mistake and saw that he was about to do something premature, and signaled him to desist. Ali b. Yaqtīn, for his turn, understood the Imam's intentions and removed his hand from the hilt of his sword. Meanwhile, Hārūn, who was not stupid, had realized that Ali b. Yaqtīn seemed to have placed his hand on the hilt of his sword, and was on the lookout to see if he was going to draw it or not. And he saw that he had not moved to draw it and that his hand simply remained there. And Imam Kāẓim ﷺ had made a sign or looked sharply at Ali b. Yaqtīn so that the latter understood that he was not to do anything to upset the cart, as it were. What happened later is a matter for another day, but after the Imam left, Hārūn turned to Ali b. Yaqtīn and said, "Hmm, it seems you were not yourself for a while there, O Ali b. Yaqtīn!" He was testing to see if Ali b. Yaqtīn would panic or would betray himself as a follower of the Imam by turning red or in some other way. But Ali b. Yaqtīn was an experienced warrior and had a response at the ready. He immediately said, "Yes, O Commander of the Faithful! I saw that you had brought that guilty party to your presence and assumed that you were about to order that he be put to death, so I reached for my sword so that I would be on the ready." Hārūn said, "Excellent! Well done, O Ali b. Yaqtīn!" (Ibn Shahrāshūb, *Manāqib* 4:307). Well, sometimes the situation turns to such a pass, which Ali b. Yaqtīn must be able to tolerate.

And finally, in another hadith report, the Imam is informed that two of his followers have been arrested. He was told that one of them disavowed him under torture and the other held out and died. The germane part of the Imam's response is that he says, "The one who died attained heaven faster." And so, sometimes the matter comes to such an eventuality as well.

In any event, there is much to say concerning this subject, and I do not have anything else to add at this point, because I think that whatever else I say will be adding details and marginalia and would be material which you might not be able to absorb or recall. So, in sum, the general discussion concerning *taqīya* and the headings of the subject that we discussed with reliance on the hadith reports about the lives of the Imams  should suffice to let you know the general outline and limits of the subject matter; i.e. that our discussion should suffice to enable you to conceive of the limits of the subject, and for you to envisage a new conception of this important tenet.

www.ingramcontent.com/pod-product-compliance
Lightning Source LLC
Chambersburg PA
CBHW071559080526
44588CB00010B/954